D1010919

Passionate
Spirit

Also by Cate Haste

Keep the Home Fires Burning
Rules of Desire
Nazi Women
The Goldfish Bowl (with Cherie Blair)
Clarissa Eden: A Memoir (editor)
Sheila Fell: A Passion for Paint
Craigie Aitchison: A Life in Colour

CATE HASTE

——— • ———

Passionate Spirit

——— • ———

The Life of Alma Mahler

BASIC BOOKS

New York

Basic Books
Hachette Book Group
1290 Avenue of the Americas, New York, NY 10104
www.basicbooks.com

Printed in the United States of America

First Edition: September 2019

Published by Basic Books, an imprint of Perseus Books, LLC, a
subsidiary of Hachette Book Group, Inc. The Basic Books name
and logo is a trademark of the Hachette Book Group.

The Hachette Speakers Bureau provides a wide range of authors for speaking events.
To find out more, go to www.hachettespeakersbureau.com or call (866) 376-6591.

The publisher is not responsible for websites (or their
content) that are not owned by the publisher.

Print book interior design by Amy Quinn.

Library of Congress Cataloging-in-Publication Data
Names: Haste, Cate, 1945—author.
Title: Passionate spirit: the life of Alma Mahler / Cate Haste.
Description: First edition. | New York: Basic Books, [2019] |
Includes bibliographical references and index.
Identifiers: LCCN 2018058720| ISBN 9780465096718
(hardcover: alk. paper) | ISBN 9780465096725 (ebk.)
Subjects: LCSH: Mahler, Alma, 1879–1964. | Vienna (Austria)—Biography. | Women
composers—Austria—Biography. | Diarists—Austria—Biography. | Wives—
Biography. | Arts, Austrian—20th century. | Europe—Intellectual life—20th century.
Classification: LCC DB844.M34 H37 2019 | DDC 780.92 [B]—dc23
LC record available at https://lccn.loc.gov/2018058720
ISBNs: 978-0-465-09671-8 (hardcover), 978-0-465-09672-5 (ebook)

LSC-C

10 9 8 7 6 5 4 3 2 1

To my grandsons, Arthur Bragg and Eric Flintoff

Contents

Preface

ALMA MAHLER WAS a woman of extraordinary complexity. Challenging, difficult, charismatic, generous, passionate, and self-serving, she was the object of veneration and of mocking disdain and the doyen of elite Viennese society for several decades. She inspired ballads, notably the satirist Tom Lehrer's 1964 classic, "Alma," which spread her fame to a new generation, as well as several plays and films. Yet none has truly captured this exceptional woman.

In *Passionate Spirit*, I address her enduring—and controversial—legend and ask why, more than half a century since her death, she still commands the fascination of scholars and readers alike. Alma was a powerful woman, a femme fatale who successfully defined her life through love. Many men fell in love with her, she was widely adored, the muse of geniuses, the generous spirit who intuitively understood the springs of creativity that inspired their work. Alongside this attractive image runs the hostile one of the seductress who used love to gain power over men, the devouring maenad, cold and calculating, who first beguiled men then ruthlessly rejected them. She becomes the self-serving egoist, who invented her own significance as a muse by grossly exaggerating her importance in the creative lives of great men. Her widely recognized musical and compositional talents are belittled and any compositions of value attributed to the influence—if not the pen—of either her teacher, Alexander von Zemlinsky, or her husband, Gustav Mahler. She is consistently and damningly accused of anti-Semitism, yet she had two Jewish husbands, one of whom she followed into permanent exile to escape the Nazis, several Jewish lovers, and a social circle composed mostly of Jews.

Clearly there are elements of truth in all these versions. My aim is to weigh the merits of these judgments against the available evidence, to portray the woman I discovered as I read her words and listened to her voice. And in so doing, I aim to reassess her legacy, to view her free from the screen of skepticism and the harshly judgmental tone of previous commentators on her life.

I like Alma Mahler. I particularly like the modern young woman who emerges from the pages of her early diaries, written between the ages of eighteen and twenty-two, when she was untrammeled by convention and bent on realizing herself and her talents despite the odds against her as a woman. And I find equally challenging and interesting the later woman who was surrounded in her famous salon by Vienna's glittering cultural elite but was tormented by longing, afflicted by terrible tragedy, and still breached the boundaries of decorum in pursuit of a passionate life lived to the full.

THE EVIDENCE IN Alma's case is controversial. She is routinely accused of massaging the facts to serve her own legacy—of suppressing or editing her husband Gustav Mahler's published letters to remove critical references to her, for instance—acts seen, particularly by Mahler scholars (for whom she was for some time their principal source), as tampering with the archive. In addition she burned all of her own letters to him, which rouses suspicion about her intent among frustrated scholars. These claims have been exaggerated into the prevalent view that *anything* written by Alma is bound to be inaccurate or self-serving, which in my view considerably undervalues her witness to her own life and the history she lived through.

With this caveat in mind, I have drawn as far as possible on primary sources. I have drawn more extensively than previous commentators on the private diaries Alma wrote in her late adolescence between 1898 and 1902, which were published in 1998.[1] I have quoted extensively, often for the first time, from the unpublished typescript of her later diaries covering July 1902–1905, 1911, and 1913–1944, which are preserved in the Mahler-Werfel Papers at the Kislak Center for Special Collections, Rare Books and Manuscripts at the University of Pennsylvania in

Philadelphia. Believed to be an accurate copy of her original diaries, they include some clear alterations in her own bold handwriting that I have acknowledged in the text. This invaluable source is the spine to my narrative of Alma's life, the voice to which I have listened to penetrate this kaleidoscopic personality.

The diaries are the record of her most intimate feelings, her ambitions, her palpitating self-doubt, her candid comments on people and events. Because I used mainly the entries written on the day or very soon after the events, they have an immediacy that conveys honesty, rather than the structure of recollection. And, because a private diary provides the space to vent feelings and to work through emotions, they are raw and sometimes shocking in their candor.

Her unpublished 614-page typescript memoir, "Der schimmernde Weg" (The shimmering path), also in the Mahler-Werfel Papers, is an interim autobiography based largely on her diaries. It covers the period 1902–1944, and though less immediate—it was begun in 1944 and abandoned in 1947—it remains an important record. I treat her autobiography *And the Bridge Is Love*, ghostwritten when she was seventy-nine and published in 1958, as a far less reliable source. It reveals a harder, more cynical persona, which lends credence to her hostile legend and has been the principal source for at least two previous biographies of Alma. Recognizing its inaccuracies, I have quoted from it only when absolutely no other source was available.

Alma's *Gustav Mahler: Memories and Letters* first published in 1940, and *Gustav Mahler: Letters to His Wife*, edited by Mahler's respected biographer Henry-Louis de la Grange and published in 1995, are valuable sources. Additionally several archive collections, in particular the Mahler-Werfel Papers at the University of Pennsylvania, include Alma's correspondence with the numerous personalities in her life.

Few firsthand witnesses remain, so I am extremely grateful to Marina Mahler, Alma's granddaughter, for several long and entirely enjoyable interviews, for her insights, for her hospitality, and for the invaluable help she has given me throughout.

I have used in evidence the voice of Anna Mahler, Alma's daughter, recorded in interviews with Peter Stephan Jungk, the biographer of Alma's third husband, Franz Werfel. Anna called her "Tiger-Mammy": "She was a big animal. And sometimes she was magnificent, and sometimes she was abominable," Anna recalled, neatly encapsulating the complexity of this remarkable and controversial woman.

Cate Haste
London, November 2018

— *1* —

Vienna Childhood
1879–1898

When Alma Mahler walked into a room, heads turned. Her magnetic presence and charismatic allure were like "an electric charge" in any gathering. She was a femme fatale who commanded fascination, adoration, and love and could enchant people in seconds. At the age of nineteen, with clear skin, an enigmatic smile, lustrous, flowing hair, and piercing, watchful blue eyes, Alma was called "the most beautiful girl in Vienna." Her personality was mercurial; one minute she was the grande dame—imposing, regal, exuding authority—the next she was jolly and good humored, revealing "the Viennese soft femininity [which] even in her most awful moments, made it difficult to really dislike her."[1] Some likened her to a demigoddess to whom her admirers and devotees brought gifts. Others loathed her.

Alma was a modern woman who lived out of her time. With an independent will, an intelligent mind of her own, and a strong sense of her own worth, she harbored ambitions that were completely at odds with the behavior expected of young women in late nineteenth-century Viennese society. Her freedom mattered as she challenged the constraints imposed on her.

Alma was deeply romantic. She needed to be loved fiercely and also to feel love with a passion that fired her being. Only superior creative talents inspired her love. She was irresistibly and erotically attracted to a series of extraordinary men of glittering talent and genius, each of whom would make his distinctive mark on the European cultural landscape. Her first infatuation was with the painter Gustav Klimt, though he never made a golden portrait of her and did not become her lover. Composer Gustav Mahler was her first husband, and, after he died in 1911, the wild expressionist painter Oskar Kokoschka openly became her lover. Her second husband, the architect Walter Gropius (with whom she had had an affair while married to Mahler) founded the modernist Bauhaus movement, her third was the then widely read novelist and poet Franz Werfel. Several other writers, composers, and artists who worshipped her praised her for her "unique gift," her "profound, uncanny understanding of what creative men tried to achieve, and her capacity to persuade them that they could do what they aimed at, and that she, Alma, understood what it was," as one associate described it.[2]

Alma had not anticipated this. At eighteen, music was her passion. Her consuming aspiration was to be a composer, an extremely ambitious goal for a young woman. Nothing moved her as much as her usual twice-weekly visits to the opera, which left her enraptured and her imagination overwhelmed by its beauty and grandeur. But women composers were almost nonexistent. Girls were taught the piano not to encourage their creativity but to burnish their accomplishments as elegant and cultured wives. Women were still barred from studying at the music and art academies. Their capacity for creativity was deemed, then and later, to be limited, parochial, "domestic," and their creative vision, by their very nature, far inferior to that of men. If, as happened to Alma, a work revealed remarkable talent, its merits were belittled or attributed to the influence or direct intervention of another—male—composer.

The adverse climate did not dim Alma's ambition. For she was compelled to create music, driven by the spirit that flows from mysterious sources. Her belief in her innately superior pedigree, descended as she was from a painter father, Emil Jakob Schindler, whom she was convinced was a genius, gave her an unshakeable confidence in her own worth. From him came her profound conviction that the pursuit of artistic excellence was the only truly worthwhile goal and that only a person of exceptional creative talent was worthy of eliciting her love or capturing her soul.

But, when she was twenty-one, Alma was faced with a dreadful dilemma. She had to choose between her passion for a genius nearly twice her age, Gustav Mahler, and the pursuit of her own precious goal, her music. She chose the genius. Why? She had become persuaded of the nobility of giving herself entirely to a superior being who would "give my life meaning," she explained. It was a capitulation of her inner being to the prevailing view of the role of the wife, and it happened, despite her stubborn nature and her modern ideas, because of the overwhelming intensity of her love.

Although the loss of her own music left a lasting wound, music would remain her source of strength during a life of passion and high drama, shadowed by tragedy with the premature loss of her first husband and the deaths of three of her four children. Love was the core of her existence and the wellspring of the power that this restless and irrepressible woman would from then on exercise over those in her orbit.

Born in 1879, Alma Schindler was brought up as a child in the bohemian artistic circles to which her parents, Emil and Anna Schindler, belonged, and, as an adolescent at the busy hub of the influential Viennese avant-garde, the Secession movement cofounded by her stepfather, the artist Carl Moll. She was a young woman of exceptional vitality and intellectual curiosity, eager and open, like a flower to the sun, to life and new experience.

The milieu of her self-discovery was fin-de-siècle Vienna, the magnet for talent and enterprise from across the sprawling Austro-Hungarian (or Habsburg) empire and the crucible for innovation and new ideas in every sphere of culture and intellectual thought. Artists, composers, writers, dramatists, architects, and scientists of the psyche all sought to express the new soul and spirit of modern man and woman, their condition of uncertainty and nervous anxiety, their rejection of ossified principles, and their search for inner truth through emotional and psychological introspection. In so doing they shaped the intellectual currents that defined the twentieth century.

Yet underlying the city's buoyant cultural energy was an ominous sense of unease. The multinational empire of Austria-Hungary, which for three centuries had held together a kaleidoscope of nationalities and ethnic minorities covering much of central Europe, had begun to fragment. Demands by minorities for greater autonomy and increased rights to control their own languages and territory were opening up fissures that threatened the empire's cohesion and stability. Faced with these intractable problems, the Viennese zeitgeist turned increasingly toward the unifying and exuberant balms of art and culture, in which pursuit the city could still lay claim to be the capital of Europe.

Within this atmosphere of cultural ferment, the guide, mentor, and polestar of the young Alma's existence was her father, the painter Emil Jakob Schindler. She would spend many hours in his studio, watching him paint, "standing and staring at the revelations of the hand that led the brush," and through this she acquired an intuitive sense of the process and struggle of artistic creation. Such intense involvement with the artist she loved unreservedly nurtured in her young imagination fantasies of patronage: "I dreamed of wealth merely in order to smooth the paths of creative personalities. I wished for a great Italian garden filled by many white studios; I wished to invite many outstanding men there—to live for their art alone, without mundane worries—and never to show myself," she wrote.[3]

Alma's love of music dated back to her childhood when her "profoundly musical" father sang beautifully his favorite Schumann lieder and her mother, Anna, a trained singer, joined in. Emil Schindler took his intelligent, growing daughter seriously. His conversation was "fascinating and never commonplace," she recalled.[4] When she was eight, he led Alma and her sister, Gretl, into his studio to tell them the story of Goethe's *Faust*: "We wept, not knowing why. When we were all enraptured, he gave us the book. 'This is the most beautiful book in the world,' he said. 'Read it. Keep it.'" Her furious mother thought it unsuitable reading for small children and removed it. As her parents argued, Alma and Gretl listened behind closed doors with bated breath. Their mother won: "But in my mind a fixed idea remained: I *had* to get the *Faust* back!" Alma wrote.[5]

Her unwavering devotion to Goethe spawned a burgeoning interest in literature and, later, philosophy. But her education was otherwise patchy. Though Alma appears to have attended school for a short period, she and Gretl, in common with other bourgeois Viennese girls, were taught at home by tutors. Alma's tutors were either "nasty" and were dismissed, or they were nice and taught them nothing. Girls had been admitted to secondary school in Vienna since 1868, but until 1892, when Alma was thirteen, they were still barred from the gymnasium—the grammar school—and access to universities was still impossible. The education of girls, including Alma, tended to focus on social skills—French, dress making, and piano, rather than the philosophy and literature that inspired her.

Alma remembered herself as "a nervous child, fairly bright, with the typical hop-skip-and jump brains of precocity. . . . I could not think anything through, and was never able to keep a date in mind, and took no interest in anything but music."[6] Later she railed loudly against this neglect of girls' education: "Why are boys *taught* to use their brains, but not girls? I can see it in my own case. My mind has not been schooled, which is why I have such frightful difficulty with everything. Sometimes I really try, force myself to think, but my thoughts vanish into thin air. And I really want to use my mind. I really do. Why do they make everything so terribly difficult for girls?"[7]

However, she had acquired through her father a deep appreciation of painting and of the arts. Schindler, though influenced by plein air painters like Jean-Baptiste-Camille Corot, Théodore Rousseau, and Charles-François Daubigny, had developed his own vision of landscape known as poetic realism—atmospheric paintings saturated with feeling, which convey a strong sense of transience in images that are both aesthetic and subjective. He focused not on the heroic panorama of landscape but on the mundane and everyday—the vegetable garden, the mill and stream near their house, the poplar tree avenue—which he transformed with fluent brushstrokes in different light and atmospheric conditions into statements of poetic truth. Although rooted in the Viennese tradition, his style reflected the new understanding of nature that was spreading across Europe. In Alma's eyes, he was the true prophet of the Austrian landscape.

In complete contrast, Alma's expansive imagination was also fired by the opulent spectacles of her father's friend and associate, Hans Makart, the most fashionable artist of the era. His dramatic, ornate representations of allegorical, historical, and classical motifs decorated Vienna's public buildings and private neo-Renaissance palaces, and he was the dominant influence on painting, fashion, and interior design: Makart

hats and Makart red were all the rage, along with the Makart bouquets—
bunches of dried flowers, ostrich feathers, and grasses that decorated the
salons of the bourgeoisie. Alma fell under Makart's spell for a time: "I
loved trailing velvet gowns, and I wanted to be rowed in gondolas with
velvet draperies floating astern," she wrote.[8] She was entranced by stories of his legendary parties, when "the loveliest women were dressed in
genuine Renaissance costumes, rose garlands trailed from ballroom ceil-
ings, Franz Liszt played through the nights, the choicest wines flowed,
velvet-clad pages stood behind every chair, and so forth to the limits of
splendor and imagination."[9]

Alongside this romantic extravagance there was in Alma a practical
young woman with a sense of the difficulties and hardships of life. For
her family's comparatively comfortable existence had been only recently
earned.

WHEN ALMA MARIA Schindler was born on August 31, 1879, her father
was a struggling artist, saturated with guilt and self-doubt and prone to
melancholy. He and Alma's mother, Anna Sofie (née Bergen), were living in penury in a cramped rented flat on the Meyerhofgasse in a poor
district of the city. They had met two years earlier in 1877 when they
sang together in a semiprofessional production at the Künstlerhaus of
the comic opera Lenardo und Blandine. Anna had just been offered a contract with the Stadttheater in Leipzig, which she did not take up, for in
December 1878 they announced their engagement. Anna was pregnant
with Alma when they married on February 2, 1879.

Money worries plagued Schindler. Still only slowly making his name
as an artist, he earned little from his work, despite having won the prestigious Karl Ludwig medal for his painting Moonrise in the Prater the previous year. "What wouldn't I do for forty gulden," he opined on March
14, 1879. His anxiety mounted to despair as he received a notice to quit
his apartment: "I tremble each time the bell rings. . . . Unlucky man!" he
wrote in his diary.[10] Later Alma reflected on her mother's struggles with
"the debts—and Papa, who, when things were at their worst, would simply roll over on his stomach and sleep round the clock."[11] With no money
to buy paints or canvas, Schindler despaired: "Death desirable . . . my
life has only deficits of money, satisfaction and honour."[12] Even worse,

he feared he had sacrificed his artistic core, his vision: he had stopped dreaming of grandeur, honesty, and immortality. "My brain doesn't work in form and colours any more, but merely in worry about bread." Schindler's consolation was his wife, Anna, for without her, "my existence would be pure agony or I would be dead by now."[13]

The birth of their first child was overshadowed for Schindler by guilt at his poverty: "Only those should marry who can lie down and die the very next day, without leaving their nearest and dearest to die of starvation," he wrote, convinced that his marrying was a reprehensible act. "All that counts is whether there is money in the house. And there isn't even enough to pay for my funeral."[14] Anna's confinement had horrified him—"a most shameful and despicable act of nature," which had made his beloved Anna a martyr. For some time, he felt only indifference toward the child whose existence had meant a partial separation from his wife. He was so tormented by his inadequacy that he even contemplated giving them both away, out of love, so he would know they were well cared for.

Anna Sofie endured his melancholy with forbearance. Her modest background had equipped her for adversity. The second of nine children, she was born in Hamburg on November 20, 1857. Her father, Claus Jakob Bergen, had owned a small brewery, but he went bankrupt in 1871, and the children had to rely on their talents and financial support from friends to survive. She told Alma of her grim youth, "how one night she [and the whole Bergen family] had to flee from the island of Veddel, . . . and they didn't even have enough money for the rent. . . . At eleven years of age, [she] became a ballet dancer, . . . she played walk-on parts for a whole year and became the breadwinner for the whole family. . . . [L]ater she became a nanny, had to wash nappies and sleep in the cooks' room. . . . [S]he became an au-pair girl, then a cashier at the baths and finally a singer."[15] Anna had a good soprano voice and was sent to Vienna in 1876 to take voice lessons with the respected teacher Adele Passy-Cornet. But then she fell in love with Emil, and her career prospects ended.

In February 1880, Schindler contracted diphtheria and blood poisoning and spent six months at the North Sea resort of Borkum. On his return he found Anna was again pregnant. The father was almost certainly his painter colleague Julius Berger, who had shared the flat with Emil since before his marriage. Margarethe (Gretl, or Greta), was born on August 16, 1880, and treated as Schindler's own child.

After his initial indifference, Schindler's attachment to his daughters strengthened into love as his circumstances improved. In February 1881 he was awarded the Reichel Artist's Prize, which carried an endowment of 1,500 gulden and enabled him to start paying off his debts and move into a larger flat. A sympathetic patron, the Viennese banker Moritz Mayer, commissioned paintings for his new apartment and, unusually, agreed to pay him a monthly sum of 200 gulden until they were finished. The following spring another Austrian financier bought the prize-winning *Moonrise in the Prater*.

Schindler took up teaching and soon gathered around him a loyal circle of talented women artists who, because they were barred from entry to the art academies, were reliant on private tuition. Marie Begas-Parmentier, Tina Blau, Maria Egner, and Olga Wisinger-Florian each later made her name in the art world. In 1882, they were joined by twenty-year-old Carl Moll, who became Schindler's assistant and a fixture in the household. He rented an apartment in the same block and accompanied Schindler, "the Master," on family holidays to Bad Goisern in the Salzkammergut and on summer study trips with his pupils to Weissenkirchen and Lundunberg. Moll's devotion extended to Anna, and with utmost discretion they became lovers. If the sensitive and intelligent young Alma ever noticed this, she did not mention it either in her diaries or her autobiography. But her aversion to Carl Moll was, and remained, potent.

When Alma was five, Schindler rented Plankenberg Manor. Situated in the countryside near the Vienna Woods, it was the "fulfilment of his most secret . . . wishes," according to Moll.[16] For Alma, it was "full of beauty, legends and dread. . . . It was said to be haunted and we children lay trembling through many a night."[17] On the stairs was a flower-covered altar on which stood a wood-carved figure and a glistening chandelier that made the girls shudder every night as they passed it. The fifteenth-century building, part of the estate of Prince Karl Liechstenstein, was two stories high and topped by a gabled roof with a baroque onion-tip clock tower adorning the façade. It was set in a largely neglected three-acre park in which "traces of planning remained visible." Surrounding the manor were "rolling hills, broad vistas, forests and fields, poplar-lined country lanes, a quiet brook."[18]

Here Alma "lived like a princess, separated from the world" amid the beauties of nature while her father, "the true prophet of this nature,"

Figure 1. The Schindler family at Plankenberg Manor c. 1890.
"I lived apart, like a princess, amid the beauties of nature." —Alma Schindler
From left: Alma, sister Gretl, father Emil, Carl Moll, mother Anna (*standing*).

painted. Carl Moll described Schindler living "like a feudal lord on practically nothing" and propagated the myth that he was "a born aristocrat,
lived as a youth with his uncle in Schloss Leopoldskron—and has now
been returned to another castle."[19] Alma imbibed the legend, describing
herself as "the daughter of an artistic tradition" and her father as "always
in debt, as befits a person of genius. He came from old patrician stock and
was my shining idol."[20]

The Schindler stock was not, in fact, patrician. Emil Schindler's
paternal great-grandfather was a scythe-smith from the Steyr Valley in
Upper Austria. His grandfather became the owner of a textile factory
and had two sons, Julius, Emil Jakob's father, who was born in 1842,
and Alexander, who became a liberal member of Parliament and published novels under the aristocratic pseudonym Julius von der Traun. A

natural spendthrift, Alexander lived in the heavily mortgaged Schloss Leopoldskron, and, when his creditors forced him to flee in the night, his ignominious departure was turned into a pageant "with his many servants escorting him out in a torchlight parade."[21]

Julius took over the family business and married a beautiful woman, Maria Penz, whose portrait hung in the Gallerie of Beauties in the Vienna Hofburg. But the family went bankrupt after a fire destroyed the factory. Then, when Emil Jakob was four, his father contracted tuberculosis. As Julius was nearing the end, he took his wife in a four-in-hand coach on a journey through Italy and Switzerland, and in his final hours he had her sit at his bedside in her gayest evening gown until he died.[22]

The beautiful widow married a captain in the Austrian Imperial Army, Eduard Nepalleck, and in 1859 she followed him on the military campaign in Italy during the Second Italian War of Independence, when Austria was defeated by Italian and French forces at the Battle of Solferino. In Italy, seventeen-year-old Emil Jakob met the painter Albert Zimmermann and became his pupil at the Vienna Academy of Fine Arts the following year. On a walking tour with his mentor in the Bavarian Alps, Schindler was overawed by the elemental grandeur of the landscape: "Everything beautiful and poetic is to be found in nature," he concluded. "In this world so full of misery it is nature, most beautiful and most cruel of all women, who bewitches us with her charms."[23] This enchantment was the inspiration for his paintings from then on.

In 1886, Schindler's reputation was enhanced by royal patronage when the heir to the Habsburg throne, Crown Prince Rudolf, the only son of Emperor Franz Joseph, commissioned Schindler to illustrate his book, *The Austrian Monarchy in Words and Pictures*. Soon, the banker Herman Herwitz paid Schindler a substantial advance to create a large picture "of the south." Alma vividly remembered the several months when Schindler took his family, along with Carl Moll and a maid, down the Dalmatian coast as he worked on the prince's sketches and made studies for the Herwitz painting, *Brandung bei Scirocco* (Breakers in the Scirocco).

When they moved to Corfu in January 1888, it was "like a dream Paradise."[24] Alma sat by her father as he painted for his own enjoyment rather than on a commission, and she "saw everything with the eyes of

a painter . . . [for] our dear father would point out every beauty to us."
They lived in a very modest stone villa in the saddle of a hill with views
of the both the Adriatic and the Ionian (Aegean) Seas. Centuries-old
hollowed-out olive trees surrounded them, and by a nearby waterfall vi-
olets and wild hyacinths bloomed. Terrific storms descended when "the
sea was a mass of silicon, and above it black clouds were penetrated here
and there by moonlight," Alma recalled with a vivid and heart-rending
nostalgia.[25]

While her mother made the house habitable and tried unsuccessfully
to teach the girls multiplication tables, Alma found a new occupation.
A pianino was sent up from the town, and there, at the age of nine, she
began to compose, "to write down my own music. As the only musician
in the house, I could find my way myself, without being pushed."[26] It was
the first tentative step toward the ambition that would later consume her.

The family returned to Vienna in May 1888. Schindler was now
ranked among the foremost painters in the empire and the preeminent
exponent of poetic realism. He was made an honorary member of the
Academy of Fine Arts in Vienna and a member of the Munich Academy in 1888, and he was awarded several prestigious prizes. His paintings
were exhibited regularly at the Vienna Künstlerhaus, and in Berlin and
Munich. The family still lived in the idyllic surroundings of Schloss Plankenberg, and Emil Jacob's steady output was reducing the pile of debts.

In August 1892, the family traveled with Carl Moll to the North Sea
resort of Sylt for a three-week vacation—according to Alma, "the first
pleasure trip he could afford after his debts were paid off."[27] Schindler
had been suffering intermittent abdominal pain, diagnosed by a Vienna
doctor as "nerves." On the way to Sylt, Anna, Carl Moll, and the children visited Anna's mother in Hamburg, and Schindler stayed with his
old friend Prince Regent Luitpold of Bavaria while he supervised the in-
stallation of his Munich exhibition. A practical joker, the prince regent
had great fun turning a cascade of water on his unsuspecting guests as
they dined on the terrace. Schindler was badly chilled, and his stomach
ailment flared into intense intestinal pains. After he arrived in Sylt, Carl
Moll reported, "The master is getting more and more unwell. . . . [H]e has
no appetite, complains of abdominal pains."[28]

Alarmed by his worsening condition, Anna summoned the local
doctor, then telegraphed Professor Friedrich von Esmarch, the famous

surgeon and specialist in stomach disorders in Kiel, who promised to send his assistant. But he arrived too late. Emil Schindler died of abdominal complications on August 9, 1892.

Alma and her sister, Gretl, were alone in a restaurant when a messenger burst in to tell them to come at once: "I knew instinctively that Papa was dead," she recalled. "In a howling wind we ran across the dunes, I sobbing loudly all the way. Moll met us at the cottage. 'Children, you no longer have a father.'"[29]

It was a devastating blow. They were locked in their room but "sneaked out and found Papa lying in a wooden box on the floor of the next room. He was beautiful. He looked like a fine wax image, noble as a Greek statue. We felt no horror. I was astonished only by the smallness of this man who had been my father, now that I saw him in his coffin."[30]

The depth of her loss gradually dawned as they traveled home for burial in Vienna with her father's coffin concealed inside a piano box to circumvent a cholera quarantine in Hamburg. Her recollections were confused, but the impact of his death was not: "I was not fully aware of all that happened. I was proud of Papa's fine, gold-embroidered pall, and at the cemetery I was bothered yet again by my mother's frantic screaming. But I grew more and more conscious of having lost my guide. My guide—and no one had known but him. All I did had been to please him. All my ambition and vanity had been satisfied by a twinkle of his understanding eyes," she wrote. "Death by the seashore, the cumbersome transport to Vienna, the Nordic grey, stormy hopelessness of nature on Sylt—all this, for me, has remained as part of the indelible memory of my father." Later, a "handsome, romantic monument to him" was erected in the Vienna Stadtpark. At the unveiling, "this coming-to-life in marble of my father's features," Alma almost fainted.[31]

EMIL JAKOB SCHINDLER'S early death at the age of fifty left an aching vacuum of love in the thirteen-year-old Alma—a wound that shadowed her life. "If only he were alive today," she sighed in 1899. "I'm convinced I would have developed quite differently. He was the only person whose love for me was genuine and selfless. Already then! How would it be today, now that I understand him?"[32]

By her own account, in her adolescence she "grew completely away from my surroundings. I became indifferent to them, engrossed in music." Still under her father's spell, she was "tantalised by all things mystical" and fascinated by "words such as 'humans at play in the locks of the deity'—a phrase my father had coined, watching the bathers on the beach at Sylt. I picked this up from him, and many other beautiful expressions my father used."[33]

They moved from Schloss Plankenberg to an apartment on Theresianumgasse in Vienna. As Carl Moll became the dominating influence in the household, Alma's resentment of him deepened. Not only had he replaced her father, but as a sensitive young girl it is likely that Alma had discerned, even unconsciously, the real relations between Moll and her mother. Carl Moll was "my father's pupil—an eternal pupil, who spent his life and wasted his small talent shifting from teacher to teacher, however incompatible," she wrote scornfully later. "He used me to test his skill as an educator . . . but all he reaped was hatred. It was not in him to be my guide."[34] In secret, she built herself a library. Because her mother "thank god had little time for me," she went out alone and exchanged

Figure 2. Alma (left) with her mother, Anna Schindler, and her younger sister, Gretl, c. 1895.

her children's books in secondhand bookshops for modern literature and philosophy, which she smuggled into the house under her wide cape.[35]

Alma was not much more sympathetic toward her mother at this time, though she is far less harsh on both adults in her diaries, written from 1898 when she was eighteen, than in her retrospective account of her life in her 1959 autobiography, *And the Bridge Is Love*. Her overwhelming feeling of abandonment and the vacuum left by the irreplaceable loss of her father's love, run as leitmotifs through the diaries, ripening sometimes into rebellion, at other times into howls of pain and despair. Crucially they underlay her strained relationships with her mother. At her core was a loneliness that she mastered by submerging herself in reading and music—playing, composing, and listening to, above all, Richard Wagner. She "yearned for the blue sky on earth," she wrote, and "found it in music."[36] As she grew older, she became more determined to pursue her independence and forge her own path. Increasingly she longed to find someone to whom she could give total love and loyalty, who could understand her and inspire her respect and devotion, and who would fill the gaping hole left by her father's death.

Her isolation was compounded when her mother married Carl Moll on November 3, 1895, three years after her father's death. Alma recorded the event scornfully in her autobiography: "The poor woman, I thought. There she went and married a pendulum, and my father had been the whole clock!"[37] He looked like "a medieval wood carving of St Joseph, doted on old paintings, and most obnoxiously disturbed the tenor of my ways." Even as her stepfather, Alma insisted, he "had no authority over me."[38]

CARL MOLL WAS a more prominent figure in Viennese cultural circles than Alma gave him credit for in her anguished account. He was the cofounder, with artist Gustav Klimt, of the Vienna Secession, the movement that challenged the hegemony of the Academicians, classicists, and historicists over the Viennese cultural scene. Its first meeting took place at Moll's house on June 21, 1897, and Alma joined in the excitement of the leading painters, sculptors, and architects who socialized there, discussed art and ideas, and "absorbed our thought and emotions for a long time."[39]

More than forty "insurgents" from across the arts spectrum had broken away from the Künstlerhaus, the official artists' association, after it failed to adopt their proposals for a more open, less parochial approach to art. Vienna's cultural style had been dominated since the 1850s by the ethos of the Ringstrasse, a massive project established by Emperor Franz Joseph in 1857 to remodel the city by removing the old walls to create a vast boulevard surrounding the inner city. It was lined with 150 ornate and imposing public buildings, including Parliament, City Hall, the Burgtheater, and 650 private apartments and palaces built for the burgeoning middle classes. Vast friezes depicted allegorical subjects, and ornate decorative motifs filled the interiors of buildings that imitated historical styles—neo-Renaissance, neoclassical, neo-Gothic, or neo-baroque. Artists had reaped fame and fortune from the commissions and patronage that this opulence generated. The Ringstrasse was an emblem of and a showcase for the grandeur and imperial splendor of the Habsburg Empire and a celebration of the new status and influence of the entrepreneurial classes.

It was this decorative extravagance and imitative ethos that the younger generation of artists, sculptors, designers, and architects rejected as they sought a style that reflected the true spirit of modern life. The Ringstrasse style appeared to them a façade disguising the true nature of Viennese society. This "screen of historicism and inherited culture with which bourgeois man concealed his modern, practical identity"[40] was compared in 1898 by twenty-eight-year-old architect Adolf Loos to the fake, cardboard Russian villages that Catherine the Great's General Potemkin constructed to disguise from her the true poverty of everyday life.

Gustav Klimt was a central figure in the movement as well as in Alma Schindler's emotional and sexual awakening. The "most gifted of them all," famous at thirty-five, and "strikingly good-looking," Alma wrote, he was "a painter of Byzantine delicacy who sharpened and deepened the eyesight I had learned from Papa."[41] Klimt had made his name fulfilling commissions for the same decorative scenes adorning the palaces and public buildings that he and the Secessionist movement now rejected.

Klimt came from humble origins. Born in July 1862 in Baumgarten, near Vienna, he was the second child of a gold engraver whose business collapsed in the 1873 financial crash, plunging the family into near penury. At fourteen, he went to art school in Vienna and later set up a partnership with his artist brother Ernst and fellow student Franz von Matsch. Among their first prestigious commissions was the design for the entrance hall to the new Burgtheater, the Austrian National Theater. When they unveiled the project to rapturous applause in 1881, Klimt was heard to mutter in Viennese dialect, "Did the work make us daft or are they?"[42] Further commissions followed, but, by the early 1890s, Klimt was reconsidering his achievements, questioning the conservative Viennese ethos, and exploring new ways of expressing his vision.

Once independent of the Künstlerhaus, the Viennese Secessionists developed their own unique style and objectives under the motto *Der Zeit Ihre Kunst / Der Kunst Ihre Freiheit* (To the age its art / To art its freedom). Vienna must be open to the stimulating artistic and cultural breezes sweeping Europe—art nouveau, French impressionism, Belgian expressionism, the English Pre-Raphaelite movement, and the German Jugenstil movement. They proclaimed a new language of authenticity, simplicity, purity of line, and clarity of purpose, a regenerative aim that was echoed in their magazine, *Ver Sacrum* (*Sacred Spring*). Klimt's *Nuda veritas* in the first issue holds up an empty mirror as the emblem of the movement's aims—in the architect Otto Wagner's words, "to show modern man his true face."[43] Klimt's poster for their first exhibition in March 1898 shows Theseus slaying the Minotaur, watched by Athena, the goddess of wisdom. The authorities censored the poster, insisting that Theseus's manhood be disguised by a tree trunk, which tended to prove the rebels' point.

The spirit of aesthetic regeneration spread across the creative and intellectual life of fin-de-siècle Vienna. In the music of Gustav Mahler, Richard Strauss, and Arnold Schoenberg; in the plays of Arthur Schnitzler and Hugo von Hoffmannstahl; in the work of *Jung Wien* writers like Hermann Bahr, Peter Altenberg, and Berta Zuckerkandl; and in Friedrich Nietzsche's philosophy and Sigmund Freud's psychoanalytic studies of the undisclosed self, there was a search for a language to comprehend the soul of modern man. Its focus was the inner, instinctual "anxious" self of "psychological man"—not merely rational but a creature of feeling and instinct who emerged at a time of painful uncertainty—of disintegrating political stability, rapid social change, and dissolving moral certainties in the twilight years of the Habsburg Empire. "Our generation sensed . . . that in the realm of the arts something had come to an end with the old century, and that a revolution, or at least a change of values, was in the offing," the writer Stefan Zweig decided. "The good solid masters of our fathers' time . . . were as suspect as the rest of the world of security . . . their cool, well-tempered rhythm was no longer in keeping with the accelerated tempo of our time."[44]

It was in this milieu that Alma Schindler was raised. From idolizing her father's poetic realism, she was now swept up in Vienna's most vibrant and revolutionary art movement as it evolved a new, specifically Viennese aesthetic and language of art. The first Secessionist exhibition in March 1898 was "simply beautiful," she decided. "There was art, true art, and real people," and she shared in the group's excitement as 57,000 attended.[45] Emperor Franz Joseph was among the first through the door, 218 items were sold, and the exhibition was extended by popular demand.[46] The modernist advocate Hermann Bahr heralded it as "an exhibition in which there is not a single bad picture! An exhibition which is a resumé of all modern painting! An exhibition which shows that we have people in Austria who can be ranked beside the best Europeans and measured against them! A miracle!"[47] Alma visited the revolutionary new Secession building designed by Joseph Maria Olbrich: "A temple of art . . . a quiet, elegant space of refuge" with "walls white and gleaming, holy and chaste," and she found "rare finesse" in the gold, white, and green color scheme.[48] The interior was "simply wonderful."[49]

CARL AND ANNA Moll's house was the hub of the febrile energy that fueled the movement. It was the background noise within which Alma formulated her own goals and ambitions as she absorbed the currents around her with an open, inquiring mind. Along with their family friends, the Secessionists—Klimt, Koloman Moser, Josef Hoffmann, Joseph Maria Olbrich—and the young leaders of culture came regularly to suppers and lively parties, where Alma entertained at the piano and danced and drank champagne and joined in discussions that lasted into the early hours.

Though surrounded by artists, Alma's overriding passion was music. Twice or three times a week, Alma went to the opera, and every Sunday to the regular Vienna Philharmonic Orchestra concerts. She recorded her powerful emotional responses in her diary. Wagner's *Die Walküre* on May 7, 1898, had "such passion, such magical sounds"; other than *Tristan und*

Isolde, her favorite opera, she had "never felt so enraptured, so breathless, so crazy."[50] Then of *Götterdämmerung* on May 18: "Wonderful. . . . The world doesn't deserve it."[51] Three days later, *Tristan und Isolde* was "incomparable, unearthly—thoughts not of a man but of a god."[52] She was bowled over by "its mad passion and boundless longing . . . for the unknown, for something that exists but which we cannot recognise."[53] When she heard the acclaimed soprano Lilli Lehmann sing in Beethoven's *Fidelio* with "such talent, such fire, such genius," her heart "began to pound so hard I feared it would burst."[54]

Alongside her rapturous enthusiasm, she was developing a discerning critical ear. Alma's first encounter with Mozart left little impression. But she "liked enormously" a performance of *The Marriage of Figaro* in April 1900: "There's nothing thrilling, nothing nerve-racking about this kind of music—in contrast to Wagner's—but it's placid, uncommonly neutral and sweet" and was thus "the healthier of the two." That Mozart moved her less than Wagner was, she perceived, "due to the times we live in. Our century, our race, our outlook on life, our blood, our heart—everything is decadent! That's why people prefer operas in which the music whips up every feeling and tears us apart like a whirlwind. We need madness—not dainty pastorales—to refresh the heart and mind. Quite honestly, *today* I learnt to respect Mozart. . . . Now I *love* his music."[55] When she played Beethoven, the twenty-year-old always felt "as if my soul were at the dry cleaners, and that the ugly black stains caused by the impurities and nervous traumas of Wagner were being removed."[56]

From 1894, when she was fifteen, she had taken weekly music lessons with the blind organist and composer Josef Labor and piano lessons with Frau Adele Radnitzky-Mandlick. Alma was an accomplished pianist and spent hours practicing. At nineteen, she knew the scores of most of Wagner's operas by heart and was frequently overwhelmed: "Yesterday I played *Die Walküre* until late at night," she reported in January 1898. "The passage where Siegfried draws Sieglinde passionately towards him is wonderful—such fire, genuine erotic ardour. Is there *anything* to equal it? My throat is very sore today."[57]

She was developing an intense interest in composition, producing each week as many as two or three piano pieces, variations and song arrangements of poems by Goethe, Rainer Maria Rilke, Heinrich Heine, Richard Dehmel, Gustav Falk, and others, which she submitted to Labor for comment at her lessons. She was overjoyed at praise and accepted criticism with humility: "He gave me a good lecture about 'time-wasting' and begged me to take things more seriously. I have to admit that he was right," she wrote in November 1898.[58] She was "thrilled" when he didn't find any mistakes and sometimes surprised when he found something particularly praiseworthy: "I played him my song and two movements from my sonata. He said that all three were good, pointed out a few mistakes."[59] She heeded his advice: when she had "crammed in too many themes in quick succession," she took notice that she should try "to derive various moods from just one theme."[60]

Her mother sang her songs in a beautiful, well-schooled voice, and sometimes they were performed in public, at concerts arranged by Frau Radnitzky-Mandlick, or more often at soirées with family and friends. "The general opinion was that they didn't sound as if they'd been written by a woman," she noted about one.[61] Complex, intense, and emotional, the songs are often a barometer of her emotional state: "It's astonishing how you always manage to find a poem that corresponds to your state of mind," her sister, Gretl, told her after she heard *Ich wandle unter Blumen*. "I know you: [but] anyone who hears your songs can feel what mood you're in." To which Alma responded, "It's true, I feel compelled to write songs only when they suit my mood. . . . Never have I written a cheerful song or a cheerful instrumental piece. I just can't!"[62] Alma did not know whether her song was any good—she "only knew that love's passion went into it."[63]

By the age of eighteen her ambition to be a composer had crystallized: "I want to do something really remarkable. Would like to compose a really *good* opera—something no woman has ever achieved," she confided to her diary.[64] "O Lord God, give me the strength to achieve what my heart longs for—an opera. . . . That would be my dream! . . . I almost despair, yet my whole being strives to achieve this one goal. I pray to you that I may suffer no defeat in the battle against my weakness, against my femininity."[65] It seems that Alma had absorbed the prevailing belittlement of women's creative powers and saw her femininity as "weakness," an obstacle to her goal. As she struggled in that climate of indifference, she was plagued by destructive self-doubt and chastised herself for her failings: "If only I were a somebody—a real person, noted for and capable of great things. But I'm a nobody, an indifferent young lady who, on

demand, runs her fingers prettily up and down the piano keys and, on demand, gives arrogant replies to arrogant questions, likes to dance . . . *just
like millions of others*. . . . In a word, I want to be a somebody. But it's
impossible—& why? I don't lack talent, but my attitude is too frivolous
for my objectives, for artistic achievement."[66]

She was acutely aware of the boldness of her ambition as a young
woman, with almost no examples to follow. When eight songs she
played to Labor received the comment "A most respectable accomplishment . . . for a girl," she fumed. "It's a real curse to be a girl, there's no way
of overcoming your limitations."[67] She was bitterly disappointed to find
that the work of woman composer Cecile Chaminade was "coquettish,
affected Parisian." She had hoped for "an exception to support me" but
concluded by capitulating to the prevailing view: "After this concert I
know that a woman can achieve nothing, never ever."[68]

Even so, Labor was encouraging: "Your pieces are better than hers.
You're unaffected, at least, & you write as to the manner born."[69] Despite her insecurities, Alma could not give up on her music. The drive
to compose consumed her. When a song went wrong she was "terribly
depressed"—"all my joy is gone"[70]—and when inspiration faltered she
was paralyzed by fear "of losing my creative gift, my sense of melody. Dear
God, it's the finest, purest, most wonderful thing I ever possessed. Don't
take it from me, I beg you."[71] When it went well, she said, "nothing can
compare with my joy when I take a song I've just finished and play it
through. I play it over and over, and in the sound I can hear my own
image. When Mama sings my songs it's something very special. When
she makes a mistake my anger knows no bounds . . . as if I'd been torn
apart."[72]

Although her formal education had been limited, her appetite for
knowledge was voracious. Reading was a passion and a solace, a defense
against an encroaching sense of abandonment. Her interests were eclec-
tic and wide ranging. By nineteen she was familiar with the works of
Plato, Socrates, and Nietzsche, with Spinoza's *Ethics* and the poetry of
Goethe, Rilke, and Heine. She had read Alfred de Musset in French and
consumed Byron's *Cain* and *Don Juan* over three weeks in May 1898.
In her secret library were the modern German writers Hermann Sudermann, Bertha Suttner, Heinrich Zschokke, and Richard Voss, along with
Émile Zola, Gustave Flaubert, Henri Murger's *Scènes de la vie Bohème*—a

"delightful, racy book, although it's dreadfully immoral. . . . [I]t won my warmest sympathy. . . . Mama is aghast that we're reading it!"—and Alphonse Daudet's *Fromont Junior and Risler Senior*, which she thought "magnificent, hideously true, brilliantly narrated and utterly moving."[73]

After evenings spent at the theater, she commented trenchantly to her diary on the plays of Gerhart Hauptmann, Arthur Schnitzler, Henrik Ibsen, George Hirschfeld, and others. When she was not playing the piano, learning French or needlework, or composing, she paid courtesy visits to relations and family friends or went to daytime concerts. The Secession exhibitions continued to generate great excitement and huge crowds. She went to each exhibition several times to meet friends and, as one of the inner circle, to do the honor of meeting and greeting sponsors and patrons and celebrating with the artists.

Alma's familiarity with and understanding of art—begun under her father's tutelage—made her a discriminating critic. Even though she was deeply engaged with the modern Secession spirit, her appreciation of the older ethos represented by her father never faltered. On a visit to the Künstlerhaus exhibition for Emperor Franz Joseph's jubilee, which included thirty of Schindler's paintings and some "exquisite" Makarts, she decided, "No matter how much the Secessionists rail or contemptuously shrug their shoulders, they have nobody to equal *him.*—The epoch of Pettenkofen, Waldmüller, Makart and Papa won't be surpassed that easily. Not by a thousand Engelharts and Klimts. *Tempora mutantur.*"[74]

As Alma steadily carved out her independence, the ache left by her father's absence did not ease. On the sixth anniversary of his death, August 9, 1898, it seemed to her that she was "the only one to have remembered. But then—I believe nobody ever loved Papa more dearly than I. Particularly now. He is my constant refuge."[75] A year later she was no less in thrall: "My thoughts are with him almost daily, hourly I wish him near me. I love him more than when he was alive and mourn him perhaps more than ever. . . . I often feel the maddest desire to speak, to lament, to seek comfort at his side."[76] During any rupture in her uneven relations with her mother and stepfather, she thought of her father and the love she so painfully lacked: "If only I had *someone* to whom I could speak my mind. I live amongst strangers. If my dear Papa were here, I'm certain he would understand me."[77]

Although she was included in the Molls' social life, Alma felt like an outsider. She still found it difficult to reconcile herself to Moll's personality and his dominating position in their household. There were tensions and explosions. She was a volatile young woman with a mind of her own, an inclination toward rebellion, and an honesty about her opinions and her emotions. When her mother once struck her during a row she fumed, "If Mama thinks she can restrain me by resorting to violence, she's mistaken. It just makes me defiant & stubborn. At such moments I wish I were far away, far . . . away."[78]

An even greater shock came in March 1899 when her mother announced that "before long you'll be getting a little brother or sister." Alma reacted with a howl of pain: "I looked at her—and burst into tears. Gretl laughed. As if in a flash, the future raced through my inner eye. Moll on the one side—Schindler on the other. Our dismissal, our estrangement from the family, our hatred of the intruder. I'd never experienced anything of the kind. I almost fainted."[79]

She felt isolated, rejected, and confused. Her plan to compose a cradle song for her mother was abandoned when "my thoughts turned to the idea that for us the little brat will signify—a loss."[80] She was deeply concerned when her mother left their summer retreat for her confinement in Vienna—"Who knows if I will ever see her again?" Alma wailed. But the deepest hurt was that her mother paid more attention to her mother-in-law and other people than to her, which unleashed another wail of outrage:

> Leaving at such a worrying time, we should mean more to her than all the others together. I told her so too. With tears in my eyes, I cycled through the village, Christine and Gustav [Geiringer] right behind. The latter invited me over and spoke very kindly to me. Dear God, he has no idea what a state I'm in! We no longer have a home we can call our own! If all goes well, the child will deprive us of our mother's affection—as is already partly the case. If anything goes wrong, the outcome will be disastrous. Wherever I look, there's no hope of rescue—except marriage. . . . Dear God—if only I had someone to talk to, someone to embrace me, a heart to love me, a soul to understand me. Never![81]

Nothing alleviated her despair: "The climate remains unchanged: our barometers still point to storm," she noted.[82] When Alma found out only by chance from a family friend instead of from her mother about plans for the newborn child's Catholic baptism, she was beside herself: "These outsiders all knew about it, but we didn't. . . . I was crying so hard, I could scarcely stand. . . . I found a bench, sat down and cried as I have *never* cried before. This is the end. The day on which Mama told us she was expecting a baby, that very day . . . that very moment, I could foresee everything. 'Children, I've got a new toy now, you should get married. And keep your opinions to yourselves. It's none of your business. You're strangers now, strangers in my house!' . . . My eyes are so sore, I can scarcely see! In my heart I felt as if I were being torn forcibly apart. *How* can I love my mother, if she abandons us for the sake of another child? We mean nothing to her now—we're just in her way."[83]

Alma stewed in frustration as she contemplated her options. One was to ask her mother and stepfather for enough money to move out, but though she often dreamed of escaping Vienna, she did not feel suited to such a radical challenge. As she reached this impasse, her other option, a mere few days after her twentieth birthday, was marriage. But as yet she did not feel the pressure to get married. Moreover, there was nobody suitable whom she loved enough.

— 2 —

Awakening

1898–1899

*O*utside the family circle, Alma was already making waves in Vien-nese society. With her thick hair, penetrating blue eyes, sensuous mouth, and strong features she had a growing reputation as "the most beautiful girl in Vienna." Vivacious, quick witted, and musically accom-plished, she could engage in serious conversations with family friends about Goethe and Plato as readily as deliver her intelligent judgments on art exhibitions and the opera, theater, and concert performances she regularly attended.

At grand social occasions, young men conversed and flirted and danced, and paid court to Moll's attractive stepdaughter. She willingly participated in the elaborate, boisterous parties common in their cir-cle: "The table looked wonderful: We had girandoles and, as a centre piece, a fruit bowl surrounded with flowers—and garlands with which they later decked me out. . . . We fooled around like children. . . . Later Gustav [Geiringer] played and everyone danced for all they were worth. [Theobald] Pollack proposed one toast after another, then [Felix] Fischer toasted Gretl and me. It was such fun."[1]

Alma was learning to flirt, to use her eyes, charm, and mental agil-ity to enchant men, discovering that she could have power over them. After one party when she stayed up till 3:30 a.m., a young man "told me that I was madly flirtatious—that I'd first turned his head, but later taken

Figure 3. Alma Schindler, 1898.
"The most beautiful girl in Vienna."

no further notice of him." She conceded immediately, "He's quite right: I'm utterly vulgar, superficial, sybaritic, domineering and egoistic!" She chided herself for her vanity and lack of seriousness: "Nothing pleases me more than to be told that I'm exceptional." And when she was, she criticized herself for being "just one of many, for I relish such shallow compliments!"[2]

Through her family connections, Alma was acquainted with the intersecting circles of artistic talent and industrial enterprise that made up the cultural life of fin-de-siècle Vienna. Mingling in the Molls' drawing room with the Secession artists and architects were singers, actresses, musicians and composers, prominent journalists and writers such as *Jung Wien* founder Hermann Bahr and Secession champion Berta Zuckerkandl, as well as her father's old family friends—Ida and Hugo Conrat, merchant and honorary treasurer of the Tonkunstlerverein; the Hellmanns whose daughter, Gretl, was a childhood friend; Theobald Pollack, a high-ranking civil servant; photographer and chemist Hugo Henneberg and his wife, Marie (Aunt Mie), whose portrait was painted by Klimt.

This diverse elite at Alma's fingertips reflected the pride in the city's artistic excellence that engaged and unified all strata of Viennese society.

"The first glance of the average Viennese into his morning paper was not at the events in parliament, or world affairs, but at the repertoire of the theatre, which assumed so important a role in public life," according to the writer Stefan Zweig.[3] To which was added the thriving opera and concert programs and proliferating artistic endeavors. Since Emperor Franz Joseph's remodeling of the city from the 1860s, the imperial and aristocratic monopoly on culture had loosened. The rising bourgeois elite who financed the architectural splendors of the Ringstrasse had become the chief patrons and benefactors of culture. And this cultural interchange between artists and entrepreneurs helped dissolve social and class barriers: "It was only in regard to art that all felt on equal terms, because love of art was a communal duty in Vienna," wrote Zweig.[4] And, as the cohesion of the empire began to weaken, cultural excellence assumed a powerful unifying purpose.

Within this thriving culture, as well as in Alma's social circle, assimilated Jews were an influential presence. Their steady emancipation since the 1860s by a series of imperial decrees had lifted previous restrictions on their place of residence, property ownership, and civic activities. New opportunities had opened up in trade, industry, finance, and the professions, though access was still barred to the higher echelons of the civil service and the army. By the 1890s, Jews had come from all parts of the empire to Vienna, where the ethos of liberal tolerance had helped bring about the effective assimilation into every level of society of Jews loyal to the monarchy and the empire.

In the cultural circles in which Alma moved, the Jewish bourgeoisie, as Zweig observed, became the benefactors and patrons of the arts; they were the audiences at operas, concerts, and theaters; they attended art exhibitions, commissioned paintings, and were the "exponents and champions of all that was new." Jewish talent powered the creative and intellectual vigor of Viennese culture as scholars, painters, theater directors, architects, journalists, scientists, and innovators gained eminence: "Because of their passionate love for the city, through their desire for assimilation, they had adapted themselves fully, and were happy to serve the glory of Vienna," wrote Zweig.[5]

But seeping into this cultivated Vienna was a swelling current of anti-Semitism. Previously contained in the casual asides that reflected deeply ingrained prejudice, anti-Jewish sentiment acquired potent political currency when Karl Lueger, leader of the Christian Social Party, was elected mayor of Vienna in 1895 on a militant anti-Semitic platform. Emperor Franz Joseph refused four times to ratify the appointment: "I will tolerate no *Judenhetze* [Jew hounding] in my empire. I am fully persuaded of the fidelity and loyalty of the Israelites and they can always count on my protection." But he gave in when Lueger, noting that "Jew-baiting is an excellent means of propaganda and getting ahead in politics," won again in 1897. His elevation to mayor heralded the public legitimation of anti-Semitism. Though no laws were passed restricting the civic activities of Jews—and Lueger was open to some accommodation on the spurious ground that "who is a Jew is something I determine"—the open expression of anti-Semitism was sanctioned in public, in the more virulent sections of the media, and in private.

Although Alma was never politically engaged, indeed there is hardly a mention of politics in her diaries up to 1902, and even though a great number of her associates were Jewish, she too was tainted by the prejudices of the age and prone to startling and tasteless anti-Semitic asides in her diaries. Her comments are not consistent and display no coherent view and no political platform; often they reflect class prejudice as much as racial prejudice. She might say of a friend she liked, "He's a Jew. But what difference does that make, actually . . . ?" but then comment, after a lively evening discussing modern literature with the "very sensible, intelligent . . . very sweet" Frau Spier: "What a pity that [she] is so conspicuously Jewish."[6] Alma's anti-Semitic prejudices would remain a taint throughout her life.

IN HER SOCIAL milieu, Alma was mostly surrounded by men. She had several girlfriends, mostly the daughters of family friends, and a practical sister, Margarethe (Gretl), with whom she got on despite having little in common. As an eligible young woman in the closed, gossip-ridden society of Vienna, Alma was minutely observed. When rumor spread that she was to be engaged to the Secessionist architect Julius Mayreder, who had become a frequent visitor at the Moll house, she was appalled: "Nothing could be more idiotic, really—engaged to *Mayreder . . . Ughhhhh!*" It was "revolting, the way people love to wag their tongues," she protested.[7]

The person who intrigued Alma was Gustav Klimt. Handsome, charismatic, the dominant figure in the Secession, at thirty-five he was older than many of his contemporaries, single but with responsibilities for his own family and, after the premature death of his brother, Ernst, for his sister-in law and her sister, Emilie Flöge. Believed to have had affairs with several women including his models, his unconventional lifestyle included dressing, when not in frock coat, in long, flowing smocks. He worked closely with Carl Moll during the Secession's establishment and was a regular visitor to his household.

Alma took increasing pleasure in his company: "Klimt is such a dear man," she decided after a party in March 1898. "He was delightful, talked about his painting etc, and then we talked about *Faust*, a work which he loves as much as I do.—No, he's a really delightful fellow. So natural, so modest—a true artist!"[8] Their encounters became more teasing, playful, and flirtatious. Returning in a cab from a visit to the Prater, she refused to speak to him after he said she was "spoilt by too much attention, conceited and superficial."[9] But he pulled such faces that she had to laugh: "I really don't understand why Klimt is considered a poseur etc.—I find him really very dear and significant."[10] The flirtation progressed at a supper a few weeks later when "Klimt gave me the idea of shaping my bread into a heart. I did so, then he formed a toothpick into an arrow and plunged it into the heart."[11]

From then on, using her diary as a confessional, she charted the "stations of my first love"—as she called them—and the chaos of her oscillating emotions. As she experienced a growing sense of abandonment by her pregnant mother, she longed for someone to understand her "instinctively & completely, whom I understand instinctively & completely, that our souls might flow side by side—that they might resound as *one* chord, as a beautiful harmony."[12]

When friends and relations began to tease her about Klimt, she brushed them off: "I really don't know what's the matter with everybody. If you talk to one person a little longer than you talk to others, everyone immediately thinks you're in love."[13] Klimt issued his own veiled warning to her: "He told me yesterday 'Look before you leap! You can't trust an artist—and a painter least of all. It's in the blood. High spirits—frivolity. Here today, gone tomorrow.'"[14] She was undeterred, perhaps even

Figure 4. Painter Gustav Klimt, "handsome and brilliant"—and Alma's first love.

excited, but her mother was becoming concerned. In August 1898, at a spa at Franzenbad, Anna warned Alma against him: "'He's involved with his sister-in-law and even if he's really very fond of you (which seems to be the case), he has no *right* to behave this way—it's unscrupulous and abominable.' I said: 'Really, what business is it of mine?' To which she replied: 'He really likes you, don't deny it, but you're too good to be merely his plaything.'"[15] Back in Vienna, her inquiries confirmed Klimt's attachment to Emilie Flöge, the sister of his sister-in-law, Helene. Alma was shocked and initially refused to believe it, but her mother was so persistent she finally resolved to break with Klimt, though she still believed with blind confidence "even if he's hitched up with his sister-in-law [*sic*], it's me that he loves."[16]

But her resolve invariably faltered in his presence. Although she behaved coolly toward him at the opening of the Second Secession Exhibition in November 1898, she relented the next day: "I actually *spoke* to Klimt. I'm so happy. . . . I consider him handsome and brilliant."[17] As her infatuation deepened she sought signs that her feelings were reciprocated. After a dinner with family friends in mid-January she reported,

"Now I know what he feels and I'm happy. . . . He's the only man I ever loved and shall ever love. We harmonize so beautifully."

Even so, Alma was not blind to his shortcomings and was capable of blazing honesty. When she asked Klimt straight out whether what was said about "the other woman" was true, "he said no, and it was patently obvious that he was lying."[18] On another occasion she observed him being blatantly untruthful and concluded, "I know he's insincere, but that he's also a coward came as a surprise. Life is full of surprises . . . especially with someone like that."[19]

In February 1899 she was thrown into turmoil when he turned to her as he was leaving after a dinner to ask: "'A.S., have you ever thought of visiting me in my studio . . . just you, on your own?' A tremor went through my whole body. I don't remember what I answered. He asked me to dedicate a song to him, and I said: 'They're all dedicated to you.'"[20] As her watching mother shot her furious glances she decided, "In future my motto shall be: 'Grasp the opportunity.'"[21] That night Alma didn't sleep a wink. She was "madly excited . . . in connection with Kl. Am I truly happy or, actually, deeply unhappy? I don't understand myself. But I think probably the latter."[22]

Within a few days she was assailed by more doubts: "Everything he told me was insincere. . . . He's leading me up the garden path, sometimes professing affection, sometimes quite the opposite. It's got to stop."[23] But she experienced a new level of sensual arousal when he spilled a glass of schnapps on her white dress: "He took my skirt on his knee, and himself washed the stain out of my petticoat. Both his legs and mine were hidden under the skirt, and inevitably they touched. Although I kept withdrawing—for I consider such behaviour vulgar—I did so with reluctance and was overcome by such a strange, sweet sensation." The young Alma was taken aback: "My goodness, what I'm writing here is madly sensual . . . [things] that cause blood to rush to my cheeks." But she could still stand apart and reflect: "Heavens! Why do I have to be so fond of *this* particular fellow? . . . Can one love a man who's so unscrupulous? Yes, unfortunately.—Artists are rarely people of integrity."[24]

For Alma, the question of marriage hovered below the surface, though always unspoken. She was shattered at a dance in March 1899 when Klimt told her "it would never be possible for him to marry me— that he was fond of me all the same. Never had we spoken in greater seclusion and solitude than in the midst of the dancers in that salon. Never had I felt sadder than in the inner circle of that waltz. Never."[25]

A month later, in April, the family departed on an extended trip to Italy, made possible by a generous gift to Moll from the art collector and Secession patron Carl Reininghaus. In Rome she decided the Klimt affair was over: this man—who she believed had "at least three different affairs running simultaneously" had "declared his love in all colours of the rainbow and—was just waiting to test me."[26] But by the time they got to Pisa, she was again imagining his eyes and hearing his voice: "Everything is in chaos!" she wailed.[27]

Carl Moll had arranged for Klimt to join them in Florence. Assuming that Alma's feeling had cooled, he warned her to keep out of his way. Klimt arrived on April 24 and their daily contact facilitated a new round of playful encounters—sitting beside each other in a cab "like a married couple," Klimt remarked—they cuddled closer, their knees touched, and she couldn't sleep for "sheer physical excitement." After her mother told her to tidy up her disheveled hair, Klimt took out the hairpins one by one until her hair was loose over her shoulders: "Kl moved back, as if in holy awe. Then he came closer, ran his hand caressingly over my head and stroked my hair with uttermost devotion, so gently, so softly, yet so firmly." When he confessed that he would have loved to burrow his hands in her hair and she asked why not, "his eyes implied that otherwise he would have lost control of himself and done something foolish."[28]

At Genoa she experienced her first kiss. He came into her room, and before she realized it "he'd taken me in his arms and kissed me. It only lasted a tenth of a second, for we heard a noise in the room next door. . . . It's indescribable: to be kissed for the first time in my life, and that by the only person in the whole world that I love."[29] Her recollection of it several weeks later was suffused with the glow of romance: "We were engulfed in dark silence, and he kissed me with such force, with such a frisson. It was so sad, we were both close to tears. It was almost a kiss of benediction. A kiss with which he begged me never to love another man and with which I gave him my promise—plied, my troth. And we rejoiced."[30]

Their second kiss was at Verona, when she delivered his shirts to his room: "He held me and kissed me again. We were both terribly agitated. Later he stood behind me and said: 'There's only one thing for it: complete physical union.' I staggered and had to steady myself on the bannister." Later that day, "he returned to the subject again. 'If two people are united, their happiness is assured. God won't object either.' I resolved to give him an answer. In the evening, on the stairs, I asked him for a copy of *Faust* and said: 'From this book I take my code of behaviour: "Do no favours without a ring on your finger." There's nobody I'm more fond of than you. But that—not yet.'"[31]

Once again, Alma elevated the kiss to a rhapsodic "spiritual union," the moment "for which I will yearn for the rest of my life," and which convinced her that "once a man has kissed you, you are his for eternity."[32] But in the midst of her great passion, she now began to have doubts about Klimt's "brutal behaviour." Standing on a bridge, staring into the black canal near the Bridge of Sighs, she suddenly felt Klimt's fingers "pulling, tearing at my collar. As I was leaning on the stone, the neckline tightened. Before I could realise what he was about, everyone moved on, . . . As was his wont, he pinched my arm, whispering: 'Silly girl, Alma, I could have put my hand on your heart—easily.' A cold shiver went through me, my heart missed a beat. He wanted to feel my breasts! Or did he want to see how fast my heart was beating! The former would have been lechery, the other love—unfortunately I'm *sure* it was the former."[33]

She retreated again. When she ignored him for a whole afternoon, Klimt grew furious and was petulantly returning her photo when Carl Moll arrived on the scene. That evening Moll confronted her about the relationship. Alma later claimed furiously that her mother had "studied the stammerings in my diary and thus kept track of the stations of my love."[34] She lay all night "thinking of nothing but that I should softly open the window and throw myself into the lagoon."[35]

Moll warned that, even if Klimt gave up his other liaison, "brutality" was his second nature, which for Alma, with her "sensitive disposition, would be most regrettable." Surprisingly, Alma took this in her stride. She gave her word to Moll that she would tell Klimt that "the affair has got to end, that people are already beginning to talk—that's the truth— and that anyway it will lead nowhere." Her own doubts had surfaced again: "I also think he'd be madly jealous, and that for me, with my spirit of freedom . . . my will to freedom!" would be a serious obstacle.[36]

The drama was not over. Alma might resolve to end it, but she could not deny the powerful hold he still exercised over her romantic imagination and her febrile emotions. As they sailed around the lagoon, Klimt sat opposite her, "his eyes begging forgiveness. I felt awful." Later "Kl. stole up to me unobserved. 'Keep a place in your heart for me, Alma, just a tiny one.' I told him: 'Klimt, it's got to stop. Everyone's talking about us, it's got to stop.' 'Yes,' he said, 'it was stillborn.'" She assured him, "'Even if I don't speak to you, you can trust me, for you know that I love *only* you.' He said: 'But not just for now, Alma. I want you to love me always.' 'For ever,' I replied."[37]

When he departed Venice, Alma was distraught. At the final lunch he behaved "very correctly" but "time and again our eyes met. A heaven opened in our gaze." As Klimt said goodbye, "I felt the ground trembling beneath my feet, the whole world darkening before my eyes. All of a sudden I could feel just what—whom—I had lost . . . everything for me has grown empty, pale and desolate."[38] Carl Moll drank a toast to her prudence and good sense. Tears welled up in her eyes at his sympathy. She was plunged into deep, inconsolable despair: "Sun, why do you wake me? Why? That's how I felt yesterday, that's how I feel today, from now on that's how I shall always feel. The romance of my life is over, all spiritual energy is spent. . . . Two days ago, at 2:00 p.m., I died secretly. A leave-taking from life and for life."[39]

Alma took months to overcome her grief. A week later in Vienna, as a storm raged outside her window, she decided she would never marry: it would be "an unscrupulous act" for it "would mean betraying the person to whom I gave my hand—betraying my heart, my entire person. For my person is no longer my own."[40] To Klimt she had sworn, "I am yours, therefore I have no rights over myself," and the idea "made me happy, it ennobled me."[41]

The lesson Alma drew from this experience—that love entailed the sacrifice of self-hood—informed her emotional and romantic makeup well beyond her immediate turmoil. She soon encountered another severe setback—the betrayal of love. On the day she marked with a black cross in her diary, Klimt wrote Moll a long, apologetic, and often disingenuous letter in which he dissociated himself from her and denied their love. He was, he wrote, an "indescribably unhappy man" who snatched at happiness "like a starving stray dog snapping at a morsel of food," but he realized his actions had brought sorrow to a colleague whose friendship he valued. He had noticed Alma's beauty as a painter and had "delighted in her," he explained, but had never courted her "in the real sense of the word" and never expected to arouse the stirrings of first love in this "beautiful, blossoming young child." He reassured himself that, for her, "it must be all a light-hearted game, a passing mood." He was certain, he added breezily, that she would soon forget it all. Meanwhile, he begged for Moll's friendship and forgiveness and hoped he might again visit Moll's household "without causing trouble."[42]

Alma was grief stricken. "He's betrayed me. I cannot write for tears." Hurt and confused, she was calmed neither by her mother's solicitude nor Moll's clumsy reassurance: "Alma, does it really affect you so deeply? Wasn't it just a diversion on your part, nothing more? Try to forget him. You can still be happy."[43] She thought only of his betrayal, his abandonment of her without a struggle—"If only I could run away—far away . . . , I wouldn't be ashamed, for I did everything for love's sake. But I'd like to run away, to banish all these false, evil people from my sight. I trust nobody."[44]

WITH KLIMT'S "BETRAYAL," Alma was completely unable to compose or play music: "The blood stagnates in my veins, my throbbing passion is spent," she wailed. "Sensibility has given way to pathetic insipidity. Where then can melody be born? Can fire issue from a spent crater?"[45] When she found her voice again it was to compose a fantasia with the motto "I was born to be lonely / And loneliness is my destiny, / For I feed off my own thoughts."[46]

To compound her woes, she continued to fear that her pregnant mother would abandon her: "Here I stand, hands clasped together . . . weeping compulsively," she wailed. "For I have lost everything: my father, my Klimt—and now I am about to lose my mother. Three people who constituted my world. . . . I feel so wretched . . . so lonely and abandoned. . . . I haven't composed a note for a week. . . . I can find neither inner nor outer repose."[47] As so often when she felt the world was against her, she turned to her father's image for consolation. On the terrace under a shining moon, she prayed, without knowing to whom or for what: "All I know is that I wrung my hands, wept and kept repeating the words, 'Father, I love you.' Never in my life have I prayed more fervently. I was so dreadfully sad. If only I had *someone* in whom I could confide. . . . And I do so long for love—for *unselfish* love."[48]

For the next nine months, though outwardly calm and absorbed in her life and her music, Alma continued to run the gamut of intense emotions, still obsessed with Klimt while struggling to release herself from him. She did not blame him for what happened: "Is it his fault that I love him more that anyone in the world? He was weak *too*. . . . But surely I was weaker by far . . . for he never duped me, never left me in any doubt that he couldn't marry me. . . . The tacit agreement was: live for the moment. He was in love with me after all. . . . For me it was the same. . . . [I] knew I'd never love anyone more than him." She oscillated wildly between resolution and renewed surrender to her romantic feelings. On June 9 she was casting out her love as "unnecessary ballast, time-consuming and nerve-racking. It's time to put paid to such folly."[49] But when at dinner her mother gave her a compassionate look, she burst into tears: "There's nothing more frightful than pity. Although I'm unhappy and always shall be, I won't ask *compassion* of anyone," she wrote defiantly.[50] But by the end of June she was again "sad, very sad. I'm thinking about what I've lost—happiness that will never return."[51]

Of one decision—to draw back from the brink of the "total union" Klimt wanted—she was clear, though "Lord knows, to utter these words was the hardest task I ever faced: my love for him was boundless, utterly devoted. My only wish was to be his, body and soul, for ever."[52] She was certain that she "would have been the happiest woman in the world—then. And now the unhappiest. How grateful I am for my steadfast character! . . . Things turned out better, but I can never be entirely happy and joyful."[53] Though later she blamed her mother and her "so-called breeding" for destroying her "first marvel of love," at the time she thanked God for having rescued her, and her mother, "who taught me to distinguish between Good and Evil. My inner voice, my instinct, fearing no retribution, steadfast in heart and soul, told me: 'This is forbidden.' . . . And yet I loved you, and love you still—my Klimt!"[54]

Later, when she heard he was having another affair, she found new resolve: "Let him be buried—for ever. Let him be numbered amongst my dead, my beloved dead. Never shall I think or say a word against him. I repeat: for me he is sacred." She could convincingly declare in January 1900:

> And so we came to the end of a romance that lasted three years. And what an ending—ha! I've lost three years of my life. But I shan't despair, for despite the cruel times I went through, Kl. made me happier than anyone else ever will.
>
> It was my first, great, beautiful love.—Amen![55]

— 3 —

Love and Music

1899–1901

*A*lma turned to music for solace. "Music, my hope, my strength, don't abandon me, as the others have abandoned me," she pleaded in her diary.[1] She worked hard at her compositions before departing in May 1899 for the picturesque Salzkammergut region, where the family regularly spent their summers. Here among the breathtaking scenery of precipitous mountains and great stretches of lakes, social life was more muted. She composed piano pieces and lieder, read voraciously the works of Emile Zola and Hermann Bahr, Richard Voss and Peter Nansen, played *Parsifal* and *Tristan and Isolde* on the piano, and entertained friends staying nearby.

In July 1899, Max Burckhard visited. A lawyer and former director of the Vienna Burgtheater, he had introduced contemporary playwrights Henrik Ibsen, Gerhart Hauptmann, Arthur Schnitzler, and Hugo von Hoffmannstahl to Viennese audiences. Now in his midforties, he was a founder of the Secession journal *Ver Sacrum*. He appeared to take Alma seriously, as her father had done before, and talked to her about *Faust* and Goethe and Wagner's writings: "A serious discussion with a man of such intellect is for me one of the real pleasure of life," she noted.[2] Accompanied by her sister and mother, they cycled through the woods and beside the lakes, and went on long walks in the mountains where Alma marveled at the beauty of nature. Burckhard arrived at picnics with extravagant

Figure 5. Alma on a cycling trip in the Salzkammergut, summer 1899.

gourmet delicacies and sometimes a punch bowl of peaches, vintage wine, and two bottles of superior Heidsieck Monopole champagne: "We drained it to the last drop and became frightfully merry. . . . We flew back home. When you've had a drop or two there's nothing better than a cycle ride."[3] Alma was increasingly intrigued by this intellectual bon viveur.

At her first excited visit in August to the Bayreuth Festival, which had been set up by Richard Wagner to perform his operas, she was over-whelmed by *Parsifal*. Then, at *Die Meistersinger von Nürnberg*, a work "so rich that it becomes divine," she at last "could sense that life is beautiful again."[4] Music had rescued her. But she was in turmoil once more when news came that her mother had given birth on August 9—the very date on which her father had died seven years earlier: "Oh what joy! Another girl! Yet another poor, unfortunate creature on God's earth. . . . There's something grey and symbolic about it. I'm so sad, I just can't stop myself crying."[5] Try as she might, she could find no warm words "for my *stepsister*."

Instead, in her distress she vented her disdain for Moll by asserting the superiority of her and Gretl's "so much richer" pedigree: "in our veins flows the blood of a genius" but "capable and hard-working" Carl would "*never* attain the rank of a true artist."[6] Already, and as she would for the rest of her life, Alma was ranking people according to a hierarchy of genius rather than of any other social, racial, or religious status.

She immersed herself in music. Over five days in September in Vienna, Alma heard *Die Walküre, Siegfried, Götterdämmerung*, and, a week later, *Lohengrin*. She composed feverishly. To her music teacher, Josef Labor, she played all her new pieces and received mixed responses: *Einsamer Gang* (based on a poem by Leo Greiner) had "very good ideas," *Hinaus* (also based on a poem) was too long, *Der Morgen* was "good." Her courage in tackling her sonata movement was "remarkable," but her étude was "dull." "You have a very fine talent," he told her. "We might be able to make something of you." Alma carried on composing daily, determined to "make a reputation for myself."[7]

As Klimt's influence waned she took more notice of other young men. The Secession architect Joseph Maria Olbrich appealed to her for the first time on an outing to the Prater: "He's such a dear sensible fellow. . . . The look in his eye is affectionate, candidly open."[8] The more she appreciated his talent, the stronger her feelings grew for him. His great achievement, the Secession building, had impressed her—the "uncommonly distinguished" façade, the "colour scheme of rare finesse" and the "simply wonderful" interior.[9] But she had not imagined Olbrich was "*so very* gifted," until she visited a villa designed by him: "A jewel from top to bottom . . . everything breathes *one* artistic spirit. . . . This is a man of stature."[10] Of all the Secession artists, she decided, only he "is *self sufficient*, he alone has the *self-confidence* of a true artist."[11] Moreover, she told him, "both as a man and as an artist," he reminded her of Wagner in "his immense pride, immense vanity, immense self-assurance" as well as his versatility and proficiency—"which can really get on one's nerves." Never one to pull her punches, Alma thought him the most talented artist, but she also resented his "well-nigh petulant vanity."[12]

Olbrich took a discerning interest in her compositions. He shared her love of music, and they went to concerts and the opera and played piano together at social gatherings. She knew her feelings for him were not reciprocated, but she rejoiced at the return of her ability to love, which she feared had shriveled in her: "Half a year has passed. I love another man—with renewed fervor—as if with a sacred, morally purified fervor. Is it unjust? Just *once*, physical union—that was what I felt with Klimt. With Olbrich I wish for physical union my whole life."[13] Gossip circulated that they were "fond" of each other.

When in January she suspected that he was in love with a woman whom Alma waspishly described as "small, cute and superficial, loves to talk about things she doesn't understand—I don't care for her at all," she sank into despair that she would never be loved: "To think that someone should prefer an insignificant little mannequin—to me!" she raged petulantly.[14] But when she heard in September that Olbrich had moved to work in an artists' colony in Germany and that he was engaged to an actress, she recovered surprisingly quickly: "Well—I draw a line beneath the affair. . . . Nor is the line particularly bold or prominent: just a delicate little flourish."[15]

Alma needed to love and be loved, to fill the vacuum at her core that could so easily suck her into gloom and self-abnegation. Creative talent in any sphere lifted her spirits, gave meaning to her life. Opera singers inspired her awe. Lilli Lehmann, the leading soprano at the Vienna Opera and a Moll family friend, was "uniquely pretty, sweet and kind. . . . When I look at her in profile, she drives me crazy—her eyes so black, her nose so fine and dainty, her mouth, her teeth. Yes, she's uniquely beautiful."[16] Her performances were "breathtaking," "brilliant," "wonderful," and she herself was "something special."

A flirtation with Erik Schmedes, the Vienna Opera's leading heldentenor, was an enjoyable diversion. He stirred Alma's adoration as he played Wagner heroes, with "brilliant . . . Teutonic verve." At thirty-one, handsome, well built, and physically overpowering, he was also vain—and very alluring. Although she thought him "dense but amusing," his physical presence could make "the blood rush to her head" but "without a hint of love. For that I don't respect him enough—it's nothing but lust."[17] With equal clarity, she found "endearing" the conceit of a man who spoke "quite calmly and without the slightest scruple, of his *talent*" and who "unashamedly considers himself and his voice the most important things in the world."[18]

They devised weekly encounters on the Ringstrasse and exchanged gossip and playful banter as he walked her home. She was pleased when he sought her out in the audience during a performance, but she quickly recoiled from her delight: "My goodness, I'm so terribly superficial and vain."[19] At a masked ball she got him to dance with her despite the furious interventions of the woman Alma cuttingly called his "little" wife, from whom he claimed to be always on the point of divorce. Siegfried "could cope with the larger dragons, but not the smaller ones," he explained.[20] Alma massaged his vanity. Seeking her reassurance of his uniqueness, he asked, "All my friends warn me: 'Watch your step, she's a dreadful flirt.' . . . Tell me one thing: are you so sweet to everyone or just to me?"[21]

Alma basked in the attention she found she could command. Although too sensible to let it turn her head, she was given to bouts of conceit as she realized the power of her beauty. At a Künstlerhaus exhibition with Gretl, she noted, "Without flattering myself I must admit that I caused quite a stir. . . . Five young academicians chased after us through all the galleries."[22] At a party of family friends, where she was dressed in a beautiful

Figure 6. Alma Schindler,
c. 1900.
"I want to do something really remarkable."

white crêpe-de-chine dress, the men "were hovering about me like midges round a lamp. I felt like a queen, proud and unapproachable, exchanged a few cool words with each in turn. . . . It was a veritable triumph."[23] She noted Secessionist Koloman Moser's view of her as "such a unique person," with "something irrepressible, invincible" about her, and appreciated the veiled but affectionate compliment of her friend Berta Zuckerkandl, as she deftly put to music a poem by the artist Fernand Khnopff: "She's good-looking—that's bad enough. She's a brilliant pianist—that's infuriating. And on top of it she composes—it makes you sick."[24]

Alma saw herself as a thinking, unconventional, and independent woman who was not afraid to be controversial or deliberately provocative and, sometimes, in strait-laced Viennese society, to shock for the sake of it. "I don't give a damn for morality," she declared, "for I love Nature. And morality is unnatural. Freedom—that's what I long for and can never attain."[25] At lunch with family friends Ida and Hugo Conrat, she alarmed fellow guests by announcing that she could "respect someone with an unscrupulous character if he is otherwise brilliant," adding that "only a few artists are honest." Their talent was rather "to offer up their soul to humanity—for the salvation of humanity, to safeguard the world against brutality."[26]

Although she put on a bold face in public, she was afflicted by self-doubt in private. Torn between her ambition to be "a somebody" and her sense of inadequacy, she was prone to give in to prevailing expectations of women's abilities: "What can a dumb woman like me achieve?—Nothing! I lack application. My head is full of other, *silly* ideas."[27] With any setback, it was only a short step to her descent into despair, for her self-doubt extended to the fear that she would never be loved, never experience passion, never love fully. The shadow of Klimt still haunted her at intervals, for nothing she experienced had entirely replaced that great passion: "If only I had someone to embrace, to kiss—to kiss to death—let me love *just once*—enjoy life—*just once*—and then die," she wailed in March 1900. "I'm in such a state of nervous agitation. I had to stop composing. . . . I can't go on vegetating like this. I must experience life. I *must*. I feel the urge to fall at someone's feet and give myself to them, body and soul. There's too much zest in me."[28] Her mother was concerned enough to consult Berta Zuckerkandl, whose husband, Emil, was an anatomist, because Alma had "lost a lot of weight, is pale and also became very silent." It worried her that Alma had also stopped flirting. The doctor had diagnosed anemia, but Anna worried more about Alma's state of mind: "She goes to the opera nearly every evening. Then she comes home tear-stained, sits down at the piano and plays for hours."[29]

When Alma met young composer Alexander von Zemlinsky at a dinner at the Conrats' on February 25, 1900, her life took on a new direction. She had seen him conduct at a concert a few days before: "He cuts the most comical figure imaginable. A caricature—chinless, small, with bulging eyes and a downright *crazy* style of conducting," but she thought his work was "quite original—very Wagnerian" and "a little immature," but the orchestration was "magnificent."[30]

Alma had "a wonderful time" seated next to him at dinner. "He's dreadfully ugly, almost chinless—yet I found him quite enthralling." They discovered a shared admiration of the conductor, composer, and director of the Vienna Court Opera, Gustav Mahler, to whom they drank a toast: "I told him how greatly I venerated him and how I longed to meet him." Zemlinsky asked her opinion of Wagner. "'The greatest genius that ever lived,' I replied casually. 'And which work of Wagner's is your favourite?' 'Tristan'—my reply. That so delighted him that he became transformed. He grew truly handsome. Now we understood each other. I find him quite wonderful. I shall invite him to call."[31]

She sent him her song *Stumme Liebe*. They next met at a party at the Conrats' on March 10. As men flocked around Alma, Zemlinsky playfully taunted her: "Fraulein, you're a dreadful flirt . . . if I weren't so sensible—you could easily turn a man's head."[32] He thought her song showed "real talent" and flattered her by offering to dedicate to her a volume of his own songs. Alma was overwhelmed with joy. She invited him to visit. Several times he failed to turn up, but she saw his opera *Es war Einmal* on March 19 and liked it "quite well." Discerning critic that she was, Alma thought it "dramatic and well-shaped," but, in the first scene, "too many scenic and linguistic fireworks" left her cold.

Zemlinsky was a leading figure among the young musicians establishing their reputations in Vienna. The son of a Jewish-Muslim mother and a Slovakian Catholic father who had converted to Judaism, Zemlinsky had studied music at the Vienna Conservatory under Robert Fuchs and Anton Bruckner and attracted the support of Johannes Brahms. By 1899, at the age of twenty-eight, he was seen as one of the most promising composers of the era. Recently appointed *Kappelmeister* at the Vienna Carltheater, he was a teacher and friend of the composers Arnold Schoenberg and Anton Webern.

When he eventually visited Alma in April and she played him her songs, he concluded that she had "much talent" but lacked technical expertise. When Zemlinsky pointed out her errors, he was "kind" and witty." One phrase he said was "so good I could almost have written it myself," but he thought it was "a crying shame—that I was full of ideas but didn't take it seriously enough to learn properly."[33]

His stringent comments challenged Alma. By May 1900 she was determined that he should be the rigorous mentor she needed to realize her talent and discipline her unruly mind. It was not an option for her to study at a music academy because women were barred from entry. As they played *Siegfried* four-handed on the piano at the Conrats' house, Zemlinsky agreed to start lessons that winter. He asked for her photograph, a gift that in the contemporary social code implied that he had a special place in her affections. She agreed. They met often at parties and soirées, sang and played duets, and went to concerts together.

Their relationship was volatile from the start. Zemlinsky was sensitive, proud, quick to take offense, and cautious of this vivacious woman whose flirtatious manner was sometimes confusing. He had a witty tongue that could turn to biting sarcasm. There were periods of closeness and significant froideurs. When Alma discovered there was a woman, Melanie Guttmann, in his life, she was furiously jealous and avoided him for a time. On an early visit, when she playfully told him to take off his hat, he was livid: "I won't let anyone subjugate me—least of all a woman," he hissed and threatened never to return.[34] During the "unrestrained" conversation that followed his outburst, he delivered an even more withering broadside: "He told me that I lacked all passion, that I do everything by halves—I can only be half a musician, only take half a pleasure in things—and only marry half-heartedly, that is, marry a man I don't care for. I shall never approach things in real depth." Alas, Alma conceded, "how *right* he is, how *very* right. I'm very worried about my half-heartedness."[35] It seems she was prepared to accept quite damning criticism from the respected teacher she had chosen as the agent for her self-improvement—and whom she needed to realize her talent. She accepted his criticisms because they mirrored her own sense of inadequacy and because they revealed that Zemlinsky took a real interest in her character. Above all, she confessed, "His reproaches spur me on."[36]

In July, Alma again departed with her mother and Gretl to the Salzkammergut, where she composed almost daily, working on a song cycle based on a text by the eminent poet Rainer Maria Rilke. She read Nietzsche's *The Birth of Tragedy* and several contemporary novels. Max Burckhard visited and on his arrival gave Alma and Gretl a lecture on Kant and Spinoza.[37] He had already impressed Alma as a "kind, sharp-witted fellow . . . robust in mind, robust in body," whose artistic candor, blunt manner, and "whole, delightful personality" she admired.[38] He took on the role of sympathetic listener and wise mentor. When she told him of the tensions at home, he advised her to bide her time, not rebel against her mother and stepfather's authority, but "learn something, achieve something—and all of a sudden you'll find a footing." It was what Alma wanted to hear: "I want to study, work hard, that's the *only* way to get anywhere."[39]

With her family they went on long cycling trips, energetic walks, boating expeditions, and picnics where Alma consumed copious quantities of food and champagne and was frequently "squiffy." They visited neighbors from Vienna: Berta and Emil Zuckerkandl, the Secession patron Carl Reininghaus, and Lilli Lehmann, who had a house nearby and promised to take Alma to see Mahler next winter—"I'd go, no question about it," Alma decided.[40] In September, life changed when her sister Gretl married Wilhelm Legler at Ischl. Alma observed this with mixed emotions. She knew that, though outwardly happy, Gretl had cried all night before the wedding and that she had a loaded pistol in her suitcase, which in a fit of depression she had recently contemplated using. As Alma waved them goodbye at the station she felt "terribly sorry for her. . . . I fear for her, my poor, dear Gretl."[41] As her sister entered the uncharted territory of her marriage, Alma remained the lone unmarried daughter, living somewhat uncomfortably with her mother and stepfather. But she had no wish to marry yet.

Alma heard little from Zemlinsky during the summer. Carl Moll had arranged as a present for her twenty-first birthday a printed copy of three of her songs with a title page designed by Koloman Moser. She sent

Zemlinsky the printer's proof, but he was "in the most dreadful state" after his father's recent death. When he eventually looked at the printer's "so-called gallery proofs," they were "simply bristling with mistakes, some in the original manuscript, others in the engraving. . . . [T]hey set my head spinning."[42] Alma was deeply upset, for it confirmed her early misgivings about Moll's "amateur" publishing effort.

It was not until October that Zemlinsky visited Alma again. After numerous cancellations followed by courtly apologies, Alma had concluded he was "capricious and unpredictable" and threatened to give up on him entirely—until she reminded herself how much she wanted the lessons and forgave him.[43] When he turned up at her house on October 18, "admittedly half an hour late," his appearance provoked "a chorus of dismay" in the household. Alma defended him to her family. He was "neither hideous nor grotesque. His eyes sparkle with intelligence—and such a person is never ugly," she insisted.[44]

At their first lesson in November, Zemlinsky repeated his assessment of her skills: she had talent but lacked technique and aptitude; in harmony and counterpoint, her capabilities were "slight—almost non-existent," even after her six years with Labor. Her lessons with Labor continued, for she was troubled by feelings of guilt at abandoning him, but she knew Zemlinsky was the more demanding mentor she needed. "What a wonderful fellow! And stimulating beyond measure," she declared. "My spirits are soaring."[45] A lesson in December was "a thermal bath. Invigorating, quickening, soothing. And his refreshingly sharp tongue. A wonderful fellow. I want to keep on working hard."[46]

She was meanwhile experiencing unexpected sexual stirrings in another direction. When she received a card from Max Burckhard, she could "scarcely speak for joy. . . . Involuntarily I kissed the card, and now I long for him."[47] When she glimpsed him at the opera she was "in a terrible state of physical excitement. . . . I was hot and cold all over," and she couldn't stop thinking about him—"those adorable eyes . . . Burckhard—my Burckhard!"[48] But when gossip linked them romantically, family friends warned her strongly against him, citing his several previous unsavory affairs. She brushed them off impatiently. As she read a letter from him, she "blushed from head to foot. . . . I grew hugely excited, I kissed it. I dream of giving my body to him, just once, even if it is only a kiss."[49]

Three days later, she was "absolutely shattered." Burckhard arrived at her home and brushed her cheek with his hand: "I resisted. He didn't desist, came closer and closer, and finally he kissed me—and this was the worst of it—touched my mouth with his tongue.—That put paid to any illusion of passion. How I had been longing for that moment—and how horrid it actually was. I shall never forget the disillusionment. . . . Klimt's kiss and Burckhard's kiss—the former was Heaven—today it was Hell— an abyss opened before my very eyes." That evening she deliberately "got sozzled" and couldn't stop shaking all over—"I really love that man, but his insidious behaviour disgusts me."[50]

Next day, confused and still in shock, she faced the facts: "My feelings for him aren't tender—it's just that he excites me physically." She was determined to make clear to him: "I'm not and shall *never* be your plaything."[51] At Christmas he reverted to his role as older mentor with a present of thirty volumes of books, including Shakespeare and Schopenhauer, which gave her "the greatest pleasure."[52] And though she knew Burckhard's intentions were "not exactly unsullied," she resolved to "never succumb to his advances. I swear it. No more than a kiss!"[53] She could not entirely quell the nagging sensual feelings she experienced in his presence and did not completely resist the occasional advances he made over the next six months.

AT PRECISELY THIS time, only a few streets away Sigmund Freud was evolving his theories of the psyche and exploring the connection between the repression of female sexuality enforced by social "respectability" and the hysteria and neurosis he diagnosed in his young middle-class Viennese patients. While Freud explored the damaging effects of sexual repression, Alma showed no restraint in calibrating with surprising honesty the awakening of her own sexual nature. Her experiences with men up until then had stirred powerful feelings of romantic love, but, when she was overwhelmed by sexual longing, she was unprepared and ignorant of the nature of physical love.

She had observed copulating dogs and been revolted by "the pivoting motions of the male" but had confidently imagined that in humans it was different—"something calm and dignified." When a girlfriend "robbed her of her last illusion"—that it was not all that different, she was horrified: "And that's what Klimt called 'physical union," this jigging about," she wailed. "It's revolting, disgusting. Do humans pull the same daft faces as dogs. Ughhhhhhh. When a man introduces himself I now imagine him rocking up and down on top of me—and can scarcely bring myself to shake his hand."[54]

Alma's escape from her revulsion was in music, which "can compensate for everything, everything."[55] During her lessons with Zemlinsky in the autumn of 1900, Alma found her feelings for him slowly shifting from respect into a deeper romantic longing. She was "endlessly fond of him," she decided in February 1901, after visiting his room, which "radiates unbelievable poetry" and contained her photograph on his desk: "Our conversation flows like honey. . . . We talk about *everything*."[56] And a month later: "His eyes are velvety. He can be so sweet. When he speaks to me, I feel a strange joy."[57] At a concert together, "when he turned to me, it caused me physical pain—sheer sensual over-anxiety."[58]

Zemlinsky was equally falling under her spell, but pride and caution held him back. With two such volatile personalities, both in different ways unsure of themselves, misunderstandings were frequent. He took refuge in sardonic mockery: "You are a sentimentalist! . . . If I listened to all your gushing critiques of the members of your circle . . . I would

Figure 7. Alma's composition teacher Alexander von Zemlinsky: "Dear Alex."

be under the impression that you only associated with demi-gods," he taunted her.[59] Once, when she had been pushing him, against his will, to play to her from his opera, he exploded: "You know, Fräulein, you are becoming tiresome. You may be able to keep all your other young men under your thumb, but with me—that won't work." He was right, she conceded but noted "how impudent, how rude the fellow can be."[60] When he turned up late for a lesson and she was cross with him because she had to leave for a dinner engagement, he took offence and declared with icy sarcasm: "Either you compose or you socialise—one or the other. If I were you, I'd stick to what you do best—socialise." Alma fulfilled her engagement but was desolate: "Our friendly, cheerful tone was gone. As if the varnish had been scratched away."[61]

When he ignored her at a concert, she was offended and feigned indifference. He withdrew, complaining bitterly about how little interest she took in his work. Fearing she had lost him for good, she railed against her "incredible stupidity and thoughtlessness."[62] In March he complained acidly about her unpredictable personality: "You are altogether curious— . . . one minute full of enchanting politeness, then again blasé indifference! Your manner, you know, is just as transparent to the interested observers as your work—a warm, feminine, sensitive opening, but then scrappy, racy passages with no style!"[63] Lessons continued, nonetheless. That same month he was "delighted with my work. Said it was a pity I wasn't born a boy, that it was detrimental to my talent," for as a girl, if she wanted to make her mark, she would experience "countless setbacks," he told her.[64] She was undeterred.

Alma's life was further complicated when out of the blue she received a proposal of marriage from the Secession architect Felix Muhr. The very next day another proposal arrived from Franz Hancke, the Secession's managing director—"the second one this week! Like in a penny dreadful!"[65] Alma was "thunderstruck," as she had encouraged neither of them. Hancke she rejected outright, but Muhr she kept for a time in suspense, even though her feelings were clear: he was "an agreeable, well-educated fellow" with money, but she felt nothing for him. It would be marrying out of friendship—for "common-sense" reasons, she decided, and shuddered at the prospect of giving her body to a man she did not love. "Never maturing, never being fulfilled. Half-measures. . . . Always half measures— it's too dreadful."[66] The proposal had reinforced her immediate goals: "I *want* to make my mark. For me, Muhr is far away. I won't even consider the possibility of getting married. I just want to study—to climb ever higher! To be a somebody!"[67]

Alma was taken aback and delighted when, in April, Zemlinsky finally overcame his caution to confess that a letter from her had now become "a necessity for me! I am happy—every time I see an envelope with your handwriting."[68] Then, on a beautiful spring day, with blossom and scent all around them, they sat together after a lesson: "He told me I was playing with him, that he thanked God for his common sense. Suddenly our gaze met and didn't waver." He kissed her hands, bent his head over them: "I laid my head on his, we kissed each other on the cheek, held each other for an eternity. I took his head in my hands, and we kissed each other on the mouth, so hard that our teeth ached. . . . He told me he had struggled all winter against his love for me."[69] Next day, Alma thought of him constantly: "I long for him. . . . I see everything in a new light. The trees are greener, the sky bluer."[70]

Zemlinsky's next letter was an unprecedented outpouring of love, mixed with intense anxiety. He was "in the midst of a great hopeless passion, my worship of you over time has become so strong but also so steadfast and total," he confessed. But his days had been marred by trembling anxiety, for he believed "a huge disappointment is inevitable," that eventually he would lose both her love and their friendship. His only happiness was that the bond of music still held them together.[71]

Alma was overjoyed at his declaration of love, carried his letter in her pocket, kissed it at intervals during the day—and noted, "Incidentally, my sexual organs are strangely disturbed."[72] His next letter, addressed in the familiar *du* form, was the first of many in which he rhapsodized: "I adore you. . . . I am so happy today, I am repeating to myself every word you have said to me, I continuously see your eyes, your lovely, lovely eyes. I continuously say one thing—why me—especially me?"[73]

But a caution had seeped into Alma's feelings after his earlier rebuffs. Doubts began to surface in what would become a repeated pattern—great surges of emotion succeeded by withdrawal into emptiness, followed by return to devotion a few days later. It was not calculated: she was as bewildered by it as the other person. She looked forward to their next meeting "warmly—but no longer as *intensely*"; she worried "that this affair won't endure much longer." Crucially, she began to doubt her own ability to love in a way that had meaning for her: to "penetrate to the depths of a true, intense passion. The ecstasy has worn off *so* quickly." Although she longed desperately for Zemlinsky, it was "no longer as *wild* as in the first week."[74]

She blamed herself. But his courtly hesitation, his reverence, and his modesty had "cooled her fire." She longed for him "to hug me tightly and *shout out loud*, 'Alma, my Alma,' as Klimt once did." Instead he still called her "esteemed Fräulein" and told her, "'I don't *dare*.' I detest people who don't dare," she exploded and descended into black despair.[75] She could summon up no feelings of love for him, no matter how hard she tried. "I *want* to love him, but I believe . . . it's already over." Returning from a friend's wedding, she rather cruelly pictured herself standing at the altar with Zemlinsky—"how ridiculous it would look . . . he so ugly, so small—me so beautiful, so tall." But she also reflected, "Since love departed from my heart, my music has died within me. I feel uninspired, am completely sterile. What a wretched feeling."[76]

When Zemlinsky detected her coolness, he distanced himself with sarcastic complaints that she lacked seriousness and was insincere and "far too superficial to return his love." Alma's despair deepened: "*Nothing* really moves me. I am truly only half a person. I'm deeply saddened—no, I'm incapable of being *deeply* sad. Tepid—just tepid! I feel sorry for anyone who sincerely loves me. I'm disgusted at my behaviour."[77] Consumed by self-pity, she spent the next day thinking "of how best to do away with myself. Slash my wrists? Tonight and by the morning I'd be dead. How lovely that would be." Zemlinsky's taunts echoed through her brain: she would "never make anything out of my life. I was born only half a person. I have only half a soul—he has only half a body. One of us should have been born *complete*. I composed and wept while doing so."[78]

In the midst of this storm, Alma was preparing to move with the family to the Hohe Warte, on the outskirts of Vienna, where Carl Moll had commissioned a villa. It was designed by Josef Hoffmann at Steinfeldgasse 8, in Secessionist style with simple rectilinear shapes, the decoration and artifacts in harmony with the architectural flow, and the exterior at one with the interior. At her first sight of the plot in February 1900, Alma had been appalled: "It's in the backwoods. . . . May I never live to see the day on which we move there."[79]

On May 1, as she bade farewell to their old house, a calm now descended on Alma. When Zemlinsky visited the next day they fell into each other's arms: "We kissed the living daylights out of each other. . . . I sank down, he on top of me. With an *insane* jolt I pushed him away. He asked: Why? He knew exactly why."[80] Two weeks later she was certain: "I want to live for him. That's my only wish. How sweet he was yesterday—*uniquely* sweet. We were sitting interlocked, my knees between his. He pressed me hard—hard—kissed my thighs."[81]

The next day, May 18, Alma departed with the family for their extended summer at St. Gilgen on the Salzkammergut. "My whole existence was centred around him and his being—and now I'm already beginning to feel the emptiness," she wrote sadly.[82] Soon diverted by the beauty around her—"snow on the mountain tops, blossom in the valley"—she felt at ease.[83] But all her calm was shattered when she received the first of his letters—an angry outburst against her treatment of him: "My pride is finally beginning to rebel!" he declared, for she never missed an opportunity "to emphasise how ridiculously small I am, and how little I have, how much there is that makes me unworthy of you . . . : I'm frightfully ugly, I have no money, perhaps not even any talent and also that I'm dreadfully stupid! I have nothing, I'm not handsome, I'm supposed, beggar that I am, to be grateful that you love me—a little." He would not, he protested, "be denigrated." He did, after all "have some standing—perhaps just as much as that entire band of artists, those poseurs and prigs, whose company you respectfully cultivate."[84]

The letter, which she had been "bursting with joy" to receive, made her "unspeakably sad."[85] On a walk with her confidante, Aunt Mie (Marie Henneberg), she was speechless. But sailing all next day with Max Burckhard, her sorrow gave way to defiance: "Didn't think of Alex *for one second. If he doesn't want me the way I am*, with all my faults, he can do without."[86] Her immediate reply seems only to have provoked him further, for two days later came another rebuke: "All the sweet things that one can read into it, if one wanted to, don't really come from your heart." He loved her "far more passionately than I have been able to show you," but he insisted on his own terms: "I have to be the master, not the slave! I can only be the master! I can humble myself before my own love, but not if it's demanded of me. Above all I can't endure knowing that you think you're the one with more to give! And it isn't true!! I always give more because inwardly I am richer."[87]

Gossip about their relationship had already provoked a barrage of objections from her family and friends. When her mother realized

Zemlinsky's love for her, she warned, "You are not the person to make sacrifices—nor is he. . . . On a diet of bread and water, even the strongest love perishes. I have nothing against him—but he should at least have a *few* groats to his name."[88] When Burckhard heard, he exploded: "For heaven's sake *don't marry* Z. Don't corrupt *good* race." For Alma, "Somewhere that rang a bell. He's right—my body is ten times too beautiful for his," but she also added, "That his soul is a hundred times too beautiful for mine—that didn't occur to me."[89]

Aunt Mie was staying nearby and normally followed Alma's progress with sympathy. But in this case she too advised, "Oh dear, you can't marry *him*. He's a Bohemian, you wouldn't feel the rift until you were married. He's still a nobody, and that won't change for some time yet, because he's so stubborn. . . . No, no, Alma. He's not for you."[90] Alma reflected, "All the fighting has turned him sour. . . . It's all running through my head." But also: "He loves me—I love him. . . . He will educate me, raise me to his level—and I will educate him—raise him to my level."[91] When her mother threatened to stop Alex ever coming to their house, her steely defiance returned—it was "Alex—or nothing! But I was deeply affected all the same. My eyes filled with tears—and I cried all evening."[92]

With her suitor Felix Muhr still pressing her for a decision, she weighed her options: a life of financial restrictions with Alex or, as Muhr's wife, "a life of luxury, respected, humoured, loved, spoiled." Unable to compose and "rudely thrust off my calm, secure path," she decided Muhr was "perfectly sympathetic but Alex I *love*! I don't love him as fervently as last spring—but still warmly . . . for me Alex is immensely stimulating. Muhr is not *in the least*," and, moreover, what use was money and comfort—"which only makes you lethargic and dull-witted, when there's not a hint of stimulation? *Never* before have I had to grapple with such an intractable problem."[93]

Alma added to her dilemma by declaring her distrust of marriage. She was an independent being who chose "to *live*" and wanted her freedom. "I *myself* shall shape my destiny. Only *myself*," she insisted, adding in a flash of self-awareness, "I'd love to know *which* of my two souls will triumph. My loving soul—or my calculating soul."[94] The arrival of Max Burckhard—"a person of whom you have to be *very* wary"— compounded her confusion.[95] He still stirred her sensuality. After his gourmet lunches—caviar, goose-liver, pineapple, and the like washed down with Asti Spumante—she found it difficult to maintain her distance. As they sat alone together, Alma experienced powerful conflicting emotions as he kissed and stroked her hand—then her knee, her face, her legs under her skirt: "It felt wonderfully tender & pleasurable," she recalled—until suddenly it was enough. She removed his hands but "would have given anything for him to kiss me—& more. . . . I was consumed with desire."[96]

Almost immediately, regret and disgust took over: "B.—as a person—leaves me *completely* cold, but my desire—my cursed, churned-up desire—seethes and boils over. . . . And this abominable seducer, who's only interested in my sweet face & my ample curves, did I *for one moment* give him my body? Shame on me—I'm disgusted with myself." She felt she had betrayed Alex and their love, but also herself. For when Alex had stroked her body and kissed her thighs she had found "nothing dishonourable in it. On the contrary, it aroused me. . . . To burn with desire, and yet feel so unsullied. . . . My soul reaches out to him, just as my body. . . . But now, today, I'm shattered. A curse on B. and his eyes (at the time his eyes were shining like a wild animal's) and his exploring hands. A curse on me and my sensual temperament, *on the whole affair*."[97] On his next visit, she couldn't take her eyes off "the bulge" in B.'s trousers: "My sensuality knows no bounds. I simply *must* get married."[98] Overcome by confusingly powerful sensual feelings, she wailed, "Why am I so boundlessly licentious? I *long* for *rape!*—Whoever it might be."[99] In the chemistry of her sexual longing, the themes of dominance and submission would recur throughout her life.

After a planned secret rendezvous at Bad Ischl failed, Alma did not see Zemlinsky until after the family had moved into the Hohe Warte and her mother had relaxed the ban on her seeing Alex, as long as he behaved "correctly and sensibly." When they met on October 5, love flared: "Our kisses were less wild but more tender than in the spring. . . . My longing for him—for his embrace—knows no bounds."[100] She wanted "to be his for eternity. . . . When he kissed me, although he twisted my spine & pressed his body against mine, I had the sensation of something holy. A powerful, searing rite—like something God-given. . . . A *drop of eternity*. I would gladly be pregnant for him, gladly bear his children. His blood and mine, commingled: my beauty and his intellect."[101]

She longed for him to be "my lord and master. . . . Yes—*he* shall command me—for ever and ever. Let me be his vassal. Let him take possession of me."[102] Later she reflected:

> I think, once I am his, he will kiss the ground I walk on. But no—*I* want to do just that! I would never have believed that I could ever so humiliate myself as to kiss a man's hand!—But I do so, do so with pleasure. I have the feeling of having climbed down from a high pedestal. But the further I descend, the taller grows my horizon. And when my descent has ended—at his feet—I shall find myself on a pedestal *infinitely* higher than the one from which I descended.[103]

Alma resumed composing in earnest; their lessons were frequently interrupted by passionate embraces, which Alma described in breathless detail. They "worked—kissed—worked again—kissed again—and so on. Once we simply couldn't separate. He pressed my right hand between his legs, & I, who love *every* part of him, had a greater sensation of bliss than ever before. I am *firmly* resolved to marry him. . . . I wish for one thing only—wedlock, union. I want to feel him within me—to open my womb to him. . . . I would *never* have imagined that I should love anyone so. Alex, my golden one."[104] She contemplated giving herself to him entirely but feared the consequences, even though "I madly desire his embrace. I shall never forget the touch of his hand on my most intimate parts. Such fire such a sense of joy flowed through me, yes, one can be *entirely* happy, there is such a thing as *perfect* joy. . . . One little nuance more, & I would have become a *god*. Once again, everything about him is holy to me. I would like to kneel before him & kiss his loins—kiss *everything, everything*."[105]

Two days before she wrote this, Alma had met Gustav Mahler, at a supper party given by her friends Emil and Berta Zuckerkandl. Though Alma thought her future lay with Zemlinsky, her encounter with Mahler would radically transform the direction of Alma's life, her love, and her ambitions.

— 4 —

Divine Longing

1901–1902

*W*riter and journalist Berta Zuckerkandl was a vociferous supporter of Vienna's avant-garde who presided over one of Vienna's most re-nowned salons. The daughter of Galician liberal newspaper publisher Moritz Szeps, she was married to anatomist Emil Zuckerkandl, who was, according to Alma, "an extremely intelligent person and full of humour." In late October 1901, Emil invited her to supper, where they were expecting Mahler as a guest. Alma declined: "I did not want to meet Mahler," she explained later. "I had purposely and with considerable dig-nity avoided meeting him that summer because of all the stories people told me about him. I knew him well by sight; he was a small fidgety man with a fine head. I was acquainted also with the scandals about him and every young woman who aspired to sing in opera. . . . At the same time, he was of importance to me as a conductor, and I was conscious of his mysterious and powerful fascination."[1]

Alma had admired Mahler for several years, both for his conducting at the Vienna Philharmonic Orchestra and for his innovative directing at the Vienna Court Opera (Hofoper). In December 1898 his rearrange-ment of Haydn for string orchestra prompted her star-struck diary entry: "As for Mahler, I'm virtually in love with him."[2] When in February 1899 she saw him conduct Richard Strauss's *Guntram* at the Philharmonic, she decided, "Everyone had been *longing* for a true conductor. Mahler

59

is a genius through and through. Music has never pervaded me as it did today."[3]

She was less impressed by Mahler the composer. His First Symphony, performed by the Philharmonic in November 1900 was in her opinion "done with talent, but with the greatest naivety and refinement, and not in the best sense of the word. An unbelievable jumble of styles—and an ear-splitting, nerve-shattering din. I've never heard anything like it, it was exhilarating all right, but no less irritating. With pulses raging—and scarcely able to speak."[4] It was only much later that she came to appreciate his music.

She had glimpsed Mahler more than once before on holiday in the Salzkammergut, for her family's rented villa at Goisern was in the same district as the Attersee, where Mahler composed during the summer. In 1899, when out cycling with her friends, they passed Mahler, who asked them the way. Alma cycled on as her friends stopped, and when they resumed Mahler followed: "He soon overtook us and we met some four

Figure 8. Gustav Mahler, composer, conductor, opera director, and Alma's first husband.

or five times. Each time, he struck up a conversation. Shortly before Hall-statt he dismounted. We were pushing our bikes, and he started up an-other conversation staring hard at me. I jumped on to my bike and rode off into the distance." Alma had felt "absolutely no urge to meet him. I love and honour him as an artist, but as a man he doesn't interest me at all. I wouldn't want to lose my illusions either."[5]

Gossip swirled around Mahler. In March 1899 the heldentenor Erik Schmedes had told Alma "the most awful things. . . . [T]he poor man is so deeply in love [with singer Margarethe Michalek]. . . . He keeps pinching her cheek and, during rehearsal, he kisses her repeatedly. All that smooching—it makes you sick."[6] At a supper, Alma's fellow guest, Hans Fuchs, son of the Hofoper's *Kapellmeister,* Johann Nepomuk Fuchs, denounced Mahler as "a scoundrel" who had taken years off his father's life. Alma put this down to jealousy because Mahler had been appointed over his father as director of the Vienna Court Opera.[7] Several dalliances with leading singers, none of which ended in marriage, had contributed to his reputation as a roué and a "degenerate," though the latter most probably stemmed from the anti-Semitic hostility that accompanied the appointment of a Jew as director of the Court Opera. None of this dented Alma's admiration, and she admitted she had been "very taken with him" when, out walking on the Ringstrasse, he had stopped to talk to her com-panion but had stared the whole time at Alma. Her reluctance to have any closer acquaintance with him would be overturned dramatically in a few short days.

BORN IN 1860 in Kališt, a village in Bohemia, Gustav Mahler was the sec-ond of fourteen children, only six of whom survived infancy. His father, Bernhard Mahler, was a brewer and tavern-keeper, and his mother Marie (née Hermann), the daughter of a soap-boiler from Letetsch. They had married for convenience, not love, and were "as ill-suited as fire and wa-ter. He was rigidity, she was gentleness itself," Gustav recalled.[8] In their modest two-bedroom house, none of the windows had glass, but Bern-hard believed in self-improvement and kept a collection of modern and classic literature in a glass-fronted bookshelf. When restrictions on free-dom of movement for Jews were lifted in the 1860s, the family moved to Iglau (Jihlava in the modern-day Czech Republic).

Gustav's musical talents were recognized early on by both his parents; he started lessons at age six and gave his first public performance at nine. Though timid and submissive to her often brutal and abusive husband, his mother provided Gustav with emotional support. He went first to the gymnasium in Prague, then, in 1875 at the age of fifteen, Gustav entered the Vienna Conservatory of Music to study under celebrated pianist Julius Epstein and composer Robert Fuchs. He went on to study philosophy at Vienna University in 1878 but completed only one year before being offered a post as conductor of operetta at the spa town of Bad Hall, then as conductor of opera at Laibach. He was briefly at the Carltheater in Vienna, then at Olmutz and Kassell, before joining the Leipzig Municipal Theater in August 1886. His reputation was growing, largely because of his innovative approach and his idiosyncratic, rigorous, and increasingly autocratic conducting style, which led to friction and admiration in equal measure among colleagues. In early 1888 he wrote his First Symphony. After two years as director of the Royal Hungarian Opera in Budapest, he moved in 1891 to be chief conductor at the Hamburg Opera. There he had a series of successes with Wagner operas and a production of *Eugene Onegin* at which its composer, Tchaikovsky, who was present, deemed him "positively a genius."

After his father Bernhard died in 1889, followed later the same year by the deaths of his mother and his sister Leopoldine, Gustav took charge of his four remaining siblings, installing them in a rented apartment in Vienna and supporting them financially. His sister Justine took charge of the household and lived with him. In 1893 he acquired a retreat in the small village of Steinbach on the Attersee, where he worked during the summer in his tiny composing hut beside the lake.

In Hamburg he fell into a turbulent and very public romantic relationship with the young soprano Anna von Mildenburg. Mahler left Hamburg after friction with the opera's director, but also to release himself from von Mildenburg. With his eye on the Vienna State Opera, Mahler converted to Catholicism in 1897, for, despite Emperor Franz Joseph's repudiation of anti-Semitism, it remained improbable that a Jew would be appointed to the highest position at the Court Opera.

After six months as *Kapellmeister* at the Hofoper, Mahler became its director in October 1897, aged only thirty-eight, on the retirement of Wilhelm Jahn. His appointment caused widespread surprise—and controversy: "Vienna was split into two camps. It's impossible to under-stand now with what level of fanaticism the Mahlerians and the Anti-Mahlerians fought against each other," Berta Zuckerkandl recalled. "For ten years Mahler fought against routine, nepotism, laziness, intrigues and stupidity. In those years he reformed the opera."[9]

BOTH MAHLER AND Alma accepted Berta Zuckerkandl's second invitation to supper on November 7, 1901. Because Mahler "had a reputation for provoking unpleasant moments," and liked only light food, Berta chose her guests carefully. Assuring Alma that she would be among friends Berta seated her between Gustav Klimt and Max Burckhard—"her past, her present [for Burckhard was in love with her] and her future," as Berta later put it.[10] From the start, Alma noted, "Mahler observed me closely, not simply because of my face, which might have been called beautiful in those days, but also because of my piquant manner." During dinner, as she, Klimt, and Burckhard laughed together in "a merry trio," Mahler looked on and listened covertly, then openly, and at last "called out envi-ously: 'Mayn't we be able to share the joke?'"[11]

The conversation round the table was lively, with all except Alma speculating on the corrupting influence of patronage on the arts. Eventu-ally she spoke up. "'Why?' she demanded, 'has the public allowed this to happen?' Mahler, who had until then paid little attention to her, looked at her carefully. 'Such a question can only be asked by someone young who knows nothing of cowardice and compromises,'" he commented.[12]

When the guests dispersed, Berta witnessed in the next room "a fu-rious Alma. Mahler is also angry. He jumps back and forth, as always when his nerves are agitated."[13] Their conversation had turned to "the subjectivity of beauty"; Mahler praised the bust of Socrates, and Alma asserted that Alexander von Zemlinsky was beautiful too, which Mahler said was going too far. Her hackles raised, she challenged him on why he would not perform Zemlinsky's ballet, *Triumph der Zeit*. She did not mince words: "You don't have the right to leave a piece of work that has been given to you—by a real musician like Zemlinsky is—for more than a year. You can say no but you should have responded," Berta heard Alma saying.[14] Mahler retorted, "Because I don't understand it." Alma offered to outline the plot: "Mahler smiled: 'I'm all ears.' To which Alma replied,

'But not until you have explained *Die Braut von Korea*' (a ballet that had a regular place in the repertoire and was a model of confusion and stupidity). Mahler laughed out loud, revealing a mouth of glistening white teeth."[15] He inquired about her studies under Zemlinsky and asked her to bring him one of her pieces—"he even wanted to know exactly *when* I would call on him. I promised to come as soon as I had something worthwhile."[16] With Berta and Sophie Clemenceau, Mahler invited Alma to the dress rehearsal of Offenbach's *The Tales of Hoffmann* at the Hofoper the next day.

Alma was buoyant at meeting Mahler: "I must say, I liked him *immensely*—although he's dreadfully restless. He stormed about the room like a savage. The fellow is made *entirely* of oxygen. When you go near him, you get burnt."[17] Mahler later told Berta that "this was the first time he felt comfortable in society." But Berta thought Alma was "shocked by her temperamental outburst. How did she dare to speak to her idol in such a way?"[18] and Alma confessed in her diary that she "was not pleased with myself. I had a distinct feeling of having put myself in a false light. Owing to my wretched, inborn shyness I could never be my real self in company and when I met people for the first time. Either my obstinate silence was broken only by distracted replies, or else, as tonight, I was as bold as brass and kept nothing back."[19]

Alma had declined Mahler's offer to escort her home. He walked instead with Burckhard, who probed Mahler's opinion of Alma: "'Fraulein Schindler is a sensible, *interesting* young lady, don't you think?' Mahler replied: 'I didn't care for her at first. I thought she was just a doll. But then I realized that she's also very perceptive. Maybe my first impression was because one doesn't normally expect such a good-looking girl to take anything seriously.'"[20] Later Mahler confessed to Alma, "Already then, it was God's will that we should be *united*. You may have been unaware of it, but I had already experienced my baptism of fire."[21]

At the opera rehearsal the next day, Mahler gave his guests a "warm welcome" and impolitely took only Alma's coat as he ushered them into his office. Alma went to the piano and turned the pages of the music as conversation went on around her: "Mahler stole glances at me, but I was in a malicious mood and would not help him out," she recalled. "I was in all the glory of untrammeled youth and not to be imposed upon by fame or position." When he asked, "Fraulein Schindler, how did you sleep?"

and was told, "perfectly," he rejoined, "I didn't sleep a wink the whole night."[22]

Next morning an anonymous poem arrived in the post. Though her mother dismissed any idea that Mahler would have sent it, Alma was convinced it was not a joke and was from him. She walked along the street in a dream. Her next encounter was at a performance of Gluck's *Orfeo* on November 18, when she looked up at the director's box and found Mahler staring down at her. As she stood at the intermission with her mother in the foyer, suddenly Mahler was beside them "as though conjured up from the floor." He asked to be introduced to her mother and invited them both up to his office: "We talk about everything under the sun—he is fascinating, kind. Mama invites him to call—he accepts. Let's hope he really does come. We shook hands with vigor. . . . We stared at each other, stared and stared."[23] As they left, she told him she would like to be engaged as a conductor at the opera: "He promised in all seriousness to let me try my hand: it would give him at least great pleasure. I replied that that was not enough: his verdict would not, I thought, be impartial. To which he replied: 'No verdict is ever impartial.' We parted in high spirits. Feeling that something great and beautiful had come into our lives."[24]

When Carl Moll heard of their encounter, he was furious that his wife had "taken an innocent girl into the private room of a *roué* like him." Max Burckhard, who was present, saw the situation more clearly and asked Alma, "'Now what are you going to do if he proposes?' 'Accept,' I said calmly." Burckhard was horrified and tried to dissuade her: "'It would be a positive sin,' he declared. 'A fine girl like you. And such a pedigree too. Don't spoil it by marrying an elderly degenerate. Think of your children—it would be a sin! And besides: fire and water go together. But fire and fire, that's all wrong! He would stifle you, not vice versa, and that would be a terrible waste of your talent.' In short, he did his best to prevent the marriage."[25]

Alma was steadily being drawn in. Though she tried to keep Zemlinsky in the forefront of her thoughts, his star was already beginning to fade: "It's just too dreadful, I should be ashamed of myself. . . . But *Mahler's* picture is graven in my heart," she wrote ten days later. "I will pluck out this poisonous weed—make room for the other again—my poor Alex.— If only the poem had come from him. If only! I could hate myself!" When

Zemlinsky called two days later, his manner was cool. "He spoke no loving word. . . . [W]e kissed each other once, just once. My longing for him again knows no bounds."[26]

The following Thursday Mahler arrived unexpectedly, announced only by a commotion downstairs and a chambermaid rushing into the room crying. "Gustav Mahler is here!" Alma was in the middle of a counterpoint lesson with composer Robert Gound but abandoned it to attend to her visitor. Having recently moved in, her room was a muddle of books, which Mahler inspected, apparently approving of her taste until he discovered her complete edition of Nietzsche's works. Alma rejected his peremptory advice that she cast them into the fire. Mahler proposed a walk, and, on the way downstairs, they met Anna Moll, who invited Mahler to stay for supper: "'There's paprika chicken and Burckhard. Do join us.' 'I'm not particularly fond of either,' he replied, 'but I'll stay all the same.'"[27]

They walked through snow and wind to telephone Mahler's sister Justine, with whom Mahler lived, to explain his absence from supper: "I can still see the sparkle in the snow as we passed each lamp-post," Alma wrote later, recalling "how we both without a word drew attention to its fairy-tale beauty."[28] Following behind as her chaperone, Carl Moll remembered them "side by side, unhesitatingly close, and yet strangers."[29] Alma recalled, "Every other minute his shoe-laces came undone and he selected the highest point of vantage to put his foot upon to tie them up. His childlike helplessness went to my heart." When they arrived at the post office, he did not know his own number so had to ring the Opera House to get it. On the way back they were silent:

> Suddenly he burst out: "It's not so simple to marry a person like me. I am free and must be free. I cannot be bound, or tied to one spot. My job at the Opera is simply from one day to the next." A feeling of suffocation came over me. He laid down the law without thinking of consulting my feelings. After a moment's silence I said: "Of course, don't forget that I am the child of artists and have always lived among artists and, also, I am one myself. What you say seems to me obvious."[30]

When they got back from the walk, they "went by tacit agreement straight up to my room. There he kissed me and went on to talk of a speedy marriage, as though it went without saying. Those few words on the way up seemed to him to have settled everything. Then why wait? And I—I was silent. He had simply made up his own mind about it." When they joined the others, she wrote, Mahler "revealed all his charm, all the resources of his mind." They argued about Schiller: "There was such a fascination in the way he rose up in his defense that I, after letting him kiss me without really wishing it, and speed on the wedding before I had even thought of it myself, knew now that in both he was right and that I could no longer live without him. I felt that only he could shape my life. I sensed his true worth and significance, which placed him streets ahead of every other man I had met."[31]

Next day Mahler sent Alma all his songs: "Everything lovable and beautiful was still resounding in me—and went on vibrating through my dreams," he wrote.[32] Alma replied warmly, agreeing it was a "uniquely beautiful & wonderful experience."[33] But the songs disappointed her: "They struck me as insincere."[34] "Truly, they don't relate to his personality. This studied naivety and simplicity, and he the most complex of characters. I'd like to tell him so—but fear he might be insulted." When she played them through next day, she began to like some of them, even though "it's pretty dour stuff."[35] But his conducting of Mozart's *The Magic Flute* on December 8 was "heavenly," and at the end of each act "he gave me such a touching smile . . . as if casting out a line to me."[36]

A battle now raged within Alma: "Alex against Mahler." After a Mahler visit when they "kissed—drank greedily from each other" and he told her how much he loved her, she confronted her "*terrible* dilemma. I keep repeating the words 'my beloved' and follow them with 'Alex.' *Can* I really love Mahler as he deserves and as I am really able? Shall I ever understand his art, and he mine? With Alex the sympathy is mutual. He loves every *note* of me." But of Mahler, she asked, "Do I really love him?—I have no idea. Sometimes I actually think not. So *much* irritates me." She questioned "whether I love the director of the Opera, the wonderful conductor—or the man. . . . Whether, when I subtract the one, anything is left of the other." She had another problem: "His art leaves me cold, so *dreadfully* cold. In plain words, I don't believe in him as a composer. And I'm expected to bind my life to this man. . . . I shudder. . . . *What should I do?*" One question plagued her: "whether Mahler will inspire me to compose—whether he will support my artistic striving—whether he will love me as Alex does. Because *he* loves me utterly."[37]

Mahler's daily letters of endearment were persuasive and passionate and by turns tender, admonishing, and didactic. "I hear nothing but this one voice, stronger than all else. . . . A voice that knows but one word and one note: I love you, my Alma!" he declared.[38] He warned her of his ambition to "replace your 'earthenware gods' with my vision of the divine, even if this may strike you at present as mere sophistry," and somewhat pedagogically he praised her progress: "Yesterday you really delighted me! . . . You made a completely changed impression and appeared far more mature. I can sense that the past five days have opened you up, have revealed you."[39]

Alma remained in a dilemma, with her feelings in chaos: "Never in my life have I met anyone as alien as he. How alien and yet so close!" she observed. "But he should let me be as I am." She worried whether she could "live up to his love," her desire for him was "unbroken," though his "immense ardour" frightened her. But she could see a path of growth and renewal through him: "Already I'm aware of changes in myself, due to him. He's taken much away from me and given me much in return. If this goes on, he'll make a new person of me. A better person? I don't know. I don't know *at all*."[40]

Mahler departed on December 9, 1901, for a performance in Berlin of his Fourth Symphony: "My new life begins here. . . . From now on I can live, breathe and exist only if I think of you," he wrote from Berlin. "My Alma, if you take me . . . you will acquire the clairvoyance of love, the omniscience of yourself as me, of myself as you."[41] But it was not quite as clear cut as his ardent letters implied. To his sister Justine he confided, "There's no need for haste. I still have many tests to complete. ~ The dear girl herself is in quite a state, finding herself in a completely unfamiliar situation, to which I have to open both her eyes and my own. As I recently realised, she will have to mature considerably before I can consider taking such a momentous decision." He asked Justine to help him, to "take a look at Alma with your cool, feminine eye."[42]

Doubts surfaced. "She's still so very young. When I think of the age difference I lose heart."[43] He was forty-one, she was twenty-two. He needed reassurance of her support, he told Alma. He had "spent the past fifteen years battling against superficiality and incomprehension, bringing down on me all the troubles, indeed all the miseries of a trail-blazer."[44] He had suffered "the insults of Philistines, inarticulate scorn and hatred" and was liable to suffer more. He must know—could she stand by him and take those burdens upon herself—"even to the point of humiliation—could you happily bear this cross with me?"[45] His other distressing concern was their age disparity. He wondered to Justine "whether a person on the threshold of middle age has the right to so much youthfulness and vigour, whether that person has the right to tether the spring to the autumn, to force his partner to forego the summer. I know I have much to offer, but that is no fair exchange for the right to be young. . . . For a while, of course, everything would be plain sailing. But what will happen when the autumn of my fruitfulness yields to winter?"[46]

The question would plague Mahler for many years, but for now the sincerity of her letters to him banished his doubts: "All my life I never dreamt I would experience the bliss of loving someone who returned my love in equal measure," he wrote to her on December 14. "Whenever I think of you (and you are constantly on my mind), life becomes worth living again."[47] He assured Justine that Alma's last "sweet" letter had dispersed all his remaining doubts about her warmth and sincerity. The two women had met and, in Alma's view, "got on quite well together." Justine had been "uncommonly kind and courteous" to Alma when she visited Mahler's apartment and acquainted herself with his desk, his bed, his books, and his surroundings.[48]

In Vienna, Alma was beset by new anxieties. Felix Muhr finally asked for an answer to his marriage proposal and threatened to kill himself if she turned him down. She told him the hard truth. Muhr responded by alerting her to the rumor, apparently based on a reputable doctor's diagnosis, that Mahler was suffering from an incurable disease and was already weakening perceptibly. Alma went into a spasm of concern for "my beloved Master." Burckhard then weighed in with his own concern that, "when two strong personalities come together, they usually fight until one of them is forced into submission," and that person, he warned Alma, would probably be her. But she wrote, "Must *I* be subdued? I can and will not. And yet I feel that I stand at a far *lower* level—and it would do me no harm to be drawn up to his."[49]

Overwhelmed by Mahler's ardor and her powerful feelings for him, Alma painfully concluded that she must end the relationship with

Zemlinsky. When he failed to turn up in person, she wrote to him, "For me, the last weeks have been torture. . . . You know how *very* much I love you. You fulfilled me *completely*. Just as suddenly as this love came, it has vanished—been cast aside. And befallen me with new power! . . . I shall *never* forget the joyous hours you have given me—don't *you* forget them either. . . . Once again: forgive me—I no longer know myself. Your Alma."[50]

Immediately, she mourned her "immeasurable loss."[51] Two days later Zemlinsky turned up unexpectedly "paler than usual and very quiet." They sat side by side and talked, "he a little sarcastic, as ever, but otherwise kind, touchingly kind. My eyes kept filling with tears. But my will stood firm. . . . Today I buried a beautiful love. Gustav, you'll have to do much to replace it for me. . . . Had [Alex] uttered just *one* angry or accusing word, I would never have begun to feel that way. Alex, I *respect* you—my respect for you is endless. My poor Alex—I could see the suffering in his face. You noble man!"[52]

As Mahler daily rhapsodized over their love, Alma's feelings for him blossomed. She had "but one wish, one dream: to be yours alone." Through him, she was convinced she would "become a better person, he purifies me."[53] Even so, tensions were growing between them. Mahler's tone was often patronizing, he assumed that all between them was "clear and indissoluble" even before he had consulted her, and he even assumed that when he returned from Berlin he should be treated by her mother as a son, dispensing with his need to ask for her daughter's hand.[54] Moreover Alma began to suspect that Justine was observing her "with an eagle eye" for signs of her faults and feared she might poison his love: "If Justi intrigues against me and his interest wanes, I shall—*not* die," she wrote, but it left her "inexplicably restless."[55]

Her anxiety highlighted other reservations about Mahler, and on December 19 she poured out her seething fears to family friend Theobald Pollack. If she was going to marry him, she "must do everything *now* to stake *my* rightful claim. . . . particularly in *artistic* questions. He thinks *nothing* of my art and much of his own. And I think *nothing* of *his* art and much of my own.—That's how it is! Now he talks unceasingly of safeguarding *his* art. I *can't* do that. With Zemlinsky it would have been possible, because I have sympathy for his art—he's such a brilliant fellow. . . . And *I* am supposed to lie, lie for the rest of my life?"[56]

She repeated none of this to Mahler, but in a letter that day she happened to say that she could not write any more, "as I had some work to finish, meaning composition, which up to now had taken the first place in my life."[57] The response was devastating. On December 19, Mahler wrote a long twenty-page letter expressing his profound disappointment that she appeared to have revoked her previous pledge to him: "to be all you *need* and *wish for*." He set out to "clarify" unequivocally the "very basis of our bond." His opening salvo was an attack on the malign influence of her circle of friends, who had flattered her because she was good looking and had made her vain. He questioned her talk of "individuality" for, though "unsullied in body and soul, richly gifted, open-hearted and precociously self assured," she had not yet reached a state of "fully reasoned *intrinsic* being. . . . [E]verything in you is nascent, latent and undeveloped." What she could perhaps one day become was "the highest and dearest part of my life, my faithful, valiant partner, who understands me and spurs me on to higher things . . . an unassailable fortress . . . a heaven, in which I can always submerge, retrieve and constitute myself—all that is so indescribably noble and beautiful—so much and so great—in a word: MY WIFE."

The core of Mahler's "fears and misgivings" was Alma's idée fixe that she must "remain true to herself" and to her own music. In the letter, she had written of "your" music and "my" music. This had to be discussed at once, and they must be clear about it before they met again: "Would it be possible for you, from now on, to regard *my* music as *yours?*" he asked, before launching into the next issue: "How do you picture the married life of a husband and wife who are both composers? Have you any idea how ridiculous and, in time, how degrading for both of us such a peculiarly competitive relationship would inevitably become? What would happen if, just when you're 'in the mood,' you're obliged to attend to the house or to something I need?" He did not hold "the bourgeois view" of a marriage, which regards the wife as a kind of plaything and at the same time his housekeeper. But he insisted that "if we are to be happy together, you will have to be my wife, not my colleague."[58]

The crux of the matter was:

If you were to abandon *your* music in order to take possession of mine, and also to be mine: would this signify the end of life as you know it,

and if you did so, would you feel you were renouncing a higher existence? Before we can think of forging a bond for life, we *must* agree
on this question. . . . I realise that if you are to make me happy, you
yourself must be happy (on my account). But in this drama . . . the roles
must be correctly cast. The role of "composer," the "bread-winner," is
mine; yours is that of the loving partner, the sympathetic comrade. . . .
[Y]ou must surrender yourself to me unconditionally, make every detail of your future life completely dependent in my needs, in return you
must wish for nothing except my love! . . . [F]or someone I love the way
I would love you if you were to become my wife, I can forfeit all my life
and all my happiness.[59]

In conclusion, he required her utterly candid reply before his return in
two days' time; he would send a servant round to collect it.

Alma was "dumbfounded": "My heart missed a beat . . . give up my
music—abandon what has until now been my life?" she wrote. "My *first*
reaction was—to pass him up. I had to weep—for then I understood that
I loved him. Half-crazed with grief, I got into my finery and drove to
Siegfried—in tears! . . . I feel as if a cold hand has torn the heart from my
breast." She found his behavior "so ill-considered, so inept. . . . It might
have come on its own . . . quite gently. . . . But like this it will leave an indelible scar."[60] She talked it over until late at night with her mother, who
"was so horrified by his unreasonable demand that, deeply as she loved
him, she urged me to break with him. Her unqualified support brought
me to my senses."[61]

Next morning she reread the letter. She recovered her calm and
confidence and, with extraordinary speed, made up her mind: "Suddenly
I felt such warmth. What if I were to *renounce* my music *out of love* for
him? Just forget all about it! I must admit that scarcely any music now
interests me except his." She had decided: "Yes—he's right. I must live
entirely for him, to make him happy. And now I have a strange feeling
that my love for him is deep & genuine. For how long? I don't know, but
already *that* means much. I long for him *boundlessly*."[62] When she went
out, she met Mahler's servant who handed her a second, more conci-
liatory letter, expressing how strong and deep were his love and his fidelity to her, and how hard and uncompromisingly truthful he could be
with the person he loved.[63]

When they met that afternoon, Mahler was "as kind and loving as ever. Our kisses were hot." Alma had become "wax in his hands. . . . I want to give him everything. My soul is his."[64] Next day her longing for him was "indescribable. Everything about him is lovable & familiar. . . . I have the *feeling:* I could *live . . . exist* for him alone."[65] She would "give everything for him—my music—*everything*."[66] His love would "elevate" her, for she stood "at a far *lower* level and it would do me no harm to be drawn up to his." He would "purify" her, for she felt "imbued with the holiest feelings" for this man who believed that "the bond that unites us has been forged in the name of a love that surpasses understanding, divine love."[67]

In a few short days Alma had been persuaded—indeed, persuaded herself—to give up the thing she cherished most, her music, to subsume herself to another being. Until then she had set herself apart from other young women by her determination to develop her own creative talents and make her name as a composer. Yet she abandoned herself and her creative power for what she believed to be a higher, nobler cause.

Alma had reached an impasse. She was under increasing pressure to marry as suitors arrived at her door. Although she was in her own self-image an independent spirit, striving for truth and "complete freedom," she could achieve independence only by leaving home—and that meant marriage. She had been so overwhelmed by her own sexual longing in response to Mahler's passion that she had relinquished her power to resist him. She was twenty-two, he was nearly twice her age. With her respect for creative genius, it is difficult to deny the connection between him and the father figure, the genius, who could elevate her to his exalted level.

With her music she gave up part of herself. "I simply believed that it was the fate of woman—that I had to give up all *that* happiness when I married," she later confessed, echoing the social imperative on women to subsume their own interests to their husband's.[68] Alma had robustly defended her ambition to be a composer against her own persistent doubts, but, faced with the humming chorus that denigrated women's creativity and reinforced barriers to their achievement, she capitulated to the social norm. Now she formulated a role that she believed could be as fulfilling as her passionate ambition had been, as the nurturer and muse to genius.

This was perhaps not an unfamiliar role for her but rather one embedded deeply in her sense of self. From early childhood she had been

patiently present, watching adoringly as her father painted. She had
witnessed and encouraged the creation of art by a man she revered
above all others. And in return he had believed in her and loved her
and understood her as no other human being had. Perhaps her return
to something resembling this role appeared less disfiguring, more comfortable and rewarding, than it might seem. Even then, a worm of doubt
stirred in Alma: "But *must* one be subordinate? Isn't it possible—with
the help of love—to merge two fundamentally opposing points of view
into—*one*?"[69]

Later she looked back on her decision: "I buried my dream and perhaps it was for the best. It has been my privilege to give my creative gifts
another life in minds greater than my own. And yet the iron had entered
my soul and the wound was never healed."[70]

ALMA AND GUSTAV were officially engaged barely six weeks after they met,
on December 23 in the presence of her mother and Carl Moll. When
the news broke in the press, they were showered with "letters, telegrams.
Everywhere my beauty, my youth & my musical talent are stressed."[71]
But she did not welcome the public attention. At her first appearance at
the opera: "Every opera-glass was focused on me—every single one. I felt
offended & withdrew."[72]

Alma was now resolute: "My life is his, he shares my joys, I his sorrows.
Amen!"[73] Their intimacy deepened. They were "all but joined in wedlock" on December 30 as "he let me feel his masculinity—his vigour—&
it was a pure, holy sensation, such as I would *never* have expected." She
could not imagine "giving myself to him before the appointed time. A
sense of wrongdoing & shame would debase the whole, sacred mystery."
But she knew he must be "suffering *dreadfully*. I can gauge his frustration
by mine," and she railed against "these *dreadful* conventions? Why can't
I simply move in with him? *Without a* church wedding. We're consumed
with longing, are dissipating our strongest desires."[74]

So Alma relented, and her diary records in startling detail their first
"sad" union:

He gave me his body—& I let him touch me with his hand. Stiff and
upright stood his vigour. He carried me to the sofa, laid me gently down

and swung himself over me. Then—just as I felt him penetrate, he lost all strength. He laid his head on my breast, shattered—and almost wept for shame. Distraught as I was, I comforted him. We drove home, dismayed and dejected. He grew a little more cheerful. Then I broke down, had to weep, weep on his breast. What if he were to lose—that! My poor, poor husband! I can scarcely say how upsetting it all was. First his intimate caresses, so close—and then no satisfaction. Words cannot express what I today have undeservedly suffered. And then to observe his torment—his unbelievable torment!

But on January 3, 1902, her entry is starkly brief: "Bliss and rapture," and the next day: "Rapture without end."[75] Mahler had woven his spell: "Yesterday I was in fifth or sixth heaven! The seventh is still in store for us," he told her.[76]

Their engagement was a surprise and a cause of concern to some of Mahler's associates. "His fiancée, Alma Schindler . . . is twenty two years old [sic], tall, slim and dazzlingly good-looking, the most beautiful girl in Vienna; she comes of good family and is very rich," wrote Bruno Walter, Mahler's assistant at the Hofoper. "But we, his friends, are very concerned about this; he is forty one years old, she twenty-two; she is accustomed to moving in high society, he is tied up with himself, fond of isolation; so there is good reason for misgivings. He himself feels very awkward and uneasy in his role as bridegroom, and when people congratulate him he gets annoyed. But they are said to be deeply in love."[77]

Others were less sympathetic. Alma's first meeting with Gustav's old friends at his Auenbruggergasse apartment on January 5 was a disaster. She felt that she was under hostile surveillance from Mahler's old flame Anna von Mildenburg and the poet Siegfried Lipiner. He "patronised me, called me 'my dear girl,' and put me through my paces. . . . I was reprimanded for reading the *Symposium*—it was far above my head. I have never before encountered such aridity in any human being—if he was a human being," Alma fumed. She responded with "unprecedented impertinence," as she put it, declined to take part in general conversation, and, when asked by Mildenburg for her opinion of Gustav's music, replied in a temper: "I know very little of it, but what I do know I don't like," at which Mahler laughed out loud, then took her by the arm, "and we went into Justine's little room. 'It was frightful in there,' he said: 'We'll do better on our own for a bit.' So here we were—together again, happy and free of care. But in the next room, my downfall was decreed."[78]

Lipiner's hostility to Alma was relentless—and reciprocated. Although Mahler had justified her behavior as that of "young, shy girl" embarrassed by distrustful strangers, Lipiner lambasted her as "an unpleasantly impudent, opinionated and hypercritical creature" who was all "unnaturalness, superficiality and heartlessness." He questioned her feelings for Mahler and announced that, as far as he was concerned, they could live in "splendid isolation," undisturbed by "troublesome, useless people."[79] With battle lines drawn, Lipiner and his circle—as Alma put it—"launched a regular campaign against me."[80] Lipiner blamed Alma when his friendship with Mahler cooled, and Alma was convinced that Lipiner and his circle contributed to the hostility she faced over many years: "Their plan was to degrade me in his eyes, to show me up in my raw immaturity; and so to wound his pride. But they had not reckoned with my fierce spirit of independence or my sensitive pride."[81] Alma gave as good as she got.

IN JANUARY 1902, Alma heard for the first time a work by Mahler rehearsed all the way through. Gustav had shown her his Fourth Symphony on January 5, and they played it through together the next day. "It really moved me—pleased me very, very much," she wrote.[82] "A work which was new and strange to me, very strange at the outset, became by degrees so familiar that I soon knew its every beauty and how each instrument came in." The orchestra rehearsals she attended were "the most unforgettable and exalted hours of my life," when she observed with interest Mahler's abrasive leadership style: "He raged, he stamped; he picked on victims for special castigation and shouted at the orchestra as a whole until they played unwillingly." Some even threatened to walk out.[83]

In the first few weeks of her engagement, Alma had been "truly happy," but she was troubled in mid-January by a change in Mahler's attitude: "He wants me to be different, completely different." Even more, she perceived a confusing inner conflict between her own two selves: "As long as I'm with him, I can manage—but when I'm on my own, my other, vain self rises to the surface and wants to be let free. . . . My eyes shine with frivolity—my mouth utters lies, streams of lies. And he senses it, knows it. Only now do I understand. I *must rise to meet him*. For I live only in him." As so often, her confusion resulted in her withdrawal: "He begged me to talk—and I couldn't find *one* word of warmth. *Not one.* I wept. That was the end." She chastised herself: "I have two souls: I know it.—Only one—which is my true soul? If I lie, will I not make us both unhappy?—And am I a liar? When he looks at me so happily, what a profound feeling of ecstasy. Is that a lie too? No, no. I must cast out my other soul. The one which has so far ruled must be banished. I must strive to become a real person, let everything *happen to me of its own accord*."[84]

At the end of January, Mahler's health caused concern. While he was on a break hiking in the mountains, he was diagnosed with dilation of the veins caused by weeks of high blood pressure. Mahler reassured Alma that it had been caught early and he would soon be restored to health, but it was not the first time. Almost exactly a year before, after conducting Mozart's *The Magic Flute*, he had suffered a violent hemorrhage that had required an immediate operation and a long convalescence. Alma recalled being present at the performance when she had noted "he looked like Lucifer: a face as white as chalk, eyes like burning coals," and had said to her companions, "It's more than he can stand."[85] This time Mahler recovered in the snowy mountain air to feel "fresher and healthier than ever," but his health was a nagging worry for Alma from then on.[86]

Mahler and Alma were married on March 9, 1902, at 1:30 p.m. at a private ceremony in the Karlskirche. As Mahler had an aversion to large social events and Alma was uncomfortable in the public eye, they had agreed on a modest affair attended only by Anna and Carl Moll, Justine, and her lover, Arnold Rosé, violinist and *Konzertmeister* at the philharmonic. Mahler arrived on foot in galoshes in the rain, dressed informally, like the others, in a gray suit, black overcoat, and a felt hat. Alma, her mother, and Justine drove in a carriage. When they kneeled, Mahler misjudged the hassock, landed on the stone floor, and had to stand up again to make a fresh start: "We all smiled, including the priest." There were six at the wedding breakfast, "a rather silent occasion, and the guests departed immediately afterward."[87] The next day, Justine married Rosé and immediately moved out of the Auenbruggergasse apartment, which as manager and housekeeper she had shared with her brother for twelve years.

On the evening of the wedding, Alma and Gustav left by train for their honeymoon in St. Petersburg, where Mahler was engaged to conduct three concerts in the vast sparkling white hall of the Assembly of the Nobles. "Once in the train . . . we breathed again. His clouded spirits cleared as though by magic; and I too, alone at last, was no longer oppressed by the need to conceal my condition." For Alma was by then three months pregnant. From being a young woman driven to compose music before all else, struggling in the doldrums of romantic and sexual love, she was now, after an extraordinarily short time, a woman pregnant and married, with a mission "to move every stone" from the path of her genius husband—and "to live for him alone."[88]

～ 5 ～

A Nobler Calling
1902–1907

The next three weeks in St. Petersburg were "unforgettably beautiful," despite some initial setbacks. Mahler had caught a feverish chill in the overheated train; Alma was aghast to see him "rushing up and down the corridor—his face as white as a sheet, incapable of uttering a syllable. He jumped out at every station and walked about the platform, in thirty degrees of frost without hat, coat or gloves." For the first of three concerts he was due to conduct, Alma was feeling unwell because of the pregnancy. For her comfort she was placed behind the orchestra "and so could see his face, which had a divinely beautiful expression. His exaltation when he was conducting was always intense and the sight of his face on these occasions, uplifted and open-mouthed, was so inexpressively beautiful that I felt a thrill of utter conviction."[1]

With Gustav's cousin, a czarist government official, they visited the city, the Hermitage Museum, and the frozen Neva River after dusk with "a merry bustle of skaters." Alma found the piety of the people "deeply moving."[2] In St. Petersburg high society, Alma found archdukes "easier and more amiable in manner than our nobility at home," though what was said "meant just as little to us."[3] Alma was neither a snob nor a social climber. Social hierarchies mattered far less to her than the hierarchies of talent and intellect.

On her return to Vienna on March 31, Alma moved into the Auen-bruggergasse apartment. She soon discovered debts amounting to 50,000 crowns, attributable to deficiencies in Justine's financial management, Mahler's continuing support for his demanding family, and debts owed to his three sisters, which he accrued when building his house at Maiernigg on the Wörthersee. Though unused to managing a household, Alma took control and claimed she paid off the debt within five years: "I had been brought up in such a modest way that the strict economies of our early married life were no hardship," she wrote, doubtless recalling the years of austerity she suffered with her parents in her youth.[4]

The hostility to which Mahler had grown accustomed was now part of Alma's life. Friction with the orchestra over his allegedly arbitrary hiring and firing of musicians was exacerbated by resentment at his exacting con-ducting style. Mahler had warned her of his lonely, beleaguered position: "I have spent the past fifteen years battling against superficiality and in-comprehension, bringing down on me all the troubles, indeed all the mis-eries of the trailblazer," he wrote from Berlin.[5] He also faced pressures as a Jew, as he warned his assistant Bruno Walter. Although he was baptized a Catholic, the anti-Semites still saw him as Jewish. Walter was appalled by the "hateful" virulence of the anti-Semitic Viennese press. But Mahler reassured him that "nothing matters less than what the press says here; they are a bunch of idiots, lapping like dogs at every new face, growling for a while and then a few years later he is 'our Walter.'"[6]

At the end of May 1902, when she was four months pregnant, Alma accompanied Mahler to the premiere of his Third Symphony at a music festival in Krefeld. They became "completely one" as she attended re-hearsals and discussed with him "this stupendous work."[7]

During the performance of the Third Symphony on June 9, Alma felt "an indescribable state of excitement; I cried and laughed softly to myself and suddenly felt the stirrings of my first child." The performance "finally convinced me of Mahler's greatness, and that night I dedicated to him my love and devotion with tears of joy."[8] It was Mahler's first major success. A tremendous ovation erupted after the first movement; people leapt to their feet and surged toward the platform at the end: "This man's inex-haustible verve never ceases to perform new miracles. Not one moment's boredom, not one second of fatigue!" declared critic William Ritter.[9]

In the audience was the composer Richard Strauss, an early Mahler supporter and now at the height of his powers. He strode to the podium at the end of the first movement, "applauding emphatically as though to set his seal on its success," but became steadily more subdued and then at the end, he was nowhere to be seen. At dinner at an inn afterward, Alma observed Strauss stride in, shake hands in a lordly way with everyone, and pass Mahler without a word. Mahler sat for some time in stony silence: "His spirits sank and the public acclamation now seemed of no account."[10]

Composer Hans Pfitzner visited Mahler in Krefeld. As Alma retired to an alcove in their bedroom so the men could speak alone, she heard a high, thin voice pleading urgently with Mahler to produce his operatic work, *Die Rose vom Liebesgarten*. Shocked by the degrading spectacle of a desperate artist being turned down "coldly, calmly, tersely," she rushed from behind the drapes to squeeze the man's hand "to show how deeply I sympathised." To Alma's astonishment, Mahler was not angry at her intervention. Pfitzner became Alma's lifelong, extremely demanding, and doting friend.

They traveled on to the Wörthersee where Mahler had a villa on the lakeside at Maiernigg, a spacious building with two large verandas and a large studio bedroom and dressing room for Mahler with a magnificent view over the lake. Isolated in the woods above the house was Mahler's *Häuschen*—a one-room composing hut, barely furnished with a grand piano, a desk, and bookcase displaying the works of Goethe and Kant.

At Maiernigg, Alma observed for the first time his life "stripped of all dross, almost inhuman in its purity." They lived peacefully from day to day, undisturbed except for the occasional letter from the opera, "which was sure to bring trouble."[11] Her days revolved around Gustav's regime— up at 6 or 6:30 a.m., then breakfast was brought by the cook two hundred feet up the hillside to his *Häuschen*. At noon he came down and swam in the lake: "I would sit on the steps and he would climb out for a chat, lie on the sun deck until his body was crimson, and jump in again." Despite Alma's anxiety about his heart, he repeated this procedure four or five times until he felt reinvigorated. After a simple lunch—the soup had to be waiting on the table—they rowed around the lake or walked for three or four hours, whatever the weather: "I climbed fences, crawled through hedges, and once shocked my mother, who came to visit us just as Mahler had dragged me up an almost vertical slope. Sometimes I felt too tired to go on; but whenever I was on the point of collapse he would take me in his arms and say, 'I love you'—and suddenly I found new strength and the race continued." Sometimes he stopped to take notes, while Alma sat patiently on a tree trunk or the grass. If an idea pleased him, "he threw me a smile, knowing that nothing on earth made me happier."[12]

Anna von Mildenburg, Mahler's former lover, was a neighbor who took to visiting them uninvited in the evenings. Once during a thunderstorm she dragged Mahler onto the terrace "for closer contact with the fury of the elements," as Alma observed. "The great Wagnerian soprano let her hair fall about her face and played Valkyrie and Ortrud in the same breath," while Alma, who had always relished the fury of nature, remained inside, terrified of being hit in her condition by branches hurtling through the air. Although stung when Mildenburg scornfully called her a coward, Alma contrived to make a musical event out of her next visit. They played and sang the whole of the last act of Wagner's *Siegfried* together: "Her voice that afternoon was truer and her singing more beautiful than they had ever been on the operatic stage; and as our concert carried right down to the lake, there was a crowd of boats in front of our house by the time we had done, and an outburst of enthusiastic applause," Alma recalled.[13]

While Mahler worked in his composing hut on his Fifth Symphony, down below, Alma played the piano very softly until he objected to the disturbance, so she took to copying out the symphony to manuscript as soon as he had finished: "I learnt at this time to read his score and to hear it as I wrote and was more and more of a real help to him," she reassured herself.[14]

Though she had resolved to subsume herself to him, Alma was soon plagued by nagging inner conflict and "a pitiful longing for someone who thinks of me, who can help me find myself." She had become "no more than a housekeeper! . . . I have lost my way, I can no longer find the bridge to the other side. Someone has taken me roughly by the arm and led me far away—away from myself. And I long to return to where I used to be." Discontent smoldered as she surveyed her "mindlessly hectic existence, the abandonment of all self-contemplation, finally the loss of all my friends—and the gain of a friend who does not know me."[15]

Matters came to a head in July, when she confronted him, and in "a bitter exchange of words—I told him everything." He promised he would help her. She knew he could not, for he was "totally absorbed in his creative work," but that day she resolved to overcome her doubts and find a way to fulfill herself—through him. She could congratulate herself that Mahler was happy, that she had "restored his peace of mind. He thanked me unceasingly and said I would not regret it. And that makes me feel better. I no longer feel so empty." With that she reaffirmed her goal and her "one purpose in life: to sacrifice my happiness for his—and to grow happy for having done so!"[16]

Aged twenty-three and six months pregnant, without an occupation to absorb her creative energies nor friends nearby to share her frustration, and lacking the attention she was accustomed to, Alma was under considerable strain. After another day alone, when Gustav emerged from his composing hut, she "couldn't share in his happiness, and tears came to my eyes again. He grew serious, my Gustav, terribly serious. And now he doubts whether I love him!—and how often have I doubted it myself." She was not only distraught but confused: "One moment I pine for his love, the next I feel nothing—nothing at all! When I love him, I can accept everything without difficulty; when I don't, it's impossible." She longed to find her inner balance, her calm, for she had never been as close to anyone as him, and he had told her he had never worked as fluently as then. So she decided, "From now on I don't want him to notice my inner struggles. . . . I will strengthen the ground on which he moves with my hard-won internal peace." But, she acknowledged, "my face, my eyes betray me. And these tears that keep flowing. Never before have I cried as much as now, at a time when I have everything that I—as a woman—could strive for."[17]

By mid-August she had recovered her equilibrium: "My pregnancy is something of a hindrance, but I can surmount every weakness. . . . My mission, to remove every obstacle from the path of the genius, is profoundly fulfilling." She was deeply touched when he gave her "something very intimate, just for you"—a love song he had composed to the Rückert poem *Liebst du um Schönheit*, with the closing line, "Liebe mich immer, immer dar" (Love me always, I will love you forever). She played it over and over: "I almost wept. The tenderness of such a man! And my lack of sensibility! I often realise how little I am and possess—compared with his infinite riches!"[18]

When Mahler completed his Fifth Symphony at the end of summer, they climbed arm in arm to his composing hut, where he played it through to her. It gave her profound pleasure to feel that she had shared in its genesis. Later he dedicated it "to my dear Almerschl, my faithful and brave companion on all paths."[19]

On November 3, 1902, Alma gave birth to a daughter, Maria Anna. The delivery, a breech birth, was long and extremely painful. When Gustav read in the face of the doctor that something was wrong, he "raged up and down in the next room, waiting in a frenzy of anxiety for the end of this frightful delivery." Alma recalled, "To bring her into the world cost me incredible pain. I don't yet feel real love for her. All, all of me belongs to my beloved Gustav. I love him so dearly that everything other than him is dead to me."[20] When it was over, Gustav exclaimed, "How can men go on conceiving children knowing that they will cause such suffering." But, when he heard it was a breech birth, "he laughed uncontrollably. 'That's my child, showing the world straight away the part it deserves.'"[21]

Alma was confined to her bed for two weeks and then fell ill for a long time with gallstones—"the cause, or perhaps the result, of my intense unrest." A governess took care of Maria, and they had a cook, Elise, and the housemaid, Podi, to ease the domestic burden. Barely six weeks after the traumatic birth, she was again in emotional torment and suffering symptoms of acute postpartum depression. The absence of her music haunted her: "It feels as though my wings had been clipped. For eight days and nights now, I have been inventing music deep in my mind; it is so loud and insistent that I hear it between every word I speak and I cannot sleep at night!"[22] She told Gustav how upset she was by "his lack of interest in what was happening inside me, that he had never even asked me to play any of my works for him, and that I am tormented by his total indifference to my feelings. My knowledge of music suited him only insofar as it served his purposes. He didn't take me seriously. He said: 'Because your golden dreams have not been fulfilled. . . . you only have yourself to blame.'" Alma was not appeased: "My God, how hard it is to be deprived so mercilessly of *everything*, to not be taken seriously about what one feels most deeply."[23]

In despair, she lamented her loneliness and lack of purpose: "Gustav lives *his* life. And I have to live his, too. I *cannot* occupy myself *only with my child!* Now I'm learning Greek . . . to fill my empty hours. But what has become of my goal, *my magnificent goal!* My bitterness is intense! I am constantly choking with tears! No-one understands this. Everyone thinks I am happy, and yet one thing is missing, the one thing which is more important to me than all the rest."[24] With no means of solace, she raged at her fate: "Gustav, why did you bind to you this splendid bird so happy in flight, when a grey, heavy one would have suited you better? There are so many plump ducks and geese who don't know how to fly!"[25]

In effusive and loving letters, Mahler assured her of his love and longing for "my *own*, the *very* one who now embodies all I belong to and all that belongs to me," while at the same time dismissing her inner torments.[26] Alma's doubts smoldered inside her: "Gustav is so solitary, so distant! Everything in him is so deeply buried that it cannot surface! Even his love; everything is muted. I need warmth! I am alone! . . . Oh, if only he were younger, younger to enjoy life!"[27]

In such a volatile state, Alma's jealousy flared easily. She had a vicious tongue when thwarted or enraged. At the first rehearsal of *Euryanthe* at the Opera House in January 1903, she observed Gustav with Anna von Mildenburg and the soprano Lucie Weidt and was horrified when he "let those whores drink out of his glass! . . . Playful, charming, cooing, like a young man he danced around Mildenburg and Weidt!" Alma's reaction was violent: "He disgusts me *so much* that I dread his coming home. My God! If only he *never* came home again. Not to live with him any more! I'm so agitated that I can scarcely write. What an idiot I was to stay at home languishing for him. The thought of him nauseates me, I can hardly express it."[28] When he arrived home and wanted to caress her, she rebuffed him. "Everything in me was cold," she wrote. Then, just as swiftly, her feelings returned, but an emptiness had appeared at her core that she couldn't dispel. "Now that I am supposed to live only for someone else, I do not feel happy. Although I truly love this man. Nothing really touches me. I cry, I rage, I rant, but all on the surface. Deep down, there is an indestructible, frightening calm. No pain affects me! No joy either! . . . Yes, absolutely nothing, nothing, nothing. Wretched half-creature!"[29]

Above all she mourned the loss of her music, which could have been her redemption and the salve to her loneliness. She played the piano:

"But for what and for whom? I can't any more. My joie de vivre has fled! . . . If only the *one* thing was left to me—*my* music! . . . I stagnate. I'm so tired!"[30] Later she was convinced that in music she could have found "a complete cure for this state of things, but he had forbidden it when we were engaged." And now she dragged her hundred songs with her "wherever I went like a coffin into which I dared not even look."[31]

Even so, there were periods of composure when her love for Mahler was rekindled and she absorbed herself in his work. But his uncertain health still perturbed her. During the performance of *Tristan and Isolde* in February 1903, Gustav retired backstage after the second act and lay on the sofa white-faced and hardly able to pull himself together to conduct the third act: "'If only someone would take it off my hands,' he said." His sister Justine was also present. As they looked down at the exhausted Mahler, Justine said under her breath, "One thing delights me—I had his youth, you have him now he's old." In this moment of extreme anxiety, Alma "lost all that was left of my love for [Justine]."[32]

Gradually Alma met Mahler's more sympathetic musical associates, including French composer Gustav Charpentier, "a complete bohemian" who captivated her during the rehearsals of his opera *Louise* in March 1903.[33] He was "the first of the Surrealists . . . as much a painter as a musician," she thought, who "talks of his music as of a mistress." In *Louise*, "the seducer now had to wear a red electric bulb beneath his dress-coat, so that when he opened it his heart was revealed. . . . All realism was very properly eliminated as being out of date."[34] Charpentier told her she was fortunate to have "so great a husband." He told Mahler, "You have there *un gamin, la clarté, la gaîté, le printemps*—we artists need that," and Alma glowed in his praise.[35]

When she did not accompany Mahler on conducting tours, he wrote her daily letters that overflowed with energy and love. They could also be didactic, treating her, as she later complained, like a child in need of guidance, admonishing her to "rid yourself of certain trivial ideas that are obscuring your vision and blinding you to reality" and demanding, "What are these 'inconsequential matters' that have become of such 'consequence' to you? What depresses you so? Can't you ever relax?"[36]

At Easter in Abbazia on the Croatian coast, Alma reassured herself that she had achieved the outward calm she had imposed on herself—"to be quieter, to keep silent when I'm hurt."[37] But during a fever in May her vivid dreams exposed her inner turmoil, her fear of losing herself. In one, a large green snake with long legs "suddenly forces its way up inside me. I pull at its tail. It won't come out. I ring for the chambermaid. She pulls with all her strength. Suddenly she gets hold of it. It slides out with all my inner organs in its mouth. Now I am hollow and empty like a wrecked ship."[38]

THE SUMMER OF 1903 in Maiernigg with its "unvarying and peaceful routine" and utter tranquility calmed her. Mahler worked on his Sixth Symphony, and they played piano duets together and walked daily round the Wörthersee. Gustav discovered particular delight in the child, "Putzi"—"carrying her about and holding her up to dance and sing. So young and unencumbered he was in those days," Alma recalled.[39]

That June she finally found the courage to play her compositions again—her piano sonata and her lieder: "I feel again—! this is what I want. I long to create again. The role I impose on myself is a delusion. I need MY Art! Everything I played today. . . ! So profoundly familiar to me. If only Zemlinsky were here to work with me but there is also Gustav's completely unfounded jealousy. And so I have nobody. These last few days, tears. . . . I don't now feel inwardly unhappy. Not at all. But I wouldn't be averse to a few more visible or palpable signs of Gustav's love."[40] On her birthday in August he apologized for not giving her a present; he had not known what to buy her: "What more can one give, when one has already given oneself?" he asked.[41]

In September, Alma was pregnant again. She cancelled her afternoon "races"—the energetic walks she took with Gustav three times around the Belvedere or the Ring in Vienna, but she still traveled with her mother to hear the Prague performance of Mahler's Second Symphony—a critical success that augmented his growing international reputation as an original, though controversial, modernist. But increasingly Alma missed her music and the intellectual stimulation she was used to. "I'm growing shallow! I must start reading again, learn more! . . . I want to lead an intellectual inner life." Reading in her diaries of her former life, so "full of new experiences," she realized "how monotonous and calm it has now become! I must have some stimulus."[42]

Alma decided to widen their social circle. She had contacted Zemlinsky about possible lessons, which he refused, but because he revered
Mahler he visited often with his pupil, Arnold Schoenberg. Bruno Walter came, but when Mahler played his Fifth Symphony to him, Alma
was distraught: "He is letting him look into the depths of his soul. Up to
now, the work belonged only to me! I copied it and we have often sung
the themes for ourselves. . . . And now it belongs to others. Bruno Walter
is the only one whose connivance I do not begrudge. . . . And yet—I had
to go out of the room."[43]

At a dinner with the now ailing Max Burckhard in February 1904,
they met the German playwright and novelist Gerhart Hauptmann and
his companion, Margarete Marschalk. So engrossed in conversation
were Hauptmann and Mahler on the long walk home that they stopped
and talked at every lamppost for fifteen minutes at a time. Margarete
and Alma "sat down on a seat and waited patiently until we could get a
word in edgeways to remind them of our existence."[44] Exhausted at four
in the morning, they completed the journey by cab and then met again
every day during the writer's visit. The empathy between the two men
was a "blessing" for Alma: "These two geniuses of dark and light were
bound to harmonise and give out a beautiful note," she wrote.[45] Hauptmann told Mahler, "People like you make it possible for long stretches
of our journey on earth to be illumined by a happy and divine light."[46]
It was the start of a lasting friendship. Alma got on well with the elfish
Margarete, but she was utterly beguiled by Hauptmann's talent.

At about this time she clarified her feelings to Mahler during a walk:

> "All I love in a man is his achievement. The greater his achievement
> the more I have to love him."
>
> "That's a real danger. You mean if anyone came along who could do
> more than I—"
>
> "I'd have to love him," I said. He smiled: "Well, I won't worry for
> the time being. I don't know anybody who can do more than I can."[47]

In June, after seeing Hauptmann's play *Der arme Heinrich*, the words
continued to sound in Alma's ears through her dreams until "suddenly I
woke, as though God had touched me with a finger. My hour had come—
and still I heard Hauptmann. I did not want to wake anyone. I opened

the window. It was 15th June; all nature bloomed; leaves rustled, birds sang. I had no fear." Mahler called the midwife and then tried to mitigate the pain by reading Kant aloud to her while she "sat at his writing table and writhed in agony. The monotonous drone of his voice drove me crazy; I could not understand a word he read."[48]

Anna Justinia was born on June 15, 1904, at midday, as Alma noted— in the middle of the week (Wednesday), the middle of the month and the middle of the year—"[it] might have been an allegory." The child was nicknamed Gucki, "from her wide-open, blue eyes." Later in the day Gustav arrived. As Alma opened her eyes, an enormous stag beetle hovered in the air an inch or two from her face. To her amusement, Mahler was holding it by a single leg and beaming with delight, despite his horror of beasts of all kinds. "'You're so fond of animals,' he exclaimed exultingly. 'I caught this fellow for you.'"[49] It seemed like a sacrificial offering. After the birth Alma was ordered to rest in bed for three weeks to conserve her strength.

Summer at Maiernigg was exceptionally peaceful, with Gustav "more human and more communicative" than usual. He took an interest in the children, told them stories, built a playground for them on the lakeshore, and could scarcely bear to be parted from them. To Alma's disbelief he worked on his *Kindertotenlieder*, based on elegies written out of the depth of grief at the loss of a child by Friedrich Rückert. She could not understand him "bewailing the deaths of children, who were in the best of health and spirits, hardly an hour after having kissed and fondled them. I exclaimed at the time: 'For heaven's sake, don't tempt Providence.'"[50]

When he worked intensively on his Sixth Symphony, neither the cook nor the children were allowed to make the slightest noise, and Alma stopped playing the piano or singing until he surfaced, "radiant with joy, as always when he had finished working and wanted to re-establish contact with our life." He was "serene; he was conscious of the greatness of his work. He was a tree in full leaf and flower," Alma observed.[51] When the symphony was completed, Alma walked once more arm-in-arm with him up to his composing hut where he played it to her, confident as ever of her musical instinct. "We both wept that day," she wrote. "Not one of his works came so directly from his inmost heart as this." He told her he had tried to express her in the great soaring theme of the first movement;

in the third movement, he "represented the a-rhythmic games of the two children, tottering in zig zags over the sand. Ominously the childish voices became more and more tragic, and at the end died out in a whimper." In the last movement he recorded his downfall—or, as Mahler told her, that of the hero: "It is the hero, on whom fall three blows of fate, the last of which fells him as a tree is felled."[52] For Alma this was a portent of Mahler's own fate.

Erica Tietze, the daughter of old family friends, the Conrats, came to stay. She recalled evenings on the terrace overlooking the lake and lying beside Alma in hammocks on the lake shore: "He doesn't know how to *enjoy* anything." Alma told her, and Erica commented, "It's true! . . . Yesterday we had to have four roosters slaughtered because their crowing

Figure 10. Glorious Alma.
"She seemed like a beautiful beast
of prey." —Erica Tietze

disturbed him while he was sunbathing."[53] As they rowed on the lake, Erica sat facing Alma: "In the setting sun her hair seemed like a halo of red flame, and she herself like some beautiful beast of prey."[54]

When they disembarked for tea, it was "like running the gauntlet," Erica observed. "This beautiful woman, this famous man, known to everyone." Alma was deeply uncomfortable with the celebrity. It heightened her "torturing sense of inferiority" that she was "nothing but his shadow," an adjunct instead of a person in her own right. In the street, people "stood stock still and loudly exclaimed: 'Look—there's Mahler with his wife.' They laughed, nudged each other and turned around to stare and made me feel so uncomfortable that I could barely walk on. But Mahler saw nothing," Alma remembered.[55]

Alma was too ill to go to Cologne in October for the world premiere of his Fifth Symphony, even though he pleaded, "Do all you can: sweat it out, drink quantities of cognac, swallow aspirins. . . . How awful it would be if I were left in my own for my world première."[56] She, too, was upset for she felt a proprietorial interest in what had been her "first full participation in his life and work, the whole score of which I had copied, and— more than that—whole lines of which had been left out because he knew that he could trust blindly to me."[57] Despite her illness, she felt at peace, happy even, with her role in his life.

Yet, in the new year, six months after Anna's birth, she was again experiencing serious depressive symptoms: "Nothing really interests me—serious things tire me out. I drag myself wearily from hour to hour—weary in body and soul." She blamed herself: "We are in fact two people. . . . and we ought to be one!" But her strength and sense of purpose revived when both her children were sick and she found that "the more you make demands on yourself, the more strength you find. All the morning I wrapped Gucki in cold sheets, took her temperature, etc. I've rarely been so cheerful and good-humoured. Suddenly it became clear to me why I am alive: my children need me. And Gustav Mahler needs me."[58]

But she still felt incapable of giving Gustav all her warmth and wondered why. They had talked about the early stages of their intimacy and how she had found his body odor offensive. "He said to me, 'That is the key to a lot of things! You acted against your nature!' I alone know how right he is. Initially I found him foreign, and in many respects this will always be so." She wondered what now kept them together: "Duty? Children? Habit? No, I know that I really love him and that without him I could not live. For he has taken so much away from me that his presence is my sole support. It seems impossible to go back to my former life. Now I must try to get the best I can out of the short span that is *life*. And what I mean by best is to BECOME SO GOOD, SO USEFUL, SO CALM, CONTENT AND SELF-CONTAINED that I can achieve my happiness from that."[59]

Alma kept up her interest in events at the opera, where Alfred Roller's new set for *Rheingold* was causing havoc: the Rhine maidens refused to sing suspended in baskets on long poles. "His settings were beautiful but awkward," she noted drily.[60] Her admiration for Arnold Schoenberg, who "for all his wrong-headedness is a very original fellow," blossomed at the premiere on January 17, 1905, of his *Pelléas and Mélisande*, when, to whistles and catcalls the audience "kept leaving in droves and slamming the doors behind them."[61] But Alma's loyalty to him was implacable: nobody who entered "the circle of Schoenberg's spirit could resist his intellectual pre-eminence or the force of his logic," she declared.[62]

After Mahler agreed to direct Hans Pfitzner's opera *Die Rose vom Liebesgarten*, Alma saw more of this self-centered and temperamental man; she alone could calm him during rehearsals. They played her songs together, and, when he complimented her on her composition and fine feeling for melody, she exclaimed, "What a melancholy joy coursed through my veins! A moment's bliss."[63] Once, they became so engrossed in playing each other's songs that they almost missed their rendezvous with Mahler and Hauptmann. "Pfitzner was in love with me that night," she wrote. "Why it suddenly blew up and promptly died out again, I do not know. . . . [H]e begged me to let him come closer to me—he touched me with his hands wherever he could and begged me finally in an enraptured voice for my photograph. We were alone in the living room. I let it happen—felt that tingle on my skin that I haven't felt in a long time."[64]

Mahler was jealous but tolerated the composer's adoration of his wife. When Pfitzner excused himself from a rehearsal and dashed off with a red rose to see her, Mahler—"both amused and vexed"—followed. On the Ring, he encountered a May Day procession of working men. Mahler was delighted that they looked at him "in so brotherly a way—they *were* his brothers—and they were the future!" Pfitzner, on the contrary, was "furious at the sight of proletarian faces" and darted off down a side street to escape.[65] When the two rivals for Alma's affection confronted each other, they argued not about Alma but about the procession.

Alma's days were now more tied to Gustav's schedule. She attended his public performances, concert tours, and festivals when she could. And, in Maiernigg with the children in June 1905, she realized how far her life had been subsumed into his. "In the lake, in the forest, his image appears everywhere. . . . I live ONLY for him. I copy music for him, play the piano to impress him—I study, read, all for the same reason." But other— as she saw it, negative and conflicting—sides to her personality refused to be suppressed: "My former pride, my imperiousness, my self-indulgent ambition, my search for glory all rise again—instead of striving to make life beautiful and tender ONLY FOR HIM. For that is my sole purpose in life, the only justification for my existence. And my dear little children."[66] Her resolve was fragile, however, and her inner loneliness persisted. Though Roller, Zemlinsky, Schoenberg, and Pollack arrived to brighten her days during that "murderously hot" summer, she complained, "I long for a husband . . . for I have NONE. But I am too lazy . . . even for that!"[67]

Throughout, she remained attentive to the rhythms of Mahler's creativity and completely bound up in his work. She routinely copied his work to manuscript, including his Seventh Symphony after he had suffered a creative block that cleared only when he heard the sound of oars playing through the water on the lake.[68] In the spring of 1906, she attended the rehearsals in Essen of his deeply personal Sixth Symphony: "None of his works moved him so deeply at its first hearing as this," she wrote.[69] That summer, when Mahler was again "haunted by the spectre of failing inspiration" during work on his Eighth Symphony, he experienced one morning a vision "that struck me like lightning, the whole immediately stood before my eyes; I had only to write it down, as if it had been dictated to me."[70] He had never written "under such compulsion," he insisted, and was convinced the *creator spiritus* that took possession of him was evidence of a higher power, perhaps divine, "which reigned over all art and life."[71]

This inspiration was no surprise to Alma, who believed that a profound spirituality lay at the core of Mahler's creativity and, moreover, that he felt "a strong leaning to Catholic mysticism. . . . He could never pass a church without going in; he loved the smell of incense and Gregorian chants."[72] His friend Oskar Fried believed that Mahler was "religious through and through, in a mystical, though not in a dogmatic sense."[73] Mahler never denied his Jewish origins, and even though he did not attend the synagogue or observe Jewish rituals or celebrations, he identified as Jewish. "His sense of being chosen by God came from personal, not racial, roots," Alfred Roller thought.[74]

Alma, who had been prone to casual and tasteless anti-Semitic asides, almost never made such comments during her marriage to Mahler. Rather, she sympathized with his bitter suffering from "the Jewish question" not only when Cosima Wagner had tried to bar his appointment at the Hofoper but routinely from the press and critics. At a festival of German composers in Graz in May 1905, when other composers "gave Mahler the cold shoulder," Alma observed, "Anti-Semitism was already in the ascendant and Mahler was made to feel it."[75] He did not deceive himself that people would forget he was a Jew because he was skeptical of the Jewish religion and baptized a Christian. "Nor did he wish it forgotten," she wrote. "Rather, he emphasised it. He was a believer in Christianity, a Christian Jew, and he paid the penalty. I was a Christian Pagan and got off scot-free."[76] Of his Jewishness, he would often say, "I am thrice homeless. As a native of Bohemia in Austria, as an Austrian among Germans, and as a Jew throughout the world. Everywhere an intruder, never welcomed."[77]

Mahler worked with "superhuman energy" throughout the summer of 1906: "He was boundlessly happy and elated," Alma recalled. His love for her was insistent, but she felt shut out from his true being by his utter dedication to his work, even though she understood the compulsion of creative genius. She had bound her life to his but rather than inspiring him, as she had hoped, she feared she had merely entered his shadow.

It was no better in Vienna, when his strict daily routine came into force, "and a profound solitude enclosed us both," she wrote sadly.[78] Even so, he found time for the children, and Alma recalled poignantly his relationship with Maria, the eldest, who—just as she had done with her father—"used to go to Mahler's studio every morning. They held long conversations there together. Nobody has ever known what about. I never disturbed them." Their "fussy" English nurse took her to her father's door "as clean and neat as a new pin," and he returned her "smeared with jam from top to toe." She was "his child entirely. Her beauty and

Figure 9. Mahler with his favorite daughter, Maria, c. summer 1904.

waywardness, and her unapproachability, her black curls and large blue eyes, foretold that she would be a danger later on," Alma wrote.[79]

That autumn Mahler faced increasing pressure at the Opera House. To add to discontent among singers and orchestra about his directorial style, the court censor banned his production of Strauss's *Salome* on moral grounds. The move signaled to Mahler that people in high places were intriguing against him. Prince Montenuovo accused Mahler of neglecting his duties as Hofoper director when he found out the number of Mahler's outside engagements, though Mahler assured him that his duties were unaffected and the Court Opera's prestige was enhanced by his tours. In January 1907, the complaints were amplified into a sustained press campaign against him. As a public figure, he felt "like a wild animal pursued by a pack of dogs," he told Alma from Frankfurt, where the papers were filled with rumors of his resignation and of a massive deficit at the opera that made it impossible to keep him on.[80] He was vilified for declining performance quality, making cuts to operas, and undermining morale by his frequent absences and his autocratic style.

Alma and Mahler withstood the storm, though the troubles did not go away. Prince Montenuovo continued to support him, and he had two successes with *Die Walküre* and *Iphigénie* in March 1907, but Mahler found the arguments and the permanent tension surrounding him and the orchestra utterly draining.

Though insulated to some extent from the crisis, Alma could not fail to be affected by Gustav's exhaustion, the hostility around him and the gathering uncertainty about their future. In her inner life, she had adjusted with considerable torment to the mission she had set herself and had managed to attain an equilibrium within the outwardly stable framework of their marriage. But that calm was about to be shattered, and the unfolding year would be "blackly underlined in the calendar of our lives."[81]

— 6 —

Grief and Renewal

1907–1910

*T*he pubic intrigues against Mahler intensified in the spring of 1907. Prince Montenuovo had affirmed his support, but when he found that Mahler planned three extra concerts in Rome, Mahler was summoned, and, after an acrimonious discussion, he agreed to hand in his resignation. When he left with Alma for Rome, both were "half-glad to be quit of the Opera, half fearful of the unknown future."[1] But Mahler hesitated to cut ties with the opera completely. It was only at the end of May, after a further dispute between Roller and the Hofoper ballet master, that Mahler finally tendered his resignation. Even then he could not depart until a successor had been found.

Alma witnessed the furor, the fierce disputes, and the rumors engulfing Gustav. Convinced that Mahler's dismissal was "the stupid idea of 'philistines.' . . . who believe that no-one is irreplaceable," she also observed that Mahler had "had enough of endless tortures, obstacles and intrigues," and decided that she must "stand steady during these hectic goings-on" to support him. As her confidante Berta Zuckerkandl wrote, "She feels she must be practical, reasonable and balanced. She needs to protect Mahler and therefore often has to bear the moods of the genius." Alma did not mind him abandoning his "envied position," because she had hated playing "Frau Director." But she reflected to Berta on her own role as the supporter to genius. Quoting Talleyrand's saying "No man is

97

a hero to his valet," she asked her, "Please, tell me honestly: is there a genius for us genius-women?"[2]

Despite the immediate uncertainty, their financial future was secure—at least in the short term. Heinrich Conried, director of the New York Metropolitan Opera, had offered Mahler the post of conductor as part of a strategy to resuscitate the Metropolitan's fortunes in the face of growing competition from the Manhattan Opera House in New York. In June Conried offered Mahler a four-year contract and an unprecedentedly generous salary of 125,000 crowns for a six-month session in New York (which compared to 36,000 crowns for a ten-month session in Vienna).[3] Mahler signed on June 21: "Everything is true. I am going because I cannot stand the riff-raff any longer," he wrote to his friend Arnold Berliner.[4]

They were to suffer an even more profound upheaval. When Alma returned from Rome, she found their youngest child, Anna, feverish and sick. Scarlet fever was diagnosed. Maria, the elder, was sent away to stay with Alma's mother. Alma watched Anna's illness reach its peak and her recovery begin before she herself underwent an undisclosed operation in a nursing home. When Anna was well enough, Alma took the children to Maiernigg while Mahler spent a week alone in the Semmering. Three days after her arrival, the eldest, Maria (Putzi) was taken suddenly ill with symptoms of scarlet fever and diphtheria. For a fortnight they lived "in an agony of dread."[5] Then came a relapse, when the child was in danger of suffocation. "It was a ghastly time, accompanied by thunderstorms and lurid skies," Alma wrote. Mahler, who "loved his child devotedly, hid himself in his room every day, taking leave of her in his heart." When it became clear that they would have to perform a tracheotomy, Alma posted a servant at Mahler's door to keep him in his room if the noise disturbed him.

Alma and the English nurse prepared the table for the doctor to carry out the tracheotomy and put the child to sleep: "While the operation was being performed I ran along the shore of the lake, where no-one could hear me crying." Alma recalled. "At five in the morning the nurse came to tell me it was over. Then I saw her. She lay choking, with her large eyes wide open. Our agony dragged on one more whole day. Then the end came."[6]

It was too much for Mahler to bear: "Weeping and sobbing, [he] went again and again to the door of my bedroom, where she was; then fled away to be out of earshot of any sound." They telegraphed Anna Moll, who came at once. "We all three slept in [Mahler's] room. We could not bear being parted for an hour. We dreaded what might happen if any of us left the room. We were like birds in a storm and feared what each moment might bring—and how right we were!"[7]

They put the funeral arrangements in the hands of a relative. Two days later Mahler asked Alma and her mother to go down to the edge of the lake:

> And there my mother suddenly had a heart attack. I contrived cold compresses with the water of the lake and put them over her heart. Then Mahler came down the path. His face was contorted and when I looked up at him I saw, on the road above, that the coffin was being placed in the hearse. I knew now what had caused my mother's sudden seizure and why his face was contorted. He and I were so helpless, so bereft, that it was almost a joy to fall into a deep faint.[8]

The doctor who was called to see Alma diagnosed that she was suffering from "extreme exhaustion of the heart." Mahler suggested the doctor might examine him too, thinking it would distract them from their gloom: "The doctor got up looking very serious. . . . 'Well, you've no cause to be proud of a heart like that,' he said in that cheery tone doctors often adopt after diagnosing a fatal disease," Alma recalled. Mahler went to Vienna by the next train to consult Professor Kovacs, who fully confirmed the verdict of the general practitioner—valvular insufficiency, or rheumatism of the heart, possibly resulting from streptococcal tonsillitis, which impaired the heart's functioning. Kovacs forbade Mahler mountain ascents, bicycling, and swimming, and ordered a course of training to learn to walk slowly: "The events, on top of his retirement from the Opera, changed our whole existence," Alma wrote.[9]

She packed up a few belongings and fled Maiernigg to spend the rest of the summer in the mountainous Schluderbach in South Tyrol, where they "revived to some extent in new and beautiful surroundings and tried to imagine our life in the future."[10] Mahler found an anthology of poems,

Hans Bethge's *Die Chinesische Flöte* (*The Chinese Flute*) given to him by Theobald Pollack. It became the inspiration for the cycle of songs, *Das Lied von der Erde* (*The Song of the Earth*), that he sketched out that summer.

On August 10, Prince Montenuovo confirmed that Mahler could be released from the Court Opera, as they had found a new director, Paul Felix Weingartner. The emperor agreed to increase Mahler's pension, with an additional bona fide payment of 20,000 crowns, and Alma would be entitled after his death to a pension not normally allotted to the director's widow.

Believing it was too full of painful memories, Alma and Gustav had decided to sell Maiernigg. The wound ran deep: "For a time, Mahler and I were alienated, our suffering had driven us apart. Without realising it, he felt I was to blame for the death of our child."[11] He seemed to believe that Maria, who had been sent away to stay with her mother when Anna first contracted scarlet fever, had been brought back home too soon, before Anna had fully recovered. Bruno Walter observed a marked transformation in Mahler: "I could sense unmistakeably the darkness which had descended over his whole being. 'I shall soon get used to it,' he would say."[12] But he was "a broken man . . . he is at the end of his tether. [Alma] seems to be taking it better, with tears and philosophy."[13] But she took a long time to recover. After several "nervous attacks," in October she retired to a spa for treatment: "You are still young—somehow you've simply *got* to get over this," Mahler wrote to her. "Heavens, what would I give to rid myself of all my maladies, and you can't even keep it up for a fortnight. . . . *Now be a good girl* and avoid the high life, even if you're feeling better. You've got to get well for America."[14]

Mahler had agreed after a meeting with Conried in September to arrive four weeks earlier than scheduled in New York, when he would conduct two performances a week for an extra fee of 25,000 crowns. At the Hofoper during September and October, he planned a series of farewell performances of his favorite operas—*Don Giovanni*, *Figaro*, *Die Zauberflöte*, *Die Walküre*, Christoph Gluck's *Iphigénie en Aulide*, and Beethoven's *Fidelio*.

As Alma prepared for their departure, friends rallied to his support. Young composers who owed much to his influence—Zemlinsky, Schoenberg, and Alban Berg—mourned his departure. Berta Zuckerkandl lauded his achievements: "For ten years he fought against routine, nepotism, laziness, intrigues and stupidity. In those years he reformed the opera. Not only the Vienna opera but opera as an art form."[15] Supporters packed the hall for his final performance on November 24, conducting his Second Symphony: "The audience simply would not leave," reported the *Neue Freie Presse*. "Mahler was called back to the rostrum time and again, to ovations, cheers and waving handkerchiefs, to which the members of both the orchestra and the chorus added their voices."[16] The praise was not universal; his detractors and the consistently hostile anti-Semitic press welcomed his departure.

Mahler visited Berta before he left and spoke warmly of the future and of his deep gratitude to Alma: "I'm taking my homeland along with me, my Alma and my child," he told her. "Alma has sacrificed ten years of her youth to me. No-one can ever know with what absolute selflessness she has subordinated her own life to me and my work. It is with a light heart that I set off on my way with her."[17] Berta believed Alma had become "the intellectual companion of the genius to whom she had dedicated her life." Unlike other women "who lose their own self and forget about their personality," she remained "very rich in individuality and managed to continue to develop independently." Nor did she let herself "be conquered by Mahler's demons." Often she would follow a different path from Mahler's, but if she detected intrigues, she would always take his side, and, on the rare occasions when she couldn't stand it anymore, she confided in Berta.[18]

The relationship looked rather different from Alma's perspective. Her turbulence was not stilled nor her independence secured, despite the outward appearance: "I existed only as his shadow. I lived his life. I had none of my own," she reflected later.

> Work, exaltation, self-denial and the never-ending quest were his whole life. . . . I cancelled my will and my being; like a tightrope walker, I was concerned only with keeping my balance. He noticed nothing of all it cost me. He was utterly self-centred by nature, and yet he never thought of himself. His work was everything. I separated myself inwardly from him, though with reverence, and waited for a miracle. I was blind. . . . In spite of having children, I was still a girl. He saw in me only the comrade, the mother and housewife, and was to learn too late

what he had lost. These carnivores of genius, who think they are vege-
tarians! I have found it so all my life. People speak of ethics, but—they
hardly practice them.[19]

On December 9, 1907, Gustav and Alma arrived at the Westbahnhof
in Vienna en route for New York. A note had secretly been sent around
to friends and supporters urging them to be at the station at 8:30 a.m.
Two hundred people turned up, including Alexander Zemlinsky, Arnold
Schoenberg, Erik Schmedes, and Gustav Klimt. Alma was amazed: "They
were all drawn up when we arrived, flowers in their hands and tears in
their eyes, ready to board the train and deck out our compartment with
flowers from roof to floor."[20] The music critic Paul Stefan recalled: "There
was no artifice: simply an overpowering wish among all of us to see once
more the man to whom we owed so much. . . . The train started to move.
And Gustav Klimt said what we had all been feeling about the sad end-
ing of a great epoch: 'It's over!' [Vorbei!]."[21]

For Alma, the departure was "without regret or backward glances.
We had been too hard hit. All we wanted was to get away, the farther the
better. We even felt happy as Vienna was left behind. We did not miss
our child, who had been left with my mother. We knew now that anxious
love was of no avail against catastrophe, and that no spot on earth gives
immunity. We had been through the fire. So we thought. But, in spite of
all, one thing had us both in its grip—the future."[22]

In Paris they met up with Ossip Gabrilowitsch, a young composer and
pianist and devoted admirer of Mahler who had visited them in Maiernigg
in the summer. He had shown no indication then of his feelings for Alma,
but when he found Alma alone in her hotel room, he confessed that he
was on the verge of falling madly in love with her: "Help me to get over it.
I love Mahler. I could not bear to hurt him," he pleaded. Alma was "too
dazed to speak," but it had an electric effect on her: "So I was still capable
of arousing love: I was not old and ugly, as I had come to think." Just as
Gabrilowitsch felt for her hand in the dark, Mahler came in, affectionate
and kindly—"and the spectre vanished. Nevertheless, this episode was my
standby for some time in many an onset of self-deprecation," she wrote.[23]

On December 12, in high spirits they boarded the ocean liner *Kaise-
rin Augusta Viktoria*. In their cabin was a telegram from Gerhart Hauptmann looking forward to their return to Europe, "which needs men like

you more than its daily bread."²⁴ The Atlantic passage was rough. Mahler spent much of it trying to avoid seasickness "by lying rigidly on his back on his bunk like a cardinal on his tomb."²⁵

Their arrival in New York on December 22 "so took our breath away that we forgot all our troubles," Alma wrote, as she recalled "the harbour and all the sights and scenes and human bustle."²⁶ For Gustav it seemed "the most colossal spectacle of man and nature."²⁷ After a siege by report-ers at the dock, they moved into a spacious suite of rooms containing two pianos—"so we felt at home"—on the eleventh floor of the Hotel Ma-jestic overlooking Central Park. That evening at a concert at Carnegie Hall, they paid their respects to the conductor Walter Damrosch, who had premiered Mahler's Fourth Symphony in New York. The next day Mahler began rehearsals for *Tristan und Isolde* at the Metropolitan Opera.

Alma was intrigued by Americans and alternately amused and dis-mayed by the wholly different ambience of the American music world. Their first luncheon party was with "the super-God Conried," who was "already disabled from tabes [syphilis] and showed unmistakeable signs of megalomania," she wrote. In his smoking room was a suit of armor that could be illuminated from within by red lights. In the middle of the room was a divan with a baldacchino (a canopy) and convoluted pillars "and on it reclined the godlike Conried when he gave audience to the members of the company. All was enveloped in somber, flounced stuffs, illuminated by the glare of colored electric lights. And then, Conried himself, who had 'made' the actor Adolf von Sonnenthal and was now going to 'make' Mahler." For Alma, the whole spectacle, and their host's "utter innocence of culture, kept us in concealed mirth until we were in the street again and could burst out laughing."²⁸

They soon found, however, that physical distance and new surround-ings had not eased their pain; they were still "annihilated by the death of our child." Alma "suffered from hallucinations. Wherever I looked I saw my doomed child." Gustav would not have her name mentioned in his hearing. Moreover, the shattering verdict on his heart now dominated his behavior. To conserve his strength he spent half the day in bed and got up only for a rehearsal or performance: "I spend the whole time lazing around," he reported to Carl Moll; and to Zemlinsky: "I really live from day to day, conduct, rehearse, dine, go for walks. . . . I am not exerting myself at all."²⁹

Alma found him "nervous, quick tempered and irritable. It was a wretched winter for me, and indeed for both of us."[30] Their suffering "estranged and separated us. Without knowing it he increased the bitterness of our loss." On Christmas Eve, Alma "wept without ceasing all day" until evening when a friend called and insisted they go out, where they could see a Christmas tree, children, and friendly faces. But when some actors and actresses joined them, one of whom was called "Putzi," their grief was renewed.[31] As it worsened and Alma was unable to get out of bed, Mahler called the doctor, who diagnosed weakness of the heart and nervous collapse. He prescribed strychnine, forbade her to move, and ordered four weeks of rest cure: "At last I was able to give way to my grief and my physical exhaustion." Mahler rallied to her support; he "felt his own sorrow less and gave all his thoughts to speeding my recovery."[32]

Despite the shadow over them, Alma found much to engage her. She attended Mahler's first performance of Tristan and Isolde on January 1, 1908—"one of the finest I had ever heard in my life," which was an "immediate triumph." Mahler's subsequent repertoire at the Metropolitan Opera included Die Walküre and Siegfried, and then in March his greatest triumph, Fidelio, staged with Alfred Roller's sets imported from Vienna.

Alma accompanied Mahler to "sedate" Boston and to Philadelphia, where, at the performance of Tristan, she sat in the front row immediately behind Mahler. There, "as though a veil had fallen," she "suddenly saw in his face marks of suffering I had never seen before. The dread of losing him gave me such a pang that I had a heart attack and fell into a dead faint."[33] A doctor, Leon Corning, carried her out into a dressing room. She had revived by the time Mahler rushed in at the end of the first act, but she remained backstage for the rest of the performance. She chatted with the soprano between her appearances, though the bass baritone, Anton von Rooy, remained "permanently Wotan" (regardless of the opera), striding silently and unsmiling to and fro with his spear, and "every inch a god," she observed mischievously.[34] It made her realize how sincere and modern Mahler was among the "stagey solemnities" of the past.[35]

Dr. Leon Corning, the millionaire discoverer of spinal anesthesia, invited them to dinner in New York. A shy, reserved man, he barely spoke but had "a constant flicker of lightning in his face," Alma recalled, with her usual flair for dramatic description. In his study—"the chamber of a medieval alchemist," "wires hanging from the ceiling crossed the room in all directions." Steps led down to "an iron-plated cell in which patients were rendered insensible by breathing condensed air. . . . His wife clad in black weeds swept through without word or look. Her face was a death mask with hollow eyes. He led us into his music room, in which three or four grand pianos stood in a row. Dr. Corning cheered up and walked up and down playing the flute."[36]

Toward the end of their stay in New York, they met the neurologist Dr. Joseph Fraenkel—"a genius both as a man and as a doctor, and we both fell in love with him the day we first met," Alma wrote. "Dazzling in his wit," he was "a daring thinker—a little splenetic perhaps, but always original."[37] He had studied medicine in Vienna, hoped to enroll in the army, but, as a Jew, balked at having to convert to Catholicism. He emigrated to America in steerage in his twenties and was taken up by a wealthy woman in first class, who sent him meals. While lodging in a poor New York rooming house, he gradually built up his reputation and advanced his career; eventually, his clients included the Vanderbilts and the Astors. Mahler fell "so entirely under his sway that he would unquestionably have done whatever he told him."[38]

Some moments were deeply moving for Alma. A young woman art student was visiting Alma at her hotel when they heard a commotion outside and saw a procession winding along Central Park: "It was the funeral cortège of a fireman, of whose heroic death we had read in the newspaper." The procession halted immediately below them, and the master of ceremonies gave a short address: "There was a brief pause and then a stroke of the muffled drum, followed by a dead silence. The procession then moved forward and all was over. The scene brought tears to our eyes." At the adjacent window Mahler too was leaning out, his face streaming with tears. The brief drum stroke impressed him so deeply that he used it in his (unfinished) Tenth Symphony.[39]

Once when Mahler was working, the silence was broken by the tremulous sound of an Italian barrel organ playing below. Alma rang reception and begged them to move him "at once at my expense. The noise ceased immediately. Then Mahler burst in: 'Such a lovely barrel-organ—took me straight back to my childhood—and now it's stopped!'"[40]

Within weeks of their arrival, they learned that Conried would be unable to continue because of illness. Mahler was offered the post of director, but he declined as it involved administrative duties. Conried appointed as general manager Guilio Gatti Casazza, who brought in his fellow Italian Arturo Toscanini to be co–principal conductor with Mahler. Despite initial harmony, tensions soon surfaced between the two conductors. But a new lifeline appeared for Mahler. Mary R. Sheldon, wife of a New York banker, was so impressed by Mahler's *Fidelio* that she formed a committee to create a "Mahler orchestra," which would restructure the ailing New York Philharmonic. Mahler agreed to a series of concerts the following spring. "Both of us have found much to appreciate in this country; people go about everything with an alertness, sanity and candour that we find most attractive. Everything has a future," he wrote to Zemlinsky. Even so, he told their friend Countess Misa Wydenbruck that he had been plagued by homesickness: "Unlike my wife, who would gladly remain here altogether, I regret to say that my heart belongs to Vienna."[41]

So, on April 23, 1908, they boarded the ship bound for Europe. "Mahler had regained much of his old physical self-confidence, and at once the world was brighter for me," Alma wrote.[42] On their return, all Vienna was busy in preparation for the emperor's jubilee celebrations in June. Mahler escaped to Prague while Alma went with her mother to look for a house to replace Maiernigg. They found Trenkerhof, a large farmhouse with eleven rooms and two verandas in a glorious location outside a village near Toblach on the south side of the lush pastoral Pustertal Valley between the Dolomites and the Alps. It would be their summer retreat for the next three years. Mahler had a composing hut built nearby in a mossy clearing surrounded by woods.

They moved in shortly afterward. Alma was amused when allotting the rooms that Gustav selected the two best and brightest for himself, then took the largest bed: "His egoism was sublimely unconscious. . . . [M]y mother and I followed him around, rejoicing in his innocent pleasure."[43] Along with Alma's mother and little Anna, they had a nanny; the cook, Agnes; and the maid, Kathi. In these surroundings Alma seems to have recovered her spirits. After a few weeks Gustav reported to Carl Moll, "Thank God, Almschi is now mobile again, and I am hoping—at last—to enjoy a calm and pleasant summer. . . . [She] is finally really doing something rational about her health, and I am quite pleased with her progress. She is also very cheerful and full of hope."[44]

Mahler worked on *Das Lied von der Erde*, completing the last movement by September 1. Superstitiously he would not call it the Ninth Symphony—neither Beethoven nor Bruckner had survived the writing of their Ninth Symphonies. By this device, Mahler "thought to give God the slip," as Alma described it. Much of her time was taken up with visitors—her mother and Carl Moll, banker Paul Hammerschlag, critic Julius Korngold, Alfred Roller, Oskar Fried, and others. Ossip Gabrilowitsch joined them. The frisson of Gabrilowitsch and Alma's Paris encounter was revived: "It was only natural that we should fall a little in love with each other. We really didn't want it, and fought hard against it." One night, when Gustav was working, "Ossi and I were leaning out of a window and looking over a moonlit meadow. The moon shone on our faces, we turned for a long time towards each other, we moved close. Gabrilowitsch left after this one kiss and whenever we saw each other again always there was this struggle. We both loved Gustav so strongly that a conscious betrayal of him was impossible."[45] Again Alma was drawn to a man of outstanding talent, who, to anatomist Emil Zuckerkandl, looked "like a Kiev Jew after a pogrom." Alma saw a different image: "Everything in his face was distorted. But it was precisely for that reason that I sought out this strangeness, and he presumably also sought me. This youthful camaraderie gave me back my self-confidence."[46]

Alma now began to face open hostility from Gustav's supporters. At the first performance in Prague of his Seventh Symphony, she was closely observed by the music critic William Ritter. At the close of "this formidable, boiling cauldron of a symphony," he watched from a distance as Mahler went up to Alma. and confidently construed merely from Mahler's reaction that Alma "had understood neither what was being said to her nor the music she had just heard, which she knew was written entirely out of reverence for her." With equally unfounded assurance he deemed that "she felt not a jot of pity for the man of genius who, prostrated and entirely absorbed in his work, was virtually dying of love at her very feet."[47] This pure speculation was amplified into fact in Ritter's accounts of the time, and it duly fed into the legend of Alma as a devouring and merciless maenad.

Further hostility came from the musicologist Guido Adler, who complained that Alma was deliberately alienating him from his old friend Gustav. Adler was not in the least reassured when she declared her great respect and unwavering friendship for him and his wife, invited them to visit, and apologized if she had appeared to neglect them during a year when she had "endured so much suffering, such unending grief, that I have shied away from everyone with whom I had not yet *spoken* in person."[48] Adler rejected her apology, then broadcast his misgivings among mutual friends. He blamed Alma for persuading Mahler—against Adler's advice—to go to America, claiming her motives were selfish and mercenary in her pursuit of luxury.

Mahler replied with an impressively robust defense of Alma: she had "*nothing* but my welfare in mind," her "sole and earnest endeavour" was to help him "achieve that independence which, more than anything, will help me to devote myself to creative work." Adler's remarks "did grave injustice" to a woman who was guilty of neither extravagance nor selfishness, who had never "let herself be dazzled by the outward glitter of my position nor ever . . . let herself be tempted to indulge in luxury of any kind." Alma was "not only a courageous, faithful companion who shares all my intellectual interests, but also (a rare combination) a sensible, level-headed manager of our domestic affairs, . . . the person whom I have to thank for all the prosperity and orderliness, in the true sense of the word, of my existence."[49]

Their departure on November 12, 1908, for America, where Mahler would work out his contract at the Met, was a melancholy affair; the band played "Tis God's Decree That We Must Part," which reduced the crew and passengers, including the Mahlers, to tears. With them this time were Anna and her English nanny, Maud Turner, who was "always exhibiting the stoicism of a samurai in her charge." As they were approaching the liner in the small tender, Anna gave a cry of delight as the ship loomed up before them. Maud advanced, held her tightly by the hands, and said sternly, "Don't get excited—don't get excited!" Mahler heard this and immediately "snatched her up and sat her on the taffrail with her feet dangling over the water. 'There you are, and now be as excited as you like. You shall be excited.' She was."[50]

In New York, they stayed at the Savoy Hotel on Central Park—much favored by the Metropolitan Opera stars including the legendary operatic tenor Enrico Caruso and the soprano Marcella Sembrich. Those leading lights in New York society, Mary Sheldon and Minnie Untermeyer, had successfully raised funds for the "Mahler Orchestra," and preparations

Figure 11. Alma
with daughter Anna
("Gucki"), c. 1908.

were being made to restructure the New York Philharmonic. Meanwhile, Mahler worked out his contract with the Met under its director, Guido Gatti-Sasazza. In February 1909 Mahler signed a two-year contract with the New York Philharmonic, and in March he conducted his last performance of *Fidelio* at the Metropolitan.

As invitations arrived to dinners and social events, Alma found new friends. At a ladies' luncheon she met women "of that incredible elegance to be seen only in America." Nobody noticed that the acclaimed ethnologist and musicologist Nathalie Curtis had arrived in an ill-fitting coat and ragged skirt, which Alma took as evidence of "the truly democratic America. Wealth bowed down to poverty if it clothed a creative, gifted mind."[51] Austrian sculptor Karl Bitter received them dressed in a white chef outfit at his house on the Palisades overlooking an abyss and cooked fish Indian-style on an open grill. Sinologist Friedrich Hirth entertained them with stories of China.[52] Anna Moll joined them on February 9 and stayed until March. Though Alma makes no mention of it in her memoir or autobiography, she appears to have had either a miscarriage or an abortion during that time: "Alma is very well," Mahler wrote enigmatically to Carl Moll in March. "About her *present state* she has doubtless written to you herself. She has been relieved of her *burden*. But this time she actually regrets it."[53]

On their return to Vienna in April, they stopped in Paris, where Carl Moll had commissioned from the sculptor Auguste Rodin a bust of Mahler's head. Alma watched Rodin work—as she had done with her father—and was fascinated as he made flat surfaces of the rough lump and added to it pellets of clay he had rolled in his fingers. Rodin thought Mahler's head was a mixture of Benjamin Franklin, Frederick the Great, and Mozart.[54]

Alma's grief still weighed on her, and, by the time she reached Vienna, her nerves were again "in a critical state." With Gucki and the nanny Maud Turner she went in June for a rest cure to the spa at Levico, near Toblach in the South Tyrol: "I was in a state of profound melancholy. I sat night after night on my balcony. I was in tears as I observed the merry and brightly-dressed crowd, whose laughter pained me. I longed to plunge myself into love or life or anything that could release me from my icy constraint."[55]

Gustav was in Toblach, coping on his own with Agnes the cook and Kathi the maid (he fell out with them both), as he worked "feverishly" on his Ninth Symphony. He wrote to Alma daily with news of his solitary life, exhortations for her recovery, and "abstract" philosophical expositions. Although often patronizing in tone, his willingness to discuss such questions with her reveals his respect for her intelligence and intellectual judgment. Her comments on Goethe, he decided, showed she was "developing by leaps and bounds—outwardly as well as inwardly," and her interpretation of the final stanza was "splendid . . . it's better than that of even the most learned commentators, who don't come close to understanding it."[56] To raise her spirits, he advised, "My dear Almschi, you have achieved all you need for your soul to expand and reach out towards higher things. . . . 'Spread your wings,' occupy your mind with all that is good and beautiful, never cease to grow."[57] But this generous gesture still did not include spreading her musical wings.

When they met again at Toblach on July 13, 1909, Alma found Gustav in a "wonderful mood," although troubled by concerns about his

heart. "Once we knew he had valvular disease of the heart we were afraid
of everything. He was always stopping on a walk to feel his own pulse,"
she recalled.[58] Visitors arrived at Toblach—the Molls, Joseph Fraenkel,
the conductor and composer Oskar Fried. Alfred Roller came and found
Mahler "very overworked. When he comes out of his cold, damp hut he
lies down or sleeps. . . . [At meal times] Alma displays a sick, hysterical gaiety which gets on my nerves. I've openly said so to them. . . . It is quite certain that Alma gets this nervous because of Mahler, but now it is she who
drives him to become increasingly nervous. He should have around him a
calm person, with a very positive nature, to soothe his breathlessness."[59]

WITH MAHLER'S REGULAR contract to work in New York, they gave up the
Auenbruggergasse apartment. Instead, they stayed with Carl and Anna
Moll before departing in October for America, on their roughest crossing
yet: "This time we derived no pleasure from travelling whatsoever. The
most incredible storms and fog," Alma reported.[60]

As Mahler fulfilled his conducting schedule of ten concerts a month,
Alma's days were filled with engagements. She attended all Mahler's
performances, including the New York premiere of his First Symphony.
Social invitations poured in as they met a variegated mix of America's social and cultural milieu. Mahler now rarely missed a dinner party, tickets
for the theater were always at their disposal, and their box at the opera
was filled with friends, including Prince Troubetzsky, "a wild handsome
Russian" who went about the streets of New York accompanied by two
wolves, and Carlo di Fornaro, a journalist "with an excess of conscience"
who had just been to Mexico and told them of the cruelty and ruthless
oppression of its president, Porfirio Diaz. He was now investigating the
shortcomings of American prisons.

The English aristocrat Poulteney Bigelow, who wrote a critical book
about his childhood friend, Germany's Kaiser Wilhelm II, introduced
them to New York literary society, though the language barrier intervened. Alma's English was not good, so "in this foreign land we built up
a world of our own, which was more European than Europe itself." Once
they had entertained five people, each of whom had come over from Europe in steerage—Karl Bitter to avoid conscription, Joseph Fraenkel for
lack of money—all on their arrival were either destitute or in flight.[61]

Ossip Gabrilowitsch came to see them one evening. After Mahler had retired to bed, Gabrilowitsch played Alma a Brahms piece she loved: "And I was sure he would never play it more beautifully." They bade each other "a sad farewell," for each time they met, "the struggle in us was rekindled; but we loved Mahler too much for any thought of infidelity to enter our minds." Mahler had heard their exchange, and, when Gabrilowitsch left, he confronted her. Alma defended herself "with spirit and conviction" and restored his faith in her. But she "stood all night by the open window, praying for the strength to end my miserable life."[62] Later that year, Gabrilowitsch married Mark Twain's daughter, Clara Clemens.

Alma found more to appreciate in the company of women. Society leader Minnie Untermeyer became a loyal friend and "guardian angel," to whom Alma turned when in difficulty. She greatly admired the "quite fearless" Nathalie Curtis, who had lived for many years among the North American Indians with her brother, camping in the open and chronicling their music. Irene Langhorne Gibson, the wife of Charles Dana Gibson, who created the celebrated "Gibson girl," intrigued her. She was "a beauty of spun gold, untarnished and vacant," and Alma was not surprised when she asked Alma "how such a beautiful girl as I had brought myself to marry such a hideous and old and altogether impossible man as Mahler. To all I said she replied merely with a contemptuous smile."[63] Louisine Havemeyer, wife of a wealthy sugar magnate, gave musical afternoons in her Tiffany-designed "fairy palace" that contained a long gallery of masterpieces: eight Rembrandts, many Goyas, and an El Greco landscape and his *Portrait of a Cardinal*. With Mahler she visited Mrs. West-Roosevelt, who lived at Oyster Bay near her brother-in-law, the American president, Theodore Roosevelt, in whose house, surrounded by sea, every room opened onto a glass veranda. The whole interior was visible from the outside, which they were told perfectly reflected Theodore, "whose life was as clear and open as his house."

Designer Louis Comfort Tiffany invited them to his palatial house. In an enormous room at the top of an imposing staircase, "coloured lustres shed a soft, flowerlike light through the gloom. The prelude to *Parsifal* was being played on an organ. Light filtered through panels of stained glass high up in the walls, which 'might be the gates to Paradise.'" Tiffany came up and murmured a few incomprehensible words: "before we could collect our wits . . . he vanished." They heard afterward that he was a hashish addict and never quite in his right mind. The music stopped, they heard a murmur of voices, and "silent footmen perambulated with costly glasses. . . . Palms and sofas, beautiful women in odd shimmering robes. . . . It was the thousand and one nights—in New York."[64]

Friends took them on excursions through the city's underground and low life. With the music patron Otto Kahn and Joseph Fraenkel they attended a séance at the flat of fashionable medium, Eusepio Palladino in "proletarian" Broadway. In a room with walls papered black and a curtained-off alcove, as they linked hands, they witnessed Palladino going into convulsions. Suddenly, phosphorescent bodies touched them, the alcove was bathed in phosphorescent light, the table shot up to the ceiling, and a mandolin flew through the air and hit Mahler on the forehead. He was "in danger," warned Palladino.[65] They left in silence.

The music publisher Ernest Shirmer and his wife drove them with an armed detective through the back streets of Chinatown to an opium den, where "a creature with the most degenerate man-woman face you could imagine" took them into rooms lined with bunks on which lolled doped addicts. Upstairs in a luxuriously furnished room, they watched a Chinese man slowly succumb. They went on to a religious sect where a man "with the face of a fanatic" played hymns to "a starving congregation" lined up on benches. "What wretchedness in those faces!" Alma thought.[66]

In the Jewish quarter it was "all life and bustle, chaffering and shouting . . . The whole street was full from end to end of old clothes and rags. The air was heavy with the smell of food." When Alma asked Mahler softly, "Are *these* our brothers?" he shook his head in despair. Then, with a sigh of relief, they entered a well-lighted street among "our own kind of people." Alma asked herself in a flash of perception, "Can it be that there are only class and not race distinctions?"[67]

They left New York in April 1910: "I've come through the year with flying colours," Mahler wrote to Anna Moll.[68] He felt "fresher and healthier with this activity and lifestyle than he had done for years," he told Guido Adler.[69] He hoped that in about a year's time he might attain "a human kind of life," living and working near a few close friends, though he and Alma had "a new brainwave every week about our future—Paris, Florence, Capri, Switzerland, the Black Forest," he confided to Alfred Roller. "Especially now that my wife's enthusiasm for America is fortunately beginning to slacken off," he thought that in the foreseeable future they would "land somewhere in the vicinity of Vienna where the sun shines and beautiful grapes grow, and never go away again."[70]

After all the turmoil of the past few years, it seemed that a new calm was settling over their lives. But their return to Europe heralded the most profound crisis yet in their marriage.

~ 7 ~

"To Live for You,
to Die for You"
1910–1911

*O*n their return journey they stopped off in Paris on April 12 where
Mahler was to conduct his Second Symphony at a concert organized by the music patron Countess Greffulhe. Mahler was shocked
when Claude Debussy, the most eminent French composer of the time,
walked out in the middle of it. No amount of praise for "a vast and colossal work" that "aspires to the sublime" was any consolation to Mahler for
the bitterness "of being so misunderstood and indeed condemned by the
foremost French composers," Alma observed sympathetically. Renowned
for his musical chauvinism, Debussy judged the work "too Schuber-
tian . . . too Viennese—too Slav."[1]

After a trip to Rome with Mahler shortly afterward, Alma was exhausted. "I was very ill. The wear and tear of being driven on without
respite by a spirit so intense as his had brought me to a complete breakdown." She was prescribed six weeks of treatment from early June at a
fashionable spa in a wooded valley south of Graz. Gucki and the English
nanny went with her while Mahler worked on his Tenth Symphony.
Alma lived "an utterly solitary life" in Tobelbad. On a diet of lettuce and
buttermilk, going barefoot and clothed in a "horrible nightgown," she

took outdoor exercise in wind and rain and "bathed conscientiously in the hot springs." The first time she took the waters, she fainted and had to be carried back to bed.

The German doctor saw her despondency and loneliness and prescribed dancing. Three days after her arrival she met the "extraordinarily handsome" twenty-seven-year-old German Walter Gropius, who, she noted, "would have been well cast as Walther von Stolzing in *Die Meistersinger*." As they glided across the dance floor, the attraction between them was immediate. They embarked on a passionate love affair.[2] Accustomed to the lack of attention to her inner feelings and starved of sensual pleasure in her marriage, she had feared that, at thirty-one, she had prematurely become a "detached, resigned old woman." She was not even sure "whether such a dried-up twig can ever come to life again but if it can—then I shall have heaven on earth," she told Gropius.[3]

As always, Alma was drawn to creative talent. The young architect who awakened her sensual nature—"the healthy element in my life"—and set her on a path of profound emotional torment, was just

Figure 12. The handsome young architect Walter Gropius, Alma's lover.

embarking on a career that would make him one of the leading influences on twentieth-century modernism. In this case she was drawn more to his charm than his drawings, an area with which she was less familiar than other artistic fields. Working in the Berlin offices of leading architect Peter Behrens, Gropius's style developed around the concept of a building as a total work, a rational and functional entity, with radically simplified designs that would combine art with the products and techniques of mass production. Nine years later in 1919, he founded the Bauhaus movement, which inspired a generation and remains a continuing influence on architecture and design.

Mahler sent daily letters to the clinic, exhorting Alma to do everything to recover from her "tormenting illness." Alarm bells rang when she failed to write: "I'm worried not to have heard from you at all today. Are you concealing something from me? I keep sensing something between the lines."[4] On June 25, he telegraphed, "Why no news am very worried please send express reply," and to Anna Moll, he wrote, "I'm so perturbed by Almschi's letters, which have such a peculiar tone. What on earth is going on?"[5] On June 30 he changed his plans in order to visit her for two days at Tobelbad, where he found her "much fresher and sturdier, and I'm convinced that her treatment has done her a power of good. Please make her stay as long as she can," he begged Anna Moll, who had joined Alma in early July.[6] Anna was not only aware of the nature of her daughter's relationship with Walter Gropius, she became complicit in it as their chaperone, confidante, and go-between.

When Alma returned to Toblach on July 16, Mahler "was fonder of me than ever." She wondered whether the young architect's love had helped her regain her self-assurance, for she felt "happier and more optimistic." Although she had "no intention of embarking on anything new," she set up a poste restante three kilometers away to which Gropius's passionate letters could be sent in secret. "Wait for me!" she wrote to him on July 18, even as she warned him she was still irrevocably bound to Mahler. When Alma could not write to him, her mother kept in contact: "My dear Walter, You are now so close to my heart that I cannot find any other way of addressing you. . . . Hold your head high—you have a splendid objective ahead of you—a thousand greetings, your devoted Mama."[7]

The situation began to unravel on July 29, when a letter from Gropius arrived addressed to "Herr G. Mahler, Toblach" but intended for Alma, in which he openly wrote "about the secrets of our nights of love." Mahler was shocked to the core: "[He] was seated at the piano when he opened the letter. 'What is this?' he asked in a choking voice and handed it to me." He was convinced "that the architect had deliberately addressed the letter to him as his way of asking him for my hand in marriage."[8]

Alma was horrified: "Please! Don't come here!!! I beg you!!" she wrote to Gropius two days later. Completely unable to understand Walter's action, she described to him the catastrophic outcome: "How many tears, Walter, have been shed since that evening! G[ustav] and I cried all day yesterday and said terrible things. It tears my heart—to see him *suffer so dreadfully*! Because it was all revealed to him more or less by accident, and not by a frank confession on my part, he has lost *all* trust and *all* faith in me! You have made us both suffer immensely." Now she waited "with *feverish* longing" for his explanation: "I am so thunderstruck, so shattered. My faith in you is so shaken—I don't know what will happen—but I—cannot—yet! Don't come here! Write to A.M.40 [the poste restante]. I am hoping that you can say something or other to get you out of this."[9]

Seemingly oblivious to the gravity of his actions, Gropius persisted: "Your letter makes me horribly anxious for you both. But don't take it tragically. I'll go out of my mind if you don't ask me to come over. I *shall* justify myself before you both and clear up the mystery." He requested only one hour "to speak, to give and receive consolation, then I will go away again and will not now force myself between you."[10] The crisis precipitated for Alma "the most difficult period of my life," she told him. For she "had to decide—about life and death. . . . I am now *forced* to make up my mind. I am experiencing something utterly unimaginable, namely that G[ustav]'s love is so infinite that if I remain—despite all that had occurred—he will live, and if I leave him—he will die."[11] Even so, she could not shut out her love for Gropius or the possibilities it opened for her: "Tell me what would happen to me in the future if I—decide for a life of love with you. Oh—when I think of it—my Walter, that I could be deprived of your *strong* love for my whole life . . . !—Do help me, I do not know what to do."[12]

Though Gropius claimed later that the letter was mistakenly addressed, his action remains a mystery. Much later he expressed a wish "to compensate for the suffering I inflicted on Gustav and you," which he attributed to "lack of mature prudence."[13] However, his biographer, Reginald Isaacs, points out that Gropius had a tendency "to take up with older women who were married or already had a male partner, and then get in touch with the husband or partner." His reason for this, "whether pangs of conscience or other motives, must remain an open question," Isaacs concludes.[14] But perhaps the phrase in his letter to Alma: "Has your husband not noticed anything yet?" suggests he wanted—out of pride or neediness—to feel he was part of the charmed embrace of their marriage, rather than peripheral to it.

One consequence was that Alma now felt able to pour out to Gustav her pent-up frustrations and the accumulated disappointments of her marriage: "At last I was able to tell him all. I told him I had longed for his love year after year and that he, in his fanatical concentration on his own life, had simply overlooked me. As I spoke, he felt for the first time that something is owed to the person with whom one's life has once been linked. He suddenly felt a sense of guilt."[15] Unable to do anything "but walk about together all day in tears," they sent for Anna Moll to help them through the crisis.

After their painfully honest confrontation Alma "felt as strongly as I ever had that I could never leave him. When I told him so, his face was transfigured. His love became an ecstasy. He could not be parted from me for a second."[16] Although they had spoken to each other as never before, Alma could not speak "the whole truth"—that her "boundless love had lost by degrees some of its strength and warmth; and now that my eyes had been opened by the impetuous assaults of the young [Gropius], I knew . . . that my marriage—was no marriage—and that my own life was utterly unfulfilled. I concealed the truth from him . . . to spare his feelings."[17] Even so, she did not regret the marriage for she had convinced herself "that my protracted suffering over all these years was necessary for my inner development and that if I had been happy I might have become shallow, like so many talented persons around me."[18]

A few days later Alma and Gustav were out driving when she glimpsed Gropius hiding under a bridge. He had apparently been in the area some time in the hope of meeting her and getting an answer to his letter. Alma's "heart stopped, but only from fright, not joy." She told Mahler at once, "and he said: 'I'll go and bring him along myself.' He found him in Toblach: 'Come along,' he said. Nothing more was said by either."[19] In silence in the pitch darkness they walked up to the house, with Mahler in front with a lantern and Gropius following behind.

Alma was waiting in her room: "Mahler came in looking very serious. I hesitated for a long time before going in to speak to [Gropius], and I broke off our interview after a few minutes because I was suddenly worried about Mahler. Mahler was pacing up and down in his room. Two candles were burning at his table. He was reading the Bible. 'Whatever you do will be right,'" he said. "Make your decision." But Alma knew she had no choice: "I could never have imagined life without him, even though the feeling that my life was running to waste had often filled me with despair. Least of all could I have imagined life with another man. . . . Mahler was the hub of my existence and so he continued to be."[20] A year later she vividly recalled "the anguished look on Gustav's face—as he left me alone on that evening. What torture he was going through!"[21]

The next morning Alma took her leave of Gropius at the station. On the way back, she met Mahler, who had come halfway "in his dread lest I had gone with [Gropius] after all."[22] Before leaving, Gropius wrote with dignity to Mahler: "We had unfortunately so little to say to each other— it pains me that I can *only* cause you pain. Let me at least thank you again for the nobility with which you treated me, and shake your hand for one last time."[23] On the train, he sent Alma telegrams from every station.

Despite her sincere commitment to Mahler, Alma continued to correspond with Gropius, sharing with him the fluctuations of her heart and the minutiae of her life with Mahler. "Gustav was waiting for me at home, in the saddest of moods.—He would [so] wish for only one day [to be] you!"[24] she wrote on August 7. Of one change she was relieved: "He does not pester me any more with his sensuality—and that is bearable— *for the time being*."[25]

Mired in conflicting feelings, she had not relinquished hope of a life with Gropius but decided she must see "whether I can put up with this life at least until I—that is to say you—call me to you, until you are ready and independent in life, so that I can follow you in full confidence and you without any anxiety can take me home."[26] But when Gropius wrote of "our future" together, she cautioned, "Walter, that *can't* come as quickly as you think—Gustav lay the whole day at my feet, and kept asking me, sobbing: 'Are you going to stay with me?' Finally I promised I would, and he said that in doing that I had saved his life. . . . But now the question is

only, will your love be strong enough to survive the most difficult thing—
that is to say *waiting and waiting*? My place is now here. G[ustav] is a sick
wonderful human being—whom I *must* not abandon in his need."[27]

Unable to bear losing Gropius, once again she proposed: "Wait for
me. I will *never* look at another man. . . . I love you without end. Your
heart's love could never go out of my life. . . . *One thing* only we can
know—let us keep ourselves pure for each other—*in every respect!* . . . if
we love each other *steadfastly* and *faithfully* nothing can happen to us."
She proposed he think of himself as her fiancé, for "what do we know of
the future—everything can proceed more quickly than we think."[28]

Walter Gropius declared his constancy: "Yes, Alma, I put my trust in
your *faithfulness* and *purity* in every respect, I thought of you as my bride
even before you did."[29] They continued to exchange letters via the poste
restante or through Anna Moll, who was staying with Alma and was also
writing to Gropius as the engaged intermediary, explaining:

> One thing is clear: Alma cannot leave Gustav for the time being.—he
> would not survive—and can you believe in a happiness that walks over
> this man's corpse?—a man of such greatness, such kindness and such
> nobility. It would be quite unthinkable! You couldn't possibly be happy!
> So what to do? You must yourselves summon up your own strength and
> be strong! You are after all both still young, you can wait for a while.
> Gustav's condition you cannot imagine. . . . He has a serious cardiac
> complaint, and it is a miracle that the shock has not killed him.[30]

The anguish he suffered transformed Mahler, who lived in constant
fear of being abandoned. He wrote poems to her almost daily. His letters
are great outpourings of love, self-abnegation, and remorse: "Breath of
my life! I smothered your slippers in kisses and stood longingly at your
door. You took pity on me, you glorious woman, but . . . the demons have
punished me for putting my own interests before yours. . . . Bless you, my
love—for what you have granted me—my heart beats only for *you*."[31]
And a few days later: "My darling, my lyre-play, . . . Here I lie prostrate
and await you; and silently ask whether I may still hope for salvation, or
whether I am to be damned."[32] He "attempted to propitiate her as if she
were some capricious goddess whose decree could be favourably influenced by giving up burnt offerings," psychologist Stuart Feder observes.[33]

Alma recalled the frightening intensity of his fears: "He was now jealous of everything and everybody. . . . The door of our two rooms, which were next to each other, had to be always open. He had to hear my breathing. I often woke in the night and found him standing at my bed-side in the darkness, and started as at the apparition of a departed spirit." She fetched him from his *Häuschen* each day for meals: "He was often lying on the floor weeping in his dread that he might lose me, had lost me perhaps already. On the floor, he said, he was nearer to the earth."[34]

Though it all, Mahler had continued working on the Tenth Symphony. His anguish is woven into the inscriptions he wrote on the final stages of the score: "Für dich leben! [To live for you!] / Für dich sterben! [To die for you!] *Almschi!*" he pleaded at the end of the finale, and in even darker mood, in the second scherzo: "The Devil is dancing with me, / Accursed madness, seize me! / Destroy me / Let me forget that I exist / So that I cease to be / So that I . . . "[35] Over the dramatic muf-fled drumbeat that ends the movement, an allusion to the New York fire-man's funeral they both witnessed, but also a portent, perhaps, of his own death, he wrote: "You alone know what this means." On the same page: "Ach! Ach! Ach! Leb'wol mein Seitenspiel [Farewell my lyre], Leb'wol [Farewell]."[36]

ONE DAY IN August 1910, Alma was nearing home after a walk with her daughter, Gucki, when "suddenly I heard my songs being played and sung. I stopped—I was petrified. My poor forgotten songs. I had dragged them to and fro to the country and back again for ten years, a weary load I could never get quit of. I was overwhelmed with shame and also I was angry." Mahler came out to meet them "with such joy in his face that I could not say a word. 'What have I done?' he said. 'These songs are good. Really excellent. I insist that you work through them again and we will publish them. I shall never be happy until you start composing again. God, how blind and selfish I was in those days!'" He played them over and over, showering her with extravagant praise. She "had to sit down there and then and work on them—after a ten years' interval! . . . Yes, he excelled himself in promises and exclamations," which she believed—with charac-teristic self-doubt—overestimated her talent.[37]

Mahler's realization of her achievements, her creativity, and her identity transformed the relationship for Alma: "Now for the first time I shall really have something of G[ustav]—he wants to read serious works with me—and make music," she told Gropius. "In short, he is another person—through these few days of suffering—wanting to live *only for me, abandoning* what he calls das 'papierne' Leben, his austere musician's existence."[38]

The most important change was that Alma could compose again, and with his support: "Yesterday I finished a song and gave it to Gustav when he returned from his hut—He went into the living room, came out again a moment later—and said with tears [on his face]: 'I am quite moved—that is wonderful!'" She was enjoying "the love and *admiration* which G[ustav] is showing for *my* music. He wants to devote his future life only to that, and I, who had already abandoned all hope of that happening, can hardly believe my luck. He spends the whole day playing my songs, and says that they are simply wonderful," she told Gropius. In a small display of pride she added, "To be *honest*—I knew that my pieces were good—and while I dragged my children *secretly* around with me for eight years—I was convinced that they were good—and simply believed—that it was the fate of women—that I had to give up all *that* happiness when I got married."[39] Inspired by his new understanding, Mahler described her "dear songs" as "like stars . . . blissful heralds of your divine being, which shall illuminate my heaven, until the sun of my life shines in my firmament once again."[40]

She now knew—as she had always known—that her music was "a bridge to life. Suddenly I find the world a pleasant place again." The minute she was alone, she worked on her songs: "I am making so many changes in one of them that it is almost a new song. Yesterday we found three [songs] in which not one note needed to be changed.—G[ustav] is terribly precise and strict and I have absolute trust in his judgement."[41] One night "an apparition" woke her in the middle of the night: "Gustav was standing before me in the dark 'Would it give you a small pleasure if I dedicated the Eighth to you?' I: 'Don't. You've never dedicated anything to anyone. You might regret it.'" But he had already written to his publisher, Emil Hertzka at Universal Edition, insisting he include on the title page the words, "To my dear wife Alma Maria."[42]

Despite the rapprochement in her marriage, in her letters to Gropius Alma's ardor was undimmed: "I know that I live only for the time when I shall be yours, and yours alone," she wrote, signing herself as "your wife." "I am *with you so intensely* that you must feel me. You *always* give me such great pleasure! . . . When will the time come when you lie beside my body, naked, and when nothing can separate us but sleep?"[43] She assured Walter that she had not had intimate contact with Gustav, and while she had confessed that all her married life "was *one* long dread of pregnancy— every month I trembled," now she told him, "My Walter, I want a child from you—and will cherish it and look after it until the day comes when without regret we sink smiling and forever into each other's arms."[44]

On the night of August 21, Alma woke suddenly and called out to Gustav. When there was no reply, she ran to his bed but found him lying unconscious beside a lighted candle on the landing. Alma carried him to bed, called for her mother, sent a servant to get the doctor, and gave Mahler "what stimulants for the heart I had in the house."[45] Alma and Anna Moll stayed with him through the night, fearing the worst, but by 5 a.m. when the doctor came, he had revived.

Aware of the possible psychological roots of his physical turmoil, Mahler decided to consult the founder of psychotherapy, Sigmund Freud. After Mahler canceled the appointment several times, Freud agreed to break his holiday to meet him in Leiden in Holland. On August 26, they spent four hours together on a leisurely stroll through the ancient town. Next day, Mahler telegraphed Alma, "feeling cheerful interesting discussion motes swollen to planks ready to depart for Toblach."[46] Freud's diagnosis "composed Mahler's mind," Alma reported. "He said: 'I know your wife. She loved her father and she can only choose and love a man of his sort. Your age, of which you are so much afraid, is precisely what attracts her. You need not be anxious. You loved your mother, and you look for her in every woman. She was careworn and ailing, and unconsciously you wish your wife to be the same.'"

He was "right in both cases," Alma decided. "Gustav Mahler's mother was called Marie. His first impulse was to change my name to Marie . . . and when he got to know me better he wanted my face to be more 'stricken'—his very word. . . . I too always looked for a small, slight man, who had wisdom and spiritual superiority, since this was what I had known and loved in my father." She claimed, though this is not mentioned in other accounts, that Freud "reproached him with vehe-mence after hearing his confession. 'How dared a man in your state ask a young woman to be tied to him?'"[47]

Much later in conversation with his pupil Maria Bonaparte, Freud described their encounter:

> He had married a woman quite a bit younger than himself. At the time the marriage was not going well although he was a normally potent man and loved his wife. . . . [H]e was faithful to her. But she no longer ex-cited him. On our walk he spoke to me of every possible thing. . . . He demonstrated an intuitive understanding of analysis . . . right away he was in his element. What impressed him greatly was when I said to him, "Your mother's name was Marie?" "But how do you know!" he ex-claimed. Of course, I could see it from what he was telling me—he had an enormous fixation of his mother. "But how was it," I asked him, "that you could marry a woman whose name was not Marie?" "But," he ex-claimed, "she is called Alma-Marie!"[48]

Later Gustav wrote to Alma: "Freud is quite right—you were always for me the light and the central point! The inner light, I mean, which rose over all; and the blissful consciousness of this—now un-shadowed and unconfined—raises all my feelings to the infinite."[49]

THAT FALL SHE briefly considered letting Gustav travel alone to America, but she soon relented: "Gustav says he cannot live one day without me—so I must go with him."[50] When she reassured Gustav of her love he was ecstatic: "Oh, how wonderful it is to love. And only now do I know what it means. Pain loses its power and death its sting. . . . I sense the bliss that springs from love when one loves with total conviction and knows one's love is reciprocated."[51] He told her, "Almschili, if you had left me at the time I would simply have been snuffed out, like a candle starved of air."[52] When Mahler left for Munich on September 3 for the world premiere of his Eighth Symphony, he wore on his finger her wedding ring as a token. He was "still crazy" and obsessively feared losing her, Alma told Walter, but his ardor roused Alma's concern: "This idolatry and veneration that he now lavishes on me can scarcely be called normal any more."[53] The situation was impossible: "*He knows* that without me he cannot live. I *know* that I will respect and protect him—but love only you. *How* can we get out of that!?"[54] She made plans to meet Walter at his hotel in Munich after she had joined Gustav for his performance.

On her arrival in Munich, Alma found Mahler's suite of rooms "smothered in roses in my honour" and the copy of the Eighth Symphony dedicated to her on the table, beside another to her mother. Of the dedication, Mahler declared, "Does it not make the impression rather of a betrothal? . . . the announcement of an engagement?"[55] But he looked ill. He had recently had a recurrence of the acutely inflamed septic throat infection and had taken to his bed, though he soon recovered. Alma met Gropius at his hotel on September 7 and then attended rehearsals. After one that ended to rapturous applause, the ever-observant critic William Ritter approached Alma: "'How happy and proud you must be!' I said to her—'Not more than usual,' she replied, with a half-sad, half-smiling look on her face"; it seemed to the ever observant Ritter "to express not so much admiration as heart-break."[56]

Mahler conducted the premiere of his Eighth Symphony before an audience "wrought up to the highest pitch of suspense," which included their friends and a substantial number of the patrons, composers, conductors, writers, and artists who made up Europe's cultural elite: Gerhart Hauptmann, Alfredo Casella, Countess Greffulhe, Alphons Diepenbrock, Willem Mengelberg, Arnold Berliner, the Clemenceaus, Bruno Walter, Arthur Schnitzler, Hugo von Hoffmannstahl, Stefan Zweig, Kolo Moser, and Alfred Roller, along with Richard Strauss, Camille Saint-Saëns, Siegfried Wagner, Anton Webern, Max Reinhardt, Lilli Lehmann, and Erik Schmedes.[57]

Alma sat in the box "almost insensible from excitement": "The whole audience rose to their feet as soon as Mahler took his place at the conductor's desk. . . . [Then] Mahler, god or demon, turned those tremendous volumes of sound into fountains of light. The experience was indescribable." As the whole audience surged toward the platform, Alma waited behind the scenes "in a state of deep emotion until the outburst died down. Then, with our eyes full of tears, we drove to the hotel," where they celebrated his triumph with friends.[58]

Walter Gropius saw Mahler conduct his work for the first time in Munich and was overwhelmed. He left the concert "with this feeling that we could not hurt him, we must bow down to this man," he told Alma.[59] His respect for Gustav now added to the potent chemistry of their entangled triangular relationship. When in January he heard the Seventh Symphony, he felt as if "a remote and alien Titan shook me and drew me after him with tremendous verve—running the whole gamut of my emotions—from the demonic to the touchingly child-like." Gropius feared "this alien strength, since my own art grows in different soil."[60]

In a letter Gropius drafted to Alma after Munich, though perhaps never sent, his tone was feverish, his emotions confused and colored by his recent discovery that Alma "had become intimate with Gustav again": "*What* I wanted to believe was that you were following him, watching over him, and going to protect him until he passed away—but not that you were his beloved. Don't think I am attaching any blame to you, this must be in my nature. For me you are the holiest, most noble person, completely *beyond reproach.*"[61]

Gropius resolved to extricate himself and to let her go. He had realized that in the face of Mahler's "superb qualities both as a man and as an artist," he was "not able so to captivate you that you did the supreme thing for me," and that "for a person like you the physical presence of a strong-willed person was inevitably more effective than my bungling scribbling from a long way off. His will was simply stronger and more mature, and compelled you to surrender. The fact that you did *that* shows that your passion for me was a mistake. I take the full blame for that," he wrote. He realized now that Gustav, to whom she had given her soul, was her man.

The decision left Gropius utterly despondent, he told her, for he had by his resolve forfeited all belief in himself: "When I had your love, I had wings. I was *simply* capable of everything. Now my gate is shut again, I can only relapse into dull indifference." His only consolation was that he had "helped two splendid people like you to go further in their lives. . . . I cancel myself out entirely and let you go free. . . . I sincerely hope that you, wonderful woman, will be happy." He left one option open—his only hope–"that you will still love me when G[ustav] has passed away and that then for us two a time for happiness can come."[62]

But his resolve was short lived. On receiving Alma's next letter, he "went down on my knees to you, O Fount of Wisdom, and gazed up at you, filled with *gratitude.* . . . What we have experienced together is the all-greatest, the all-highest, that the human soul can ever know. . . . I must . . . bring down *superhuman* sacrifices to you, without complain-ing."[63] For Walter, too, she resembled a goddess.

They arranged to meet when Alma was traveling alone to Paris en route for America: "I'm leaving here by the Orient Express on Friday 14 October at 11.55 in the morning. My compartment is No 13 in the second sleeping car," she told him.[64] Walter boarded the train in Munich, and they traveled together to Paris, where they enjoyed "hours of bliss" and days of "sheer joy—completely *untroubled*. There was never a single discordant note in our love," she wrote to him from New York. "Your beautiful eyes are lighting up my path. . . . When shall I have you before me again, physically? . . . *When* shall I see you again, just as a god created you—for only a god can achieve such a thing. *I want* to absorb all your beauty. Our joint perfection cannot but produce a demi god."[65]

In New York, Mahler faced a heavy schedule of sixty-five planned concerts and the reorganization of the orchestra to improve its standard under a new manager, Laudon Charlton. Though the season was ulti-mately deemed a critical success—with receipts increased by a third over the previous season—Mahler faced disagreements with the Guarantors Committee over the choice of program and the dismissal of an orches-tra member.[66] Alma complained later, in a probably ill-advised burst of bitterness after Gustav's death, that whereas in Vienna he was "all powerful—even the Emperor did not dictate to him," in New York, "he had ten ladies ordering him about like a puppet."[67]

When the orchestra was playing in Buffalo on December 9, Alma drove with Gustav on an icy day to Niagara Falls, where "the strength of the greenish light . . . the thunder of the water beneath the roof of ice . . . had a dreamlike beauty."[68] Mahler is said to have exclaimed at the roar of the falls, "Endlich ein Fortissimo!" (At last a fortissimo), although later, after conducting Beethoven's *Pastoral Symphony*, he concluded that "articulate art is greater than inarticulate nature. . . . Nature, as it ap-pears in Beethoven's music [was] greater, more sublime that the Niagara Falls."[69] Alone on the train back, Alma reread Dostoyevsky's *The Brothers Karamazov*, then telegraphed Gustav from New York: "Splendid journey with Aliosha," referring to one of the characters in the book. He replied at once, "Journey with Almiosha much more splendid."[70]

The torments of the year seemed to have abated. "We were very close together in those days," Alma remembered.[71] An unfamiliar contentment entered their lives, even while Alma remained torn between Mahler and her longing for Walter's sensual love. But the longer they were apart, the more Gropius's image began to fade. Alma's devotion to Gustav flowered as his fear of abandonment abated, his attentiveness to her needs and interests grew, and he became an affectionate and considerate spouse. "Particularly during this winter, their harmony was of almost unbelievable intensity," an American friend, music critic Maurice Baumfeld, observed. Mahler "shared everything with her completely. . . . For his wife above all, he composed, conducted, created, lived. . . . I seriously believe that he thought she was powerful enough to fend off death itself."[72]

At Christmas, to Alma's surprise, and in stark contrast with his previous custom, Gustav showered her with presents. She was "touched to the heart by all the lovely things he had thought of without any regard for his own likes and dislikes."[73] They spent Christmas alone with Gucki, and Joseph Fraenkel joined them on New Year's Eve. At midnight they heard the sirens wail from all the city factories and boats in the harbor, while the bells of all the churches "united in an organ-note of such awful beauty that we three who loved each other joined hands without a word and wept. Not one of us—then—knew why."[74]

With her new freedom to compose, she worked on her old songs, *Licht in der Nacht* and possibly *Erntelied*, and developed a new choral work. "The winter was *wonderful*—and I felt young and fresh. . . . [W]e understood each other so completely," she recalled.[75] Mahler insisted on copying out her score, praised her work, and reported to Anna Moll, "She is really blossoming—is keeping to a splendid diet, and has *entirely* given up alcohol, looking younger every day. She is hard at work and has written a few delightful new songs that mark great progress. This, of course, also contributes to her well-being. Her published songs are causing a furore here and will soon be sung by two different singers."[76] Soprano Frances Alda Gatti-Casazza had seen Alma's published songs and wanted to perform one at her forthcoming recital. Mahler pressed her to sing all five and got angry when she insisted she had room for only one. When they rehearsed, Alma was "so nervous I could scarcely open my mouth."[77]

Mahler was working on *Das Lied von der Erde* and played it to her over and over again almost daily until Alma knew it by heart. Gucki observed him—as Alma had done with her father—as he scratched out notes: "'Papi,' she said. 'I wouldn't like to be a note.' 'Why not?' he asked.

'Because then you might scratch me out and blow me away.' He was so delighted that he came at once to tell me what she had said."[78] Gucki was already displaying a very original imagination. After visiting the leading occultist May Field, Alma had begun practicing the occultists' rites— "We started shutting our eyes to see what colours we could see." When Gucki was found walking up and down with her eyes shut, and was asked what she was doing, she replied, "I'm looking for green."[79] Gucki would later become an exceptionally gifted sculptor.

ON FEBRUARY 20, 1911, Mahler was struck down with inflammation of the throat and high fever, similar to an attack he had quickly recovered from the previous December. When Dr. Fraenkel diagnosed influenza, Mahler ignored his advice not to conduct a concert the next day and went ahead, wrapped in thick woolen clothes. It was the last concert he would conduct. Over the next few days, the inflammation came and went, and his temperature fluctuated. Mahler canceled all his concerts. When he collapsed, Alma called in Fraenkel, who consulted an endocrinologist and ordered a blood test, which confirmed Fraenkel's diagnosis of endocarditis. Later it was verified as *Streptococcus viridans*, which had infected an existing heart valve lesion, giving rise to bacterial endocarditis. The heart was increasingly affected, Kollargol treatments brought no improvement, and as the bacteria multiplied the infection spread through the whole body.

Alma looked after him "just as if he were a little child. I put every bite into his mouth for him and slept in his room without taking off my clothes. We got so used to it that he said more than once: 'When I'm well again we'll go on like this. You'll feed me—it's so nice.'" Meanwhile he joked about "his little bugs," the streptococci infection ravaging his body, "which were either dancing or sleeping."[80] Often he was convinced he would recover, at other times he despaired, and sometimes he joked about his death: "'You will be in great demand when I am gone, with your youth and looks. Now, who shall it be?' 'No one,' I said. 'Don't talk like that.' 'Yes, but let's see, who is there?' He went through the list. . . . 'It'll be better after all, if I stay with you,' he always quipped. I had to laugh with tears in my eyes."[81]

Sometimes friends took Alma out for a drive. When Frances Alda Gatti-Casazza was due to perform her song *Laue Sommernacht* in a recital, Alma went with Fraenkel to hear it from the back of the gallery. Gustav awaited her return in "the keenest suspense. He said he had never been in such a state of excitement over any performance of his own works. When I told him it had been encored he said, 'Thank God,' over and over again. He was quite beside himself for joy."[82]

Alma had ceased writing to Gropius when Mahler was first taken ill. But she was still in thrall to Walter and soon resumed her letters. In a tangle of profound emotions, she wrote on March 11, "Gustav has been ill for three weeks. . . . I do what I can. I would sacrifice my life . . . to help this *wonderful, glorious* man. I sit helpless by his bed for all the hours of the day. Be patient, my heart. In Tobelbad we *lived* a work of art—*without knowing it.*"[83] Three weeks later, she wrote again, affirming her love for Walter even in the depths of her anxiety for Gustav: "At present my feelings are numbed. To my great astonishment I was able to perform superhuman feats. For twelve days I literally did not change my clothes—and was nurse—mother—housewife—everything—and on top of everything, filled with sorrow—fear and care . . . but I know that when I see you, everything will blossom and bloom again. *Love* me! . . . with the feelings that made me so utterly happy. I want *you*!!! But you??—Do you want me?"[84]

It was decided after consultation with doctors that Mahler should be sent to Europe to see a leading bacteriologist. When Alma heard this she fainted and had to be carried out, diagnosed as suffering from exhaustion. Anna Moll was summoned; she left Vienna the same day, caught the fastest ship, and arrived in New York six days later on March 31. She shared the nursing with Alma as they packed and began preparations for the return to Europe, where Fraenkel had recommended a consultation in Paris with the eminent French bacteriologist, André Chantemesse.

A stretcher was prepared for Gustav to leave the hotel, but he waived it aside and walked unsteadily to the lift, leaning on Fraenkel's arm. The lift boy turned away so they would not see his tears. The foyer was empty. Alma discovered that the manager had cleared it—"We knew Mr Mahler wouldn't want to be looked at," he told Alma.[85] Minnie Untermeyer's automobile was waiting to take them to the quay. Onboard, Fraenkel bade farewell to Gustav, knowing it was the last time. The cabin was heaped with presents and flowers. Alma and her mother nursed, fed, and dressed him. Almost every day they carried him to the deck, which had been screened off for their privacy. "Mahler's beauty was staggering," Alma observed. "'Today, you're Alexander the Great again,' I used to say. The beauty of his black shining eyes, his white face, his black hair and blood-red mouth struck terror into my heart."[86]

Carl Moll met them at Cherbourg on April 16 and traveled with them to Paris. At the Hotel Élysée Palace the next morning, Alma found Gustav up, dressed, and shaved, sitting on a balcony ready for breakfast: "'I always said I should recover as soon as I set foot in Europe. I'll go for a drive this morning and in a few days, when we've got over the voyage, we two will set off for Egypt.' I stared at him in utter astonishment. It seemed literally to be a miracle. . . . We all laughed and wept for joy. It seemed he was saved," she wrote. It was not to be. He ordered an electric automobile and drove to the Bois de Boulogne, getting paler and paler: "He got into it as a man recovered, and got out, after an hour's drive, as a man at death's door."[87]

Later he collapsed. Chantemesse moved Mahler to a clinic in Neuilly. He was weakening visibly but with bouts of feverish excitement. He wept as he told Anna and Carl Moll his wishes for burial without pomp or ceremony beside their daughter Maria at Grinzing cemetery, with a simple inscription on his headstone: "Mahler." When Alma came in, he talked of the past: "'My life has all been paper!' He said this again and again, as though speaking to himself: 'Ich habe Papier gelebt.'"[88] Writing to Gropius, Alma distractedly betrayed her despair: "Such a noble human being is struck down and must slowly and *miserably* perish—everything is done for him. We have the very best doctors—he is being treated with serum—it offers a possibility of recovery. That is all."[89]

Alma's concern intensified. She called Professor Franz Chvostek, the most celebrated doctor in Vienna, who arrived next morning and immediately arranged for Mahler to travel by train back to Vienna. When Alma went to Gustav's room, she had never seen such joy on his face. They packed and set off that night. "'We're coming home in poor trim this time. But we'll soon be on our feet again,' Gustav said, and Alma, as she sat on a suitcase beside him, laid her head on his hand and kissed it." Chvostek called her out in the middle of the night. "'No hope,' he said solemnly. 'And may the end come quickly. If he did pull through, which is not likely, he'd be condemned to a bath-chair for the rest of his life.' 'Better than nothing,' I said. 'I can't face life without him.' 'Yes, but then the whole nervous system will go too and you don't want to wheel a senile idiot about.'" Alma "refused to submit" and resumed her watch over him.[90]

At every station journalists boarded the train to obtain the latest bulletin—"and so Mahler's last journey was like that of a dying king."[91] He was transferred to the Loew Sanatorium in Vienna. Friends arrived as he lay completely still. Gradually his mind was becoming confused. One evening "two attendants lifted his naked emaciated body. It was a taking down from the cross. This was the thought that came to all of us."[92] He cried out, "My Almschi!" hundreds of times in a voice Alma had never heard before. He had difficulty breathing. Chvostek was summoned: "Mahler lay with dazed eyes; one finger was conducting on the quilt. There was a smile on his lips and twice he said: 'Mozart!' His eyes were very big."

Alma was moved to the next room when the death agony began. The "ghastly sound" of the death rattle ceased suddenly at midnight on May 18 during a thunderstorm. A torrential downpour changed to hailstones as lightning flashes lit up the sky and great thunderclaps tore the air, Alma recalled, "With that last breath his beloved and beautiful soul had fled, and the silence was more deathly than all else. As long as he breathed he was there still. But now all was over. I shall never forget his dying hours, the grandeur of his face, which grew ever more beautiful as death drew nearer. His genuine struggle for eternal values, his ability to rise above everyday matters, and his unflinching devotion to truth are an example of a saintly existence."[93] Alma was not allowed back into his room: "I was moved that night from my room next to his. The doctors insisted. But I felt it a humiliation not to be allowed to stay near him. I could not understand it. Was I alone? Had I to live without him? It was as if I had been flung out of a speeding train in a foreign land. I had no place on earth."[94]

She was taken to the Hohe Warte with her mother, where she remained under medical supervision. The next morning she prepared to tell Anna, who interrupted her: "Don't! I know." On doctor's orders she was prevented from going to the funeral. It took place on March 22, 1911, in pouring rain at Grinzing cemetery. Hundreds of friends and mourners attended the simple ceremony. At one point, wind "buffeted the trees so violently that they roared and bowed low. It was as though a deep sigh, a shudder were escaping from the whole of nature," one journalist noted. Then, "as the thud of the first two handfuls of earth hit the coffin's metal cover, a ray of sunlight broke through the clouds." Another mourner recalled a rainbow and the song of a nightingale.[95]

— 8 —

Tempest
1911–1914

*A*fter it was over, faced with the "deadly silence," Alma broke down completely, she told Gropius. When Chvosteck warned her that her lungs were weakened and if she went on like this, she would "soon be where your husband is," she felt "the first happy moments since Gustav's death. I *wanted* to follow him."[1] Chvosteck ordered her to bed where she remained, suffering "a long period of mental and spiritual agony": "I simply could not grasp that I was now separated from him for ever. I felt completely rootless."[2] She lay in bed listening to bells tolling and talking to Gustav's picture. When he had been the center of her life and it had seemed to her that "only for him and his illness [am I] in this world," their new closeness had nourished her. Now that she was alone and exhausted, she reflected how "time seemed somehow to have passed by while I had been Mahler's wife and noticing nothing but him."[3] But she did not wear mourning clothes, for Gustav had forbidden it.

Music once again saved her: "Music was left to me and opened its arms," she wrote. With seven-year-old Anna she played music all day long. The cook had to drag them away for meals. Gradually she found a path to recovery: "I want to catch up on what I have failed to do for nine years—to get well," she told Gropius. In those years, she now realized, she had become "more and more depressed. . . . Nobody can have any idea of the nervous torments of my married life."[4] By July, she began to "live

135

the life I ended nine years ago. I live from one day to the next—work the whole day, play the piano, walk a little—in short do as much as I want to and what interests me—an hour is never too long— . . . my life has now been colossally simplified."[5]

Alma did not immediately resume relations with Gropius. A distance had opened up between them. The closeness Alma experienced with Gustav in the last months overshadowed her feelings for the absent Walter. After Gustav's death, her own grief and ill health consumed her. Gropius, too, withdrew emotionally. In February that year, his father had died, leaving him feeling helpless, disoriented, and often depressed. In June, he wrote from a beautiful Ostsee resort that he was thinking "with great melancholy" of her and Gustav and what had happened: "If only I could care for you here! You would get well again." It was the anniversary of the day when "all unknowing—I glimpsed you for the first time. It seems as if a decade has passed since then, because our hearts have experienced so much."[6] But the distance between them widened. Their first meeting in Vienna in August was passionate but also strained: "Yes—my behaviour must appear strange to you," Alma wrote to Walter. "Even to myself I am sometimes a mystery, Now I tremble about what might have happened to me, and what I should do. Do keep writing to me in your lovely way."[7]

When they were due to meet in Berlin in September, Gropius pulled back:

> I can *not* be in Berlin on the 25th. Your letter was as touchingly *sweet* as you yourself—but since I have been away from you a burning shame has risen up in me which compels me to avoid you. I must go away for a while to discover whether my eyes are blind—to cloak my love in such a beautiful form that it could do justice to you and compensate for the sorrow that I caused to you and Gustav out of my lack of mature prudence. Today I am *not* sure, and I am deeply saddened about myself.[8]

Slowly Alma was recovering. She had found order in her life and a new apartment, she told Gropius in November and invited him to visit. But he put off meeting her again, complaining he had a tooth infection and was staying in a sanatorium "in a pitiful state," after his recent travels.[9] They didn't meet until December, in Berlin. Alma felt uncomfortable and the visit was a disappointment. Walter introduced Alma to his sister and his mother, Manon Gropius, to whom Alma took an almost instant dislike, a reaction which was soon reciprocated.

Letters became scarcer after this. In January 1912 she asked, "Are you remaining faithful to me?" then wanted to know why he was not replying to her letters.[10] In April she told him she was living a life of almost monastic calm, and in May, on the first anniversary of Gustav's death and Walter's twenty-ninth birthday (which she failed to mention), she wrote praising him as an honorable, good, and generous man. He appears not to have replied. In November when silence greeted Alma's request for the return of some magazines she had lent him, she persisted, rather sadly, "Aren't we human beings who once completely understood each other?"[11] His final, cool reply came on December 3, 1912:

> I am so pleased that you have thought of me lovingly. [However] . . . you have moved too far away from me and that's why the closeness of our mutual understanding suffered. . . . No, it cannot be like it was before and everything has changed fundamentally. Can one really at will turn deep feelings of togetherness into friendship? . . . What will come later I do not know. It does not depend on my actions. Everything is whirring together, ice and sun, pearls and dirt and devil and angel. So one just follows. Perhaps in some happy hour you will cross my path again.[12]

ALMA MEANWHILE WAS leading an eventful life of which Gropius knew nothing. Her recovery was greatly assisted by the glow of adoration of a series of suitors. At thirty-two, she was a statuesque beauty with a magnetic charisma, left comfortably off by the pension she received as Mahler's widow. She began to crystallize her goals: "Unwittingly, while looking for greatness in men, I was facing life—tempting, seductive life." She could now "realize my childhood dream of filling my garden with geniuses."[13] Talented men soon appeared. In the fall, for a while she saw much of Franz Schreker, an "immensely gifted" composer and the founder of the Vienna Philharmonic Choir, but "he played no part in my life; I walked beside him for a stretch and left him at the right time."[14]

Joseph Fraenkel, who had sustained both Alma and Gustav during the terrible final months, arrived from America after a decent interval to declare his love for her and to propose marriage. Alma had then thought him "the most wonderful accomplished brain . . . everything he says is stimulating, witty . . . never a commonplace word," and admired him for his "touching" progress from penniless Jewish émigré to eminence as the physician to millionaires.[15] But in Europe he appeared as "an elderly, sick little man quite unheroically nursing a fatal intestinal ailment."[16] They traveled to Corfu together, but illness confined him to his cabin.

Alma was intent on renewing her inner independence and burning to experience life again. She had moved on: "Wandering in souls had become my greatest joy."[17] She was not ready to tie herself to Fraenkel or anyone else. Her response to his courting was muted. She saw him as "sheer intellect," the one man "for whom even I was too earthy," which convinced her that their relationship was doomed. "The fact that separates us is the divergence of our own souls," she wrote in a farewell letter.

> What is salvation to me is unthinkable to you, with your cerebral make-up; what is salvation to you strikes me as madness. That's how different we are!
>   My watchword is: Amo—ergo sum.
>   Yours: Cogito—ergo sum.[18]

Later, a night in Corfu came back to her in a vivid dream: "The window was open . . . the souls spoke . . . the bodies yearned, but there came a donkey scream, ridiculously vulgar. But near me lay a brain on two legs—and a misplaced red heart. In which ticked a golden clock."[19]

On November 20, 1911, on the train back from the first performance in Munich of Mahler's *Das Lied von der Erde*, conducted by Bruno Walter, she encountered by chance the biologist Paul Kammerer—"one of the oddest individuals I ever came across."[20] With considerable fuss and élan, he had several years before turned up at Maiernigg pleading to serve his idol, Gustav Mahler. Both Alma and Gustav were soon worn down by this demanding being. On the death of his beloved idol, the grief-stricken Kammerer announced to Alma his intention to transfer his love for Mahler to his wife and daughter, explaining that Mahler's exalted position was also an accomplishment of his extraordinary wife, one of "the rare breed of brilliant Viennese women."[21]

He now proposed that Alma should give up music to become his laboratory assistant at the Institute for Experimental Biology. Surprisingly she agreed. When she squirmed at feeding live mealworms to reptiles, he put her in charge of studying the molting habits of the praying mantis. Alma spent days monitoring their exact movements, trying unsuccessfully to persuade them to eat in the dark at the bottom of the cage, as Kammerer wanted, when they preferred to eat in sunlight at the top.[22] When her daily visits to the laboratory became too time consuming, Kammerer had a terrarium installed in her apartment and came regularly to check on the various reptiles and retrieve the salamanders and lizards that had escaped down the stairs.

Soon Kammerer declared his all-consuming love for her: "I valued him as a friend, but as a man I always found him disgusting," she recalled. "Every day he wrote me the craziest letters. . . . Every other day he would run out of my house threatening to shoot himself—preferably on Gustav Mahler's grave." His behavior made him the clown in her circle: "When I got up from a chair, he would kneel down and sniff and stroke the spot where I had been sitting. He didn't care at all whether or not there was a stranger in the room."

Eventually Alma approached his wife, Felicitas: "I advised her to take more care of him and above all to remove the pistol he had been brandishing constantly, endangering me and himself. I told her, 'thank God that he brought his lonely heart to me—for I don't want him, and so you have not lost him.'"[23] Felicitas thanked her "profusely," and it seemed to Alma that their marriage improved. Subsequently Kammerer fell passionately in love with all five sisters of an artistic family. He committed suicide in 1926 after his reputation was ruined over allegations of falsifying scientific evidence, though it was also said that it was because the last of the sisters had refused to accompany him to Moscow.

ALMA HAD BEEN living with her parents on the Hohe Warte and had just settled into a new apartment at Pokornygasse 12 when her life was turned upside down again. On April 12, 1912, she met Oskar Kokoschka, a twenty-six-year-old painter who was fast making his reputation as the enfant terrible of the Vienna art world. Her stepfather, Carl Moll, suggested "the poor, starving genius" might paint her portrait. Alma had seen Kokoschka's work at a Kunstschau exhibition and noted his "original, grandly conceived design." She agreed to sit for him. He was invited to dinner at the Molls' house

Kokoschka had brought rough paper and started at once to make drawings. After a short while Alma felt uncomfortable being stared at and suggested she play the piano. They withdrew to an adjoining room where she played Isolde's *Liebestod* from Wagner's *Tristan and Isolde* while he drew, "interrupted by coughs: on the handkerchief he tried to hide were flecks of blood. He hardly spoke, and yet he seemed unable to draw. We stood up—and suddenly he embraced me passionately. But this kind of embrace was strange and alien. I did not respond at all—and exactly that seemed to affect him. He stormed out."[24]

Kokoschka was "dazzled by her, she disturbed me," he later recalled. "How beautiful she was. . . . How seductive behind her mourning veil!" (although Alma did not wear mourning clothes). "She quite enchanted me! And I got the impression that she was not exactly indifferent towards me."[25] Both claimed the other had been the one to fall in love at first sight. Within days, Kokoschka delivered to her "the most beautiful love letter" addressed to "My dear friend," in which he pleaded with her to "strengthen me with your joyousness and purity so I will not succumb to the decline which threatens me." He declared he would be

> lost if my life should stay so unclear. I know that I will lose my abilities, which I ought to be directing towards a goal that is greater than myself, that would be sacred to you and to me. If you can respect me and wish to be as pure as you were yesterday, when I recognised that you are superior to and better than all other women, who only ever brought out my baser self, then you will be making a true sacrifice for me and will be my wife, in secret while I am still so poor.

From the very outset he saw her as his muse and savior: "I believe in you as I have never believed in anyone but myself. If you with your woman's strength would help me out from my mental confusion, then that beauty beyond our understanding, which we worship, will bless *you* and *me* with happiness," he wrote.[26]

Alma felt that he had consciously cast a spell over her: "I had to see him again." They soon became lovers. He was "a strange mixture, as a

man and as a human being"; in a surprisingly detached description of the
man who so powerfully roused her erotic nature, she later wrote,

> Although his form is beautiful, something hopelessly proletarian in his
> structure is disturbing. He is tall and slim, but his hands are red and
> often swollen. His fingertips are so congested that when he cuts himself
> while trimming his nails, the blood comes spurting out in a high arc.
> His ears, though small and finely chiselled, stick out from his head. His
> nose is somewhat wide and tends to swell up. The mouth is large, and
> the lower jaw and chin prominent. The eyes somewhat angled, which
> gives him the expression of someone on the prowl. But as such the eyes
> are beautiful. He holds his head up really high.[27]

Kokoschka was still a student at the Vienna School of Arts when his
work was first noticed at the Kunstschau exhibitions organized by the
Wiener Werkstätte. He elicited both praise and outrage. Gustav Klimt
called him "the greatest talent of the younger generation," one critic
called him *Oberwilding*—the "chief savage," while Archduke Ferdinand,
the heir to the throne, wanted "to break every bone in the young man's
body." In his paintings, as well as in prose plays and illustrated poems,
notably *The Dreaming Boys* and *Murder, Hope of Women*, he explored the
subconscious, the hidden self of irrational impulse, and the "bitter struggle between mind and sex, a battle won by sex," as Kokoschka declared.[28]

When Alfred Roller, head of the Vienna School of Arts, was instructed to expel him, he was rescued by the modernist architect Adolf Loos, who introduced him to Herwarth Walden, editor of the Berlin
expressionist magazine, *Der Sturm*. Kokoschka's drawings in *Der Sturm*
between 1910 and 1912 "seemed to shake the edifice of modern art like
earth tremors," artist Oskar Schlemmer wrote. Kokoschka lived in abject
poverty, on biscuits and tea, until a gallery owner, Paul Cassirer, offered
him a contract and a regular income, which enabled him to engage in
Berlin's social life: painter Georg Grosz recalled him appearing at a ball
"with a real ox-bone dripping with blood, which he gnawed at from time
to time."[29] When he returned to Vienna in December 1910 he had decided "my whole life is hellish. . . . I am a bad-tempered weakling desperate for any sympathy that comes my way."[30] Shortly afterward Carl Moll
stepped in to support him.

Alma fell deeply in love with the provocative, savage, eccentric artist. They became inseparable. "Oskar Kokoschka is a genius. I loved him for that, and I loved the ill-bred, stubborn child in him," she later reflected.[31] "I saw all the purity in the world confronting me in Oskar Kokoschka, but I could not bear so much light."[32] Eventually she would describe the three years she spent with him as "one violent struggle of love. Never before had I experienced so much strain, so much hell and so much paradise."[33]

He satisfied her yearning to be loved and worshipped for herself. He validated her self-worth because he depended on her presence to inspire him and nourish his creative powers. She glowed in the knowledge that she had power over genius—for that had become her greatest wish. But she also discovered the sacrifice of self that went with the towering self-absorption, the overbearing need to control and possess that lay at the core of geniuses such as Mahler and Kokoschka.

In daily letters to Alma, Kokoschka poured out his love, his possessive adoration, and his dependence on her: "I must soon have you as my wife, otherwise my great talent will go to rack and ruin. You must re-animate me in the night like a magic potion. I can work all day, spending what I have absorbed at night. . . . Tonight, working on the red picture I

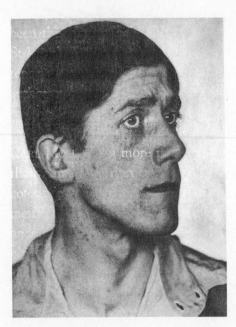

Figure 13. Painter Oskar Kokoschka. "I must soon have you as my wife, otherwise my great talent will go to rack and ruin."

have seen how strong you make me and what I will amount to when this force is constantly active."[34] She must bind herself to him "more strongly than any human being to the earth. . . . Your inner virtue, which I recognised, has conquered my mistrust and disarmed my cruelty which lay always ready like a hound to separate me from my dearest," he wrote in May 1912.[35]

The corollary of his love was his intense jealousy of everything in her life. When in early May 1912 she went to stay at Scheveningen, a seaside resort on the Netherlands coast, he warned, "You may not slip away from me, not ever, not for one moment." "Whether or not you are with me, your eyes must always be directed toward me, wherever you are."[36] When he left after visiting her, he did not immediately go home but instead walked up and down under her window, "and toward two, sometimes not until four o'clock in the morning he whistled, and that was the sign I had been longing for, that he was finally going away. He left in the comforting awareness that no 'lad,' as he gently put it, had come to see me."[37] Sometimes a more visceral savagery surfaced: "Alma, I just happened to come by your house at ten in the morning, and could have wept in fury because you can stand there surrounding yourself with satellites, while I withdraw to the filthy corner again. And if I have to take a knife and scratch every single alien idea inimical to me out of your brain, I would do it, before I find myself sharing the redeeming flame of joy with you—I'd rather starve, and so will you. I will have no other gods before me."[38]

His controlling intrusiveness precipitated their first disturbing crisis. As she played and sang *Parsifal* for him, he stood behind her chair and "adroitly switched the words he hated. A new, eerie text was whispered into my ear, and I was to accompany it. I began to cry, to scream. He did not stop. I fell from the piano; like Miracolo in *Tales of Hoffmann*, he kept coming after me. With my last ounce of strength I dragged myself into my bedroom and swallowed a large dose of [toxic] bromine. Now he was frightened, too, and got my doctor on the phone at four in the morning." Alma would not allow the trembling creature in for two days, then on the third he arrived with both hands full of flowers, which he strewed over her bed, and was forgiven.

Still her feelings could soar in his presence. She never doubted his genius and acknowledged that the price was his obsession. After years of feeling neglected by Mahler, Kokoschka's intense attention and all-consuming love, his daily worship, his need for her was irresistible and possibly addictive: it made her indispensable to a genius. And it was never dull. He amused her, and she delighted in his eccentricities. Early on he bought her a pair of flaming red pajamas, which she disliked because of their vulgarity. He took them over and wore them as he wandered around the studio and received shocked guests. They were something of a fetish: "He spent more time in front of the mirror than he did in front of the easel," Alma noted.[39]

. But sometimes she had to escape his flaming and fluctuating passion. After Mahler's death, Alma had found a traveling companion in Henrietta Amalie (Lilly) Lieser, whom she had known at a distance, as they inhabited the same social circles. A prominent patron of the arts, Lilly came from the wealthy Landau family and had married the entrepreneur Justin Lieser in 1896. She had two daughters of similar age to Gucki. In April, at the start of Alma's affair with Kokoschka, they had spent several days visiting Paris. For three years from 1912 to 1915, whenever Alma needed to get away from Vienna and Kokoschka, it was with Lilly that she traveled.

In July, they went with Gucki for two weeks to Scheveningen, leaving Kokoschka "completely apathetic" without her, for she was "truly the only person who has a good, brightening effect on me, where so often lurks in me wild perversity," he told her.[40] In Scheveningen Alma met up with Joseph Fraenkel: "I did not feel this was disloyal to O.K., because he was already a long way from me. I just wanted to make it clear to myself one last time that it was all over between us," she explained, though not to Kokoschka, whose jealousy of Fraenkel had taken on a dark character: "Oskar Kokoschka could only make love to me with the most peculiar game playing," she recalled.[41] "As I refused to hit him during our hours of love, he began conjuring up the most appalling images of murder in his brain, while whispering murkily to himself. I remember that he once evoked Fraenkel in that connection, and I had to take part in a revolting fantasy murder. When he fancied he had been gratified, he said: 'If that hasn't killed him, at least he'll come away from it with a little heart collapse.'"[42]

Alma then joined Kokoschka in Munich. They "met, loved, quarrelled, and saw a film about Christopher Columbus," which inspired him to create one of the many intimate and agonized representations of their relationship, in the lithograph series *Gefesselter Columbus* (*Columbus in Chains*).[43] At Mürren, near Bern in Switzerland, they spent "some strange, wild, ghostly weeks" at in a hotel overlooking a valley, where Oskar painted her portrait and they experienced mysterious visions: "The valley below us suddenly began to glow—the mist—which had been white before—became blood red." A candle left on a chair outside "was swept away in the mists like a lost soul."[44] On her birthday Kokoschka gave her the first of the seven fans on which he charted the progress of their love—another form through which he could "capture" her.

But there began a terrible struggle, as Alma resisted Kokoschka's pressing efforts to claim her as his own. Kokoschka even made secret preparations to get a marriage permit in Switzerland and asked his mother to send his baptism and nationality certificates. Alma "trembled upstairs in the hotel at the possibility he might succeed."[45] He postponed his plan only when it appeared unworkable. When she thought she was pregnant, Kokoschka was overjoyed: "Should you have a precious child from me, so is great Nature compassionate and . . . will never more tear us apart for we will rest in and support one another."[46] But Alma did not want his child: she "feared what might grow in me. I was afraid it might inherit Kokoschka's ferocity."[47] Alma left for Vienna to get immediate medical advice, though her fears were this time groundless.

Kokoschka's jealousy was unbridled. He was incensed at any sign of her continuing emotional attachment to Mahler. Though it was barely a year since his death, he complained that she continued to venerate Mahler: "Wherever I looked, I'd see pictures of him looking back at me. Or his death mask, or Rodin's bust of him, or even the objects he had been fond of."[48] In a fury in June, he refused to go with her to rehearsals in Vienna of Mahler's Ninth Symphony: "I can find no peace in you as long as I know someone else, dead or alive, is a part of you," he spluttered. "Why have you invited me to a dance of death, and why do you want me to stand mutely, for hours on end, watching you, while you, a spiritual slave, obey the rhythm of the man who was and must be a stranger to me, knowing that every syllable of the work hollows you out, mentally and physically?"[49] One day he suddenly got up, "gathered up Mahler's photos one by one, and kissed Mahler's face in every one. He said it was white magic, and he wanted to use it to transform his jealous hatred into love. But I cannot say it helped," she recalled.[50] Perhaps to exorcise his demons, Kokoschka expressed his jealousy of his rivals in drawings "Alma Mahler Caressing Hans Pfitzner" (1913) and "Alma Mahler Being Importuned by Lovers" (1913), while representing his own torment as the victim in drawings such as "Alma Mahler Spinning with Kokoschka's Intestine" (1913).

Alma's relations with Kokoschka's mother, Romana, who adamantly opposed their affair, were particularly strained. "No-one would believe how much I hate that person. An older woman like that with eleven years of family life behind her attaching herself to such a young boy," Romana fumed, and he called Alma "Circe"—a cocotte who would ruin her son.[51] Kokoschka recalled how his mother once promenaded for several hours outside Alma's apartment with her hand moving suspiciously inside her coat pocket (where he suspected a gun was concealed) while Alma looked on.[52]

In September Alma visited her sister Gretl, whose health had roused Alma's concern. After her marriage in 1900 to the painter Wilhelm Legler, Gretl had moved to Stuttgart, and contact between the sisters had become less frequent. Since February, however, after wildly erratic behavior and several suicide attempts, Gretl had been confined at a psychiatric hospital in Baden Baden, where she was diagnosed with chronic premature dementia. It was the start of several decades in mental institutions.

After her visit, Alma barely mentioned her sister in either letters or diaries, though she recorded a disturbing visit at Christmas 1925: "The haggard, brown head rose from the pillow, and I recognised with absolute certainty the face and head shape of the painter Julius Berger."[53] It was shocking confirmation that Gretl was not the daughter of Emil Schindler, but of the painter Julius Berger. When confronted, her mother confessed to the affair with Berger when Schindler was away being treated for diphtheria at Borkum. Alma was incandescent. For years she had been told that her father's diphtheria was responsible for Gretl's mental illness and had "trembled thinking that I too might go mad . . . until I finally broke through the clouds." In the certain knowledge that she alone bore her father's special—and healthy—legacy, she found herself "inspired . . . as if born anew."[54]

During her visit to Gretl at Baden Baden in 1912, Alma discovered that she was pregnant. She rushed back to Vienna, went to the flat—alone with the child—and in this flat I suddenly felt: I am not Oskar's wife!—While I was away Gustav's death mask had been placed in my living room—the sight of it almost completely robbed me of my senses. This smiling, forgiving, distinguished face—made me seem ridiculous to myself and the whole situation somehow unreal. O.K. came—found me dissolved in tears and could not calm me until I had his permission—to have the child taken away. He gave it—but he would not recover from that blow.[55]

Alma had the abortion in the middle of October 1912 in a Vienna sanatorium: "It is horrendous. . . . I longed and wished for [it] . . . only when it was here . . . I was close to madness," she wrote distractedly.[56] Kokoschka visited her: "He took the first bloodied cotton pad from me and then took it home with him.—'That is, and will always be, my only child'—and after that he always had with him that dried out cotton pad."[57] Over and over in his work he represented a bloodied, murdered child. He never entirely forgave her: "The coming into being of a living creature may not intentionally be impeded because of indolence," he wrote, pointing out that "it was a decisive event in my own development as well—that really is obvious."[58] He became even more possessive of Alma, who "began to curse his sweet innocence because it gave him the right to sit in judgment over me. I was not allowed to look at anyone, to talk to anyone. He insulted my guests and lay in wait for me everywhere and opened my letters. My dresses had to cover my arms and my throat."[59]

Kokoschka was still set on marriage and longing for "the beautiful happy world . . . when you will be my wife, and will no longer be separated from me."[60] Since October 1912 he had been working on a double portrait, intended as an engagement picture, with the two recognizable figures sitting in close intimacy, their hands touching. When Walter Gropius, unaware of Alma's relations with Kokoschka, saw it at the Twenty-Sixth Munich Secession Exhibition in the spring of 1913 and discerned its clear message, any thought of further communication with Alma was banished.

At first Kokoschka accepted Alma's regular trips away with Lilly Lieser. She often used the excuse of ill health to explain her absence, and Kokoschka appreciated the care "the Lieserin" took of her. But he became increasingly wary of this "stranger" who so regularly deprived him of Alma's presence. His waspish jealousy stirred in May: "Frau L. should be aware of what your friendship means to her, that I must surrender to her my joy and my ability to work whenever she desires to lead you away."[61] His objection gelled into petulant fury: "She is not worthy of your innocence. The person of whom you write will be so far ignored by me that I won't remember what she is doing for your sake."[62] By July, he was mounting a full-blown attack against "truly the most pitiful tragic woman, who harbours long term grudges for which she accepts no responsibility. She certainly does not have your soul, but is only mundane."[63] None of this had any impact on Alma, for whom Lilly was a valued confidante and companion.

When she was away in Paris in July, Kokoschka, who was still obsessed with marriage, stole her documents and without her knowledge posted the marriage banns announcing their intention to marry in the Döbling parish hall. To avoid a confrontation, Alma made herself scarce, and, when the marriage was due, she was away spending two weeks at Franzenbad spa, after consoling Kokoschka with the promise that she would return to marry him after he had created a masterpiece. When he turned up unexpectedly at the spa and found that his self-portrait, which he had insisted she take "for her protection," was not on the wall, a storm erupted. Alma was furious with him, but Kokoschka seemed immune to her anger: "Your letter today pelted me with hailstones of obscenity again," he wrote to her in apparent innocence, "and I am so fond of you, and I don't know why you are so cross with me."[64] When she returned from her cure, the walls of his studio were painted black and covered in white crayon sketches, while two lamps, one red and one blue, illuminated the room. She found him "in such a strange state of mind" that she insisted that they see each other only once every three days: "It was in self protection that I relaxed our bonds, at least the bonds of habit," she recalled.[65]

Between the storms were pleasant periods of calm. On a trip to the Dolomites in August they walked in the woods and devoted their hours to his work, which increasingly formed a parallel disturbing narrative of their love affair. In the seven fans he made for her and in his drawings and illustrations, he mined elemental, sometimes savage, emotions— love, jealousy, salvation, remorse—with Alma always the central figure, sometimes the savior, the maternal life-giver, and sometimes the devourer or tormenter. It seems that Alma accepted these depictions of herself without demur.

His masterpiece, *Die Windsbraut* (*The Tempest*), is the most famous depiction of their love. It shows two figures in a storm-tossed boat, the woman, clearly Alma, lying calmly, trustfully clinging to the man, who, in Alma's words, "despotic of face, radiating energy, calms the mountainous waves."[66] When the poet Georg Trakl saw the painting in Kokoschka's bleak studio, he made up a poem on the spot, which gave the picture its name: "drunk with death the glowing tempest plunges over blackish cliffs."[67]

In the spring of 1914, Alma completed work on the country house at Breitenstein in Semmering in Lower Austria, which she had been building on the plot bought by Mahler before his death. It was her own house, built to her own design, and it gained her a space and a certain peace of

Figure 14. Oskar Kokoschka, *Self-portrait with Alma Mahler*, 1913 (© Fondation Oskar Kokoschka/DACS 2018).

her own. Surrounded by balconies, it looked out on the massive Schnee-
berg and the mountains around. At the center of the house was an enormous fireplace, above which Kokoschka painted a fresco four meters wide,
which showed Alma "pointing to the heavens in their spectral radiance,
while he, standing in hell, seemed surrounded by death and serpents.
The whole thing is based on the idea of the flames continuing up from
the fireplace," she wrote. Gucki watched him as he worked, and asked,
"'Can't you paint anything else except Mommy?' Kokoschka only looked
at the child, who never took her great eyes off him when he painted, who
had her own chair in his studio so as to see each of his pictures grow. 'That
child hasn't got any face,' he said to me. 'She's got nothing but expression.'"[68] Peace prevailed as Alma settled in: "No clouds marred the beauty
of our days. Work was going on in every room: curtains were sewn and
hung. Mother cooked in the kitchen. In the evenings we sat around the
fireplace, read aloud or made music—in short, the time was totally devoted to reconstruction."[69]

That calm did not last. Under the force of Kokoschka's ungovernable
jealousy, Alma began to doubt her love. She fled to Paris with Lilly Lieser
and for a time withheld her address. Kokoschka lashed out at "die Lieser"
who had taken Alma away "in *my* time."[70] He pleaded for Alma to

> find new heart for him. . . . I shall be completely lost if you don't have
> the patience for love. . . . Even if I turn into a wayward monster, you
> have to be loyal to me. . . . One cannot switch back and forth at will
> from being foolish one minute and wise the next. . . . And you're be-
> coming a Sphinx, who wants neither to live nor to die, but who mur-
> ders the man who loves her and is too moral to withdraw this love or
> to betray someone for his own well-being. . . . I must have someone
> to communicate with! And you should lure *me* back and cradle me in
> safety.[71]

His demanding neediness had become too much for her. Alma withdrew: "Well—now that's all over, too. Something I thought would last!
Oskar is lost to me. I can't find him in myself any more. He has become
an undesired stranger to me. I am surrounded by silence," she confided to
her diary. "We get on each other's nerves. I WILL forget him! We haven't
improved one another, but rather made one another mean."[72] Alone in

Breitenstein she achieved a strengthening calm: "I am filled with courage; my soul is light in this world. Nothing tears at my nerve strings, and that's how it should remain. No-one shall again disturb the stillness of my true consciousness."[73] For a time she contemplated escape to India, to join Annie Besant and the theosophists, or the Buddhist mystics.

When Kokoschka was confronted by Alma's withdrawal, he promised to change: "But it will take weeks and months until I have changed to the person you need."[74] His promises only made her more exasperated: "He fulfilled my life and destroyed it at the same time," she raged. "Why, alas, did I forsake the quiet hearth for the blazing castle? What should I do with all these 'becomes' and all these 'maybes' from this person? . . . Do I still love this person? Or do I already hate him?"[75] Yet she maintained the edifice of their relationship, while Kokoschka, seemingly blind or unable to acknowledge the darker currents disturbing Alma, still protested his need for her: "I must have security in you . . . or my creative strength will be held back and never mature."[76]

In April, Berta Zuckerkandl had told her of the success at the Cologne Werkstätte exhibition of a brilliant young architect, Walter Gropius. As she sought order in her life, she turned again to Gropius. Alma wrote to congratulate him, and then in early May she wrote again: "After struggles and losing my way—I am myself again! I am wiser—freer—above all I now know that I don't have to search for anything—because I have found so much—everything." She offered him her friendship and confessed she had "a great desire to speak with you. . . . [P]eople who have experienced such strange and beautiful things together must not lose each other. Come—if you have time and it gives you pleasure—come and visit."[77] Walter's reaction is unknown, but she wrote again on May 24 to let him know she was lonely and would like to meet him in July. This met with no response, so her life with Kokoschka continued.

ON JUNE 28, 1914, the calm of Breitenstein, as everywhere throughout Europe, was shattered by the news that the heir to the Austrian throne, Franz Ferdinand, and his wife, Sophie, had been murdered at Sarajevo. The perpetrator was a young Serb anarchist, Gavrilo Princip, who had connections to the Serb nationalist movement. The murder was the violent culmination of a simmering revolt by Serbian and the other minorities that made up the empire, for increased ethnic and minority rights and greater autonomy, or independence, from the dominance of Austria-Hungary. The emergence of nationalism had now escalated into a dangerous threat to the empire's survival.

Austria responded to the outrage by issuing a harsh ultimatum to Serbia to rein in its nationalist "terrorists." When Serbia rejected the ultimatum, Austria declared war on July 28. The dominos fell fast. Russia mobilized in support of fellow Serbian Slavs on July 30, and on August 1, Germany backed Austria-Hungary with its own mobilization. The hostilities soon sucked in the entire European continent, and then the world.

Faced with the imminent danger, on August 1, Kokoschka advised Alma, who was in Breitenstein, to escape with Lilly Lieser to neutral Switzerland. Instead, she returned to Vienna to rent a ten-room apartment on Elizabethstrasse in the First District. In an astonishing flourish of self-aggrandizement, she co-opted these dramatic external events to her inner state: "I sometimes imagine that I was the one who ignited this whole world conflagration in order to experience some kind of development or enrichment—even if it be only death."[78]

As political order collapsed around her, Alma had reached a barren plateau in her emotional life. She was desperately lonely and intent on breaking with Kokoschka. But she still could not release herself from his demanding, magnetic presence. And, like everyone else, Alma had no idea of the disastrous consequences of the war on the ailing Austro-Hungarian Empire, already weakened by internal conflicts, which would remove the very foundations of their secure existence and radically alter the perspective on all their lives.

— 9 —

War and Marriage
1914–1917

*I*n Austria, as in all the nations of Europe the declaration of war was greeted with jubilation. After fifty years of peace under Emperor Franz Joseph, the doctrine of war as the means to resolve disputes had gained currency. Only war, it was widely believed, could resolve the conflicts multiplying within and outside the borders of the empire. That it would spread so rapidly to engulf the nations of the world was not anticipated.

In the initial euphoria, both sides glorified war as an honorable and heroic adventure: it would renew the nation's strength and exalt its manhood, purify the body politic and cleanse it of decay, and unite the people under the banner of patriotism. "There were parades in the streets, flags, ribbons, and music burst forth everywhere, young recruits were marching triumphantly, their faces lighting up at the cheering," wrote Stefan Zweig, who, though he loathed war, acknowledged something "majestic, rapturous and even seductive" in Vienna at its outbreak: "A city of two million, a country of nearly fifty million, in that hour felt that they were participating in world history, in a moment which would never recur, and that each one was called upon to cast his infinitesimal self into the glowing mass, there to be purified of all selfishness. . . . Each individual experienced an exaltation of his ego, he was no longer the isolated person of former times, he had been incorporated into the mass, he was part of the people . . . and his life had been given meaning."[1]

The euphoria did not last. Alma's friend, composer Alban Berg, observed that life was going on much as usual in Vienna four months later: "To watch this is as nauseating as the war is painful. . . . If the war should do what it is supposed to do—to act as a cathartic element—it is very far from achieving this. The dirt remains as before—only in a different form."[2]

It was soon clear that this would be a war not of heroic cavalry charges or rapid conquests but of stalemate on both the Austrian-Russian and the western fronts. "The terrible war goes on. The earth is soaked in the blood of the best," Alma wrote in despair in September 1914. "Austria CAN not win—only lose."[3] As the German troops threatened Paris, she spent an entire "sweet lovely evening" alone playing Wagner's *Die Meistersinger von Nürnberg*: "Music is everything to me. Since the beginning of this war I have not dared to play—but now I know—even surrounded by death I must SING!" This "accursed war" would purify even music, she decided, for it "must teach us to love our most accomplished talents again. It will smother the rotten seedlings." In this mood, alone, she discovered her inner strength: "I can be handmaiden to no man, because . . . my happiness comes from WITHIN ME. . . . My room is my concert-hall. Everything glows. . . . I fly."[4]

Alma continued her relationship with Kokoschka. Even though her emotional attachment to him was strained, she still could not bring about the final break: "I'd like to settle the score with Oskar. He is of no use in my life anymore," she wrote in the privacy of her diary. "He keeps dragging me back to the libidinous level. I can't do anything with it anymore. And however dear and helpless as this big child is, he is also unreliable, even treacherous, as a man." But she still struggled to "tear him out of my heart! The stake is embedded deep in my flesh. I know that I am sick because of him—have been ill for YEARS—and have been unable to tear myself away. . . . Away with him! He still PLEASES me too much! God has punished me by sending HIM into my life. Physical distance must surely bring me relief."[5]

Her disillusion intensified after a sleepless night in October when she realized "the scales have fallen from my eyes. Oskar Kokoschka is the EVIL SPIRIT in my life. He alone seeks my destruction. . . . One cannot make pure what is soiled—and when he embraced me the first time—everything in me warned me of his EVIL eye—but I wanted to make him GOOD—and might through him have almost been made evil myself. Oh—by this evil fascination! My nerves are shattered—my imagination ruined. What fiend sent HIM to me?!"[6]

With the war already at a standstill in its third month, Kokoschka came under increasing pressure to join up. After observing young men at the railway station departing for war in July, he had been afflicted by "a bad conscience as if I were partly to blame for everything because of my hedonism and frivolity, enjoying myself while others were compelled without being asked. And when there are numerous victories, this will be the greatest sin."[7] His guilt stirred again in September in a letter to his friend Kurt Wolff: "If I could be paid something in order to keep my relatives' heads above water, then I will volunteer for the army, for the shame of just having sat at home would otherwise be eternal."[8]

So Alma was probably prompting an already susceptible conscience when, according to her daughter Anna—who was aged ten at the time—Alma "kept calling Kokoschka a coward until in the end he finally 'volunteered' for military service. . . . Kokoschka really did not want to go to war, but she was already fed up with him by then."[9] By December 1914, Kokoschka knew that, at twenty-eight he would soon be called up: "It seemed to me better to volunteer before I was conscripted," he wrote.[10] He had told Alma of his rather dramatic desire "to be under fire for so long that all the evil in me has fallen away" and began preparations, with the help of his friend Adolf Loos, to enter the Fifteenth Imperial Royal Regiment of Dragoons, one of the most prestigious cavalry units in the monarchy.[11]

Released from Kokoschka's intense possessiveness, Alma opened herself up to the social life around her. Suitors soon arrived at her door. At the house of wealthy industrialist and art patron Carl Reininghaus, she experienced the unfamiliar sensation of being almost happy: "After the isolation of the last years with Oskar, this evening was like a salvation for me." Gustav Klimt was there with the cultural historian Josef Sczrigowski, who praised Mahler: "There was humanity in his every word—never merely intellect," and he turned to Alma: "But do not forget HOW you helped him with this! When he was with you—he was somehow brighter." At these words, Alma "trembled with pleasure. I had always

felt THAT, however I was happy that I finally heard this word from someone else! I did make him *brighter*! So my being with him was a mission
accomplished after all. That alone—was what I wanted all my life! To
help! To make people brighter!"[12]

Carl Reininghaus arranged another "lovely . . . serene" evening for
her and Lilly Lieser in November, with pleasing guests and a string quar-
tet in the background, but when she realized he was courting her, she
fled silently into the night. Composer Hans Pfitzner's reappearance in
her life was considerably more challenging. Although she was ill with a
fever, he insisted on immediately moving in with her. He played her his
new opera *Palestrina*. Then in the evening "he took my foot in his lap
and stroked it. That was the first evening." The next evening, he laid
his head across her breast: "I stroked his hair—what else should I do? He
wanted 'to be kissed'! Finally out of emotion I did this [on his forehead]
for this poor man! Tormented to death by the coldness of the world! He
wanted more. . . . [T]hus I began with great superiority to show him the
way to pure sensation—Yes—this DELICATE poet and musician said directly: 'What should we do now? Shall I possess you—or not?'" Alma
found him "just funny in this moment," but later she railed in exasper-
ation, "Thus are the artists—Faced with Life—they become dilettantes!
Everything flows into their work. But deep gloom must be their end. They
can find no pure echo in life, because they ring false."[13]

By December, Kokoschka had made the necessary arrangements to
join the dragoons. This included the purchase of a horse and expensive
uniform, which he financed by selling *Die Windsbraut* to a Hamburg phar-
macist for 400 kronen. He gave into his mother's safekeeping a necklace of
red beads, his memento of Alma, which Romana Kokoschka immediately
buried in a flower pot "to avoid looking at it as it reminded her of blood,"
but also presumably of Alma, for whom her dislike was undiminished. Despite Alma's private feelings, and perhaps out of compassion, Alma spent
New Year's Eve with Kokoschka at Breitenstein prior to his departure on
January 3, 1915, for training at Wiener Neustadt. "When you again took
me to your bed, you were unforgettably beautiful and noble in the way you
advised me so carefully and well," he wrote the next day. "By your words I
gave up my whole wayward will into your sweet beautiful hand."[14]

Alma's intermittent letters to him at the army base were sometimes
loving, at other times vitriolic, which left Kokoschka bewildered: "Your

letters are as rare as they are dissimilar," he wrote in January, "so that I don't know what you really want, and what annoyance motivates you to say these things."[15] Eventually he received in June a letter "which hurt me more than anything so far. I wept because I now see that I have no refuge. . . . And when I cry out, you rather shower me with scorn than draw me to your heart."[16] He insisted on being sent to the front, where in Western Ukraine in August he was severely wounded by a bullet in the head, then a bayonet thrust through his chest by a Russian soldier. His wounds were so severe that his death was announced in the Vienna papers.

Alma immediately rushed to his studio to retrieve her letters, which were presumably morally compromising for a widow at that time, and she also took, according to Kokoschka, several drawings. Kokoschka, however, survived and spent months in a field hospital before being transferred in the autumn to a military hospital in Vienna, from where he sent a message to Alma asking her to visit him. When she declined, he conceded sadly, "Really, I knew that any attempt to recapture the past must be in vain."[17] In February 1916 he was discharged and deemed well enough to return to the Italian front. When a bridge he was crossing was blown up, he suffered shell shock, which finally removed him completely from active service. But for Alma by then, Kokoschka had "become a strange shadow to me. Nothing in his life interests me. And I did love him!"[18]

When Kokoschka visited his mother and asked about the red necklace, she "took the flowerpot with its withered flowers from the windowsill, shook her head as if to chase away an unpleasant thought, and dropped the pot on the floor. With her bony fingers she pulled out from the mass of potsherds and earth the necklace of red glass beads—triumphantly, as if secretly pleased that she had been proved right. There was the source of all our misfortune!" In Kokoschka's account, he "suddenly felt cured of my tragic love, and embraced my mother: 'That's all over, I'm alive, I'm back,'" he recalled telling her.[19] But it was not entirely true—Alma would remain an obsession in Kokoschka's life for some time yet.

Alma had meanwhile found out that Gropius was in a field hospital "in a state of nervous shock." The news had unexpectedly affected her: "I sense—he is or may become something important for me," she mused.[20]

On New Year's Eve when Alma and Kokoschka had been together at Breitenstein, she had written a long letter to Walter Gropius expressing her ardent wish "that you may return safely from the battle, everything else your dear beautiful nature itself will take care of, and then I need wish for no more." She longed for the time when she "could bring you out here—here, where once you measured the ground for me with your steps. I press your hands."[21]

At the outbreak of war, August 5, 1914, Walter Gropius had joined the Ninth Hussars, the cavalry regiment where he had been a prewar volunteer. He was immediately sent to France, where he was engaged in dangerous reconnaissance duties in the Vosges region of Senones. By the end of September, the war had reached a standstill as the combatants faced each other in trenches often only two hundred meters apart. In November Gropius was promoted to the rank of lieutenant in acknowledgment of his bravery, and his regiment was moved to support on the front line at Moussey. Here he lived in an earthen cave often in three feet of mud, witnessed the regular deaths of his comrades, and at one time did not sleep for eight days. By the end of 1914, he was suffering nervous collapse and was sent to a field hospital to recuperate.

Gropius had mixed feelings when he received Alma's letter, but he agreed to meet her in February when he was on convalescent leave. Alma traveled to Berlin "with the shameful intention of straightening out this bourgeoisie son of art." Their passion was rekindled. They spent their days in "WEEPING questions, nights in TEARFUL justifications," for he still could not get over her infidelity with Kokoschka. Finally, she reported, he fell in love with her anew during a whole hour at Borchard's restaurant, where "wine and good food heightened the atmosphere and our feelings."[22]

Gropius was due to catch the night train to Hanover to visit his mother. Alma went with him to the station. There, "love took hold of him so powerfully that he spontaneously pulled me up onto the train as it was already moving down the track and I found myself, whether I wanted to or not, travelling with him to Hanover. Without a nightgown, without the slightest comfort or aids, in this way I become rather violently the booty of this man. I must say, I really didn't mind it a bit."[23]

She returned to Berlin where Gropius joined her for three more days. She had decided that "from Walter I desire children," and so he "took on the manners of a husband—did everything to ensure that I was expecting, and I tremble even now, that it happened. Then he travelled light-hearted and proud, as if after a mission accomplished, to the battlefield."[24] Though their passionate encounter had not borne fruit, it strengthened Alma's most ardent wish—"to become your own, your wife, forever," she told him.[25] In her regular letters, Alma addressed Walter as her husband and signed as "Your wife."

After Walter's departure, Alma stayed on in Berlin with Lilly Lieser, with whom she had traveled from Vienna. But something happened between them that left Alma "in no doubt about [Lilly's] predisposition. My dread of perverse people was always very strong," she wrote, "and LL's tendencies had until a *faux-pas* in Paris always been properly held in check." On a previous visit to Paris, Kokoschka had demanded that Alma return to Vienna, but Lilly had insisted, in what seemed a test of her power over Alma, that they go on to London instead. They were at the opera at the time, and, when Alma resisted, Lilly appears to have fainted. Alma took her back to the hotel where Lilly, somewhat deranged and by then lying naked on her bed, insisted that Alma feel her pulse and guided Alma's hand to her breast, which registered with Alma as a lesbian pass. Alma left promptly for Vienna the next day, but not, she insisted, because of Kokoschka's demand: "Not O.K. but my erotic health had prevailed."[26] Now in Berlin, Lilly had booked them into a shared room, and, when Alma realized the possible implications, she booked herself into a separate room, then resumed her planned visit with Lilly. Neither incident ended their relationship.

Together they went to see Arnold Schoenberg, who was living outside Berlin and in deep financial straits. Both gave him moral and financial support. Alma provided funds through the Mahler Trust, which she had set up to help composers including Alban Berg and Anton Webern. Lilly Lieser became Schoenberg's chief patron, providing him for several years with a steady income and, from September 1915, an apartment in her house at Gloriettegasse in upmarket Vienna. But sometimes Alma's patience with her revered artists ran out. When a concert she arranged in April 1915, directed by Arnold Schoenberg and underwritten by Lilly Lieser, led to serious rows with Schoenberg and turned out to be "a hopeless fiasco," she fumed to her diary.[27] "I have had enough of wayward artists. I want to call out to my soul: 'Put away your precious silver spoons—the artists are coming!'"[28]

In Vienna, she had another demanding visit from Pfitzner, who insisted that he could only do his greatest work if she lived with him, and he told her of the agony he experienced through his love for her. But Alma was troubled, for, although "desired by so many creatures," she was "STILL SO ALONE . . . ALONE."[29] To still that loneliness, at her red salon in Elizabethstrasse. Alma built up what would become her legendary salon and surrounded herself with talented friends and admirers. Siegfried Ochs, the distinguished Berlin choral conductor and composer then in his late fifties, brought her splendid presents—a Goethe autograph, a retouched version of Bach's B-minor mass, a copy of Albrecht Dürer's *Christ*. Alma admired Ochs, but she found his "trembling insane passion" unbearable and "dreaded his rather avaricious desire."[30] When Gerhart Hauptmann visited with his wife, Margarete, Alma was overjoyed to see this writer whom she admired so much, with his "large blue child-like eyes" his "noble" and worldly-wise manner. An outspoken nationalist with three sons fighting in the war, Hauptmann was burning with enthusiasm for the conflict: "Nothing is as ugly as an unventilated room. The people are renewed, become stronger," he declared.[31] Alma was beguiled.

But when she was alone with Gucki in Breitenstein, she was overcome by weariness and the hopeless feeling that she had "forever lost the possibility of happiness."[32] She was "full of fear in the world—with no man's hand in mine—anchor of my life . . . hopelessly stranded."[33] Gropius, her new hope for love, was away, fighting on the front line, stationed between Nancy and Épinal on the Upper Mosel. On March 12, 1915, he was on a reconnaissance trip to locate the enemy when he stood up to purposely attract enemy fire. Miraculously he avoided being shot and was awarded the Bavarian Cross First Class for bravery. It was only "his good fortune," he told his mother, "that all the bullets in this war had gone around me. One is in my fur hat, one is in the soles of my boot, one through the right side of my coat, another through the left and—the grenade."[34]

For long periods, Alma's only contact with him was by letters. Often she attributed their irregularity to his absence of affection rather than the consequence of war. "Dark thoughts" crowded in: "W.G. does not love me—he only thinks he does," she decided in April.[35] When she heard nothing from him for a fortnight she was "ill with longing. . . . I know what is wrong with me. I love W.G."[36]

Separated from him, living alone in times of such uncertainty, her feelings toward Gropius oscillated wildly. A blunt, angry letter from him on April 8 left her deeply agitated, hurt, and then furious: "More and more I feel this person is not what my life is all about. His jealousy of O.K. is boundless! That much Aryan thoughtlessness could be bearable if paired with genius; but paired with philistinism, there is no justification for it."[37] To console herself, she spent a "completely independent, happy evening FULL of music," and railed, "What do I need with these masculine pests???? And if ever, then not such a vain, empty creature as this W.G."[38] She summoned a steely resolve: "I am wounded, and I want to become independent of him. Yes, I will soon succeed." But she added wanly, "Where then is my joy? I am *already* SO alone!"[39] For Alma's greatest fear was a vacuum of love.

Within a week, however, she had recovered: "Glorious Night! Glorious morning! Without terror! Without threat! Without the horrendous vacuum because that is the *most terrifying*! I love Walter."[40] But at Franzenbad spa in June, she was again in turmoil, wandering around "like my own ghost. . . . He is certainly kind to me, but he is just tepid, and I am hot—that will never work. . . . If he loves me enough, he will win me over! If he doesn't love me enough then I will continue to hurry along my sunny, dusty, shadowless path."[41]

She wooed him again with renewed determination when she thought she might be pregnant: "I am with you—not a second away from you. I am walking around with a *single* idea—if only it might have happened now. I am trembling at our wild passion—which perhaps was depravity, but which was so *divinely* beautiful."[42] She soon realized that she was not pregnant, but in letters full of longing she now pressed him to marry her. "If you get leave I will come to where we can most quickly meet up and I can bring my papers and we can get married without a soul knowing about it. . . . I will remain your wife incognito until you return and can give me your protection." She signed herself as "AlmaMGropius. AMaria Gropius."[43] But when she got no immediate response, gloom and confusion descended once again: "I don't understand anything anymore. I am lying in bed, crying, and Gucki is bewildered. She has no idea what to make of this. This child is my blessing."[44]

Her mood was not helped by Walter's mother's attitude toward her. When Manon Gropius heard rumors that her son intended to marry

Alma—an older woman, a widow with a child, recently involved in an immoral affair with a scandalous painter—she was shocked.[45] But her response only amplified the already existing differences between mother and son—a generational divide that sometimes appeared unbridgeable. Walter rejected outright his mother's bourgeois views: "Do you see that I have in my *young* life tried to sincerely test the accepted views which today lie partially fossilised and dead in you, and discarded things that are outmoded and short-sighted . . . to make them compatible with the present day life, which is the only one that counts," he protested, as he vowed to pursue his own life and unique artistic vision. "I follow my beliefs and seek pure actions and it hurts *bitterly* that my mother does not recognise this." Had she wanted to understand him, he declared, his devotion to Alma—"this woman full of inner freedom"—would not have shocked her as it did.[46]

Manon Gropius remained implacably opposed. When Walter took Alma to meet her in Berlin, it was a disaster: "The embattled days we lived through with you and Frau M came over me like a hurricane and left me bent over and completely exhausted," Manon wrote.[47] Alma did not take at all kindly to Manon Gropius's disapproval. She shared Walter's disdain for her bourgeois values and found the barriers between them insurmountable.

Alma's uncertainties about Gropius were at last resolved when they agreed to get married. No family members were present at the ceremony on August 18 in a Berlin registry office, and it was witnessed by two passersby plucked from the street, a twenty-eight-year-old stonemason and a twenty-one-year-old army pioneer. "Yesterday I married. I've *landed*—" she wrote in her diary. "Nothing shall deflect me from my course—My will is pure and clear, I want nothing other than to make this noble human being happy! I am free, calm, excited, blessed—like never before. *God preserve my love for him!*"[48] Both Alma and Gropius had agreed it should be secret. When Manon Gropius discovered and objected that it was both ill mannered and dishonorable, Walter countered, "We see the conventions as a necessary evil, even a great evil, not as a joy. Try to understand, for the sake of your and our happiness."[49]

Two days later, Walter returned to the front where he would remain for several months. "I am alone—I am hopelessly in love with him. Golden days lie behind me. I feel free and happy and I am married," she mused on the train back to Vienna. "It is surely the strangest marriage that one can imagine. SO married, so free and yet so tied down. Nobody appeals to me. I almost prefer women at the moment because at least they are not so aggressive. But FINALLY I would like to reach my haven."[50]

Relations with her mother-in-law were still strained. "What should I do? I seem to come from the Circus—as it is so foreign to me. . . . She is very overbearing and I am . . . of too passionate a nature—because everything about her appears rather too narrow," she wrote to Walter in September, though she advised him to continue his "well-mannered" letters to her, to restore their good relationship and to "*Be a complete son!*"[51] But when she learned that Manon Gropius had asserted her superior social position because her husband was a privy councilor, Alma's patience snapped. Summoning her own profound sense of innate superiority she retorted:

> Tell her for a start that the gates of the whole world which are open to the name Mahler slam shut before the completely unknown name Gropius. Has not she ever given one thought to what I have given up for this? . . . I know what you are and what you are to me, but for the world you are a blank sheet. . . . It might perhaps be high time to let her know there are tens of thousands of privy councillors walking around—but there has only been one Gustav Mahler, and there is only one—Alma. Your letter has annoyed me even more than that of your mother.[52]

Though eventually Alma and Manon came to an awkward truce, it was some time before either became reconciled to the "foreignness" of the other.

The marriage remained secret in Vienna, where Alma continued to receive visitors in the red salon of her Elizabethstrasse apartment. But the long periods without her husband heightened her emotional volatility and her irritability: "I hate the war! Dear God—let the war be over soon! I can't take it anymore," she raged to Gropius.[53] Her letters described the trivia of daily life, the hardships suffered on the home front, her social activities, her increasing longing for him: "My faith in your strength is endless. . . . Beloved Walter, *when* will you walk around *here*—to consecrate my rooms for eternity."[54] She was not reticent to express her vivid erotic longing for him—"for those outrageous things—I'd like to surround you like an octopus and suck you in—drain you dry, my love. . . . Pour your sweet stream into me. I am languishing," she wrote.[55]

> The first time we see each other again, I shall sink down on the ground before you, remain on my knees, and, kneeling, beg you to take your sacred appendage in your hands and place it in my mouth, and then I will use all the finesse, all the refinement I have learned with you to give you a raging [illegible]. . . . Then you will go wild, clutch me in your arms and with all tenderness lay me down on the bed, which is as wide as the two of us are long—there are flowers in the room, and candles burn, and you will lay me down and afflict me with hideous tortures, because you always make me wait—until I burst into tears and implore you! Please!!

She asked him to tell her his erotic fantasies, for "You help me—no, us, when you meet my flaming sensuality halfway." And she suggested, "If this letter tempts you to touch your sweet appendage with your illustrious hand then at least send me the part of it that belongs to me, and I will put it into myself—this way it won't be lost."[56]

Sometimes her impatience and volatility overcame her. She needed constant reassurance of his fidelity. After five days without a letter, she exploded, "If you are cheating on me—then I'll do it, too—mark my words!—and I always find people! It's just that lately I haven't felt like it."[57] When he inquired about some reconstruction work at her Breitenstein house, she flew into a disproportionate rage. And though she was angry when she thought he had forgotten her thirty-sixth birthday, she was "mad with joy" when an onyx necklace arrived—"just when Gretel C[oudenhove]. and Baroness v Therlitz were here. And both were consumed by jealousy."[58]

At Christmas they spent an idyllic three days together in Vienna: "I was so spoiled by being enclosed in such warmth and sensitivity that I really don't know how I have deserved such love and joy," Walter told his mother. His one desire was to satisfy Alma, who "in her perpetual longing for perfection will make the most of me."[59] Alma greeted the New Year with the hope "that I will be BLESSED, our hours of love extended for months."[60] At the beginning of February 1916, Alma knew she was pregnant.

In Vienna her social life flourished. Though she tried to put Walter first, she was still susceptible to the charms of talented and adoring men. The thirty-seven-year-old poet Albert von Trentini visited her, she reported in February 1916, and, when they discussed his book, "he fell on one knee before me, laid his head in my lap and wept. He said: 'Since I have known you, I have every time exactly the same feeling. When I look at you tears rise in my eyes.'" Alma felt that "something like holiness floats round him. I feel happy in his presence, beside him."[61] She had gained "much, much joy through this man. And a PURE joy," she confessed after he had left for the battlefield. She was concerned that Walter had faded within her during this interlude but was relieved when her feelings for him returned. Even so, she missed Trentini: "A life, *without* men to live for is for me more impossible than for other people, because I live so intensely in the present," she decided.[62]

Alma settled into her pregnancy with only occasional outbursts against the war and the mounting deprivations on the home front. Summer was for Alma a period of calm during "this WONDERFUL time of pregnancy. . . . Love gives meaning to everything." She was "longing for the birth. It will give me new insight. It must introduce once again a new, incredible, overwhelming moment of ecstasy into my life."[63] Alma's relations with her mother-in-law eased when Manon visited her in Breitenstein in June. "We have grown very close. Yes—even more. I have grown fond of her. Her company is extraordinarily soothing,"[64] Alma told Walter. Manon reported to him that she now thought he had found "a treasure," and an "unusual and spiritually rich human being." Her "habit of being over-indulged" worried her, but Alma was "amiable and very gifted," and her music was "splendid, but also overpowering." She seemed to Manon to be "continually shimmering in a new light, outwardly and inwardly. I have never seen anyone with so manifold a personality."[65]

When she was alone in Breitenstein, Alma took more pleasure in the company of her women neighbors. Lilly Lieser had a house nearby; Nora Traskowitsch, "the most beautiful woman I know . . . only beautiful because she was so full of spirit" visited; and her old friend Gretl Coudenhove came "ever closer to my heart. Her warmth is incomparable."[66] Her closest friend, Helene Berg, visited with her husband, Alban: "difficult people, oversensitive, self-sacrificing to the nth degree, and both so beautiful!" Helene, "a creature of seraphic loveliness, inside and out," was the illegitimate daughter of Emperor Franz Joseph and Anna Nahowski, a woman fifty years his junior, whom he had met by chance in a park.

Over everything, the war cast a darkening shadow: "Humankind is holding its breath—because of fear of what is to come. What is STILL ahead of us all??" Alma wrote in 1916.[67] She rejected Walter's suggestion that she move to Berlin—for what could she do alone among strangers?—and decided "I must surround myself with cheerfulness for a bit."[68] In Vienna, despite the war, distinguished visitors continued to flow through her red salon at Elizabethstrasse: Klimt and her friends Duchess Coudenhove and the Wydenbrucks joined the charmed circle drawn from all sectors of society who gathered round her.

The conversation was always lively and thoughtful and wide ranging. After one stimulating evening with a publisher, a composer, and a professor, Alma was prompted to reflect on the nature of creative artists: "The more eminent artists are as human beings the greater is their art, but they are measured with a different yardstick, their world is a world created by them, they can't uproot out of their world into reality," she concluded. "That's why such human beings are so rough and without understanding in their relationship to women. They don't SEE the person opposite them. Not to mention feelings. The woman will always be short-changed next to an influential artist. He experiences himself, as does she, only as the instrument through which he can establish and realise *his* thirst for dominance."[69]

When Alma was due to go into labor in September, Gropius got two weeks special leave from the front at Nancy. But he was disappointed; the child was overdue: "I have been waiting for my child for fourteen days now," Alma wrote on September 19. "Walter visited and he has left again—sad and lonely: he and I. I had longed to put his child into his arms. Alas. . . . I am waiting—waiting—and hoping."[70] Back at the front, Walter was anxious: "We don't understand what is happening. This child seems to have no urge to enter this world which has become so mad," he wrote to his mother.[71]

Finally, on October 5, 1916, Alma gave birth to "a new, sweet girl," accompanied by "the most horrific pain—but now that she is here, I am happy. I am IN LOVE with this human being!" she wrote. "A different, new, calmer life is ahead of me."[72] At the front, Gropius greeted the news of his daughter's birth with joy and frustration: "Now my child has really arrived in this world. I cannot see it, I cannot hear it, only a short tele-gram, announcing the birth 'after difficult preliminaries.' I cannot rejoice until I know how she is."[73] He managed to get two days leave and was "enraptured by the child—our sun" who had "constantly changing, beau-tiful, intelligent large eyes which already look knowingly at the world, and hands with long, thin, aristocratic fingers."[74] But Alma was "frighten-ing" in her defense of her "maternal responsibilities" and behaved "like a tigress. I refused to let him approach her. . . . Only after a long pleading did I allow him to glance at her from a distance." Later Alma justified her strange behavior: "I would not let him share possession of the child because my fears had come true—because my feelings for him had given way to a tired twilight relationship."[75] It was becoming steadily clearer to Alma that she could not sustain a marriage at long distance.

Living alone and nursing a child under the strained conditions of war, she now feared for her future with Gropius: "He is at the front—we have been married well over a year and we do not *have* each other, and sometimes I am afraid that we will become strangers to each other. Soon I shall be fed up with LIVING IN THE FUTURE. Everything is provisional!" But she resolved to go on because she was sure she still loved Walter, and she did not want to lose him.[76]

Gropius got leave for Christmas 1916 in Vienna. Manon Alma Gro-pius was baptized into the Protestant Church on Christmas Day with masses of white lilies, candles on stands, and the Christmas tree. Walter's mother had been unable to get there because of travel restrictions, but Alma sent a New Year message to "my dearest Mama Gropius," thanking her for her gifts and for the "joy you have given me! . . . that after all you are a little fond of me."[77] To celebrate Manon's birth, Walter gave Alma a painting, *Summer Night at the Beach,* by Norwegian painter Ed-vard Munch.

Manon became Alma's saving grace. In early 1917, Alma was unwell; her weak heart was causing concern. But whenever she feared she was sliding into depression, a glance at Manon reminded her that she was "still necessary." The child delighted her: "The sweet child. No-one can know how I love this creature. I am in love with all my senses. I want all day to kiss her hands and her feet, to kiss her tiny mouth—I hardly dare."[78] Thirteen-year-old Anna needed her no more, Alma decided, for "she is wise," but Anna still intrigued her. "Yesterday evening she lay with me in bed. 'It's strange . . . how differently you and I see nature—you on a much larger scale, and I in more in detail,'" she said to Alma. "'We feel music differently too. You remember what you HEAR, I what I SEE' . . . : This went on ad infinitum. 'It's why I prefer blue, and you red. It's why I love Lao-tse, and you—?' And so it goes on. And she is 13 years old. But I love her so much, although she often seems very alien, and will become even more so."[79]

THE WAR DRAGGED on with no end in sight. One ray of hope for Alma, the proposals for peace put forward to the Allies by the Austrian foreign minister Count Ottokar Czernin, had come to nothing. In mid-November, Alma was feeling wretched and ill. Alone in wartime with two children and an absent husband, she was running two houses, one in Vienna and the other in Breitenstein. Food shortages were by then acute. With the Allied blockade, failed harvests, and any available food supplies diverted to the troops, malnutrition and starvation were widespread throughout Europe. "We had hardly anything to eat during the war," Anna remembered. "Our cook—her name was Agnes—used to prepare a kind of *ersatz* meat for us, a concoction of mushrooms and tree bark, with polenta and potatoes on the side. That was more or less it."[80] Preoccupied with domestic affairs, Alma began to fear that the drudgery of the housewife, "which makes you stupid and mean," was taking her over: "I am starting to worry about the affairs of dusters—that should not be."[81] Then, fear of human beings beset her—"I send visitors away and then get upset when I am lonely." She had, she decided, in a burst of self-recrimination, "no right to live as a parasite on the feelings of humankind. The only person that has a right to live is the one that lives in the external world—not a tired, weak person. . . . Such a human being—as I currently feel myself to be, should disappear out of shame and a sense of probity. But I continue to vegetate."[82]

Above all, hope in her marriage had faded. "The brief healing I had experienced through Walter is now vanishing because of this constant solitude: in fact being separated from him has now reached the point where I can almost no longer imagine a life together with him. I am irritated—everything upsets me—very sad. I really need some great joy!"[83]

Her mood lifted only when her social life became "beautiful and rich again." Paul Kammerer turned up, Josef Strzygowski spent an evening with her, and on November 14 she visited Helene von Nostitz, the wife of the Saxon envoy, who was in mourning for the tragic death of her young son. When Alma returned, she found that a new acquaintance, Franz Blei, was waiting for her. With him was twenty-seven-year-old poet Franz Werfel—"and with this I gave my destiny a new direction," she wrote.[84]

Franz Blei had joined her social circle that autumn. Though initially deterred by the reputation of "this dubious individual," she soon fell for the charm of the essayist, playwright, critic, publisher of literary journals, and friend of Franz Kafka. He became a regular visitor. His knowledge was vast and his intellect so wide ranging that "everybody got cross with him." When Klimt, "who finds words difficult," colluded with Alma to discuss at supper a topic of which Blei knew nothing, they decided on botany: "But lo! Blei opened a special box in his brain and out of it rolled a number of names and terms which were foreign to us and which silenced us. That's always how it was. He took control of every discussion. But finally he got tired of his own shimmering brilliance. He felt that he started to bore us."[85]

Alma knew of Franz Werfel. His poems had "already touched her." In 1915, while Gropius was in a shop buying leather boots for the front, she had found outside on a book peddler's cart a copy of Werfel's poem *Der Erkennende*. "[It] engulfed me . . . one of the loveliest I have ever known in my experience," she recalled. "I was spellbound, a prey to the soul of Franz Werfel."[86] She was so inspired that, in a rare return to composition, she instantly set the poem to music.

When they met in November 1917, Werfel had recently been transferred from active service on the Russian front to the Military Press Bureau, where he wrote newspaper propaganda articles alongside such literary luminaries as Robert Musil, Rainer Maria Rilke, and Hugo von Hoffmannstahl. An admirer of Mahler with an intense interest in music, Werfel had anticipated the afternoon with excitement. Alma's first impression was of the young man spouting "some terrible social democratic jargon," but, during the evening, "he became greater, freer, and more pure." She noted, "Werfel is a stocky, bow-legged somewhat fat Jew with sensuous, bulging lips and slit, watery eyes! But he wins you over, the more he gives of himself. His extraordinary love for mankind and his words—such as 'how can I be happy—if somewhere a human being is suffering' (which word for word I have heard from an egocentric—namely Gustav Mahler)." Alma was intrigued: "It immediately felt as if he was at home in my house." And the encounter enthused her: "It is wonderful to always have contact with intellects, how joyous for me to be touched by them. I thank God on my KNEES. IF ONLY THIS WILL BE PRESERVED FOR ME. ONLY THIS!"[87]

As Alma saw more of Franz Werfel, it began to dawn on her that she might, after all, have found her haven.

— 10 —

Intertwined Souls

1917–1920

*F*ranz Werfel became a regular visitor at Elizabethstrasse. At twenty-seven, he was already seen as one of the foremost young writers of the age. His ideas intrigued Alma, he sang with a heavenly tenor voice, and he recited his poems with spellbinding fervor. As his friend, writer and journalist Max Brod, wrote, "He knew all his poems by heart. He spoke them from memory, without falter or mistake, with fire, and a throbbing, intense or triumphant voice, whichever was appropriate—now loud, now soft but always very rich, varied modulations. And he wouldn't stop. I've never heard anything like it. I was captivated."[1]

A pioneer of expressionism, Werfel spoke with deep humanity and simplicity to the anxieties of a younger generation disillusioned with materialism, hypocrisy, and corruption, and with conventions that stifled the human heart and the purity of truth. Brod had championed Werfel since first reading his poems—"none of which was futile, none full of the meaningless phrases common to all the poetry that beginners usually brought me. Everything moved in a new light."[2] Brod's friend Franz Kafka had thought he was "going off his head with enthusiasm" for Werfel's "tremendous ability."[3]

Born in 1890 into the German-speaking Jewish minority in Prague, Werfel was the eldest son of a wealthy, self-made glove manufacturer. Though a poor scholar, Franz took an intense interest from an early age in theater and music. A visit to Prague by the charismatic operatic tenor Enrico Caruso opened his eyes to opera; he learned Verdi and Donizetti arias by heart and performed them impromptu at many a social occasion. By his midteens he was reading voraciously and writing a poem each day, as well as dialogue for the plays he performed with his sisters and friends.

Instead of academic study, Werfel passed his time in the coffee houses and nightspots of Prague with his friends Willy Haas, Paul Kornfield, Ernst Deutsch, Franz Janowitz, and Ernst Popper—all former classmates at the Catholic Piarist monastery school to which Jewish boys were sent, then later at the Stefansgymnasium. They too wrote poetry, prose, and plays; read their works to each other; discussed literature, philosophy, and politics at the Cafe Arco; and spent their evenings at beer halls, nightclubs, or the then-popular séances. In 1908, Werfel's first poem was published in the Vienna daily paper *Die Zeit*; it attracted enthusiastic support from Brod and Kafka.

His father, Rudolf Werfel, was appalled at his son's failure to prepare for a solid profession, and so Franz was dispatched to the family glove factory in Hamburg as an intern. At this he failed miserably. He continued to write, and in 1911 the influential critic Karl Kraus published several of Werfel's poems in his magazine, *Die Fackel*. He was exiled once again from his literary cafes and beer halls when he was called up for a year's military training. But, with Max Brod's support, a collected edition of his poems, *Friend of the World*, was published. It sold out immediately.

When his military service came to an end, he was rescued from a return to the glove factory by Kurt Wolff, who employed him as an editor in his Leipzig publishing house. With hair combed straight back but "looking remarkably dishevelled at all times," Werfel was soon associating with his fellow poets and thinkers at Wilhelm's wine cellar or Cafe Felsche and visiting the city's theater, bars, and cabarets. He became known, according to his biographer, Peter Stephan Jungk, "as an extremely unreliable and forgetful person who often misplaced important things and was apt to burst into Verdi arias or recitation of his own poems, a dreamy visionary who adored beautiful women." Werfel began to read his poems in public, and in private he and his friends, including Franz Kafka, read their latest works to each other.[4] His second volume of poems, *We Are*, was published in the spring of 1913 and earned praise from Rainer Maria Rilke, the poet whom Werfel revered as a saint.

When war broke out in July 1914, Werfel was immediately called up. He returned to Prague but managed to get himself declared unfit for active military duty for almost two years by feigning either physical illness or nervous instability. Meanwhile, he continued to write. In 1915 he met surgical nurse Gertrud Spirk; they became lovers. Eventually in early 1916 he ran out of excuses to avoid the front, was declared fit for combat duty, and was sent with the Nineteenth Heavy Field Artillery Regiment to the Russian front, where he served as a telephone operator and dispatch rider at regimental headquarters. He soon found a peasant's house to rent and managed to write daily, read widely, and keep up correspondence with his literary circle, even though he was interrupted by somewhat irksome telephone operator duties: "When I have to work, I am in such a foul mood that I have become the holy *telephone terror* of this entire sector. I don't believe the most hysterical lady operator in Prague is my match in delivering threats, insults and libellous remarks."[5]

In the middle of a great artillery battle in June 1917, he was suddenly transferred to the Military Press Bureau in Prague, assigned to do a lecture tour of Switzerland. By August he was writing regular newspaper articles with uplifting stories from the front, while spending days, and often nights, with literary companions at the Café Central—a high-ceilinged space, dimly lit and filled with cigarette smoke. Meanwhile, he assigned to Gertrud Spirk the role of savior, declared his longing for purity, rigor, and discipline, and beseeched her to save him from "the atmosphere of corruption" into which he had fallen since his return to Vienna.[6] But, when she visited him after a long absence, they found their passion had drained: "I must live through this period of moral crisis in which a new man beats against my old grimaces, struggling to be born," he explained. "You mustn't think that I am changing in regard to you."[7]

FRANZ WERFEL HAD just been assigned by the bureau to a trip to Italy when he met Alma Mahler. "It was really wonderful. . . . I learned much about Gustav Mahler—and sensed that he had all my conflicts," Werfel enthused to Gertrud Spirk. "They were interesting hours; she is tremendously warm and alive, a woman of quality."[8] He departed almost immediately on his assignment, but on his return his visits became more frequent. Alma enjoyed his company and even fleetingly considered that

Figure 15. Alma Mahler and Franz Werfel, 1919.
"We were in tune immediately."

he might be a suitor for her daughter: "Werfel pleases me. I'd like him to be a husband for Gucki. He is one of the finest minds I know—and so free and sophisticated. A great artist!"[9]

Alma's life acquired a new tone: "Joy—joy—and why—I do not understand it?!" she wrote after she had confided to Lilly Lieser the possibility of a new love.[10] "Many wonderful things are happening. There was one night—one divine night—Werfel, Blei! We CELEBRATED music, Walter was there. *Louise, Meistersinger* etc. Werfel recited a few of his poems, above all *Der Feind* [*The Enemy*]. This man is a wondrous miracle!"[11] Much later, embroidering with hindsight, Alma recalled, "The evening on which Werfel and I played music together for the first time and we were so in tune immediately through our very own medium that we forgot everything around us and in front of the eyes of the husband committed spiritual adultery." Gropius appears to have discerned no threat from Alma's young acquaintance but enjoyed the company of Blei, Werfel, and the other guests.

When Gropius arrived on leave from the western front for Christmas 1917, Alma's feelings toward him had changed irrevocably. The separation had become unbearable. The possibility of a new love with Werfel breached the bonds entirely. To Alma, Gropius seemed "reduced by the war and even quieter than usual and everything about him irritated me. . . . His stiffness which I previously liked as a contrast with me, how it displeased me now!"[12] When he spoke, she "was ashamed of him." When Blei and Werfel stayed the night during a snowstorm, Alma "returned to the bedroom of my husband with strange feelings. . . . I felt degraded with him and by him during this night."[13]

She had been longing for the hour of his departure, and when on December 30 it came, and Gropius hurried down the stairs, she forced herself to give him her "best possible smile in order to help him with the difficult farewell"—even though "my heart was jubilant!"[14] That evening she was to attend a performance of Mahler's *Das Lied von der Erde* conducted by her old friend Willem Mengelberg.

But Gropius missed his train. When she heard the doorbell ringing loudly, Alma realized the truth about her feelings for Walter: "My face turned to ice. His return gave me complete understanding that my love for Walter Gropius had forever disappeared. Yes—even more my feelings were comparable to a bored hatred."[15]

She refused to let him come with her to the concert. At the meal afterward with her mother and stepfather, Carl Moll, and Gropius, "everything was quiet and subdued and nobody present completely understood the depth of the hopeless grief. At the end Gropius sobbed that he could never measure up to my past and did not have the strength to battle forever against it." Gropius left that evening; in a letter from the border, he exhorted her to "break the ice in your features." It was a line from a Werfel poem—"Even he was beholden to the higher human being," Alma commented.[16]

Gropius, too, had put up a façade to hide the corrosive effects of war on his spirit: "I am gradually crumbling to pieces, and the moment has come when I must make an effort not to lose everything," he wrote from leave to his friend Karl Ernst Osthaus. "I must get out for a little time and do a little work, otherwise I shall collapse as an artist and be completely forgotten."[17] From the western front—"this grey world"—he wrote to his mother on January 7, 1918, "I can hardly bear [it] any longer. My spirits are totally starved and my nerves are getting worse."[18]

His anguish was translated into fury against those commonly perceived as scapegoats for the stalemate in the war—the traitors on the home front who stabbed the army in the back: "However hard and heroically we fight the weaklings and swine at home destroy our efforts and everything we have accomplished," he wrote to his mother. "The Jews, this destructive poison, which I hate more and more, are ruining us. Social democracy, materialism, capitalism, profiteering, all their creation and it is our fault that they have been able to corrode our lives so much. They are the devil in the world, the negative element of the world."[19] For Gropius, according to his biographer, this was a single isolated outburst born of his despair about the war and the future, and it never was repeated. But it was a potent theme of anti-Semitism resonant at the time, which later fertilized the ground in which National Socialism grew, though Gropius was never associated with it; indeed, he was ostracized by the Nazi regime.

After Gropius left, Alma resumed her life. After a glamorous New Year's Eve party at the Hotel Bristol, she gave a grand reception on New Year's Day in honor of Mahler's great supporter Willem Mengelberg, which was attended by the literary, musical, and intellectual elite of Vienna: Alban Berg, Franz Schreker, Julius Bittner, banker Paul Hammerschlag, painter Johannes Itten, music critic Ludwig Karpath, Lilly Lieser, Countess Wydenbruck, Gretl Coudenhov, Franz Blei, and, of course, Franz Werfel. The evening "was really a great success," Alma decided, but her greatest moments of happiness had been "when I was able to speak to Werfel unnoticed. Because this was the most WONDERFUL! I have to hold on tight to my heart . . . otherwise it will fly away."[20]

On January 4, at a performance of Mahler's Fourth Symphony conducted by Mengelberg, Alma's feelings soared as, from her box, she exchanged sensuous glances with Werfel. They left discreetly at the intermission: "Our eloquent silence took us to the edge. It happened as it had to, he took my hand and kissed it, then our lips found each other and he stammered words without sense or meaning, and yet those words were so absolutely true." She enthused, "I love my life. I CAN not feel regret. My deep spiritual connection with Werfel—IT HAD TO BE that I love him. The last days made complete by Gustav Mahler's music and Mengelberg—AND love—love!"[21]

Later she reflected on her first embrace by "MY MAN": "The men I had chosen in my life had never aroused my real [erotic] woman-hood. . . . Franz Werfel embraced me that first time and immediately I KNEW—HERE is my joy. . . . [E]very one of my cells anticipated him fever-ishly." Their first days together were "incredibly beautiful": "We loved each other on and off, day and night. We never tired. It was difficult to be ourselves in front of other people. Actually we were always absorbed in each other even in front of others. And our music. With our minds and our music, we are one! It must come, as it came."[22] Now, "the music I make with him has become the air I breathe."[23]

Within a fortnight, Werfel was summoned back by the Press Bureau for a lecture tour in Switzerland. He went via Prague, where he began to disentangle himself from Gertrud. To Alma he wrote ecstatically, "Homesickness, ceaseless homesickness on this entire trip, I yearn end-lessly for your letters, for the touch of you—Alma, Alma Alma Mahler, mysterious being who has revealed herself to me through music . . . you who gives me life, keeper of the flame!!!"[24] Already Franz Werfel saw in her his muse and his strength: "I am longing for you. . . . I believe you can help me because you are strong, because you want a lot from me. I am so homesick."[25] And in February: "You have to help me MORALLY. Build a wall around me. Through other humans and my own inclination I have become a pale ghost.—When I am with you I am whole."[26]

By then, Alma knew she was pregnant, though she was unsure who was the father—whether Gropius in December or Werfel in January. But she was sure of her love for Werfel: "This wonderful human being! This entirely true human being," she wrote. "I love Werfel and want the best for him. If only I had the strength to show him all the beauty of a pure existence. I feel NO REGRET! I must BURN my own path. . . . This bourgeois existence KILLS ME. Only now am I living truly according to my heart. May God please preserve THIS LIFE."[27]

Werfel returned in March. He had been recalled from his lecture tour when news of several speeches with anti-capitalist, anti-militarist con-tent reached the bureau. "Speculation is rife whether he has been hanged or beheaded on his return to Vienna," Berta Zuckerkandl reported in her diary. In Zurich, Werfel had lectured to young workers and tried "to state his pacifist faith in a not too tempestuous form; after this debut the relations between him and the Vienna Authorities were broken off."[28] In Vienna Werfel resumed his regular visits to Elizabethstrasse: "Werfel and I continued living in rapture and had very little care for the growing fruit inside me. We lived fully, intoxicated and regrettably without care," Alma wrote.[29]

Despite their uncomfortable Christmas, Alma had continued to write regularly to Walter. After a brief spell on the Italian front training Austrians in communication, he was now on the western front at Soissons. News of Alma's pregnancy (even though Alma gave no hint that it might not be his child) failed to lift his desolate spirits: "I cannot find joy in Alma's new condition. The circumstances of life are so comfortless, and I am afraid of what is to come," he told his mother.[30] Alma, too, confided to Manon: "I am as desperate now as I was happy the first time. The precarious situation we are all in—Walter's insecurity,—travelling difficulties— continually increasing problems with food—Walter's increasing inability to help me—in short—I am very depressed . . . , black clouds hang over us."[31] In a possible hint at her changed feelings, she added, "This eternal war and its upsets, and the fact that Walter is not with me forces me to think only of myself. That is sad for both of us."[32]

Alma maintained the outward façade of her marriage, and in June she left with Anna and Manon for Breitenstein. Gropius was then in a field hospital, recovering for the third time in the war from severe wounds, received when a direct hit from a grenade on the building his troops were occupying killed everyone except him. Buried for several days under rubble from the collapsed roof, he was spared suffocation because he was next to an air vent. In the hospital after his rescue he wrote to his mother praising Alma, who "does everything with foresight and clarity. . . . She is constantly responsible. You can scarcely imagine what it means to bring a child into this world now and the care for the household is immensely increased by the addition of such a tiny creature, and there is no support. It is a sad fate, to sacrifice for an ever more dubious patriotic ideal profession, money, family life—actually everything. If Alma were not so full of nobility towards me I could no longer stand the passive condition to which I am condemned."[33]

In fact, in Breitenstein Alma was only just managing to get by: "My little household was reduced almost to a minimum. . . . I had to work hard physically to be able to manage everything. With scarcely any food we scrabbled about for a meagre existence . . . the farmers who only knew me a little . . . gave us nothing—so we lived on old seed potatoes, polenta, meat substitute and mushrooms which Anna found in the woods."[34] But, even so, she felt contentment: "Soon I will give birth to my child—what change. Everything has renewed itself within me. I live, I love endlessly."[35]

At the end of July, Werfel visited Alma at Breitenstein. She had a guest, Emmy Redlich, the wife of a wealthy sugar manufacturer "to whom I was in some way indebted." After an evening of music during which Alma played the entire second movement of Mahler's Eighth Symphony and Emmy Redlich insisted on a long conversation about Mahler, Werfel was eventually able to join Alma in her room: "Under the moonlight we talked . . . and made love and I forgot all my tiredness and my worries," Alma recalled.[36] "We made love! I did not go easy on her. In the small hours I returned to my room," Werfel wrote.[37] Alma described what happened next: "He left and I remained standing and suddenly in the moonlight I saw black liquid running down my legs—a big black mark formed on the carpet. I turned on the light with shaking hands and saw that I was standing in a pool of blood."[38] She roused the household.

Werfel was dispatched to get the doctor. He ran through the fields praying, "Let Alma live," vowed never to desire any woman other than Alma, and then lost his way in a marsh. Anna too had rushed out to telegraph Gropius. Werfel returned eventually with the local doctor, who wanted to operate there and then and not risk moving Alma. She took one look at this man with "his butcher's hands" who wanted "to undertake one of the most difficult operations by candlelight" and forbade him to touch her. Alma and Werfel agreed that Werfel should leave. When he insisted that he must bear the entire guilt for the misfortune, Alma brushed him away—"I'm just as guilty. Anyway what is guilt? I don't know that word."

As Werfel stood on the station platform waiting to leave, he saw Gropius step off an unscheduled military train. Gropius had been woken up and told to go immediately to Semmering and had caught the next train. On his arrival he sent for the eminent Professor Joseph Halban, who ordered Alma's immediate transfer to Vienna, first with her head down in a car stuffed with mattresses, and then by rail in an empty cattle wagon, finally in a hearse with Gropius and the doctor with a salt infusion holding vigil beside her.

The child was induced straight away in the sanatorium and born at seven months on August 2: "When I finally heard the first sweet cry of the child I thought I was in a dream. The child appeared to be very small but capable of life. . . . I lived for this child for months," Alma wrote.[39] In the sanatorium, Gropius observed Alma "in amazement . . . such self-control, such ability to rise above problems, always thinking of others, not of herself. She has a great, splendid heart, and it is not by chance that people love her so; she deserves it."[40]

Meanwhile, Werfel, sick with anxiety, vowed his eternal fidelity as he despaired over his own shortcomings and waited for news. A telegram informed him that Alma had been taken to the sanatorium; when he telephoned, Walter Gropius answered with news of the birth of a boy. Eight days after Werfel's departure from Breitenstein, Alma waited "feverishly" for his first visit: "The door opened and at the same time through the window a terrible grieving music was heard from some funeral. . . . We remained standing as if frozen and did not dare to go to the cradle in which Werfel's son was lying with his small fists clenched."[41] When he saw the child's face, he immediately recognized his own features—and those of his father. He visited often and wrote daily paeans of praise: "You holy mother! You are the most magnificent, the strongest, the most mystical, most goddess-like I have ever encountered in all my life. At every moment, in every test of life, you are perfection."[42] His powerful feelings for her were crystal clear: "She gets her insight from sibylline core, by leaps of instinctive association that are pure genius. She is one of the very few magical women there are. She lives in a light magic that contains much will to destroy, much urge to subjugate, but it is all cloudy and moist," he wrote in his diary.[43]

Once, as he stood beside Gropius in the hospital room, "the *deep poignancy* of the situation made me tremble." Werfel was overcome with guilt that a man he considered "the most distinguished and noble of men" was "living in ignorance."[44] But they did nothing to change it. Alma now signed off her daily letters to him as "Alma Maria Werfel." Though she continued to behave with Gropius as his wife, she found it increasingly difficult: "Poor W[alter] is suffering terribly. He feels that every word he utters gets on my nerves, doesn't understand why I am so cold and has no idea what to do. But I can't simulate something I don't feel—just can't. He knows I don't love him any more. He is racking his brains over how he might change things—I'm at my wit's end."[45]

Three weeks later, on August 25, "when everything looked as if it was getting better," Alma was on the phone to Werfel when Gropius suddenly arrived through the door with a large bunch of flowers. "He overheard the 'du' and, full of foreboding, he asked me with whom I was having a conversation. When, unable to lie, I mentioned Werfel's name his legs buckled as if he was struck by lightning." It changed everything: "Up till now all battles had taken place behind a veil, now everything could be seen openly and unpleasantly revealed in the light of day. I was at his mercy, defenceless and was only concerned about the life of the child."[46] She decided "I will stay with Gropius—which my duty demands—but my heart belongs to Werfel."[47]

That afternoon Gropius went to Werfel's apartment, but he was asleep and did not hear him. Gropius left a card: "I am here to love her with all the strength at my command. Take care of Alma! The worst might happen. The distress—if the child should die on us!" The "very nobility" of "this somewhat posh" card unnerved Werfel: "The whole day and night I was having doubts whether my love was enough and whether I had the right to inflict such pain," he confided to his diary.[48] It was an eerie echo of the crisis eight years before, when her then lover Gropius had been torn between his respect for her husband, Mahler, and guilt that his actions had caused pain to a noble man.

The next day the two men met calmly. Gropius stressed to Werfel their joint duty to support Alma in her precarious condition, and a correspondence followed. Gropius had read Werfel's poems and was greatly moved by them: "I am getting progressively closer so you, so that the bad feeing will disappear," he wrote to Werfel from the front. "Through your stature and honesty you are winning me over more and more. . . . I know that we will be friends even if our souls must wrestle with each other." Gropius was convinced: "We will be healed through her love, you and I . . . our beings drawn together the more we love her."[49] Werfel told Alma, "I love him and feel friendship for him" and wondered whether it might be possible "that we do not have to be jealous? That there can be a brotherhood of love for the divine being Alma?"[50] Gropius shared this sentiment: he urged Werfel that they should each bury their own pain to protect Alma from distress and help her through her suffering. With a nobility acknowledged by both Werfel and Alma, he told them he would accept whatever decision she made.

At the beginning of September 1918, Gropius was called suddenly back to the front. The German offensive in the west had collapsed, and the army was in retreat. Gropius felt only bitter disillusion with the war: "I don't believe in our cause any longer; a dreadful awakening is coming," he told his mother in August. "I no longer feel sympathy with the cause. Others can now leap into the breach."[51] He endured several more months at the front until October, when he was released from military service on medical grounds. He returned to Berlin to rebuild his architecture practice, pursue his career—and decide on what the future held for his life with Alma and the children.

Alma had still not decided between Werfel and Gropius. As so often, her feelings for Werfel vacillated wildly. At one point she ecstatically claimed to be "under the spell of his wondrous magic. He is close to my spirit and feelings as if I was him myself. . . . His face has become unspeakably beautiful because of the concern he has for me and because of his own inner transformations. I see a shimmer and halo round his head."[52] She reflected, "How incredibly similar we are—he called it Panerotic. . . . How am I ever to cut myself off from this wonderful human being? I love him. I love him with utter peace of mind! He doesn't harass me to death like the others—he has a moving calm—like the sea. So unreliable—so rolling, swaying in all directions—to become how we BOTH are!"[53]

But when Gropius very deliberately took her to see Werfel in the apartment he shared with Blei, she was shaken: "Werfel is a-moral without knowing it. . . . He lives in a shrine to shabbiness, the likes of which I have seldom seen. . . . I was paralysed by fear. The room shouted vice. . . . I felt that I had entered the room of the mistress of an art dealer."[54] After she left with Gropius, she asked herself, "Is THIS how it is going to be? I am sure I would not be able to live with such a lax man! . . . I know less than ever what to do." Even more confusion followed: "Today I committed a mortal sin. I took pity and made love with my husband without the slightest of feelings or arousal. I was lying with closed eyes and yearned like a mad woman for a REAL man—the father of my son, Franz Werfel." Gropius sensed her "deep distaste at his touch" and was "distraught"—"God please forgive me," she pleaded.[55]

In November, Gropius proposed to Alma that he take custody of Manon and that she, Alma, live with Werfel. Alma was furious and promptly announced that she had decided to "renounce BOTH of them and follow my path on my OWN." Gropius fell to his knees and begged her forgiveness. Werfel "spoke a few calm words—true, sincere words which calmed me down. How immeasurably free and wise this human being is. I WILL LOVE HIM BEYOND DEATH. His noble face was calm . . . because he KNEW that I could not let go of him. He was right. I know where my destiny lies."[56]

In November 1918, the war came to an end. Austria signed an armistice on November 3, followed a week later by the general armistice on November 11 between Germany and the Allies, which doomed the Austro-Hungarian Empire to extinction. Austria was reduced to a small rump of territory adjacent to the new republics of Hungary and Czechoslovakia and the now autonomous Balkan nations.

The Bolshevik Revolution in Russia, which overthrew the monarchy with the murder of Czar Nicholas II and his entire family and established a communist Soviet state, had taken Russia out of the war in November 1917. The success of the Russian Revolution encouraged the spread of radical left-wing ideologies throughout Europe. In Germany, civil unrest sparked by a sailor's revolt in November 1918 led to the nationwide proletarian revolution. Kaiser Wilhelm II abdicated the throne, and a republic was established.

Austria faced similar radical pressures. In Vienna, as the war reached its close, Werfel was actively involved with the newly formed Red Guard, which called for the overthrow of the monarchy and its replacement with a socialist republic. He made fiery public speeches and engaged in heated discussions with soldiers and workers. On November 12, Emperor Karl, who had succeeded Franz Joseph on his death in 1916, relinquished power. A huge crowd rushed into the Ringstrasse as the Republic of Austria was proclaimed by the Provisional National Assembly from the steps of the Parliament Building. At the announcement, Red Guards bearing red flags and demanding the establishment of a socialist republic surged toward the building. Shots were fired, and a riot ensued, which left two dead and forty injured. Several days of disturbance followed before order was restored.

Alma was a conservative and a monarchist. When by chance she had witnessed the last royal Trooping of the Colour, with uniformed soldiers parading in splendor before the emperor, she had sensed the tide of events and had wept alongside the other bystanders. On November 12, Alma observed "the proletariat's march to the Parliament" from her red salon at Elizabethstrasse: "red flags—ugly weather, the stupid rain!—everything grey and grey. Then there were shots from the parliament—*Attack!* The same orderly colourless row of human beings now stormed back, shouting and undignified." When she went out that night, she took the pistols she had acquired for her safety: "The street was full of *rowdies*—all young men under 20—with wild looking faces."[57]

The next day, the crowds gathered again. Werfel burst into Elizabethstrasse in an old uniform, looking "terrible," and begged Alma for her "blessing" before joining the crowds outside the Parliament: "He didn't want to leave until I had taken his head and kissed it." When he returned later that day from the riots, she was "horrified": "His eyes were swimming in red—his face was puffed up and filthy, his hands, his uniform all was destroyed. I sent him away—it was disgusting. I said to him: if you had done something beautiful then you would now look beautiful."[58] In a curious twist, when Werfel was being sought by the police, Gropius intervened with the authorities on his behalf and warned him in advance of raids on his apartment. Their journalist friend Berta Zuckerkandl publicly declared her support for "our greatest poet": "Werfel's human value must be upheld, for he is one of the morally untainted."[59]

Their very different reactions to these events was the curtain raiser to a lifelong disagreement over politics between the left-wing Werfel and the profoundly conservative Alma. On this occasion, Alma overcame her disapproval. In December, she enthused, "He is the only really great *true* happiness that I have experienced. . . . He is the be all and end all of my life."[60] She began to influence the direction of his work when she sent him away to write his new play, *The Mirror Man*, in "the tremendous peace of Breitenstein," which "will provoke him to a strong wave of production."[61] It would also isolate him from the influence of his "coffee-house rowdies," into whose absorbing company he had again returned.

Alma's main concern was now for her infant son, who had developed water on the brain. His head had swollen so alarmingly that it was necessary to conduct brain and spinal punctures: "Only when OUR child becomes healthy—will all be well," she wrote in desperation.[62] He did not improve. In February she realized: "The child is ill, more than ill, hopeless." She blamed herself—"that this child must go to the earth is the curse of my thoughtlessness." It was decided the child needed permanent hospital care. On February 20 she "gave my poor little son into the hospital. . . . Now he lives but I am completely without hope. It is all past. I love this child so much!" Before he left he was christened Martin Johannes in a church ceremony. Though she had asked herself, "To what end?" the ritual "touched me strangely. As if now nothing can happen to him any more. This powerful eternal symbol! . . . —My poor sweet child."[63] A month later, she wrote wanly, "Somewhere lies an ignorant child with staring eyes, and I continue living and start to forget—the young egg despite everything."[64] Dreams tormented her—"I saw my sweet poor boy lying in a coffin—flowers all around him. The coffin stood open. It snowed meanwhile over his open face. It is so dreadful—never again to put right what happened to me—with this child, with MY boy—my laughter has gone from me."[65]

The pain of her loss affected her feelings toward Werfel. In a pattern that would recur throughout their relationship as, indeed, it had with all her men, she withdrew. The tragedy of the child's inevitable death had come between them. "Am I caught up in a huge mistake?" she asked in January 1919.[66] Then, as previously with Kokoschka, came the sudden realization "that Werfel must go out of my life, that he is the source of all my unhappiness. . . . High time for a change." He must remain at Breitenstein; she had "no desire ever to see him again."[67] But by March she knew she could not stop loving him, for he was the first to have "fulfilled ALL my desires for life. . . . He is Mensch—He is man—He is a lover like none [other]—He is a poet, yes, all—everything!"[68] Isolated with his work, Werfel did not despair: "We are tied to one another by an incomparable physical enchantment," he asserted, though it did not still his dread of losing her.[69]

In Vienna, she resumed an "informal, free, convivial" social life, with open days on Sundays when friends brought their own guests to

Elizabethstrasse. Schoenberg came with his wife and daughter and several pupils who played music for her. With composer Julius Bitten she discussed the dichotomy between intellect and heart, which she rather simplistically defined, as she had done before with Fraenkel, as the divide between Jews and Christians: "Werfel the Jew stood alone and preached the value of reason, whereas we [Aryans] praised love," she sweepingly observed.[70] Berta Zuckerkandl visited with painter Johannes Itten, and they talked of Gustav Klimt, who had died the previous year.[71] "With him a very bright piece of my youth has gone out of my life," Alma wrote. "How I loved him!"[72]

During the spring of 1919, she felt she was in limbo. Unsure of her immediate path, she feared she had completely lost her direction. She no longer loved her husband, but it was "SENSIBLE with Walter Gropius in Weimar, my life vegetating to its end . . . [t]o be interested in art of a moderate talent and be a brave Frau, O how sensible!" she wrote bitterly.[73] But she was still not certain of Werfel, this kindred spirit to whom she was passionately drawn but who caused her such turbulence: "What peril this sense-intoxicated young man brought into my life. I CAN not tame him; I would not, should not, tame him. But why should my entire future be a fearful trembling over his fidelity? He is so easily seduced by everything around him."[74]

Alma longed for calm. She no longer wished to be with "one of these young gods, whether it's O.K. or Werfel, where life is always spinning around, from cliff to precipice, HORRIBLY great and horribly painful."[75] She was indeed suffering—whether from longing, dissatisfaction, or confusion—for in February, she realized with frightening clarity that "I love Gustav and always only Gustav, and that since he died I have been forever seeking, and never finding and I never will find." All around her were "pygmies—and trivial"; Kokoschka and Werfel were splendid artists "but mites next to him." When she heard his Second Symphony she was so "wounded to the heart" that she resolved to kill herself; she had hallucinated that "Gustav beckoned me with his finger. I saw him."[76]

Then she remembered Kokoschka, and her regrets stirred again: why had she not understood his genius? They had turned the world upside down. When she read his letters she found "a marvellous boy, whose youth I poisoned. . . . Was I too old for him? . . . Wasn't his slavery a sweet burden for me?"[77] A mutual friend, Baron von Dirsztay, told her that Kokoschka still loved her as fervently as ever and wished to renew the relationship: "He can paint ONLY ME—whenever he starts another, always my picture comes through." But she rejected his overture with the curt message: "I've landed on another shore."[78] Finally, in a fit of frustration, she wailed, "What drives me around the world,—like a flame in too much wind. I am forever yearning! And the best vanishes out of my open hands! *Poor susceptible me!!* Always I allow myself to be led astray from my path. AND WHICH IS IT?"[79]

By that point, Kokoschka's obsession with Alma had taken on a bizarre form. In July 1918 he had commissioned a doll-maker in Dresden, Hermine Moos, to make a life-size replica of Alma: "Please make it possible that my sense of touch will be able to take pleasure in those parts where the layers of fat and muscle suddenly give way to a sinuous covering of skin," he instructed Moos, and bought dresses and lingerie from the best Parisian houses to dress it with elegance equal to Alma's.[80] When it arrived in February 1919, although initially disappointed that it lacked some of the sensual qualities Kokoschka had anticipated, he was "enraptured—it was just as beautiful as Alma, even though the breasts and hips were stuffed with sawdust."[81] A young maid dressed and looked after it. Guests found her sitting in splendor, dressed in shimmering white, in his living room. Rumor spread that he took the doll out for rides in his carriage, though he denied the claim that he took her to the opera. He drew and painted "The Silent Woman" over and over again.

Eventually, Kokoschka "put an end to my inanimate companion." He gave a huge champagne party with chamber musicians, and the maid paraded the doll in its beautiful finery for the last time. During the revelry, the doll lost its head and was doused in red wine. The next day a police patrol arrived to investigate a report of a headless body seen in the garden, covered in blood. In the grey morning light refuse collectors carried away his "dream of Eurydice's return. The doll was an image of the spent love that no Pygmalion could bring to life," Kokoschka wrote.[82]

IN THE SPRING of 1919, Alma took Manon to visit her father, Walter Gropius, in Weimar. She was still there when she learned that Martin had died in a Viennese hospital on May 15: "This poor, tortured flame was snuffed out," she wrote.[83] She did not return to Vienna.

In April 1919 Gropius set up the Bauhaus school, the realization of his vision of a modern architecture for the future. The core of his mission was the synthesis, the breaking down of divisions, between art, craft, design, and technology, which would utilize the materials and techniques of manufacturing and mass production to create a holistic unity in harmony with society and the environment. It was a new relationship between art and society. With a radical, cross-disciplinary approach to teaching, he gathered around him an egalitarian community that included painters Johannes Itten, Paul Klee, Franz Marc, Wassily Kandinsky, Oskar Schlemmer, Lyonel Feininger, the sculptor Gerhard Marcks, the photographer László Moholy-Nagy, along with architects, engineers, technical experts, and specialists in artisan crafts and design. Gropius's vision and the Bauhaus school had a profound and lasting influence on modernism and architecture in the twentieth century. Alma visited the Bauhaus with Manon and observed the energetic ferment of new ideas around her. Although she was "baffled" by Gropius's charts, graphs, and calculations, she recognized in the work of Chagall, Klee, Marc, and Kandinsky "a new artistic courage . . . a soaring, passionate faith."[84]

During the course of her stay with Gropius, she decided to put an end to her marriage. "Through no fault of his, I was lost to him forever—and this despite my own feeling that no-one nobler, more generous had ever come into my life," she wrote.[85] She rejoiced that in Manon "all our good Aryan characteristics were merged. A godlike lovable being, a creative energy, such as I have never seen. . . . She was the elemental, most beautiful and most pure creature that I have ever met."[86] But the fierce arguments that ensued between them over who should have custody of Manon reached such intensity that at one point Alma fainted. The doctor who was summoned told Gropius, "She can't stand much more." Gropius telegraphed Werfel, who came immediately and met Alma and Manon in Dresden. Werfel had found Manon a nurse, Sister Ida Gebauer, who lived with Alma from then on. They traveled to Berlin, where Alma and Werfel appeared openly in public together.

In mid-July she wrote to Gropius to formally ask for a divorce: "It is the only possible and decent thing that I can do. With my love for Franz Werfel, who was the father of my child, I ought no longer to be called Gropius."[87] Within two weeks he had agreed, but he wanted custody of Manon. It was Alma's worst fear: "The unique Mutzi, the sweet child—this is my only anxiety because without this little elf I could not live!" she wrote.[88] She could not countenance his terms: "You say: 'Give me our child!' Don't you know what this means to me? Then you might just as well put a loaded revolver next to me!" she told him.[89]

The issue was unresolved as Alma joined Werfel at Breitenstein. In the first postwar summer, food and fuel shortages remained acute. Alma was occupied with hard physical work on the land to provide basic food needs: "I have done a lot of work in the last days, digging potatoes, storing apples on straw in the cellar, pulling beets—in short, playing farmer's wife. It was fun, but my heart no longer tolerates these heavy physical demands."[90]

Here, she experienced "complete marital happiness, like never before." As Werfel worked in the "beautiful airy" attic room she had converted into his study, Alma "pampered him like a child."[91] She was now certain of her love for this "man-child" as she called him—who was "just a tiny bird in my hand . . . with trembling heart and with open and blinking eyes. I must protect him from weather and cats"; but he was simultaneously "an enormous hero with wise whiskers and a club in his hand. He is a little bird and a gigantic mountain—both in one spirit—touchingly childishly awkward and at the same time, considers everything with wisdom and the strength of knowledge."[92] Franz reciprocated her love with his adoration: "To win you forever and tie you to myself, that is now my only goal in life," he told her. "Alma I implore you, help me during these coming years! Do not leave me for a minute!"[93]

But a temporary calm did not entirely banish her turbulence and restless longing: "I torment Franz—and he me—without realising that there will never be anyone who can make me happy. Against my mind's confusion no remedy has evolved."[94] Eventually she found an equilibrium in the knowledge that "I'm deeply attached to Franz. We have a frighteningly powerful love for each other, and hate each other with a passion. We torture each other too, and yet we are happy."[95]

Their closeness was intensified by their sensual intimacy. When Franz "first admitted his perversities to me and then very skilfully deployed them as phobias," Alma was "so excited" she couldn't sleep: "I kept seeing cripples and him, and intoxicated myself on them. A one-legged person—lying down. He and I. I as a spectator, boundlessly excited, so powerfully that I had to touch myself." Alma was concerned to "create a situation for him to give pleasure to both of us. I am not jealous, because there is no love, but something else of which I know nothing."[96]

She shepherded him through intense mood changes, including his fear of madness: "I am a captive in a prison—under the heavy roofs of my own self," he told her one day. Alma feared his brain may be "going soft." He had, since the age of ten, "driven himself to his lowest ebb through masturbation before he met me.—it happened up to three times a day. That's why he is also quite often tired and exhausted and his brain cells are morbid." She despaired: "Why are these wonderful examples of humankind so intent to destroy themselves?" and concluded it was her role "to safeguard his strengths, and without him noticing to create an ascetic life alongside me."[97]

ANNA (GUCKI), WHO had stayed with them that summer, was barely sixteen when she announced that she had become secretly engaged to Rupert Koller, an aspiring conductor and the son of a Breitenstein neighbor. "Her happiness is mine," Alma wrote, as she accepted the engagement. "I only wish that . . . they will continue to live this beautiful fairy tale, pure and beautiful to the end." To Rupert she advised, "Make something beautiful out of it; it's up to you." It dawned on Alma that "suddenly I had become a mother-in-law!" but just as she began to feel old she received two love letters, one from a musician, the other from a poet. She immediately "re-discovered her gaiety and balance."[98]

When in February 1920 Alma took Manon to Weimar, the issue of custody was still unresolved. They stayed at the Hotel zum Elephant before moving into Gropius's new apartment. But discussions with this man she had previously thought "honorable" became extremely acrimonious: "Gropius with his evil and ugly face wants half of the child.—Also wants half of me. Then I will have to leave her with him altogether because I cannot share her!" she protested.[99] She was tormented by bearing the name Gropius which "covered me like barbed wire," she told Johannes Bitten. "Well," he replied sensibly, "that is far too aggressive. A slatted fence would be more appropriate."[100]

While they were in Weimar, on March 13, 1920, Germany descended into chaos. Right-wing radicals, led by a Prussian civil servant, Wolfgang Kapp, whose followers wore the inverted Indian swastika on their steel helmets, attempted a putsch to overthrow the newly formed Weimar Republic. They intended to establish a right-wing authoritarian government supported by conservative and nationalist groups and the Reichswehr. After they occupied the administrative buildings, the government called a general strike, which was supported by Social Democrats, trade unions, and 12 million workers across the country, including in Weimar. It led to riots and bloodshed. The country was paralyzed. The putsch collapsed after four days, but it was the opening salvo in the stark and violent divisions between right- and left-wing elements that would scar Germany during the subsequent decades.

Alma was trapped in Weimar during the chaos: "How am I to get out of this mousetrap?" she exclaimed, as from her hotel room she observed what appeared to be a play from the Middle Ages. "Dusk and excitement filled the market place under our windows. Workers spat on the helmeted, motionless young men of the Kapp forces, and the mob howled. . . . Night fell. There were no lights anywhere, and in the darkness the masses looked even more menacing than in daylight. Here and there a match flared."[101] Conditions in the city deteriorated: no sewage was disposed of, water had to be fetched from far away, the dead could not be buried, bodies were dumped against the cemetery walls. On March 21 she watched the funeral of the workers killed in the fighting—"an endless procession, carrying banners with inscriptions: 'Remember Liebknecht! Remember Rosa Luxembourg!'—the Communist leaders whom a rightist mob had killed a year back in Berlin." The slain officers of the putsch "were left for days unburied," she noted.[102]

When she eventually got out, she fled to Berlin, where she met up with Werfel, who had been sick with anxiety about her safety. While there, Werfel read his new drama *Spiegelmensch* (*Mirror Man*) to Max Reinhardt, the groundbreaking director of the Deutsches Theater, who responded enthusiastically to the play. After all her anxiety in Weimar, Alma experienced with Werfel an evening of "beauty and intimacy as never before. . . . The rhythms of our souls were so intertwined that any greater intensity seems impossible. We are ONE SOUL."[103]

Shortly afterward she traveled to Amsterdam, where she was the guest of honor at Willem Mengelberg's celebrations to mark the tenth anniversary of Mahler's death. While there she realized that she had completely failed to play the role of grieving widow. She did not miss Mahler, and the remembrance dates had lost their meaning for her. She spent most of the time with Arnold Schoenberg, whose "towering intellect" again thrilled her.[104] When she returned to join Werfel in Breitenstein, her love for him burned strongly: "I love him more deeply the more I get to know him," she wrote.[105] But she was troubled that Gropius at their last meeting had commented on "a new expression in your face—a horrifying depraved look." She realized her imagination had become filled with perverse images as a consequence of her collusion with Werfel's sexual fantasies: "In the happiest moments I have blended in more and more ugly hours that excited him." Now she resolved to "guide him back, not allow myself to be pulled down. Thank you Walter—thank you."[106]

As she reflected on her erotic experiences, she came to the sweeping conclusion that "the more significant the man, the sicker his sexuality." Mahler "was so afraid of womankind that he became psychologically impotent. His way to make love to me became more and more an attack in the night during sleep," so in the last years she had locked her bedroom door. Kokoschka "was only able to make love having the most frightening fantasies. As I refused to hit him during lovemaking he started to conjure up the most horrifying murder images while he quietly whispered to himself." Then there was Werfel "with all his craziness." It was only lesser human beings, upright citizens, it seemed to her, who are "jolly, good-natured and concerned about their pleasure."[107]

Meanwhile, a disturbing tension developed in Alma's relations with her daughter Anna. Her fiancé Rupert's inability to make love to her one night in Frankfurt had triggered in Anna deep feelings of inferiority. A letter from Rupert to Alma revealed that Anna had complained to him about her mother. Alma was deeply upset that "Anna had betrayed me," and declared: "These last few days were painful, a complete disaster." She confronted her daughter, and, after a heart-to-heart during the night, there was "some light, but I am no longer the same and nor is she. The innocence between us has gone." Alma was so depressed that she was unable even to play music. Anna, however, played nonstop on the piano downstairs: "She has become a stranger to me, cool—superior and Jewish," Alma protested.[108]

Even so, Alma blamed herself. In a curious expression of mystical omnipotence, she felt with horror and absolute clarity that "everybody who comes into the vicinity of my aura, falls victim to me. . . . Now I am afraid because SOMETHING in me has yet again put a curse on someone I love—Anna."[109] Alma had been haunted for years by the thought that she had contributed to the death of her and Mahler's firstborn, Maria, the child he had profoundly loved, and that, because of her jealousy, she had in some way willed it. When Anna contracted scarlet fever, they had taken Maria away to stay with Alma's mother. As Alma drove away with Mahler past the window of her mother's house and saw Maria—"her beautiful dark curly hair pressed against the windowpane," Mahler had waved up to her "like a lover." And suddenly, Alma "KNEW this child has to be removed . . . AND IMMEDIATELY. . . . And the child was dead after a few months." Though Alma had tried to banish "this cursed way of thinking," it still haunted her.[110]

By October 1920 she had reached a harmonious understanding with Gropius. In the most honorable manner, he agreed to go through the charade of being caught by a private detective in flagrante delicto with a prostitute in a hotel room—the necessary evidence for adultery—even though Gropius had by then a new lover, a war widow, Maria Bene-mann, whom presumably he did not wish to subject to public gaze. By this not uncommon process, Gropius took responsibility for the failed marriage, and Alma emerged blameless—and she also gained full custody of Manon.

They were divorced in Weimar on October 11, 1920. Alma returned to Vienna with Manon to begin a new life as a free woman.

～ *11* ～

Conflict

1921–1931

ranz Werfel was overjoyed and relieved at the news of Alma's divorce: "I could just weep incessantly," he told her and took her to meet his parents, Rudolf and Albine Werfel, in Prague.[1] Given Alma's track record with her lovers' parents, it was an unexpected success: "You left a wealth of enthusiasm behind. My parents love you . . . they obviously adore you!" Werfel wrote enthusiastically. To his mother, Albine, Alma was "the sole true queen or monarch of our time."[2] From Prague they went on to stay in a hotel on the Grand Canal in Venice, a city that would assume increasing importance in their lives.

Anna married Rupert Koller in November 1920, and they moved to Elberfeld in Germany, where Koller was a conductor to the Municipal State Opera. Alma's hopes for her daughter's happiness were short lived, for Anna soon tired of the marriage, and, in late August 1921, she retreated to Breitenstein, where she spent a healing month with Alma. "I was so happy with her. And now everything is empty," Alma wrote when she left. "I love her passionately and this is why I was so desperate last summer. She is unhappy—suffering. . . . If she would leave him and come back to me *I would be happy beyond belief*. My heart is aching with love for her."[3]

Anna did not come back but went to Berlin to study painting. Meanwhile, Alma maintained a lively social life full of art and music in the red room at Elizabethstrasse. Olga Schnitzler stayed with her while deciding whether she should divorce her playwright husband, Arthur, and Alma held regular musical evenings. At one, a small orchestra performed two versions of Schoenberg's *Pierrot Lumaire*, each with separate singers, one conducted by Schoenberg, the other by Darius Milhaud, before an audience of eighty people who "listened intently to the brittle wonders of a-tonality."[4] Composers Darius Milhaud, Francis Poulenc, Alban Berg, Eduard Steuerman, and Cyril Scott spent a spirited afternoon together discussing and comparing their works.

Alma had meanwhile decided to buy a house in Venice. In March 1922, she found a small palazzo with a garden beside a canal near the Basilica dei Frari in San Tomà. "Casa Mahler" required extensive renovations— the addition of several bathrooms and an enlarged room for Werfel—and Alma was forced to sue the current tenants when they refused to vacate the property. While there, she bumped into Oskar Kokoschka for the first time since the war. He was showing at the International Exhibition—the Venice Biennale—and they went to the Cafe Florian in St. Mark's Square: "We were strangely close to each other and far away," Alma recalled. "His face has become that of a child. Dorian Gray. His vices have been etched somewhere outside of him." His presence made her so anxious that she "cried continuously," until her mother interrupted them and took her away.[5] But he would continue to haunt her.

News now reached her that Anna was "living with some fellow in Berlin. . . . [I]t is the highly talented cannibal Ernst Krenek, also a composer," Alma wrote.[6] They had met in February at a ball at the Academy of Music, where he was studying under Franz Schreker. Alma went to Berlin to meet the new suitor and failed to hide her disdain; years later he waspishly recalled, "I believe she liked me every bit as little as I liked her." She had "the knack of turning life into a dizzying carousel" and reminded him of "an extravagantly festooned battleship . . . [with] the same style as Wagner's Brünnhilde transposed to the atmosphere of *Die Fledermaus*." The lavish meals she gave them in expensive restaurants were in his eyes merely the means of "making people into helpless subjects of her power."[7]

Krenek attributed Alma's dislike of him to jealousy, for he was "potentially one of the fellows who could alienate her from her daughter for ever."[8] Certainly Anna believed that her mother's jealousy was a key to her character. "She was wildly, possessively jealous, and that dictated her behaviour to people." Anna told her own daughter Marina, "And if she wasn't at the centre she lashed out."[9] It led to tensions with the families of all her lovers—Mahler, Kokoschka, Gropius—as well as with her sons-in-law, each of whom believed, like Krenek, that Anna got married to "escape from her mother's oppressive influence."[10] Anna herself may well have contributed to this impression for, she later explained, despite her mother's love for her, Alma's high expectations had disfigured their relationship: "I know she loved me," she told biographer Peter Stephan Jungk, but she also "despised me. . . . I didn't fall in love because somebody was well-known or famous or significant, but rather because somebody had pleased me. Appalling! She despised me. I had no success, no money."[11]

During the spring of 1923, Alma supervised the alterations to Casa Mahler, an enterprise that strained the family finances at a time when hyperinflation was crippling the Austrian economy. Mahler's royalty payments, by then modest, were rendered almost valueless. Werfel's earnings were small, and his publisher, Kurt Wolff in Leipzig, was struggling after being badly hit in the disastrous economic climate. When Paul Zsolnay, the twenty-eight-year-old son of a wealthy tobacco magnate, came up with plans to start his own publishing house, Alma suggested he publish Werfel's current novel if Werfel could be released from his existing contract. Zsolnay offered him an advance of 5,000 Swiss francs—a sum made more valuable by the relative stability of that currency. Werfel became the mainstay of Zsolnay Verlag's first list.

Alma had made her own plans to publish Mahler's edited letters and also, despite Bruno Walter's resistance, the facsimile manuscript of Mahler's Tenth Symphony. Walter had opposed the Tenth's publication because of the very personal nature of Mahler's tortured notes, written when he thought he was losing Alma and was close to death. Zsolnay agreed to publish both the letters and the facsimile in 1924 to coincide with the world premiere of Mahler's Tenth Symphony at the Vienna State Opera. They also agreed to publish simultaneously five of her own songs that she had recently discovered among her papers, while Universal Edition reissued the 1915 edition of her Four Songs.

During an extended stay with Anna in Breitenstein in the summer of 1923, Alma invited Krenek to edit the unfinished Tenth Symphony.

Despite protesting this "repulsive" idea and accusing Alma of "common avarice," Krenek nevertheless felt "chained to the golden cage" and set to work on editing the adagio and the purgatorio, though he left untouched the other three movements. Werfel, who was working on his novel *Verdi*, formed an unusually intense dislike of the young man: "K. is an idolator of Nothing," he declared, and if he represented "the youth of our time— then heaven help us!" Werfel's nerves "had been . . . *outraged* . . . by his mechanistic Satanism!" for "only the devil could see the world" as this young composer did.[12] His animosity had no impact on Anna, for on January 15, 1924, she married Krenek in Vienna City Hall. By September, however, the marriage had broken down, and Anna had fled to Rome to study painting under Georgio de Chirico. The couple were divorced in August 1926.

IN APRIL 1924 Werfel had his first major commercial success. His novel, *Verdi*, a fictional account of his favourite composer's life was published by Zsolnay in a large print run of 20,000 and sold out briskly. In the same month Alma moved in to Casa Mahler in Venice: "Own house, sweet garden, paradise. Everything just as I wanted it."[13] Alone there with Werfel in June, her equilibrium was restored. She was happy, "without longing, without wishing for other things—I can live beautifully with him—and it is a sin when I am sometimes in a state of longing."[14]

Alma's life with Werfel was taking on a rhythm, alternating between anxious introspection, intense exaltation, and despairing withdrawal. In spring she had been confident of an inner equilibrium: "I have many people around me, am held in great esteem, I walk my path confidently."[15] Summer had been "beautiful, harmonious, joyfully loving, apart from a few disagreements," but by the New Year she felt "ill, sad, down-trodden, wretched, alone, alone—oh so alone!"[16] and her love for Werfel had fled: "My inner life no longer chimes with his. He has shrunk to a small, ugly, obese Jew of the first impression. I am alone and yet so completely tied. Worse than being married. Werfel also doesn't love me any more. . . . I dream of living alone in my house in Venice, completely detached behind the stone wall." But she was fearful and uncertain "whether I can bear the last great loneliness."[17]

By July 1924 at Breitenstein, she was again deeply content as Werfel worked upstairs on his new drama, *Juarez and Maximilian*, "every night pacing back and forth above our heads until early morning." Her commitment to him was now total. Never again would she want to be unfaithful to him, she declared.[18] But the past could still crowd in on her. Alma had been working on a memoir of her life with Mahler when she suffered a sudden physical collapse. After a terrible pressure on the front of her brain, the room had turned black, later green. Both of her hands had gone numb, the right part of her face was paralyzed, and a boil developed on her cheekbone. She had regained her strength by the evening; though she suspected that "at the bottom of my consciousness lies FEAR OF DEATH. . . . I have been touched by death. May God help me!" After the doctor forbade her to work, she attributed her collapse to profound disturbance caused by "*my writings about Mahler* which during the last weeks have enraged me close to madness. I have literally written day and night out of fear *I could lose my ability to remember and would not be able to finish before then.*"[19] She continued to work on her memoir, but it was abandoned soon after Zsolnay requested some changes. Several decades passed before it was eventually published in 1940 in German and in 1946 in English as *Gustav Mahler: Memories and Letters*.

Increasingly Werfel retreated to Breitenstein to work in concentrated isolation. But he always needed Alma to spur him on. She was indispensable to his work. Her daughter Anna attributed this to his weakness, but perhaps, as his biographer Jungk suggests, there was a masochistic strand in his personality that "thrived when he was suffering under her influence." Werfel was convinced of his need for a muse. If she was angry he feared his powers would be weakened, so he pacified her. Anna thought "his weakness, his tendency always to give in—those were negative aspects of his character. He submitted to Alma, consciously. It wasn't good for either of them—a lot of the time she really treated him as if she were his governess."[20]

Alma had been entranced by Werfel's talent and was determined his genius should not be dissipated. "She made him into a novelist, that's for sure," Anna judged. "Without her—I'm pretty sure of this—he would have remained a poet and a bohemian to the end of his life." Werfel knew this. He told a friend, "If I had not met Alma, I would have written a few more good poems and gone to the dogs, happily," Albrecht Joseph, Werfel's secretary (and Anna's future husband) recalled.[21] Joseph believed Alma's "unique gift" was a "profound, uncanny understanding of what it was that [creative] men tried to achieve, an enthusiastic, orgiastic persuasion that they could do what they aimed at, and that she, Alma, fully understood what it was." It was this uncanny and unique understanding that "made those whom she loved regard her as a demi-goddess."[22]

Werfel's dedication did not endear Alma to his coffee-house friends, who "strongly condemned the influence of Alma Mahler on Werfel," recalled journalist Milan Dubrovic, who had hung out with Werfel and his old friends Ernst Polak, Anton Kuh, Alfred Polgar, and others at the Café Central and the Herrenhof. Dubrovic greatly admired Werfel, this "truly fascinating man", with "exceptionally large eyes and a strong erotic aura . . . a splendid person, obsessed by ideas and ways to present them. He was like a fireworks display," who could entertain friends for hours "telling stories, impersonating people, reconstructing situations."[23]

After Werfel met Alma, they saw him less and less, which doubtless contributed to the hostile legend of Alma. They blamed her for taking

Figure 16. Author Franz Werfel, c. 1929.
"If I had not met Alma I would have written a few more good poems and gone to the dogs, happily."

him away from them but, even more, for having the power to lead him away from his true vocation, poetry, to become a commercially successful novelist and playwright. "We used to say, 'That's a different Werfel, he's become a "success boy"!' But he seemed happy. One evening we were sitting there discussing what those present would term the highest happiness on earth. And Werfel said, quite openly, 'Success! To me, success is practically identical with happiness.' He had to admit that."[24]

AN ENTIRELY NEW experience opened up for Alma when, in January 1925, she traveled with Werfel to the Middle East on a trip she had longed to make for some time. During three weeks spent in Upper and Lower Egypt, they explored bazaars, mosques, and museums; saw a performance of Verdi's *Aïda* at the Italian Opera in Cairo; and visited Heliopolis, Memphis, the temples of Luxor and Karnak, and the royal tombs at Thebes. On February 10, they moved on to Palestine, then governed under a British mandate. In Jerusalem, they were met by the Zionist Executive— "superior, intelligent and not responsible for their hot-blooded young followers," Alma reported later.[25] She was "enthralled" by the country. Although not impressed by the "insufficiently planned" kibbutzim, where she refused an invitation to sleep on the ground in a tent, she relished Jerusalem and their trips to Tel Aviv, Nazareth, Haifa, and the Sea of Galilee—"the old Biblical countryside immediately affects you." But she found "the new Judaism there was in all its ambitions completely foreign to me." And she added opaquely and without explanation, "*I believe the Jews are in danger there!*"[26]

For Werfel it was a period of uneasiness and conflicting emotions about his Jewish identity: "From the very first moment I felt torn. My hand is no longer free. My mind is no longer at peace. . . . [T]hose were days of deep anxiety," he wrote.[27] Werfel's relationship with his own Jewishness as well as with Zionism and Theodor Herzl's dream of a homeland for Jews had been equivocal. Even before he met Alma, he had believed himself alienated from his Jewishness, avoided both ritual and scripture, and felt more sympathetic to the Christian religion: "What do I have to do with these people, with this *alien world*? My world was the great European artists with all their contradictions, from Dostoyevsky to Verdi," he wrote in 1920.[28] But his experiences in Palestine led him to reassess his own identity as a Jew. When Alma made casual anti-Semitic comments, he found himself defending a position he did not wholly believe in: "Alma is against Jewishness in itself here, additionally, of course, against the communist Jewish, and I am endlessly in the wrong role of the go-between, a polemicist torn between both sides," he wrote.[29] The experience led him in the following months to an intense study of his Jewish origins. Inspired by his own internal conflicts on the trip, he returned to Breitenstein to begin work on a drama, *Paul Among the Jews*, about the moment when Christianity separated from Judaism. Alma proudly witnessed Werfel's dedication: "Franz has grown so serious—so full of the highest responsibility to himself, that it is a joy to watch the LIFE within him. . . . When I think what a young rapscallion he used to be!"[30]

As Werfel's works garnered wider acclaim as well as commercial success, Alma's financial worries of the previous few years receded. He was awarded the prestigious Grillparzer Prize from the Vienna Academy of Arts and Sciences, and Max Reinhardt's production of *Juarez and Maximilian* proved a huge hit at the Deutsches Theater in Berlin in January 1926. Alma had been laid low by one of her periodic depressions, "crying and crying day and night," and was mortified to miss the premiere.[31] But she managed to accompany Werfel on a reading tour of Germany, and in Prague they attended the successful premiere of her friend Alban Berg's controversial opera *Wozzek*, which he dedicated to her after she had helped finance its publication.

At the end of June 1926, Zsolnay signed a contract, payable in Swiss francs, that made Werfel the highest-paid Zsolnay author. In a poll that year by a prestigious German literary magazine, the great majority of readers voted Franz Werfel their favorite writer in German, above Gerhart Hauptmann, Stefan Zweig, and Rainer Maria Rilke.[32] In autumn, Werfel was made a member of the Prussian Academy of Arts and Sciences by, among others, Heinrich and Thomas Mann, Arthur Schnitzler, and Jacob Wassermann.

THE VOLATILE POLITICAL atmosphere of the late 1920s increasingly intruded on their lives. The fragile postwar economy of Austria had been stabilized with the help of foreign loans, and a succession of coalitions led by the Christian Social Party had given the government an appearance of stability. But this was threatened by the political extremism of opposing paramilitary organizations. Violence broke out regularly between the left-wing Social Democratic Schutzbund—a well-trained force numbering around 80,000 by the 1930s—and those of the right-wing anti-socialist paramilitary Heimwehr, led by Ernst Rüdinger von Starhemberg. In so-called Red Vienna, stronghold of the socialist-leaning Social Democratic Party, conservative Alma found herself increasingly at odds with the radical Werfel: "It is very sad . . . but the political divide between me and Werfel is getting *boundless*," Alma lamented in July 1926. "Every conversation, every single one, leads without fail to that, and our radical difference offers very poor prospects for the future."[33]

Alma was neither politically astute nor well informed, but her innate conservatism flared into overt anti-Semitism as tensions escalated. On July 15, 1927, workers marched on Parliament to protest the acquittal of members of a right-wing group who had been accused of the murder of a worker and an eight-year-old boy during a clash the previous January. The march turned into a violent and bloody battlefield. Police fired into the crowd, killing eighty-nine and wounding more than two hundred. The Palace of Justice and newspaper offices were burned down, and a general strike called by the Social Democratic leaders lasted two days before calm was restored. Alma routinely identified any left-wing creed—socialism, communism, even liberalism—with the Jews: "The mob unleashed. THE EVIL SEED OF JUDAISM BLOSSOMS," she declaimed to her diary, dismissing out of hand those left-wing "literary ideologues" who were deploring "the mass murder of ideals."[34]

The diary continues with a violent, ugly, and confused diatribe that reflected the climate of growing anti-Semitism but was deeply contradictory coming from a woman whose life was so closely bound to Jews, through her first husband and now her Jewish lover. The Jews "are excellent intellectuals, artists, financiers but they should not touch politics," she declared. "They inflame the world through their *lack of imagination*. People should FINALLY put a stop to it before it is too late!" The Jew in politics, she wrote:

> is the most serious misfortune for Europe and Asia. . . . He is forced to secure the sympathy of the masses through flattery. Flattery inevitably makes the masses stupid. . . . Without realising what ill they are doing in

the world, [they] show clearly the ONE PATH into the one subject which
the masses who are tired of promises of heaven, follow only too gladly.[35]

She railed against the current assault on the social order as evidence
that "the Jews TOGETHER and worldwide are experiencing their ascen-
dancy and their victory over the white master race . . . and Christendom
stands by sorrowfully and is allowing the leadership of the world to be
wrenched from its hands."[36]

On the more specific political front, she was convinced that "Austria
is ALREADY lost. It can only be saved by Caesarean section: affiliation with
Germany." But, for Alma, a conservative Austrian patriot, brought up in
the Austro-Hungarian Empire, the idea of affiliation with Germany was
anathema, a path strewn with pitfalls: "[Austria] will wake up then and
not comprehend its blood anymore . . . and Austria will be a vassal of
Germany."[37] Moreover, it was clear to her that Moscow, "with its dirty,
bloodied fist," was behind the July events.[38]

Then, after her furious and frustrated series of outbursts, she decided
to distance herself from the political morass and find refuge and personal
salvation in her inner life and private goals: "What do you idiots of this
world know of the vast happiness I imagine, partly in the intoxications of
love, of music, of wine. . . . With iron claws I cling to my nest. . . . Every
genius is acceptable to me, as a catch for my nest."[39]

Just as Alma was looking for distractions from politics, she found her
social horizons expanding. On the Italian Riviera she discovered the Imperial Hotel in Santa Margherita Liguria, the perfect location for Werfel to retreat to work. It was a popular spot for German writers. Alma's
friend, the author Fritz von Unruh, owned an old fort nearby built on vertical cliffs, and novelist Hermann Sudermann stayed in the same hotel.
Helene and Alban Berg joined them. During evenings filled with drink
and laughter at Gerhart Hauptmann's house in nearby Rapello, Alma
warmed to this "godly being! His blue eyes, deep like the sky mirrored in
a mountain stream." One day Hauptmann said to Alma, "It is terrible, it
is wretched that we two do not have a child together! That would have
been something! The two of us!"[40] On another occasion he decided "in
another life, we two must be lovers. I make my reservation now." His
wife, Margarete who overheard this, intervened: "'I'm sure Alma will be
booked up for there, too.' He and I only smiled," Alma recorded.[41]

Although Alma had tried to banish Kokoschka from her mind, at intervals, and especially whenever her love for Werfel faltered, she was still haunted by the man she referred to as "this monstrous nightmare."[42] While in Venice with Anna in October 1927, she glimpsed Kokoschka and found her vulnerability severely tested: "What devil is after me?" she fumed, even as her restless longing revived. "Oskar Kokoschka. . . . Incomparable—and terrible! I will never get over this person . . . ! Since I've seen O.K. I feel as if I've been destroyed. . . . I couldn't live with him. Intellect was lacking. Living without him, something is eternally missing!"[43]

When she saw him again, he was "red in the face and looked rough." Anna and Alma let him pass. He sent a card apologizing for his short sightedness, and "all the composure and all the hate melted away through this piece of paper. This wonderful human being once belonged to ME," she moaned.[44] In St. Mark's Church she prayed and begged God to guide her, then as she stepped out in the bright sunshine she met a friend who, like a sign from God, railed against Kokoschka. As if purged by prayer, Alma felt healed: "I'm again steady in life. It is stupid that I have let myself be thrown out of the saddle."[45] When a card from him arrived, she was unmoved. It seemed to her "something is waving as if from afar, . . . and it doesn't concern me anymore. Franz is my life and I do not want another one."[46]

During an evening in November discussing with the playwright Arthur Schnitzler "the strange marginalisation of women from their own self—through marriage"—something, she suggested, "that is strange to man!," she reflected on her own relationships. She realized how far, with Mahler, she had abandoned her interests, schooled herself in his "language" while forfeiting her own, and adopted his literary tastes and his philosophy. She had become unfaithful to her own inner being.[47]

With Werfel it was different, for she exercised a powerful hold over her "man-child." He depended on her love, as he often told her, but he also had the power to torment her—just as she could torment him. Their highs and lows had a frightening intensity. Their rows could leave her desolate. Once, during an evening at the theater, Alma was so appalled by the obnoxious "third rate gutter play" that she insisted on leaving. Werfel was furious with her and let rip his anger in the street: "I ran to a car and I drove home. He hissed after me, 'But remember—I'm not

coming home this evening.'. . . . I lay on the bed, fully dressed with my
teeth shaking."[48]

Alma's whole life seemed suddenly in the balance: "Have I gone this
far so that a man can talk abuse like any old slut. Am I not to be allowed
to form my own judgement in this day and age—to have free will to act!
So I am not allowed to leave a painful play which I don't like, have to
suffer being offended, being shouted at, being mistreated." She had "had
enough of the slavery to Man."[49] Her distress persisted for a fortnight: "I
had a crying fit. And I still haven't quite recovered from it. . . . [Anger]
makes my blood go black and causes doubts about life. Since then a string
inside me has broken and will not sing again. Brutality was the reason
why I left Kokoschka—brutality will create a distance between Werfel
and me."[50]

Christmas Eve with Werfel and Paul Zsolnay in Santa Margherita
was a desultory affair. She emerged only slowly from her angry distress.
On Christmas Day, a visit from Hauptmann with his wife, restored her
spirits. They were together again at New Year's Eve. When he said goodbye, Alma recalled, "He kissed me deeply on the mouth. He said: 'Finally
we are alone'—and suddenly his secretary was standing in front of us. I
also embraced her and made a general joke out of it."[51] There were more
evenings with Hauptmann, von Unruh, Zsolnay, and later Alban and
Helene Berg, when they all "drank a little too much" and were "filled
with great hilarity and beauty."[52] As so often, the company of glittering
creative people—of whatever nationality, race or religion—could restore
her energy and her equilibrium.

ALMA LEFT SANTA Margherita in February 1928 for a holiday in Sicily
with Anna: "Seeing nature and art with Anna is sheer bliss. She has an
unfailing sense of quality in these matters," Alma wrote as they visited
the ancient historic sights. But her daughter's men were "something else
again; there she tends to go wrong because she does not see—and there-
after will not find—the superior type."[53] Anna was still studying painting
with Georgio de Chirico in Rome and was now in love with an impoverished young Italian aristocrat. Alma hoped the liaison would help Anna,
who had strong left-wing sympathies, to appreciate the innate nobility of
the aristocracy.

Eleven-year-old Manon continued to delight her. During the Easter holiday with her in March 1928, Alma experienced a "MURDEROUS flight across the Alps" from Venice to Vienna. The plane hit a storm: "There were points where the choice was whether to be smashed against a white ridge or to descend into the depths with the plane rolling over like a ball at a height of 3000 metres."[54] Faced with the terror of near death, she promised herself she would once again become a Catholic. But Manon had remained serene throughout the flight: "The child was a heroine" Alma wrote proudly, and the pilots applauded her off the plane.[55]

Shortly afterward, Alma escaped from Venice to Rome, where she visited Margherita Sarfatti, journalist, arts patron, and mistress of Benito Mussolini. Reclining on a chaise longue, Sarfatti greeted Alma with a "curious, not too encouraging smile," and they discussed fascism.[56] Both agreed "that an international fascism—is ONLY possible if the fascism of the other countries is as wise as Mussolini's—and stops talking of the Jewish question. The Jews are after all so clever, and we need them. They must be accepted on an equal basis," Sarfatti insisted. "History shows that the Jew has often been more patriotic than the native." They concurred that it was "Italy's luck to have a genius at the helm. Finally we have a leader."[57] Alma would see more of Sarfatti years later in Paris, when she was no longer Mussolini's mistress but an embittered refugee whose hero "was swallowing Hitler's dust, and all that she had found so lovable about him appeared despicable."[58]

Back in Venice, the house was soon full of guests. Hans Pfitzner arrived, then Max Brod—"a salvation to me following Pfitzner's harsh and spiky manner."[59] Tragedy struck in August, when Lilli, Arthur Schnitzler's eighteen-year-old daughter and Anna's close friend, committed suicide by shooting herself in a gondola in front of her husband, an Italian army captain with whom she had fallen passionately in love. She did not die immediately, but the bullet was rusty; as sepsis set in, Anna nursed Lilli through her final days. When Alma visited Schnitzler, she found "a yellow, extinguished old man," deep in sorrow, who recalled to Alma how, after her daughter Maria's death in 1907, he had seen Mahler sitting alone on a bench, in mourning, his head bowed, and had thought to himself, "How can this man survive this?"[60]

Alongside this, Alma was experiencing a new low in the cycle of her relations with Werfel. Feeling a "strange emptiness, she decided she had been "*unhappy* for 10 years," simply playing a role to the outside world of "the so-called happy lover of a highly regarded poet. But I am neither his lover—nor his wife. I feature very little in his life and he in mine."[61] She was drinking "to be happy, perfectly happy"; often she got through a bottle a day of the sweet high-proof liqueur, Benedictine. As usual, Kokoschka, the genius, the lost soul mate, the tormenting spirit, surfaced in her mind to fill the vacuum: "My heart is always looking for him everywhere subconsciously—*and this can never stop.*"[62]

She had recovered sufficiently by the time they got back to Vienna to contemplate marriage, which Werfel had persistently proposed, but she again refused. It is perhaps a measure of her magnetic presence that she, a divorced woman, had for ten years lived and socialized openly with a man to whom she was not married. And yet this irregular relationship appears neither to have raised eyebrows nor accrued social opprobrium or disapproval even in the respectable circles of Vienna's social élite. But Alma had still not rid herself of doubts about marriage. "Perhaps I shall marry Werfel. He is the kindest but not the most loving man in my life," she decided in a rather lukewarm diary entry in September.[63]

Before she could change her mind about marriage, politics once again came between them. In Autumn 1928, the tensions between left- and right-wing groups escalated to the point where civil war threatened. In Wiener Neustadt on October 7, both the nationalist right-wing paramilitary Heinwehr, and the Schutzbund, the Social Democratic paramilitary group backed by workers' organizations, gathered in massive rallies, each of more than 30,000 drawn from far and wide. The communists were banned, and the town was under siege, with a huge military presence to control any confrontation. In the end, violence did not break out, but the demonstrations signaled profound conflict at the core of the republic. It unleashed from Alma another wide-ranging anti-Semitic outburst. In her diary she described the current political moment as "THE JEWS' REVENGE," for she identified Jews as the begetters of all left-wing ideologies that aimed "to overthrow everything and re-interpret what until then had been regarded as secure." Even "non-Semites take on the customs and attitudes of the Jew," she ranted, but "most perplexing" was "the herd of workers of the entire world, who let themselves be told willingly that there is bliss to be found on earth!"[64] Both workers and ideologues exhibited "an opium-like addiction to making everything the same."[65]

Neither her political nor her racial prejudices, however, impeded her friendships with people of opposing views, and the great majority of her friends were Jewish. Prominent socialist Julius Tandler was an old friend; Karl Renner, leader of the Socialist Party, was a regular guest; as was the left-leaning Catholic prelate Karl Drexel. On one occasion, as Renner conferred with Werfel, the leader of the right-wing Heimwehr, Ernst Rüdiger von Starhemberg, arrived to speak with Alma. She quickly got rid of the man "whose radical rightist attitude was not mine—though the red sparks flying in my living room were not mine, either," she commented.[66]

Despite their differences and her uncertainty, in June, after his many entreaties, Alma decided to marry Werfel, but she made it a condition that he withdraw from the Jewish community. He agreed, but hesitated to take the step of baptism, though rumors spread nevertheless that he had converted to Catholicism. Unknown to Alma, he reconverted to Judaism in November the same year. The night before the wedding, Alma was too anxious to sleep, unsure that this was "the right decision. I'm doing this for public show not for myself. My freedom, which I had protected despite everything, has suffered a blow. The love I felt has given way to a deeply entwined friendship."[67]

Alma and Franz Werfel were married without fanfare, like her previous weddings, on July 6, 1929, at Vienna City Hall. The ceremony was witnessed by Maria, her half sister, and her lawyer husband, Richard Eberstaller. Manon, who was blossoming into an elegant, willowy, enigmatic young girl and was installed at a boarding school for girls in Vienna, now acquired an official stepfather, "Uncle Werfel." They traveled on to Breitenstein, where Anna arrived from Paris. Anna renewed her acquaintance with Werfel's publisher, Paul Zsolnay, whom she had known distantly as a young girl. It developed into a love entanglement, and by the end of the summer Zsolnay declared he could not live without her.

ON AUGUST 31, Alma turned fifty. Age oppressed her. Two weeks before, as she waited for her menstruation, she had anticipated—"not the terrible, blessed fear of a possible pregnancy—no, it was the knowledge of the imminent failure of my female being which was eating into my soul. The 'cessation'—all cessation is terrible. And now this! Because there is no more beginning. Never again, can I entertain the thought of having another child! Never again. . . . And what do I get in exchange? Calmer blood—wiser insights into life—Ugh! There would be nothing left for me to yearn for."[68] She was not well physically: "Failure in all areas. The eyes don't want to go on, the hands are getting slower when playing the piano, I find food difficult to digest, standing and walking is difficult." Only by drinking—"of which I often do too much"—was she able to "overcome the chills and shivering inside my body."[69]

Once she was married, her restlessness was rekindled. Werfel seemed even more distant: "He is starting to ignore me—so I am starting to hate him. . . . Since he has become famous he believes he can do without me," she complained to her diary.[70] "I am experiencing my new marriage as something I am being forced into. Much *more* than I had imagined. I continuously want to get out of the net I am caught in, the net I entered willingly and in which I felt happy for such a long time."[71] She wanted both to leave and to stay. In a spin of confusion, when calm and composure had deserted her, she described her complex dilemma: "I would not be able to live without Jews—after all I live with them constantly, but my soul is so full of anger against them that I often, defiantly rail against it. Why can I never be happy—never content to enjoy what I have—and always seeking the other? *The other!* . . . Why have I given away my sweet name—my grand name, which I have viewed as mine for 30 years. Where is *my* life—that I have wasted?"[72]

Werfel's devotion was unwavering as he negotiated the choppy and unpredictable tides of her affection. After another ugly row he wrote abjectly from Breitenstein,

> Because you taunted me and because of the drink, I behaved in an unmanly and abominable way to you. I suffer from those things I said which were stupid, angry and despicable . . . [but] I know deeply without doubt that I love you, will love you eternally, whatever bad things you plan for me. . . . It pains me when I think of how you felt yesterday, UNSPEAKABLE PAIN! . . . Whatever you feel and do, I know that I *will never*

be able to live without you . . . because one hour when you are not here is
to me worrying and unbearable. . . . I know to the very end that I need
you not just for my peace of mind, but for my whole being. But perhaps
you don't need me? It all depends on that![73]

As usual, the company of friends absorbed Alma. She was cheered
when Yiddish poet Sholem Asch and his wife visited: "What a different
world! One immediately felt at home. I can't tell how IMPORTANT he is,
but he thrills me every minute," she wrote. They were on opposite sides
politically, "but I love enemies such as this—they are of my kind, even
if they were aborigines from Australia!" On a trip alone with Asch to
a nearby lake, suddenly "with hot breath he told me that he loved me
wildly." Alma calmed him, but he insisted on immediately returning to
the city. In a village he asked in Yiddish where he might get a car. The
atmosphere of anti-Semitism was already smoldering in the country, as
Alma knew: "That did it—Yiddish rather than German! The populace
glowered menacingly and I, fearing a pogrom, told him to get back in the
car swiftly, and we fled the mocking youths."[74]

ALMA HAD REVIVED her dream of visiting India, but when Werfel objected
to the long sea voyage, they returned to Egypt instead. From there they
traveled on to "a Palestine that had strikingly grown, developed and become far more interesting" since their last visit five years before.[75] She felt
so at home she thought of buying a house in Jerusalem amid the "pulsing
cultural life which we could understand and sympathize with." Painters, poets, and philosophers "were striving to re-establish its culture. . . .
[E]lectrification was in progress, swamps were being drained and forests
planted everywhere."[76] After Lebanon and Syria, they went on to Damascus. At a carpet-weaving factory, they witnessed the horrific scene of
"emaciated children with El Greco faces and enormous eyes" picking up
spools and threads from the floor. They were "the children of Armenians
killed off by the Turks," who would starve on the streets if no one took
them in, the manager told Werfel.[77] They visited Baalbeck and Mount
Lebanon, before moving on to Beirut, Mount Carmel, and Jerusalem. But
Werfel was unable to rid his mind of the image of the Armenian children.

He began amassing evidence of the Turkish massacre of the Armenians and of the resistance by a group of Armenian rebels on the Mountain of Moses, Musa Dagh.

On their return Alma found Anna pregnant and living at a level of grandeur that surprised her, in a castle built by Habsburg empress Maria Theresa. After a rapid courtship, Anna had married Paul Zsolnay quietly in Paris in December, despite Alma's misgivings about her marrying Werfel's publisher. She was even more concerned by the "game of betrayal" that she felt Anna was always playing against her: "The tangible feeling of loss of respect and darkness behind my back is growing."[78]

During that summer in Breitenstein, she felt calmer: "I am pulling myself together—taking a journey around my soul—I am almost happy. Occupied with sorting out my outer life my inner life has become more

Figure 17. Summer at Breitenstein with Anna, Werfel, and Carl Moll, early 1930s.

orderly."[79] She was less interested for the time being in politics: "The only thing that remains is the creative spirit. Whether the man on the right, whether the man on the left, whether shots are fired or there is peace—A STORM IN A TEACUP! My previous anxiety in respect of these things has given way to an unwavering peace. More important to me have become the things of MY life, MY heritage. My family."[80]

The Zsolnays had encouraged Alma and Werfel to move into a grander house that befitted her social standing. Despite her initial resistance, in January 1931, she found a splendid villa to her taste on Steinfeldgasse on the Hohe Warte. It had been designed for a Viennese construction magnate, Edward Ast, by her old Secession friend, Josef Hoffmann, and had a large veranda, an ample garden, and more than twenty rooms, with furniture by the Vienna Werkstätte. A hall with a black wooden staircase was lined floor to ceiling with marble and built-in cabinets, and colors were harmonized between rooms—dark green for the study, gray-green Cipolino marble in the oval ladies' salon. While Werfel was away in Santa Margherita working on his novel *The Sisters of Naples*, Alma refurbished the villa with a new music room and a large study for Werfel at the top of the house. Glass cabinets were filled with autographs and manuscripts, including the original score of Anton Bruckner's Third Symphony, which he had given to Mahler to make a piano arrangement. The project seems to have released in her a new energy and a revival of her love for Werfel. At Santa Margherita in late February, she was ecstatic: "Werfel! Sometimes he moves me so much that I can hardly look at him. His incredible generosity and luminescence!"[81]

But when she returned alone on March 29 for her last night in her old apartment at 22 Elizabethstrasse, she was filled with trepidation and too anxious to sleep. Death had stalked their new villa; two of the Asts' children had died there, a son of leukemia and his daughter, aged twenty, in childbirth. "I will have to muster much strength to fight the dead that are there. Will my cheerfulness be able to dry the tear-soaked walls?" she wondered.[82] At least in the short term, her fears were unfounded. When she moved in, "the house welcomed me with open arms and I stayed the night in my own bed with the feeling I had never slept elsewhere before."[83] Manon joined her from her boarding school, and they fell asleep together in the huge bed. Even though the villa was unfinished, she was persuaded by Felix Salten, the critic and author of *Bambi*, to hold a large party, with guests including the actor Conrat Veith, famous for his role in *The Cabinet of Doctor Caligari,* and other film and theatrical luminaries who drank and danced all night.

It was only the first of the many fabled social evenings hosted by Alma in the opulent mansion, where the elite from across the whole of Viennese society and culture—politicians, artists, religious leaders, writers, composers, poets, academics, intellectuals—all mingled in Alma's grand salon. But as the political landscape in Germany shifted dramatically to the right in the next few years, the contours of Austrian society and the fortunes of Alma and her immediate circle would change irrevocably.

— 12 —

Gathering Storms
1931–1936

For the first months at Villa Mahler, Alma entertained visitors almost daily—"tall, always in ankle length dresses, her hair glowing, her jewellery glittering prominently," as one guest noted. "Alma knew exactly how to make a beautiful and pleasant evening for her guests."[1] Her daughter Anna recalled her powerful allure: "When she entered a room, or just stopped in the doorway, you could immediately feel an electric charge. . . . She was an incredibly passionate woman. . . . And she really paid attention to everyone she spoke to. And encouraged them. . . . She was able to enchant people in a matter of seconds."[2]

Her salon was soon legendary. Old friends Arnold Schoenberg, Alban and Helene Berg, Bruno Walter, Ödön von Horváth, Hermann Broch, Franz Theodor Csokor, Egon Friedell, and Ernst Bloch mingled with artists, industrialists, scholars, and politicians of all political persuasions, including the future chancellor, Kurt von Schuschnigg, socialists Karl Renner and Julius Tandler, and the right-wing Anton von Rintelen. "In one corner of the boudoir, people discussed in a whisper about some appointment to a high government position, while another group of people were making up their minds whom to cast in a new comedy at the Burgtheater," Karl Mann recalled.[3]

Writer Carl Zuckmayer brought along a friend, Albrecht Joseph, who had first heard of Alma in 1921 at rehearsals in Frankfurt for Oskar

Figure 18. Alma pays close attention at her salon to composer Otto Klemperer, 1930s.

Kokoschka's play *Orpheus and Eurydice,* based on his life with Alma. Joseph remembered Kokoschka sitting in the theater day after day, "weeping quietly, incessantly . . . the rivulets of tears streaming down his face."[4] When he finally met her in Vienna, Joseph was taken aback "that this matron had ever been cast in the role of a seductress." Her figure was "simply a bag of potatoes veiled in flowing robes," but her bearing was "still imposing, regal, radiating authority," and she had "a good, even beautiful face" that, he sniped, expressed "more intelligence than she really had."[5] Perhaps sensing hostility, Alma told Zuckmayer: "Unfortunately your friend is lacking in sex appeal."[6] From then on, Joseph rarely missed an opportunity to qualify a compliment about her with an acid barb. When she failed to provide the promised help with a friend's play, he concluded bitterly that it was "a myth" that she was "queen of culture" and could "pull wires behind the scenes."[7]

Even so, he recognized the uniqueness that attracted so many to her. She possessed "the conviction of being a beauty, and this conviction radiated from her with great force." Though she "could act the haughty grand dame" at her salon, she was usually "jolly, good humored, smiling, ready to laugh even at poor jokes, drinking a lot of liquor (she did not smoke) and keeping the talk going," though for Joseph this was "never very interesting since, in a typical Viennese manner, she preferred to deal in generalities and would not be pinned down to details." He did acknowledge her expertise in music; when she once talked to him about a Mahler concert, she went "immediately, almost ruthlessly, to the core of the matter and talked with the enthusiastic knowledge of the thorough expert. . . . I had heard the concert myself on the radio but Alma's interpretation lifted my awareness to a much higher level. It felt like being whirled round in a mental storm."[8] She had the ability, "in a flash, with the speed of a rocket . . . to leave the common ground of everyday life and hover for a long time in the higher sphere of the mind which appeared to be her natural environment."[9]

Ever since Alma had moved into the new house, her social life, which had included preparations for the twentieth anniversary of Mahler's death, had been relentless. "From Whitsun onwards I was in bed and could hardly speak from exhaustion. I pretended I wasn't at home and finally had peace," she wrote.[10] Although she had a brief respite from the social whirl with Werfel in Venice, she had dropped everything to take care of her friend Albert von Trentini, who was dying of cancer. But after a short spell back in Vienna, perched on the Hohe Warte high above the city, she felt cut off: "This peace, away from town, is very monotonous and I don't know for how long I can bear it. As monotony tends to make me ill again. I need a lot of life around me—a lot of activity—and opportunities for stimulating exchange!" With nothing left to do in the house, she did not want "to become acquainted with boredom."[11]

Stimulating opportunities returned during summer at Breitenstein, when the usual stream of visitors passed through. On a visit to a spa near Padua in September, Alma read Romain Roland and André Gide, whom she liked, and Ilya Ehrenberg, whom she didn't, and evolved another grand theory, this time about Italian opera: "Nature is not close to the Italian. There is always laughter, no conflict. No mystical fog, no grey and black clouds. . . . Verdi is only interested in what is happening inside human beings. Every situation of the soul he masters successfully, nature does not intrude like, for example, always with Wagner. . . . The Italians only suffer from their own passions not from the demons of nature."[12]

Werfel's novel *Die Geschwister von Neapel*, published in October, was, like his previous one, an instant success. He was now ranked among the most widely read authors in the German language. Alma joined him on his extended lecture and reading tour to Germany in November, but the trip was interrupted by a call from Vienna. Anna was ill. Then came a telegram clarifying that Anna was physically healthy but suffering from "illness of the soul." Andy, Paul Zsolnay's mother, then called: Anna and Paul were divorcing. Alma was on a train within an hour, leaving Werfel to continue the tour. In Vienna she discovered Anna had been having an affair with the writer Rene Fülöp-Miller (Philipp Jakob Müller), who was in Alma's view "that most repulsive of all literati."[13] They had attempted joint suicide when their affair had been discovered.

On her arrival, Alma found "nothing but ugliness, vulgarity and slander" as accusations flew between the parties. For a month she "stood naked in front of this bore" as she "fought to free Anna from [Fülöp-Miller's] fangs," while he in revenge told Paul Zsolnay's father that Alma wanted Anna to stay with Zsolnay only for his inheritance.[14] Alma was in despair: "Not since the days of O.K. has so much ugliness been poured over me." She was upset with Anna, suspecting that she was the source of the slanderous comments against her: "My child has shamed me and defamed me in the ugliest way. I have spent days in bed and half the tears I shed were out of anger and the other half out of melancholy. I don't care any longer what happens to those two!"[15]

Nevertheless, when the drama subsided, Anna took refuge for a while with Alma. When she found she was pregnant but was uncertain of the paternity, she had an abortion. Zsolnay eventually fetched her back to a secret location near Vienna, where she discovered her great talent for sculpture, which became her life's career. Later that year she returned to her marriage with Zsolnay, their two-year old daughter, Alma, and the beautiful Marie Theresa house. Alma's faith in her daughter was renewed on her twenty-eighth birthday. Although Anna had had to make amends to the Zsolnays for her "lies and betrayal," Alma knew that "this beautiful gifted, young creature" would triumph beside "these mites."[16]

Alma now paused to reflect on her own life. Looking through her musical compositions one day in March 1932, she became "so absorbed with the heyday of my talent, that when I woke up I was completely distraught, I had to cry. Why did I allow myself to be diverted so far from my path? My path, which is so different from the one I have followed." She tormented herself with her familiar regret: Why had she never again achieved the great love, the intimate unity, the oneness, she had felt with Kokoschka? She found consolation in the thought that she was "surrounded by many men and I drink a lot to silence my suffering soul," but she would make more music from now on—"the music that makes me happy."[17] Werfel helped restore her faith in their love: "Franz said today: 'If ever I like a woman other than you, I would, like the heroin in *Der Maskenball*, go and find the blue herbs to cure me of love.' This has deeply moved me."[18]

Their political differences remained unresolved, however, as Austria's stability fragmented. In May 1932, with a coalition government in crisis and a worsening economic outlook, the thirty-nine-year-old leader of the Christian Social Party, Engelbert Dolfuss, took over as federal chancellor, heading a conservative coalition dominated by the parliamentary branch of the right-wing Heimwehr. Within a year his leadership would lead to the establishment of an authoritarian Christian corporate state—the Ständestaat—and, in 1934, to the end of parliamentary democracy in Austria.

This shift in the political landscape initially made little impact on Alma: "Life just keeps flowing on . . . hardly anything worth knowing or important for me. One just plays along," she noted in her diary.[19] Her most pressing concern after much soul searching was her decision in June 1932 to return to the Catholic Church, which she had formally left in August 1900. She had been increasingly tormented by "the feeling of being rejected by the community of the saints." While her decision was a wholehearted expression of her spirituality, it was perhaps also part of a personal struggle to reassert her clear identity as a conservative Christian during a time of extreme economic and political division. Werfel drew closer to his religious roots during the same period. Having lived all his life as an assimilated Jew, he rarely engaged with ritual and felt sometimes estranged from his faith. During the 1930s he identified ever more closely and firmly with his Jewishness; he "could no longer be expelled . . . from his Jewishness, not by Christians or even by Jews."[20]

At Breitenstein that summer, Alma was concerned that Werfel had lost direction in his work, as he spent his time amending his poems, with no major new project. After a fierce argument with Alma about the nature of heroes, Werfel found the inspiration for a different kind of hero in his next novel. Ever since he had encountered the emaciated Armenian orphans in the Damascus carpet factory, he had been probing the horrendous details of the Turkish massacre of the Armenians between 1915 and 1918. The heroes of his new novel, *The Forty Days of Musa Dagh*, would be the small group of oppressed people who resisted the destructive might of a nationalist power. Werfel would write "about a hero, how HE sees him . . . [and] throw a light on Turkish nationalism," Alma reported, pleased that "once again I am an inspiration for his work."[21]

As visitors arrived at Breitenstein, Alma was thrust back into the mainstream of political debate, which focused increasingly on events in Germany. Since 1930, Adolf Hitler and the NSDAP, the Nazi Party, had made steady electoral gains in Germany. With spiraling economic depression, rising unemployment, and widespread loss of confidence in the Weimar government, Hitler appealed to the masses with the call for strong leadership, unity, rebirth of the German nation, and the purge of "enemies of the Volk"—socialists, Marxists, and, in particular, Jews.

Previously an insignificant minority party, the Nazis had become the second-largest party after the Social Democrats in the 1930 election, with nearly 6.5 million votes and 107 seats in the Reichstag. They made further gains in state elections. In February 1932, Hitler ran for president but failed to oust the aged General Paul von Hindenburg from the post. In the summer of 1932, armed Nazi storm troopers of the SA and SS rampaged through the streets of Germany wreaking havoc, sacking Jewish shops, and engaging in violent street battles with the paramilitary forces of the left-wing Schutzbund. In the Reichstag elections in July, the Nazis won a substantial electoral presence with more than a third of the seats. President Hindenburg, who disdained Hitler as "the Bohemian corporal," maneuvered with Chancellor Franz von Papen to limit Nazi power and block Hitler's demand to be made state chancellor and seize control of the government.

Alma, Werfel, and their guests viewed events in Germany with unease: "Everybody calms down when the subject turns to Hitler whom *first and foremost they no longer trust* . . . and of whose anti-Semitism they are respectful. They are Jews, so they must know!" she noted in August about the reactions of her friends.[22] Her own deeply conservative, anti-Semitic, and often contradictory conclusion was that "in Germany everything is topsy turvy. More and more it is not a battle between North and South— between Protestantism and Catholicism—but simply a confrontation between Jew and Christian. With communism, the WORLD DOMINATION of Judaism stands and falls BECAUSE they have world domination with the help of the proletariat which they have radicalized. . . . At the helm of nearly all countries sat beastly Jews. . . . It is, after all, understandable that the different nations and countries can't stand for this. But there will be bloodbaths before the world is cleansed." At some time later she crossed out from the diary typescript: "*And therefore, I am for Hitler.*"[23]

Though tainted by the prejudices prevalent in Austria and Germany at the time, in her own mind Alma was clear: "I am not, what one calls an anti-Semite. I love the Jews and their brilliant characteristics." But "they should not have world domination. This would bring chaos. Because they don't know how to govern . . . their main characteristic is impulsiveness. Not suitable to keep a calm hand on government." When she read this in her diary ten years later, she added in her bold, purple handwriting: "*What followed was so terrible, awful and stupid that I have to completely take back everything I have said previously!*"[24]

Werfel's response to the gathering crisis was an impassioned lecture, "Can We Live Without Faith in God?" an unequivocal warning that loss of faith in the divine, the weakening of Christianity, was opening the way to the ersatz religions of communism, with its promise of paradise regained in the image of the classless society, and nationalism—"this raging monster," the herald of "dark primordial forces," which "speaks like an oracle [but] . . . serves not as truth but as magical incantation."[25] Werfel's recognition of the "raging monster" did not, however, alert him to the immense danger that lay ahead.

Despite the rising social tensions, Alma could draw figures from all shades of the political spectrum to her salon. In September, while staying with sixteen-year-old Manon at Schloss Velden on the Wörthersee, she met the newly appointed minister of education, Anton von Rintelen. A former governor and a leading figure in the right-wing Christian Social Party, he had strong links to the extreme militant and anti-Semitic elements of the Heimwehr. Rintelen paid court to Alma: "He was hopelessly in love with me. He followed me into my bedroom and pulled me out onto the balcony and courted me passionately like an impertinent youth. What he understood as love. . . . Immediate surrender! Mutzi and I laughed half the night over this clumsy old fool."[26] Back in Vienna, Rintelen soon joined the social throng around Alma. "Nearly all the members of the government visited me," she noted proudly, except Dolfuss, whom she had met elsewhere and reported witheringly that "it was relatively interesting from the beginning, *not more*."[27] That autumn Alma stopped drinking alcohol for a few months, only to find to her surprise that "the one I adored I no longer WANT"[28]—an echo, almost, of her relations with lovers.

She extended her political contacts when, on a three-week lecture tour of Germany with Werfel in December, she met Heinrich Brüning, a "seraphic being . . . incredibly modest and likes listening," who had been ousted the previous May from the German chancellorship. He prophesied that, despite their loss of support and of Reichstag seats in the November elections, the NSDAP remained the strongest party. The era of the current chancellor, Julius von Schleicher, "was coming to an end soon and 'Hitler will have won.' He said that a man who can wait for such a long time absolutely *has to* win," she reported.[29]

In Breslau on December 10, she witnessed Adolf Hitler address a huge political rally: "The whole city was in turmoil. I waited for hours to see his face. I did not go to Werfel's lecture but went and sat by myself in the dining room and drank a bottle of champagne. Well prepared like that, I then stood with many others and waited for him. A face that has conquered 13.000.000, that has to be some face. And that's right. IT WAS A FACE! Kind, soft, but all-embracing eyes, a young, terrified face. NO DUCE! But rather a youth, who will never mature, nor find wisdom."[30] When Werfel returned from his lecture, he glimpsed Hitler as he "disappeared with long strides up the stairs through an open door at the top. I asked Werfel about his impression. Werfel said: 'Not all that unappealing.'"[31]

On January 30, 1933, Hitler was appointed German state chancellor after von Papen had deftly maneuvered to remove General Schleicher, as Brüning had foretold, and force President Hindenburg's capitulation. There is no mention in Alma's diary of Hitler's accession or of the triumphant massed ranks of storm troopers who marched under the Brandenburg Gate and through Berlin, cheered on by ecstatic crowds.

IN THE NEW Year, Alma's own life was turned upside down by a new love. Her religious conversion had strengthened her links to the Catholic establishment, presided over by the arch-conservative Cardinal Theodor

Innitzer. The previous autumn Alma had attended his enthronement as archbishop of Vienna at St. Stephen's Cathedral. Among the dignitaries whom Alma invited back to her villa was the professor of divinity Johannes Hollnsteiner, with whom she soon felt "an immediate affinity." By February, she was suffering "a certain confusion within me. A little unimpressive priest can shatter my composure? With what powers?" And handwritten beside it in her diary: "JOHANNES HOLLNSTEINER!" At his third visit, she "had the feeling that all the other people around us were just grey silhouettes. . . . And now I don't know where I am anymore. God in heaven! The incomprehensively long night of this winter has given way to a balmy sense of awakening spring. It is hardly possible to endure!"[32] Soon he was visiting every day.

Johannes Hollnsteiner was a thirty-eight-year-old priest with ambition and influence. He had entered the St. Florian Monastery of Augustinian Canons near Linz at age nineteen and was ordained five years later. His study at the University of Vienna led him to a professorship in canon law, and by 1933 he had accrued enough power within clerical circles to be seen as Cardinal Innitzer's successor. He had also cultivated political connections as confessor and spiritual adviser to the future state chancellor, Kurt von Schuschnigg. Hollnsteiner's contacts made him an intermediary of influence in the political arena.

At the end of February, Alma spent a brief ten days with Werfel in Santa Margherita, where she listened with complete delight to the first two-thirds of Werfel's new novel, *Forty Days of Musa Dagh:* "I am praying that it will be the great work that we both dream of," she wrote.[33] When she returned to Vienna, once again she felt a deep sense of community with Catholic leaders. "THIS is where I belong—from my innermost being. The exclusive existence with Jews has removed me from myself, if that was possible. Now I am once again at home with myself." She had found in Hollnsteiner a guide and mentor: "I want to benefit from Hollnsteiner. He has profound knowledge and intellect—and a noble, unintrusive way to offer his knowledge as a gift."[34] He enlightened her on the Mass and other biblical issues: "Every word from him to me is like a song. The everlasting happens in His memory!" she enthused. They discussed indulgences and Luther's Reformation. Hollnsteiner viewed Hitler as "a type of Luther, despite also the great distance between them," Alma noted.[35]

Alma was in love. She was also certain that "we are both bound. He to the Church, I to Werfel who I love so much . . . who is so close to my spirit." But temptation was strong. "He is so free. . . . Never yet has he uttered the word SIN. He doesn't feel it as that. . . . And I . . . must I be more Catholic than the Pope?" she wondered. "J.H. is 38 years old and has not known a WOMAN until now. He wants to be and IS only a priest. He sees me differently and I bless myself for this. He said: 'I was never close to a woman. You are the first and you will be the last.' I respect this human being to the point that I fall on my knees in front of him. Everything within me is yearning for submission but I always had to dominate against my will. Here is the first man who has conquered me."[36]

Hollnsteiner was a regular visitor at the Hohe Warte, and for a time, according to Anna, Alma rented an apartment where they would meet.[37] Away working in Santa Margherita, Werfel wrote to her reassuringly, "I am pleased that Hollnsteiner is with you. Please pass my heartfelt greetings on to him. He is a magnificent human being. I have a lot of love for real and serious priests."[38] But his tolerance was soon stretched; in May, Alma complained that Werfel was "making one mistake after another. . . . Today he wouldn't let me go to church—and that was an injustice. *This is because of his jealousy.* THERE I am not unfaithful to him! Or perhaps ESPECIALLY there—where he will NEVER have access."[39] Even so she was sure that "in reality he does not believe in [my] betrayal—and OF COURSE THERE IS NONE."[40] Much later, she affirmed the perfect understanding between them, "despite the currents that now and then might tend to sweep me away; after a while these currents invariably turned out to be placid brooks in which I was reflecting my own image. [Werfel] knew that well. He was never jealous of the individual."[41]

By July, Alma's initial burning infatuation for Hollnsteiner was weakening: "Whatever the little priest has been able to teach me, he has already done [it]. I have regained my independence again and I will make sure to keep it. You pay extra when you give yourself to somebody spiritually." With a hint of disillusion, she decided "Hollnsteiner is either an Angel or a scoundrel. Out of instinct for self-preservation I decided to see him as an angel."[42] It seems that Hollnsteiner's commitment to God had taken precedence over his attention to her. She part resented, but even more admired, this dedication: "When I examine the tough, invisible work of a Hollnsteiner, who doesn't care if and when he sleeps, or eats, whose duty it is to keep his eyes fixed towards God, then I see the ENORMOUS difference in the races and philosophies." In his dogged zeal, she chose to find comparison with Hitler, "who was 14 years in the shadows, always working his way up, and again and again retreating, because his time had not yet come, . . . a genuine Teutonic manifestation of the zealot—which among Jews would be almost unthinkable. Unfortunately he [Hitler] is *stupid!*" she wrote.[43]

Alma's embrace of Catholicism highlighted a further dichotomy in her life. Alma admired, needed, and lived almost exclusively among Jews, despite her anti-Semitic prejudices. Two of her husbands were Jews, as were most of the artists, creative spirits, and innovators with whom she felt the closest affinity. "I could really write a book about 'MY LIFE AMONGST THE JEWS'—like others write about their life amongst the wild people. Because they are the wild people of the desert these Jews." One evening as she sat with Werfel and their old friends, Julius Tandler, Bruno Walter, and Ernst Polak, she had felt "alien, separated through insurmountable barriers. These barriers lie IN me. I know it. And they have increased."[44]

Political developments in Germany intruded steadily on their lives. The consolidation of the Nazi hegemony proceeded swiftly. An emergency decree in February suspended the rights of freedom of speech and association and the freedom of the press. In March the Enabling Acts abolished the Reichstag as a democratic body and established the Nazi dictatorship. Alma immediately perceived the danger to Austria of Hitler's expansionist ambitions: "Our Austria hangs by a thread—in the spider's web in *Germany's claws!*" she wrote. "Schuschnigg is a weak, cultivated little man. I have no confidence in the strength of our current leaders." Without "a miracle"—ideally, the restoration of the Habsburg monarchy—she could see "no way forward."[45]

Citing Austria as a country where anti-Semitism was "even more insidious than in Germany," she counseled that Jews should prove "through their dignity and achievement that the others are unjust" and warned that those "fantasising Jews running around and wailing in Austria . . . are now destroying the last remnant of respect people still had for them." It was a statement dangerously close to blaming the Jews for their fate, but one shared at the time by many assimilated Jews. To her diary she confided, "I fear—all is already too late!" Her opaque comment on the political situation in November 1933 was that "HITLER is just a feeble little man—not particularly intelligent. And 40 million people dance to . . . no, not his tune but something much louder . . . the loudest tune!"[46]

The web was tightening on their lives. On May 10, Werfel's books, along with 25,000 others by Jewish, religious, pacifist, liberal, socialist, or communist writers, were publicly burned by Nazi storm troopers outside the State Opera House in Berlin and by students and some teachers in university towns throughout Germany. On the orders of the propaganda minister, Joseph Goebbels, works by Arthur Schnitzler, Max Brod, Alfred Döblin, Lion Feuchtwanger, Ödön von Horváth, Franz Kafka, Robert Musil, Heinrich and Thomas Mann, Stefan Zweig, Karl Marx, Sigmund Freud, and Albert Einstein—and by many of their friends, acquaintances, and literary idols—were immolated. When a circular arrived from the Prussian Academy of the Arts Literary Division in Berlin clarifying that it was the duty of members to exclude "political activity against the government" and participate loyally in "nationalistic cultural duties," Werfel signed it; nine of the twenty-seven members of the Literary Division did not.

Werfel fell into a deep depression: "A child of fortune from birth till well beyond his fortieth year! Nothing went wrong for him, parents, sisters, wealth, continuously growing fame, and now, suddenly, the persecution of Jews in Germany." Alma wrote. "His books were burnt—he is no more courted, he is a small, cheeky Jew with moderate talent for those that now dictate success. Now even more I must stand by him."[47] She resolved that she would "never leave Werfel and the worse he is treated the less likely I will leave him! You cannot brush aside fifteen years from your own life. Even less when a being like him is and was to me so totally good and pure and noble."[48]

In October, Werfel emerged with the final version of his novel *The Forty Days of Musa Dagh*, a harrowing account of the resistance of a persecuted Armenian minority to the terror, deportations, and massacre perpetrated by a fanatical nationalist power, the Turks. It had powerful resonance for the time, as Alma knew: "It is an enormous achievement for a Jew, in SUCH a time to write such a work."[49] Although published to almost universal acclaim in November, it was confiscated in Germany and banned as a danger to public order and safety: "In the so-called best years of my life and after working without pause, I now stand on the ruins of myself," he wrote to Anna Moll in February 1934. "In Germany I have been deleted from the book, and the books, of the living, and since I am, after all, a German author, am now suspended in empty space."[50]

News of Alma's daughter, Anna, had meanwhile arrived: "She is in love—and as always it is with THE wrong one, a total phoney. This time it is a half-crippled, nihilistic Jew who will hardly let her go once he's got her. I am trying everything to help her—in every sense. It is the sparsely gifted poet, Elias Canetti," Alma spluttered in June 1933. "It is tragic how she always associates herself with people deficient of heart and soul, complete intellectual destroyers. . . . As far as I'm concerned, she can leave house and home—and me too!"[51]

The now familiar pattern with Anna's lovers ensued. Writer Elias Canetti, later a recipient of the Nobel Prize for Literature, reciprocated Alma's withering dislike. Even before he met her, he had taken against her. Later he deployed his talents to pen his coruscating, if occasionally entertaining, impressions of Alma—with the dramatic flourish of one who delights in hyperbole and often cruel caricature. On their first meeting he found "a molten dowager . . . a rather large lady, overflowing on all sides, fitted out with a cloying smile and bright, wide-open, glassy eyes." This "inebriated individual who looked much older than she was" had gathered around her "trophies" of her life, including Mahler's scores, Kokoschka's portrait of her in which Canetti saw "the composer's murderess," and her daughter, seventeen-year-old Manon, who "came skipping into the room a short time later, a light brown-haired creature, disguised as a young girl."[52]

Alma meanwhile was in turmoil as she wavered between her continuing attraction to Hollnsteiner and her commitment to Werfel: "Today Werfel is calmer and so much closer to me. Mahler always said: 'In a closed ring nothing can come in.' Here was the opening and the little *Pater filucius* is already in. But now he sits outside. I hope, for always." She resolved to detach herself from Hollnsteiner, the intruder: "I will direct all my strength, my good will to live my life along MY path, not influenced by clergy to live a barren life of subjugation. I am in fact not calm yet, may never be, as these piercing brown eyes have a strong influence on me. God! Take the blindfold now completely from my eyes, so I can see again how I was, forever and forever. AMEN."[53] But it was not resolved, and on November 27 she was "just thinking . . . should I slash my arteries or throw myself somewhere out of the 5th Floor. I am so deeply unhappy—as never before. . . . I seek joy to lift me out of my present state of mind. . . . Why this being affects me so deeply, I don't know."[54]

On Christmas Eve, she surveyed the recent "harsh, boundlessly harsh" times: "My intense love is broken against the girdle of light—of my lover. I have a sea of tears in me and, where words fail, a river flows through. Unstoppable. . . . I must learn to be content or I lose him and my new support. In his intense work life he does not need the hysterical moods of a woman." Alma was feeling uncomfortably sidelined to her lover's higher purpose—a purpose that, fatally, she admired. "The calm of my 'great' experience has been shattered. But the spring was the happiest time of my life."[55]

THE POLITICAL ATMOSPHERE in Austria remained precarious. With the dissolution of Parliament in March 1933, Dolfuss had established a one-party dictatorship in which nationalist and conservative elements and the increasingly influential Heimwehr joined together in the Fatherland Front. The Communist Party was banned, the National Socialist Party was dissolved, and its members expelled from the country. To the nations' mutual benefit, Dolfuss entered into an alliance with Italian dictator, Mussolini, who endorsed the increasingly authoritarian regime and agreed to guarantee Austrian independence against any attempts at unification with Hitler's Germany. The chancellor's measures did not, however, resolve the profound underlying fissures in Austrian society.

Alma often went with Manon to a cafe in town, where she read the newspapers and was regularly outraged at the way the workers' press "continually agitated for civil war."[56] She also had scant sympathy in her Catholic conservative heart for "the enormous mistakes" made by Social Democrats such as her friend, Joseph Tandler, who, as welfare minister, had challenged the influence of the country's clergy when he barred crucifixes from the hospitals and allowed priests in only during visiting hours. Later Alma blamed the Social Democrats for preparing the way for Nazism in Austria: "They uncoupled the relationship between the farmers and the priests. Free from the church, so, empty in their goddam heads—they were easy prey for the bacillus of the Nazi idea."[57]

On February 12, 1934, simmering conflict exploded into civil war after the Heimwehr, on the pretext of investigating an alleged arms cache, raided the Social Democratic Party headquarters in Linz. The Social Democratic leadership issued a call for resistance, ordered a general strike, and mobilized the outlawed but still clandestinely active Schutzbund. Several days of violence and street battles ensued.

Alma was at a friend's house when she heard that the general strike had been called. She left, bought candles, and raced home. "There was already no telephone, no electric light etc etc. and we were so completely alone in the Hohe Warte." Minister of Justice Kurt von Schuschnigg, a regular visitor, contacted Alma immediately to urge her and Manon to stay with him, but she declined: "The fierce shooting [we were in the firing zone] moved me terribly and almost excited me," she wrote. Outside, for two days, a desperate battle raged: "In the small lane in which our house is located a mass of people came in waves up and down. The workers tried to take the government guns from the rear. Shots were being fired out of all workers houses and if one shot of the *Heimwehr* strayed there, the ruffians screamed murder."[58] Attacks by the military on workers' houses were met by fierce resistance; their homes became virtual fortresses.

Order was not restored until February 16. More than three hundred were dead, and seven hundred were wounded on both sides. Social Democratic leaders were either arrested or exiled. Several were executed, and their party and the trades unions were banned. Chancellor Dolfuss enacted a new constitution that effectively removed all remnants of democracy. In Alma's judgment at the time, the events had damaged the Dolfuss government, but the real beneficiary was Hitler: "The Nazis—developed a strong movement amongst the workers and these, resentful from their experience of the February happenings, sank blissfully into their arms."[59]

After all these upheavals, Alma retreated with Werfel in March to Venice. Werfel was "very good and loving towards me." Alma declared herself "almost without any desires. . . . I must stand above these things. I won't allow any man to devour me and spit me out anymore." Her relationship with Hollnsteiner had reached an impasse: "Holl. doesn't need me, he doesn't need anyone. He has his *idea*. For him it's as if I have grown around his life like a rose with its thorns."[60] Her mood improved in Milan, where, at a performance with Werfel of Verdi's *La Forza del Destino*, she felt "how well we live with each other, how well we get on and enjoy music together although he is more inclined to song and I to the purely musical." But there was a drawback: "Physically—I am miles away from him. What it reveals—is that for years,—despite great physical harmony, a discrepancy has developed which is for me insurmountable," she wrote opaquely.[61]

Alma's daughter, sixteen-year-old Manon, had grown into a tall, slender young woman with waist long hair and a natural elegance, who was attracting the admiration of her friends. Bruno Walter had been beguiled on a visit by "this unearthly apparition before me, which offered itself to us as we sat still at brunch, an angelic, beautiful girl . . . with a deer at her side."[62] In Venice, when fifty-seven-year-old Anton von Rintelen, newly appointed ambassador to Rome, visited them, his amorous attentions turned on Manon. This did not unduly trouble Alma, and Manon cannily kept her distance: "She was as immune [to him] as I was," Alma wrote.[63]

The career of the ambitious suitor Rinteln was to be short-lived. On July 25, 1934, Chancellor Engelbert Dolfuss was assassinated by a group of Austrian Nazis in a failed putsch. Dressed in police and army uniforms, they stormed the radio station, central government offices, and the Federal Chancellery. Dolfuss was shot in the back and died

Figure 19. Manon Gropius. "A godlike lovable being, a creative energy, such as I have never seen." —Alma Mahler-Werfel

from his wounds. Rintelen, who was believed to be heavily implicated in the Nazi conspiracy, had returned to Vienna and was waiting at the Hotel Imperial for the call to take over the government as chancellor. The coup failed, the government regained control, and Rintelen was arrested. The night before the coup, Rintelen had put Alma in a potentially compromising position by inviting her to have a beer with him at a famous Viennese tavern. As an associate and possible accessory, she was called as a witness, but her testimony was so "innocuous" that she was not called to the main trial. Rintelen was sentenced in 1935 to life imprisonment for high treason.

Kurt von Schuschnigg took over as chancellor after five days of refusing the post: "He said to me, 'I am only a first-rate second but not a first-rate first,'" Alma recalled. "And so it came that Schuschnigg and his followers fought for five years against the larger next-door enemy who was already spreading his pestilence."[64] Schuschnigg maintained the autocratic Ständestaat regime in Austria.

In April 1934, tragedy overtook their lives. When Alma returned to Venice with Werfel from Milan on April 6, she found Manon looking pale, though otherwise well. At the Fenice restaurant, she had no appetite. Staying with them was writer Ernst Lothar, whose daughter had died of polio eight months before. When he saw Manon, "slender and gentle" coming to join them in St. Mark's Square, Alma noticed in his eyes a shadow of pain, which caused a shock to run through her. Then she suddenly realized she had lost her valued emerald cross, a present from Hollnsteiner. In vain they searched the square, the alleys. A terrible fear came over her: "Uneasily I sensed an evil omen," Alma remembered.[65]

A week later, on April 13, despite feeling unwell, Manon went with her governess to the train station, where "with her slim, beautiful hand," she waved off Alma and Werfel on the 5 a.m. train for Vienna: "It was the last time I would see her well, standing, walking, in her incredible beauty," Alma recalled.[66] That evening Alma was guest of honor at a performance of Mahler's *Das Lied von der Erde*, conducted by Bruno Walter. The next day she cabled Manon, who replied, "Stomach upset almost better, come hopefully Thursday." But Alma was anxious: "In her condition we should have taken her along with us to Vienna . . . , but she was very strong-willed when she wanted something. The whole day, on our trip, I had a feeling I should have taken her along."[67]

After the performance they joined Schuschnigg and Walter for supper at the Grand Hotel. When an urgent phone message came through that Manon was not well—"something in her head"—Alma called Manon's governess, who kept sobbing, "Camphor—Camphor." Alma booked tickets on the next plane back. When they got to Venice—"how we got to the house, I do not know. We rang, the maid screamed for joy above at the window and Mutzi hugged me, crying, then kept saying: 'Now all is good, when my Mami is here.'"[68]

The doctors diagnosed poliomyelitis and ordered an immediate lumbar puncture. Alma paced the room, unable to concentrate on anything. Two days later, paralysis of the legs set in, and, within a few days, Manon's whole body was paralyzed. The neurologist who arrived from Vienna administered twenty-one injections to ease the excruciating pain as the disease spread. Then respiratory paralysis began. "It was an utter death before death," Werfel recalled, "an incredibly terrible hour."[69] Anna, who had flown with Werfel and Zsolnay to be by her side, rushed round Venice and, with her admirable resourcefulness, found an oxygen apparatus and cylinders, which saved Manon's life. Their friend, art dealer Adolf Loewi, kept his motor launch at Alma's disposal for the entire time.

When they decided in the first week of May to transport Manon home to Vienna, Schuschnigg requisitioned for them a special car—the former railway ambulance of the Emperor Franz Joseph, equipped with an operating room and oxygen tent. Gropius had been told of the onset of his daughter's illness on his way to lecturing in England, but travel restrictions had become so tight and expensive that it was impossible to get to Vienna immediately. He kept abreast of her progress and wrote regular encouraging letters to her. When he was eventually able to visit for a week in June, he found her in good spirits. He adopted the approach shared by those around her, of determined optimism about her eventual recovery—despite the evidence. His position in Berlin had become steadily more precarious under a regime implacably hostile to modernism, the Bauhaus included.

As Manon's condition stabilized, she gradually regained some use of her upper body and arms. Confined to a wheelchair, she developed her talents as an actress, the career she had set her heart on. Their friend Franz Horch, drama coach and manuscript reader for Max Reinhardt, tutored her in acting. Horch brought actor Werner Krauss, famous for the film *The Cabinet of Doctor Caligari* (and later infamous for *Jud Süsse*), to rehearse his parts with her. He was impressed by her artistic instincts. "I'm really desperate," he told Alma. "I've read the soliloquy four times now, and Manon still isn't satisfied!"[70] Playwright Carl Zuckmayer, who had gone into exile in Salzburg when his plays were banned by the Nazis, was captivated by Manon, who shared his love of the novels of Karl May—and of snakes, which he brought her as gifts.

Hollnsteiner visited almost daily, a calming presence in all their lives, and sent her encouraging and drolly witty postcards when he was away. Manon's best friend, Susi Kertész, who had enrolled in drama school, enlisted her help with her lines. The aspiring young politician Erich Sepp Cylhar, a consultant to the federal chancellery and in line to be personal secretary to the minister of social administration, became her suitor and at the end of the year proposed to her. From China, Julius Tandler, who had been imprisoned following the February purge of Social Democrats, encouraged her to draw and write, and expressed his love by thinking of her every day at 3 p.m. Vienna time. When Alma discovered that Katherine, the daughter of the American publisher, Harry Sherman, was Manon's double—uncannily like her in looks, in "her reserve, her serious way with people," and in age—she invited her to stay in July and August and be her daughter's companion. By August, Manon had recovered sufficiently to write in her own handwriting to her father: "I'm now getting much better. My back is almost entirely free supporting. Things aren't so dull anymore. . . . I'm already eating at the table and getting visitors. Yesterday I had supper downstairs at table for the first time."[71]

On April 14, Manon was well enough to perform before an audience a monologue from Shakespeare's *Twelfth Night* and another from Schiller's *Joan of Arc*. It was, Werfel thought, "an inexpressibly matchless artistic achievement."[72] Even Manon colluded in the hope that one day she would sit again, even perhaps walk. However, the specialist gave Werfel his blunt diagnosis: "The lower limbs are totally dead. Experience shows that in spite of all our modern therapies, any improvement is illusory."[73] Manon would never walk again, but it was some consolation that she had regained the use of her arms and hands.

On Easter Saturday, April 20, 1935, there began the waves of nausea and cramps that signaled the final stage of the disease. On Sunday, Manon asked to see Hollnsteiner, who drove at speed from the monastery to which he had retreated in Upper Austria to be beside her. Physicians were called. On Easter Monday, "the horror happened. . . . [M]y most beautiful, sweetest child was snatched away, after a whole year when we fought for her recovery." Her last words to Alma had been, "Let me die in peace. I am not going to get well any more and my acting, you just persuaded me into it out of compassion. You'll get over it, the way you get over everything," and as if to correct herself, "like everyone gets over everything."[74]

Alma was inconsolable: "INCOMPREHENSIBLE ARE THE WAYS OF GOD," she wailed. "Nobody who knew her could forget her. We who remain behind are completely destitute."[75] Hollnsteiner "made the ugliness after the death beautiful" and ensured that she "was buried like a queen, just as she also lived."[76] To the crowds gathered for her funeral in Grinzing cemetery on April 24, he gave the eulogy: "She bloomed like a glorious flower. Pure as an angel she went through the world. . . . She has not died; she has gone home with open eyes."[77]

Walter Gropius, who after closing his Berlin office the previous October, had moved in penury to London, was informed by telegram on April 22 that she was gravely ill and immediately made preparations to fly to Vienna. The next day came a telegram announcing her death. No longer able to get the dispensation to bypass bureaucracy because of a sick relative, he and his wife, Isa, were waiting for a visa in Berlin when they learned that the funeral had already taken place. They returned to London, distraught. "The pain rooted deep. And came back to life with all its original sharpness whenever he thought of Manon," his biographer, Reginald Isaacs, noted.[78]

Alma was not present at the ceremony. Since the trauma of her father's funeral, she had attended neither Mahler's funeral nor those of her two dead children. This did not deter Elias Canetti from penning a vivid portrait of Alma supposedly at the graveside, a description that has been widely quoted and helped form the legend of Alma as a shallow, dissembling creature consumed with her own image. Canetti imagined Alma's tears—of which "there weren't too many, but she knew how to cry so that they flowed together until they were somewhat larger than life-size, tears the likes of which had never been seen before, like enormous pearls, precious jewellery; you couldn't look at her without being awestruck by so much motherly love."[79] But she was not there! When Alma made enemies among the literati, they did not ration their scorn.

Tributes flowed in for Manon, the child who was "too celestial to be able to live on earth," as Bruno Walter wrote.[80] "Something irreplaceable had vanished from my life," Carl Zuckmayer sighed. "I cannot think of any plants or flowers growing this spring without thinking of Mutzi."[81] To Alma's closest friend, Helene Berg, Mutzi "was not only your child, she was also mine. But we must not grieve that God has seen fit to take her, for she is now an angel."[82] Her husband, Alban, asked Alma's permission to compose a requiem for her, a violin sonata, *In Memory of an Angel*.[83]

Alma was desolate: "I desperately long for Mutzi," she wrote in July. "I can no longer live without her. She was the closest to my heart, closer than all the people I have ever loved. *I think only about the nature of my death*. I want to travel to Venice—put myself in her poor bed and open the gas tap." Hollnsteiner calmed her. He and Werfel tried to bring her around, "but neither succeed in leading me out of my fixation with death":[84] "I see Mutzi day and night—she is to me so present—so close—so unforgettable in and with me—*I love her*—she was my most special and as Hollnsteiner says, the meaning of my life HAS gone."[85]

Unable any longer to bear living in Casa Mahler, Alma went in August with Anna and Ida Gebauer to Venice to pack up the house in which for eleven years she had been happy: "But how hurt we were. The whole recent past stood before our eyes and I often could not hold myself back, just burst into tears." Rage occasionally broke through the depths of her mourning: "How awful this God is—if He exists, how despicable. Destroys my posterity in the purest form! For she was mine, my better self, blended with a very good essence from the other side. *But* this child, who knew each of my thoughts, yes, anticipated—this child had been torn from me and I stand here as a beggar."[86]

In an attempt at diversion, Alma went with Anna and Werfel on a tour of Italy, visiting Rome and Florence. In Viareggio, they stayed with Kurt von Schuschnigg, whose ally, Italy's dictator, Mussolini, was still the guarantor of Austria's independence from Germany, and provided Schuschnigg's party with a state limousine for their day trips to places of interest, including composer Giacomo Puccini's house beside a Tuscan lake.[87]

At Breitenstein in September Alma was "indifferent to everything, my life and that of others. Why bother? When death grins at you with its pitiless illogicality."[88] As she recalled the awful deaths of her other children—Maria, Martin, and now Manon—she comprehended only transience: "When I see a child, I see immediately in their features the rapid ripening, growing, passing of life, the nearness of death. When I see an animal—death. When I see plants—death looks through them, at me. It is frightful."[89]

In November she traveled with Werfel to New York, where Max Reinhardt was putting on a vastly expensive production of Werfel's Old Testament play, *The Eternal Road*, which taxed everyone to exhaustion. The voyage for Alma was "like a retracing of my ascent which had begun with Gustav Mahler," but now everything she had loved "lay entombed, decomposed."[90] She did not regain her calm until, with the American publication of *The Forty Days of Musa Dagh*, they were honored and celebrated by New York's Armenian community. On Christmas Eve they went to a banquet in the catacomb of an Armenian church. "We were a nation, but Franz Werfel gave us a soul," declared the priest in his sermon.[91] But Alma was profoundly shocked when she read in the newspaper that her old friend Alban Berg, at only fifty, had died suddenly that day of blood poisoning induced by an insect bite. "Quietly, by myself, I wept for Alban, whose last work had been a requiem for my child. Now it had become his own."[92]

Consumed by her loss and her loneliness, Alma turned her distress onto Werfel: "My marriage has long since ceased to be a marriage. . . . I live in deep sorrow beside Werfel, whose passion for monologues knows no bounds. HIS opinion, HIS words, HIS, HIS, HIS. . . . My self confidence, never very strong, is completely gone. I am only free when he is not there. . . . Suddenly I want to be away from him. Somewhere where I would like to be, to live."[93]

Nevertheless she returned to Europe with Werfel in February 1936. It would be some time before Alma regained her equilibrium—or her prodigious energy for life. When she did, it was directed not toward enjoyment or fulfillment but to survival.

— 13 —

Flight
1936–1941

*I*n April 1936, a year after Manon's death, Alma spent two weeks in Locarno with Werfel, who had been unable to work and was suffering from "the horrors of the last year."[1] Hollnsteiner joined them in Zurich, and all three had tea with writer Thomas Mann, who was living in exile and in danger of losing his German citizenship after speaking out against the Nazi regime. There was "much discussion of Hitler, Vienna and Schuschnigg. We sent off a card to the latter," Mann wrote.[2] On the anniversary of Manon's death, April 22, Hollnsteiner read a Mass for Manon, but it did little to console Alma: "The pain and incomprehension is like the first day. I feel her every moment all around me."[3]

Werfel went on to Bad Ischl in the Salzkammergut to immerse himself in the Bible and Jewish and Egyptian writings for his new novel about the prophet Jeremiah. In Vienna Alma was involved in preparations for the twenty-fifth anniversary of Mahler's death. Bruno Walter organized a program of concerts, supported by Schuschnigg, who saw an opportunity to demonstrate that Austria still celebrated its eminent Jewish cultural figures.

Her rapport with Bruno Walter was severely tested, however, when in June she read in manuscript form his monograph of Mahler. It was "highly unsympathetic . . . a conglomerate of received opinions. . . . Mahler comes out as banal." And, worst of all, Alma was "simply not present.

This wound to my ego ruined the night." She was furious that Walter had sidelined her and completely ignored her place in Mahler's life. And she was relieved that, despite Walter's objection, she had made public the evidence of his devotion in his anguished notes to the Tenth Symphony: "It was right to make facsimiles of these sketches to 'X' [the Tenth Symphony]. There seems to be no way these old opponents of mine can get over this: 'To live for you,—to die for you—Almschi!'" Thoroughly roused, she launched into an alarmingly overwrought diatribe against her "opponents" who "still hate the unsullied, beautiful Christian in me. For the Jews cannot forgive us our brighter nature . . . BLACK OF SOUL and devoid of compassion. It isn't enough for Mr. Walter and friends to have poisoned my youth—they want to get at me in my old age as well."[4] The incident fueled Alma's rising despair. "I no longer love anyone. My heart is parched. I love at most only my little patch of life. The works of men who were close to me no longer seem of paramount importance. They no longer need me, either."[5]

Outside the confines of their lives, political division hardened over Europe. In July 1936 the Spanish Civil War erupted after military-backed nationalist, conservative, and monarchist forces under General Francisco Franco mounted an insurgency against the left-leaning Republican government. Alma and Werfel supported opposite sides in the conflict, which led to tense arguments: "Time and again I try to get close to Werfel because he is close to me emotionally . . . [but] these days everything is politicised, we become enemies in no time. It is hard to live in peace in this world," Alma wrote sadly.[6] Their frequent rows threatened to break the marriage: "Werfel kept trying new arguments. It was stupid of him to try to convince her," her daughter Anna recalled. "Then after hours of embittered yelling, he lost his patience and ran out of the house, still seething, while Alma proceeded to attend to entirely different matters with the utmost composure, paying no attention to the fight they had had. He would come back, still upset, not relaxed in the least, and would start roaring again. Alma, fresh and in a good mood, received him graciously, as if she had won the argument. That was her strength: she didn't really take the political disagreements seriously, while Werfel was ready to shed his heart's blood over them."[7] Anna passionately shared Werfel's support of the Republican cause, and commiserated with him behind closed doors: "He would tell me every time, that he couldn't stand living

Figure 20. Alma with her daughter Anna, mid-1930s.

with Alma anymore and wanted a separation. . . . But he didn't have the strength to do it. He went back to her every time."[8]

Feeling embattled and isolated, Alma turned on Anna and, not for the first time, accused her of betrayal: "The leader of my opponents is always Anna. It is such a sorrow for me to have given birth to a 150% Jew." She turned again for consolation to her priest: "Yesterday Holl.[nsteiner] was close to me, like the Archangel! At the moment convivial togetherness brings no joy."[9] A cure at Marienbad spa did little to dispel her dark inner thoughts, which drifted back incessantly to Manon: "She was so very beautiful, altogether too pure to represent a creature upon this Earth."[10]

Alma decided she had to get out of the "disastrous house" on the Hohe Warte: "Buying [it] was a mistake for which I paid with Manon's death. . . . There have been guilty and innocent houses and homes in my life: wherever a loved one died there was guilt."[11] Werfel had never found the grandeur of it comfortable and had often escaped elsewhere to

write. They decided to rent it out. After packing up 10,000 books and
5,000 sheets of music, their paintings and furniture—"in reality junk for
eternity, and baggage during everyday life"[12]—she threw a party on June
11, 1937, that lasted from 8 p.m. in the evening until 2 p.m. the next
day. A band played Viennese folk tunes for members of the aristocracy,
Burgtheater stars, publishers, composers and conductors including Bruno
Walter and Alexander von Zemlinsky, writers, painters, diplomats, and
politicians. Franz Werfel fell into the pond, and Carl Zuckmayer bedded
down in the dog house "to get closer to nature," Alma reported. "Our
dear guests slept on every couch in the house, only to return refreshed to
the festivities." Franz von Papen, the Reich ambassador, "chatted with an
Austrian monarchist leader. 'If we were living three hundred years ago'
he said, 'I would have Hitler and his men burned at the stake. Since that
isn't done any more, we must wait for him to burn in his own fire.'"[13]

With Anna, Alma visited Berlin for three days, where she witnessed
the transformation of the city under Nazi rule: "A whole nation was
under arms, while in other countries people were drinking and gorging
and screwing and sleeping. . . . sleeping. . . . sleeping. The (other) nations tackled their national defence grudgingly," Alma noted.[14] In July
she returned alone to Breitenstein. As so often in Werfel's absence, her
yearning for Kokoschka returned. As she stood on her balcony, "an incredible rainbow spanned the valley over the mountain into infinity,"
which she interpreted as a sign: "'Oskar, you have forgiven me'—I mum-
bled and I opened my arms and was enveloped in him and his forgiveness. . . . It was the strangest most beautiful experience—of my life."[15] But
within days she had again "decided wholeheartedly for Werfel," to whom
she always returned, despite the tensions and torments they inflicted on
each other.[16] It was as if her obsessive recourse to thoughts of Kokoschka
whenever she felt lonely had become her way of testing, and then renewing, her love for Werfel.

That year, Anna achieved international recognition as a sculptor
when she was awarded first prize at the Paris World Fair of 1937 for an
impressive seven-foot-high female figure. Her marriage to Zsolnay had
proved less successful, and they had divorced in 1934; Zsolnay was granted
sole custody of their seven-year-old daughter, also called Alma. Faced
with an increasingly uncertain future, in November Alma consulted a
palm reader. Noting her "impressive artistic talent," her religiosity, and

great inner strength, he predicted with uncanny accuracy that she would leave Vienna at the age of fifty-nine and live with her husband in tranquil friendship in a foreign country, perhaps on another continent.[17]

Christmas of 1937 was "ghastly." Werfel had bronchitis, both he and Anna were "strangely out of tune with me," and the festivities only reminded Alma of Manon: "I cannot celebrate it without her. She surrounds me always but on days like this, I suffocate with pain."[18] Communion and midnight Mass with Hollnsteiner did not console her. She spent New Year's Eve with Werfel in rooms once used by Verdi at the Grand Hotel, Milan, and was restored by almost nightly performances at La Scala. They moved on to Capri, where, in a corner room with a balcony in the best hotel, Werfel "started writing poetry for the first time in years."[19] Calm was restored as they visited the opera in Naples, walked, and took excursions to Roman ruins.

A DARK CLOUD of anxiety hovered over their lives, however. Since 1934, despite Schuschnigg's policies to contain the Austrian Nazis and to resist Hitler's ambition to incorporate Austria into the Reich, the German threat had been building. Only a few perceived the danger. Stefan Zweig emigrated in 1934, soon after Hitler took power, and urged others, including Carl Zuckmayer and Werfel, to do the same, but his warnings fell on deaf ears.[20] Nor did the alarm bells ring when Schuschnigg made his first concession to Hitler: the agreement of July 1936, whereby Germany guaranteed Austrian independence but only in exchange for the release of the imprisoned leaders of the July putsch and the inclusion of representatives of the "national opposition"—in other words, Nazi supporters—in Schuschnigg's cabinet

Werfel and Alma and most of their associates had trusted in Schuschnigg's ability, with Mussolini's declared backing, to defend Austria's sovereignty. But in 1936 Mussolini entered into the alliance with Hitler, the Rome-Berlin Axis, that severely compromised continuing Italian support for Austria. By January 1938, Hitler's demand, backed by the threat of force, for a controlling influence on Austrian politics was building to a crisis that would be catastrophic for Austria's future.

While they were in Capri, on February 12, 1938, "the bomb exploded, and Werfel came hurtling into my room with the newspaper.

Schuschnigg had gone to Berchtesgaden."[21] At Hitler's private retreat in the Bavarian Alps, it was Schuschnigg's last vain attempt to resist Hitler's claims on Austria. Alma instantly grasped the implications—Austria's independence would end, and Werfel's life was in danger. She "got up and started to pack," then departed on February 28 for Vienna, where she spent two days incognito—"looking at my Vienna, which stared back at me with utterly strange eyes," as she planned their escape.[22]

Outbreaks of Nazi violence scarred several provincial towns as Schuschnigg received what was in effect an ultimatum from Hitler: under threat of invasion, the government must immediately release all Nazi prisoners, appoint the Austrian Nazi Arthur Seyss-Inquart as minister of the interior, in charge of the police and public order, and align Austria's policies more closely with Germany. The ban on the Nazi Party was to be lifted, the Nazi salute legalized, and the display of swastika flags permitted. When Alma contacted Hollnsteiner, however, he "radiated optimism." In his opinion Alma had been "overexcited by the foreign press."[23] Carl Zuckmayer, celebrating his newly acquired Austrian citizenship, also brushed aside Alma's foreboding. The Molls were jubilant: Carl Moll, his daughter Maria, and son-in-law, lawyer Richard Eberstaller, were already committed members of the Nazi Party.

Alma went to the state bank, cleared up her financial affairs, and withdrew the balance of her account in fifty-schilling notes, which were sewn into the girdle of the faithful Sister Ida Gebauer, who had agreed to smuggle the money out to Switzerland. The Edvard Munch painting, *Summer Night on the Beach*, given to Alma by Gropius on Manon's birth, had since 1937 been on loan to the Belvedere Gallery. Alma had at that time asked Moll to explore the possibility of selling it, but the gallery was unable to raise the 10,000 schillings she wanted. She left the painting in Moll's care, along with the house at Breitenstein and the Hohe Warte villa, both of which were soon festooned with swastika flags.

Werfel waited anxiously in Capri: "Please write INSTANTLY; is my gloom and sorrow to continue, shall I perhaps leave Capri? Write and tell me what to do . . . and write and tell me the truth about Vienna. . . . I am in a fever for an answer, and that's no understatement. My Almerl, I had really no idea how much love I have for you." Without her, he "truly felt like a man with only one arm and one leg."[24] Alma spent her "last happy evening" with the Zuckmayers, Ödön von Horváth, and Franz Theodor

Csokor in a popular but now all but deserted Jewish restaurant in Vienna. In front of a portrait of Hitler in the German Tourist Office, she observed banks of flowers piling up each day and overflowing into the street, placed there by processions of kneeling women. In a downtown bar she met Carl Zuckmayer, who was already some way into a drinking session with the cultural historian Egon Friedell. Ten days later, Friedell saw two SA men entering his apartment building and feared they were coming for him; rather than be arrested, he committed suicide by throwing himself out of the apartment window.

In an attempt to salvage control over Austria's destiny, Schuschnigg on his return from Berchtesgaden insisted that a plebiscite on Austria's independence be held on March 13, 1938. Anna campaigned energetically for it, while Alma observed the streets strewn with leaflets covered in hopelessly optimistic slogans: "Nobody picked up the leaflets; only the wind played with them, showing no mercy."[25] Two days before the plebiscite, Hitler demanded its cancellation and threatened invasion if it went ahead. With German troops massing at the border, Schuschnigg resigned that day, March 11, at 7:15 p.m., informing the nation "that we are giving way to brute force . . . , we have ordered our armed forces, should an invasion take place, to withdraw without resistance."[26] The federal president Wilhelm Miklas capitulated to Hitler's demand and appointed the Nazi Arthur Seyss-Inquart as chancellor.

Alma packed two suitcases and made ready to leave: "We knew— Austria is lost." The next day, March 12, the Wehrmacht marched into Austria and was greeted by jubilant crowds. People shook their fists at Alma as she insisted on driving in a car without a swastika flag to say goodbye to her mother: "I left her convinced that I would only be away for eight days," but Alma knew she would never see her mother again.[27] In Capri, Werfel despaired: "My heart is almost breaking with pain, even though Austria is not my country."[28] Anna refused to leave, and it was only after much persuasion that she packed a small suitcase. In her hotel room, Alma spent the whole night of March 12 talking with Hollnsteiner and Anna. Outside "the sky was filled with the drone of planes heralding Hitler's arrival."[29]

Perceiving no danger to himself, when Hollnsteiner was warned by Alma to destroy his politically incriminating papers, he replied, "Why, I haven't done anything."[30] It was a misconception shared by many, including Zuckmayer, who had no intention of leaving because, as he wrote in hindsight, "I hadn't 'done' anything, . . . I hadn't 'committed any crime' that would justify persecution. Yet by then justice had vanished from Germany and persecution was raging blindly, barbarously under the cloak of 'order and discipline.' There was no safety in having done nothing against the tyrants; one's crime was not having joined up with them."[31]

Alma departed on the morning of the invasion and traveled with Anna by train for Milan. Carl Moll came to the station to see them off "and appeared to be moved. He looked at us with his sad, doggy eyes." Alma did not believe for a minute in his sincerity: "He had always been an ARCH enemy."[32] They took a circuitous route to avoid "Hitler's newly extended domain." At the border they were searched, stripped naked to their stockings, and required to show baptismal certificates. All Jews were turned back. In Prague they met up with Werfel's sister, before proceeding on an overcrowded train to Budapest, where the Austrian consul booked a room for them. He had filled it with roses but would not be seen with them, as "the streets were filled with white-stockinged youths [Nazis]."[33] They proceeded via Zagreb and Trieste to Milan, where they were reunited with Werfel, who had traveled from Capri.

Carl Zuckmayer was still in Vienna on March 12, the day of the invasion: "That night hell broke loose. The underworld opened its gates and vomited forth the lowest, filthiest, most horrible demons it contained. . . . The air was filled with incessant screeching, horrible, piercing, hysterical cries from the throats of men and women," he wrote. "In the course of my life I had seen something of untrammelled human instincts, of horror or panic. . . . What was unleashed upon Vienna was a torrent of envy, jealousy, bitterness, blind, malignant craving for revenge. All better instincts were silenced. . . . It was a witches' sabbath of the mob. All that makes for human dignity was buried."[34] The arrests and persecution began: "Already Jews, as well as aristocrats. . . . were being herded through the streets and forced to wash the election slogans from the pavements. . . . I saw a frail old gentleman with a scrub pail and a far too small brush kneeling in the filth of the streets, kept at his task by an SA guard with a group of hoodlums standing around him. . . . People were taken away; afterwards they might be found in hospitals, horribly beaten or mutilated. Others disappeared forever."[35]

Within hours, Zuckmayer, Csokor, Horvath, and most of their circle had left Vienna. Hollnsteiner was picked up on March 30 by two Gestapo officers at the monastery at St. Florian, arrested for being an enthusiastic Schuschnigg supporter, held for eight weeks, and on May 23, 1938, deported to Dachau concentration camp, where he remained for eleven months doing menial tasks and heavy labor. Schuschnigg was immediately arrested, held in solitary confinement at Gestapo headquarters, then sent to Sachsenhausen concentration camp, where he remained for the rest of the war. Jews throughout Vienna were brutally assaulted and publicly humiliated by SA storm troopers in an orgy of atrocities.

After Milan, Alma and Werfel stayed with Werfel's younger sister, Marianne Reiser, in Zurich. It was "a terrible time, the only nasty time of our emigration," Alma recalled. "Was it their fault or ours?—I don't know!" There, "in our own family," Alma "found out, for the first time, what it means to be an emigrant."[36] Werfel believed Alma's anti-Semitic remarks, which had "burned . . . like vermouth" on Marianne's "wounds" were a major factor in the rift with his "passionate, torn, ecstatic" sister.[37]

In Zurich, American visas could still be obtained, as the quota was not yet filled. But Werfel continued to believe that their safety lay in Europe and that the continent could be defended against the Nazis. When their friend Franz Horch strongly urged Werfel and Zuckmayer to apply immediately for visas and, with Alma's support, arranged an interview with the American consul, both Werfel and Zuckmayer turned it down: "One flight is enough. We're Europeans and we'll stay in Europe," Zuckmayer insisted. "What would we do in a country where people pour ketchup on beef and where our greatest linguistic achievement would be to say in English: 'I am not able to express myself.'"[38]

Despite tightening travel restrictions, Alma and Werfel chose to go to Paris. With Werfel's Czech passport, they acquired the necessary papers and headed by train for the border. There, Alma "drew my first happy breath since the flight from Vienna."[39] Anna left for London while they settled into the modest Hotel Royal Madeleine in Paris, before going on to Amsterdam where Willem Mengelberg was conducting Mahler's Eighth Symphony and Alma was feted as the guest of honor. She was delighted when the Amsterdam-based publishing house Allert de Lange made an offer for her memoir, *Gustav Mahler: Memories and Letters*, the book that she had abandoned in 1924.

When they joined Anna for three weeks in London, however, it was a disaster: "I had a nervous breakdown . . . no books . . . no piano . . . nobody had any comprehension of Austria's fate. It was unbearable," Alma wrote.[40] But it was a success for Werfel, who, unlike Alma, spoke some English, talked with publishers, attended dinners, and took an interest in the city. Later, Alma attributed her nervous breakdown to her emotional devastation as she realized that she had become an émigré and was forced to abandon her past and her security to face an uncertain future.

On their return to Paris, Alma installed Werfel in a large room in the hotel Pavillon Henri IV at Saint-Germain-en-Laye in the suburbs of Paris while she stayed at her small hotel. A bizarre tragedy had struck on June 1, the day they arrived back. Ödön von Horváth, one of Alma's favorite young writers, was struck by a falling branch from a tree during a violent storm on the Champs-Élysées and killed instantly. Werfel joined Joseph Roth, Carl Zuckmayer, Walter Mehring, and other exiles at the funeral—"people without hope in a strange land. . . . In all their faces there was so much pain, so much distraction and destruction."[41]

In June, Alma left Paris bound for the south of France in search of a house in a climate she thought more equable for them both. Sanary-sur-Mer near Marseilles was already a haven for many of the writers, painters, and composers who had left Germany since 1933; Berthold Brecht, Heinrich and Thomas Mann, Lion and Marta Feuchtwanger, Ernst Bloch, Arthur Koestler, and art historian Julius Maier-Graefe had all sought refuge there. Alma soon found an old Saracen tower high up overlooking the bay. On the second floor, Le Moulin Gris had a large, circular room with twelve windows that rattled in the wind, with a spectacular view of open sea. This would be Werfel's study.

Then came an urgent message from Paris that Werfel was seriously ill. "My head feels as if it were full of water. It threatens to explode from interior pressure," he told her.[42] Alma took the next train for Paris. Werfel had had a heart attack; he was weak and suffering from extremely high blood pressure and agitation that might last for months. Alma was distraught: "Now Franzl is seriously ill. If ever I have turned my eyes away from him now this has been erased from my heart. I live and feel only for him who is the last remaining beloved that I have. I'm with him day and night." While his blood pressure was forcibly lowered and his smoking prohibited, Alma slept next to him on a sofa, "so that he is not afraid. . . . I feel at ONE with his inner being even if we are also diametrically opposed beings. I would not survive his death."[43]

Werfel's recovery was slow: "It took him a long time to get over the fear of death," Alma recalled.[44] After four weeks he was well enough to move back to Sanary-sur-Mer and begin writing again. They had applied for visas to the United States, he told his parents, but still they would emigrate only when "political necessity arrives at the door."[45] Alma was despondent on her fifty-ninth birthday: "What will become of us? . . . I only play Bach at the moment because he is the only one who frees me from the prison of my thoughts."[46] "God in heaven. One CAN'T live so without hope," she exclaimed the next day.[47]

Alma's fears grew as Hitler threatened the invasion of the German-speaking Sudetenland, in Werfel's Czechoslovakia: "It is grey in the world and frightening. For three weeks we have been between war and peace. And we are here in exile from home . . . unable to speak the language. . . . Complete estrangement! I often yearn for home! For Vienna." To add to her anxiety, Werfel had "joined the political journalists," writing polemics against Hitler's actions in his country and events in Germany: "He is very good at it but I would prefer him writing poetry," she wrote.[48]

When, after protracted negotiations, the four great powers—Britain, France, Italy, and Germany—agreed in Munich to Hitler's annexation of the Sudetenland, Alma was horrified: "Peace has broken out—but at what price!! . . . Now it is bringing Hitler new prestige and the German Volk inflate themselves like bull frogs. When will the strength of this Genghis Khan be broken and where, where will he break his neck . . . ? He must of course now be intoxicated by his own greatness."[49] A week later she reflected, "The world is experiencing huge events with bated breath. A genius [later changed to 'a single man'] at the helm of a great people. It started with Lenin, Mussolini continued it but Hitler has finished it. Though I am inseparably bound up with the fate of others, I have not lost my just, objective view. I know for sure that he has no opponents—but currently merely puppets created out of wax [later replaced with 'DIRT']—or even worse."[50]

Privately they could now "breathe a sigh of relief that there is no war coming. We would not have known where to go. The pressure of recent days has been terrible. None of us have slept.—We feel the ground has been pulled from beneath our feet."[51] Now her fate was to "wander with a people alien to me to the end of the world and even though I have lost my home, my intellectual and material possessions, the people who I love—my mother, whom I might never see again, I can't do anything other than with great astonishment look upon this hero—like, oafish individual, as he strides in triumph over human kind. Where to? *God alone only knows this.*"[52]

Throughout the autumn her "completely senseless life" continued—"I am currently living here in a Jewish-communist clique. And I don't belong to them."[53] Though Alma might disagree with her fellow émigrés politically, she was also clear that she had no sympathy with the other side: "When I see the wickedness that the Nazis are perpetrating—do I belong there? No. Never, ever."[54]

In November she learned that her mother had died of pulmonary edema. Carl Moll had been so distraught he had to be restrained from killing himself: "Why don't they just let him do it. He is absolutely right," Alma snapped.[55] She had thought blood ties meant little to her, but now "it speaks in a loud voice."[56] She decided she must visit Anna in London, but it was "so chilly and damp that we almost froze to death."[57] Werfel had gone to a family reunion in Switzerland, where his eighty-year-old father, Rudolf, scolded him for not emigrating earlier and offered them $5,000 to tide them over in America. Though Werfel had gotten as far as applying for visas he still had no intention of leaving yet.

Werfel and Alma met up again in Paris, where they had decided to spend the winter months. To Alma's delight, the manuscript of Bruckner's Third Symphony turned up. Ida Gebauer had smuggled it out in a package with the unsuspecting wife of a Viennese music critic. Hitler, a Bruckner fan, on hearing it had been on display at the Hohe Warte, wanted to possess it, and Alma's half brother-in-law and Nazi functionary Richard Eberstaller was instructed to retrieve it. But it was by then out of the country, and though Alma for a time considered selling it to the Germans for a large sum, and indeed offered them a deal, it never happened.

In January 1940, in the suite of her hotel in Paris, Alma revived her salon of émigrés, which now included George Duhamel, former ambassador Count Clauzel, the composer Franz Lehár, the director Erwin

Piscator, and Bruno Walter. She renewed her acquaintance with the journalist Margherita Sarfatti, Mussolini's former mistress, once known as "the uncrowned Queen of Italy" but now "the crowned beggar of the exile. . . . Brave, witty as always and full of bitterness."[58] She was a vivacious and lively presence.

ON MARCH 15, 1939, Hitler invaded Czechoslovakia: "yet another infernal outrage . . . Prague occupied by the *boches*!" Werfel raged. His family in Prague was in immediate danger. Alma had heard from a diplomat about Hitler's planned invasion and alerted Werfel's sister with the message "The Uncle would arrive next day." But it was too late. Werfel's family was trapped until they could escape in April, when his parents settled in Vichy in France. By then, Alma was pressing Werfel to leave France for America. Her life seemed to her not only precarious but empty: "Why sleep, why wake? Nothing matters any more. . . . My erotic relationship with Werfel turned into a dull marital backwater a long time ago. Why do I get up, why do my hair, for whom do I dress? There are people around us. All shadows of their former selves."[59] Her mood improved as she absorbed herself again in writing her book—the memories and letters of Gustav Mahler, which would finally be published in 1940.

But history moved rapidly. Hitler invaded Poland on September 1. Britain and France declared war on September 6. "From one day to the next our lives changed," Alma wrote.[60] They were now enemy aliens in France, subject to daily arbitrary visits from the local police, house searches, and regular inquiries about papers. When Werfel used a torch to look for a manuscript in the dark, he was reported to the police for spying. Once he was hauled in for an interrogation at nearby La Seyne and thought he would faint from fear. It turned out to be a mistake, but he was severely shaken. Alma had turned up with a photograph of Werfel from a reputable magazine with the caption "One of the greatest contemporary authors." They carried it with them everywhere from then on.

When Werfel's father had a stroke in Vichy, they spent days traveling back and forth to Toulon to get the necessary documents—a safe conduct pass—to visit him. Sitting in a restaurant at Lyon station, they were approached by an undercover officer who ordered Werfel to go with him. Alma "sat filled with fear: people were arrested on the street without reason."[61] But Werfel returned unharmed after another inspection of his papers. In Vichy, which was "unutterably bleak, no light," they found Rudolf Werfel bedridden and unable to speak clearly; they feared they would never see him again, though he held on for another year.

They visited Paris for an extended stay in January 1940. While Werfel worked at the hotel at Saint-Germain-en-Laye on a new novel reflecting the tragedy of Austria and the Anschluss, Alma was joined in her salon by her old friend Berta Zuckerkandl, who later emigrated to Algeria, and another group of exiles: Darius Milhaud and novelist Annette Kolb; biographer Emil Ludwig; Guido Zernatto; several escaped former German and Austrian ministers of state; Otto von Habsburg, pretender to the Austrian throne; along with Bruno Walter, Fritz von Unruh, and the composer Franz Lehár. Werfel managed another visit to his parents in Vichy before they moved south. Back at Sanary, while Werfel worked upstairs, Alma reflected, "Time trickles away . . . and life. One can't do anything but wait. And that is the most infamous. This Hitler kills the rest of my life. Our life, here in the tower—is completely lonely, one could say it's almost beautiful if it was not an enforced existence. One is always in a prison, in this life—but now more so than ever."[62]

In April 1940 Hitler's troops occupied Denmark and Norway, and, in May, they advanced on Belgium, the Netherlands, and Luxembourg. Now all Germans, including Austrian nationals, had to register with the authorities. Several friends, including Lion Feuchtwanger, Friedrich Wolf, and Walter Hasenclever had already been sent to internment camps. In June, Hasenclever took his own life with an overdose of Veronol. The house searches and checks on their papers intensified.

Finally realizing the threat, Alma and Werfel packed up their belongings. They left Sanary on June 2 for Marseille where, "tired and ill and completely without hope" they spent a fortnight trying to get French exit papers and American visas.[63] In early June, Hitler marched into France with almost no resistance. The government capitulated on June 13. Alma and Werfel stood with a group close to tears in their Marseille hotel as the French prime minister, Paul Reynard, broadcast on radio his final speech.

Paris fell on June 14. "Now we are searching like a mouse in its trap for a way out of the hole. But none is open any more and we are hopelessly caught," Alma wrote.[64] When they heard on June 18 that the

Germans were approaching Avignon and the French army was in flight southward, they decided to head for Bordeaux, the new headquarters of Marshal Pétain's Vichy government. From there they intended to travel to Biarritz and escape to Spain.

Their odyssey was just beginning. Having found a car with a driver, at his insistence they drove first to Avignon, then headed at a snail's pace on deserted roads through "countryside frozen with fear" for Toulouse.[65] With roadblocks every quarter of an hour and wrong turns that took them in circles, they found themselves after nightfall for the second time at Narbonne. As no hotel would take them, they ended up sleeping in an insanitary former infirmary. The next day they pressed on for Carcassonne, where they had to abandon the car at a road block (it had by then cost them 8,000 francs) and, as no trains were running, they were trapped for two days in the city—"beautiful on postcards but in reality a dirty hole."[66]

Finally they escaped on the last train out to Bordeaux, which was due to leave at 2 a.m. but arrived late overflowing with retreating French troops and frightened refugees. At six o'clock that evening they entered the chaos of Bordeaux. Half the town had been destroyed in recent bombing raids. The station platform was a sea of suitcases and people desperately running in the opposite direction to escape. As Alma waited in the pouring rain for Werfel to collect the luggage, she was approached by a young woman who, for a large fee (1,000 francs), offered them a bed for the night in what turned out to be a brothel; in the sweet-smelling rooms were hastily abandoned suitcases and the "necessary utensils of their trade." Alma and Franz had their first food for twenty-four hours at a bistro where the hostile clientele "regarded us with cold hatred."[67]

Next day, they checked in their luggage—clothes, books, all their possessions including the Mahler manuscripts and the score of Bruckner's Third—at the Terminus Hotel in Bordeaux for safekeeping. Werfel secured a taxi to take them to Biarritz, where they found a room in a "dreadful" hotel while he went daily to Bayonne to spend hours queuing in vain at consulates. Also in the queue were Viktor von Kahler and his wife, old friends from Prague. When it was rumored that the Germans were at their heels at Bayonne, they decided to travel together to Hendaye on the Spanish border, where it was alleged that the Portuguese consul could supply visas. When they arrived, they discovered the consul had lost his mind and thrown all the passports in his care into the sea.

Their options had run out. When they heard that the Germans were disembarking at the station at Hendaye, Werfel "threw himself on the bed, sobbing convulsively." Alma was "terribly concerned about him. . . . He is dying a new death every hour."[68] Kahler found a taxi that took them to Saint-Jean-de-Luz, then another that took them on, in pouring rain with no lights and after numerous checks by police, to Orthez. When no lodging was available, they slept crammed in the car—a lucky break as the Germans took over Orthez that night. At Pau they learned that the only place where hotels were available was Lourdes, the town made famous as a Catholic shrine, as yet unoccupied by the invading forces.

On June 27, 1940, they arrived at Lourdes, cold and stiff from the damp and with almost no possessions. They had had to ditch their suitcases at the roadside on the way. As they were being turned away by a second innkeeper, "*without wanting to*, the tears rolled down my cheeks," Alma recalled, and the innkeeper's wife took pity and gave them a room "about the size of a closet, with a view to a yard full of stinking garbage."[69]

They spent five weeks at Lourdes waiting as if in a prison, without a change of clothes, for the safe conduct papers that would allow them to leave for Marseille, where they hoped to obtain documents and visas to travel to America. Werfel sent telegrams to the American Guild for German Cultural Freedom, pleading their case. Alma became interested in Bernadette Soubirous, the fourteen-year-old miller's daughter from the village who had seen visions of the Virgin Mary. Twice a day Alma visited her grotto at Massabielle, for early Mass and the evening sermon: it had "a healing effect on our souls while we are here. If I move away from it the healing fades," she wrote.[70] Once, she was "suddenly so swept away that I had to cry, and cover my face. It really affected me deeply—for no discernible reason."[71]

They often drank the waters of the sacred spring, hoping for "some stroke of luck to help us get out of the town."[72] After two weeks, they moved into a larger room at the Hotel Vatican with twin beds, having previously slept in one narrow bed, and Werfel began to write again. On one of his last visits to the grotto, he made a pledge: if he and Alma ever got out to America, he would write a book, dedicated to Manon, in honor of Saint Bernadette.[73]

Their safe conduct passes finally arrived on August 3, and with the Kahlers they set off by train for Marseille. The first thing they saw outside

Figure 21. Alma's passport photo for her flight from the Nazis to America, 1940.

the Hotel Louvre et Paix was a line of six gleaming cars. Although the town was not occupied, German agents and officers were ostentatiously present. Alma and Werfel entered the hotel by a rear door and waited until the Germans departed. The next few weeks were "unbearable": food was scarce, and new regulations that demanded the immediate return to Germany of German refugees put them in constant danger. One bright moment came when, after the owner of the Hotel Vatican had used his connections in Bordeaux, the suitcase containing the Mahler and Bruckner manuscripts turned up. Miraculously the suitcases they had dumped by the roadside also found their way back.

Werfel spent hours each day in savage heat at the consulates queuing for American visas, transit visas, and the French exit papers. When they were not queuing, they went to the sea, where "the seagulls screeched, and mist over the water gave off its smell afar . . . blessed hours—as if there was nothing evil or scary in the world or lying in wait for us."[74] They were joined by Marta and Lion Feuchtwanger, who had been released from an internment camp near Nîmes after the intervention of the American consul; Heinrich Mann, the leading liberal intellectual and author, who had been deprived of his citizenship for writing against the "Nazi menace"; his wife, Nelly; and Golo Mann, their son and Thomas Mann's nephew, who had recently escaped from a Vichy concentration camp. Golo was a dedicated admirer of Werfel's work, knew every one of his poems by heart, and later praised Werfel for his "kindness, his sweetness, his utterly good nature and capacity for friendship. . . . There wasn't a trace of envy in the man."[75]

In the middle of August, Varian Fry, a thirty-two-year-old American Harvard-educated classicist, visited them. He was the representative of the Emergency Rescue Committee set up on independent initiative by US citizens, with the support of the First Lady, Eleanor Roosevelt. Their goal was to assist the escape of more than one thousand artists, musicians, scholars, writers, scientists, intellectuals, and politicians who were threatened by the Nazis. Each refugee had been selected by the President's Advisory Commission on Political Refugees and cleared by the Justice and State Departments. On the list alongside Werfel were André Breton, Marc Chagall, Marcel Duchamp, Max Ernst, Alfred Döblin, Hertha Pauli, and Lion Feuchtwanger.

American visas for Alma and Werfel finally arrived through the intervention of Cordell Hull, the US secretary of state. They now queued for hours in heat so stifling it brought Werfel close to collapse, to acquire transit visas for Portugal and for Spain, but the promise of French exit visas had not materialized. After discussing it with Fry, Alma and Werfel agreed that, with time running out, they would leave the country illegally and as soon as possible, rather than wait for their exit visas. Their initial plan to sail on a small vessel to North Africa was abandoned. Instead Fry would take Alma and Werfel; Heinrich, Nelly, and Golo Mann; and Marta and Lion Feuchtwanger on a risky journey by train from Cerbère across the Spanish border.

At 5 a.m. on September 12, after Werfel had burned his anti-Nazi essays in the hotel fireplace, they met Varian Fry and his colleague Dick Ball at the railway station. Alma was trailing twelve pieces of luggage. Lion and Marta Feuchtwanger opted to stay behind when it was discovered that new customs regulations prohibited stateless persons from crossing the border. Having been deprived of his German citizenship, Feuchtwanger did not want to jeopardize the chances of the others in the group. Fry assured him he would—and did—arrange their later escape.

Now began another, if possible, even more demanding journey. The group traveled via Perpignan and reached Cerbère in the evening. However, customs officials refused to let them go on to Spain without exit visas. They found an eerie, abandoned hotel and stayed until morning when the same message came back: their American papers were not enough, and moreover, new regulations would shortly oblige customs officials to detain every refugee. Their only option was to cross the mountains on foot. Varian Fry, who had an exit visa, would take their seventeen pieces of luggage across the border by train while Ball guided them over the mountains.

Alma was sixty-one, Heinrich Mann was almost seventy and unwell, and Werfel had a severe heart ailment when they set out in boiling heat on the hazardous journey across the Pyrenees. Werfel panicked when he realized it was Friday the thirteenth and insisted they go the next day, but Alma calmed him: "That's nonsense," she said, and he fell silent.[76] It was Carl Zuckmayer's view later that, "without her, Franz would simply have stayed lying there, and that would have been the end of him."[77] Alma "managed surprisingly well," Golo Mann remembered.[78] "She was always ahead of us."[79] They had scarcely left the village when Ball turned off the road uphill onto a stony trail that was rising steeply and soon disappeared. "It was sheer, slippery terrain that we crawled up, bounded by precipices. Mountain goats could hardly have kept their footing on the glassy shimmering slate. If you skidded, there was nothing but thistles to hold on to," Alma recalled.[80] They climbed for two hours before Ball left them to go back for the Manns.

Standing alone, at an altitude of seven hundred meters on the top of Mount Rumpissa, they saw in the distance the Spanish border post, a small hut shining white against white stones in the glaring sun. They decided not to wait for the others as it seemed wiser to attempt the border alone. "Laboriously we crawled downhill; trembling we knocked on the door which was opened by a dull-faced soldier." Despite the packets of cigarettes thrust at him, "this idiot" escorted them back to the French border post, where they were taken before an officer: "I was wearing my oldest sandals and lugging a bag which contained the rest of our money [the flight had eaten up almost 100,000 francs], my jewels and the score of Bruckner's Third. We must have looked fairly ridiculous, only slightly less picturesque than the smugglers in *Carmen*. After the march in the broiling sun we felt utterly wretched." The chief officer, in a sudden burst of kindness, waved his hand to let them through. "Dripping with sweat and dog-tired, we re-traced our steps, clambered over the dramatic iron chains that separate France from Spain, and continued our descent."[81] Alma found a half horseshoe, which she kept as a lucky charm.

No officials were visible at Port Bou customs post, but the porters who brought them wine ranted against Mussolini for taking away their grain and fat, and against General Franco because they were anti-fascist Catalonians. They became even more helpful after a generous tip. When Alma and Werfel's travel companions, the Manns, turned up, they all sat in trepidation "like poor sinners on a bench" as their papers were checked at passport control. Nelly Mann had half carried the aged Heinrich over the thistly mountainside; her stockings hung in shreds from her bleeding calves.

After an excruciating wait their passports were stamped and returned, and they made their way to a hotel in town that was riddled with bullets from the Civil War and looked, as did the whole country, "like a bleeding wound."[82] In the gathering dusk they found Varian Fry, who had transported the luggage across the border. At 4 a.m. they caught the train to Barcelona: "a war-devastated, desolate, starved, impoverished city that must have once been beautiful," Alma recalled. "As we sat outside a cafe, poor children licked the ice cream from our plates . . . everything is crumbling and desolate."[83]

Two days later, they caught an overcrowded night train to Madrid, then flew to Lisbon on September 18. During six grueling months, Alma had shown remarkable calm, stoicism, and resourcefulness—and an almost complete absence of debilitating introspection. Their "first step on free soil" in Lisbon was "unforgettable"—"heavenly calm in a heavenly country," she recalled.[84] After two weeks at the Grand Hotel d'Italia in Estoril, they obtained a passage with Heinrich, Nelly, and Golo Mann, on an expensive though undistinguished and overcrowded Greek vessel, the Nea Hellas—the last Greek ship to make a regular run to New York before Greece joined the war. Most of the journey they spent in their cabins.

Finally, on October 13, 1940, they approached the Statue of Liberty. "Now America lies before us, an entirely new continent. I hope that it will be favourably disposed toward me," Werfel wrote to his parents.[85] Their arrival in New York was "as grandiose an experience as ever. A mob of friends awaited us on the pier: all of them were in tears, and so were we. . . . At last we set foot on soil that was really free," Alma remembered.[86] Friends, relatives, and journalists thronged the pier to welcome the newly arrived exiles.

Alma and Werfel checked into a suite at the St. Moritz Hotel on Central Park. Their social life that autumn consisted, with some tragic absences, of the same friends who had sustained them in Vienna. Lion and Marta Feuchtwanger, Carl Zuckmayer and his wife, Anton Kuh, Franz Blei, Alfred Döblin, Hermann Broch, Count Richard Coudenove-Kalergi, and Otto von Habsburg had all survived the flight from the Nazis. All were now exiles together in a strange land.

Alma and Franz stayed in New York until Christmas 1940. "It was a little too busy, but the time spent there was beautiful and enriching. Much love, much joy, much activity," Alma summarized.[87] Werfel spoke at fundraising dinners, gave lectures, and wrote essays and articles. "Our Road Goes On" was an impassioned warning to the Jewish people that the Second World War was "the greatest and most dangerous moment" in the history of Israel. The enemy's mission was "the complete extermination of the Jewish spirit on this planet." They must mobilize the forces of democracy to save the Jews, for with the collapse of Israel would follow the destruction of Christianity and the descent of all civilization into barbarism.[88]

The American edition of his novel *Embezzled Heaven*, published by Viking Press, was an instant bestseller. A Book of the Month Club choice, it sold 150,000 copies in the first week alone. "We're doing *wonderfully* here, even though we pay for our happiness with a bad conscience," he confessed to his parents. "My latest book . . . is a hit. For the time being, this good fortune has freed us from all worries."[89] His parents, who were now stranded in Bergerac, were a constant concern. Powerless to get them out despite his efforts, Werfel sent them regular food parcels. Both his sisters had escaped with their husbands—Marianne to New York and Hanna to London.

Alma and Werfel moved on December 29, 1940, from New York to Los Angeles, where antique dealer Alfred Loewi and his wife, who had been by their side in Venice during Manon's illness, had found them a beautifully furnished "small, sweet house" in the Hollywood Hills above the Hollywood Bowl.[90]

In the new year of 1941, Alma and Werfel settled into an extremely uncertain future as émigrés. With Alma now in her seventh decade, they had emerged unscathed from a dangerous, war-ravaged Europe to a new life. Werfel began work to fulfill the pledge he made to the past during the dark days at the grotto at Lourdes, and with that novel, *The Song of Bernadette*, he established his name and their future in America.

— 14 —

Exile

1941–1946

To Alma's relief, after two years of upheaval, Werfel started work on his new novel in early January 1941: "Thank God! It is such a miracle that he is already able to concentrate again."[1] As soon as she settled into their new home, she resumed her social life among the expanding colony of European émigrés on the West Coast. Heinrich, Nelly, and Golo Mann had joined Thomas Mann and his wife, Katia, who, with Arnold Schoenberg, writer Alfred Döblin, and composer Erich Wolfgang Korngold, became regular guests at the Werfel household.

With the success of *Embezzled Heaven*, Werfel had established a sound financial footing, although, he told his parents, "I regard my success and fame as *undeserved;* most of the others are in poor shape and have to fight hard for a livelihood, with little hope."[2] Emigration, which Alma called "a disease," had inflicted its toll. Only a few lived much above subsistence level. Max Reinhardt, the groundbreaking theater director in Berlin in the 1930s, was struggling: "He has grown old but he still looks beautiful. He has been side-lined, sad but not bitter. An indestructible genius," Alma wrote.[3] Her visit to conductor Otto Klemperer's house was "painful, one feels that a broken mind resides and works there . . . the walls are weeping."[4]

By contrast, Alma was buoyant: "We live here from one blue blossoming day to another and praise God."[5] The house at 6900 Los Tilos

Road, surrounded by gardens fragrant with orange blossom and oleander, was modest by Alma's standards. The front door opened directly into the living room where Alma had her grand piano, and down a flight of narrow stairs, known as the "chicken ladder," were Werfel's study and the bedrooms. Their antique dealer friend, Alfred Loewi, had found a butler, August Hess, who chauffeured them in his Oldsmobile and was Werfel's personal valet and Alma's drinking partner. A "slight, middle aged man of medium height, with greyish blond curly hair and the watery eyes of a happy alcoholic," as a contemporary described him, he was born in Heidelberg and had made his way as an operatic tenor with a provincial theater company until, on a tour of America, the company went bankrupt and he stayed behind.[6]

In May 1941 Werfel finished the first draft of *The Song of Bernadette*, which they celebrated "like a great holiday." For the next draft, Werfel hired as his secretary forty-year old Albrecht Joseph, a former theater director and screenwriter, who as a Jew had been forced to leave Germany in 1933 for Vienna, where he had met Alma, then fled again in 1938. Joseph turned up daily in his old Packard and sometimes paused outside to listen to Alma on the piano: "She could play Bach magnificently with a great deal of emotion and power, and I was really sorry when she finally stopped and I had to ring the bell."[7] He worked with Werfel in his downstairs study—a small whitewashed room sparsely furnished with a narrow bed, wardrobe, desk, and two chairs. Often at the end of the day, Alma invited Joseph for a drink: "'Don't act like a Jew,' he quoted her as saying. 'Sit down and have a little glass of schnapps!'"[8] By that time she had regularly consumed the greater part of a bottle of her favorite Benedictine.

Joseph observed his employers closely. He admired the "rotund" Werfel, with his a "big head with a really beautiful forehead and bright blue eyes . . . penetrating and observant," who "spoke very well, almost like an actor . . . in a strong youthful voice."[9] He thought Alma was "probably an almost ideal partner. . . . She could give him what he wanted, what he was asking of her without having to put it into words." Although Alma could be "hard, ruthless, even cruel," Werfel's success as a novelist "was unquestionably due to her influence," Joseph believed.[10] She loved arguing and fought in conversation "with fair and unfair weapons." Werfel would answer with politeness or with feigned agreement "to get out of an uncomfortable position."[11] Once, after some particularly bad news from

Figure 22. Alma and Werfel in Beverly Hills, c. 1944.

Europe, when Alma took the position that "it could not be otherwise since the Allies—America was not in the war yet—were weaklings and degenerate, and the Germans, including Hitler, supermen," Werfel challenged her. After ten minutes of pointless argument, "he clapped me on the shoulder and said: 'Let's go downstairs and work.'" Halfway down the stairs, he stopped, turned to Joseph "and said, with a tinge of real sorrow, 'What is one to do with a woman like that?' He shook his head: 'One just has to remember that she is an old woman.'"[12] Anna too recalled how Werfel confided in her, "I don't know whether dear Alma is my greatest joy or my greatest disaster."[13]

News from Europe filtered through. Alma was shocked to hear of Hollnsteiner's fate. He did not join the Nazi Party after his release from Dachau, as was rumored, but his monastery, the Augustinian Brothers of St. Florian was closed down. He resigned from the priesthood on May 5, 1941, and had been living with a woman, Almut Schöningh, whom he married in September of that year.

To Alma, leaving the church was an unforgivable betrayal of the very mission and ideals that had drawn her to the priest. He instantly dwindled in her eyes to a man who "once had influence over me" but forfeited this by his "great betrayal" of everything that was once sacred to him and to her. His "wall of faith," which had appeared insurmountable, had now crumbled. Power had been taken away from him—mere everyday life remained, and her priest had become "a citizen like any other—uninteresting." Even worse, his betrayal had made her question her Catholic faith "in my innermost self"; she now wondered, "Perhaps this God HAS never existed, everything was an imagined fantasy—far away from real life!" and for this she could "NEVER forgive him."[14]

Further news came in July of the death at eighty-two of Werfel's father, Rudolf. He had been in Varian Fry's care in Marseille waiting for visas to travel to America. Fortunately, Werfel's mother, Albine, escaped, and in September Werfel and Alma traveled to New York to meet her off the boat and then remained for four months in a suite at the St. Moritz Hotel. While Werfel set up his mother in an apartment, Alma absorbed herself in the music and culture of the city: "Then as now I am in heaven here and only here. Nature and music—all else is worthless. . . . I go to the theatre and listen to music whenever possible," she wrote.[15]

Back in California she made new friends, mainly among the German-speaking émigré community. One of her closest was Friedrich Torberg, whom Werfel had known casually in the days of the Café Herrendorf in Vienna, and their paths had crossed briefly in Estoril, Portugal, on their flight. Alma cast her spell on this promising young writer, and soon his admiration for her verged on idolatry. Through her "he felt protected from collapsing and going completely to rack and ruin"; she praised him and chided him and said things "*that nobody else but you can say to me*," he told her.[16] With Werfel he shared a nostalgic familiarity with the vanished cultural life of Vienna. They collaborated on a film script that went nowhere, and both Alma and Werfel lobbied to get Torberg's writing published.[17]

AT THE TURN of the year, Alma's concern about their financial situation increased. Werfel's novel *The Song of Bernadette* was not due to be

published until May 1942. The Book of the Month Club had not taken it
up. They were apparently "scared of its Catholicism . . . an utter misconception, as he wanted to show only the strength and effectiveness of *any*
faith," Alma snapped.[18] No film studio had shown any interest. Moreover,
demand for work by German and Austrian writers plummeted when, after the Japanese bombing of Pearl Harbor in December 1941, America
entered the war. They were now enemies in a nation gripped by patriotism: "Everything has gone wrong," Alma moaned as she surveyed their
position. "[We] have arranged our lives in great style . . . have almost no
money . . . no capital."[19]

Even so, she acknowledged, they were better off than most of their
struggling compatriots. Stefan Zweig, who was in exile in Brazil, had
suffered a nervous breakdown the previous autumn, and then in February 1942 committed joint suicide with his wife. Werfel was shocked and
appalled: "Later generations will judge the tragedy of those poets and
writers who have been exiled from their language, to cower, like Aha-
suerian beggars, before the threshold of an alien grammar and culture,"
he declared at Zweig's memorial service at a Los Angeles synagogue.[20]
The German press celebrated Zweig's death as if it were "the sinking of a
British cruiser."[21]

Alma's worries lifted when, in March, *The Song of Bernadette* was after all selected by the Book of the Month Club. Viking Press printed a
first edition of 200,000 copies for its publication on May 11, 1942. Three
weeks later it was fourth on the best-seller list, and Viking Press printed
another 100,000 copies. In July it knocked John Steinbeck from the
top spot, where it remained for several months. Werfel was inundated
with requests for interviews, articles, and press appearances. By July, the
book had sold 400,000 copies; it would eventually become one of the
best-selling books in American publishing history. By then Twentieth
Century Fox Studios had bought the film rights for the unexpected sum
of $125,000.

His novel about a Catholic saint provoked rumors of Werfel's conversion to Catholicism. "I have dared to sing the song of Bernadette, although I am not a Catholic, but a Jew," Werfel explained, for his aim
had always been "evermore and everywhere in all I wrote [to] magnify
the divine mystery and the holiness of man."[22] The great mysteries of the
spirit were not confined to the followers of any one church, and though

he believed the Catholic faith was "the purest power and emotion sent to the earth by God to combat the evil of materialism and atheism," he was born and, he insisted, remained a Jew. He would not, especially at this time, deny that he belonged to "an unfortunate, cruelly persecuted minority" and would not enter a Catholic Church that had played an active part in the persecution of the Jews—and never disowned such activities.[23] Even so there were some who wished to convert him to Catholicism. At the Franciscan monastery in Santa Barbara, Werfel had often consulted Father Cyrill Fischer on religious matters. Fischer now believed Werfel's conversion was his duty and attempted to enlist Alma to his mission: "Perhaps you should be the angel who shows him the way to the Christ child. St Bernadette will guide you in this task."[24] How far Alma accepted this mission was not clear at the time.

A visit to New York in June for a week of interviews and publicity for the book publication was marred for Alma by tensions within Werfel's family. Although in part traceable to Alma's growing aversion to his mother, Albine—"a poor lamb . . . with no opinion of her own. Her face is strangely ugly, everything is crinkly"—the major stresses came from Werfel's sister, Marianne Reiser, who persistently rebuked him for not using his influence to get her play, *Eugenia*, performed on Broadway.[25] Her husband, Ferdinand, had always disliked Alma and, to Werfel's outrage, insisted on dismissively calling her "die Mahler." "It is a constant cackle, croaking and gossiping, the likes of which I have never seen anywhere before," reported Alma, scornfully dismissing her sister-in-law as "a proud peacock who believes herself to be a genius and is not," who was "envious of anyone who, in her view, has it easier than she does."[26]

On their return to California, Alma approached her sixty-third birthday on August 31, 1942, with trepidation: "Another one of these filthy birthdays, which brings one closer to death. Why the fuss? . . . The pleasure becomes ever more modest . . . and the barrenness and confusion then grow."[27] She decided to move to a smaller house in Beverly Hills, which she secured after tense bidding against other prospective buyers: 610 North Bedford Drive was a "charming" bungalow with a large garden near Santa Monica Boulevard. Originally built for the Australian actress May Robson, it was, in Albrecht Joseph's acid words, "one of those typical upper-middle-class ticky-tacky houses, cute from the outside, dark inside and furnished in atrocious taste."[28] After some initial grumbling about its lack of space, Werfel settled in. A new Steinway piano was installed for Alma, and she gave Werfel a wonderful new radio: "Everything is very much suited to us and *only* us two," Alma wrote with satisfaction.[29] But the past could still break through to shatter her composure. Her grief over Manon had been slowly healing as her life changed, but she was still vulnerable. When their Siamese kitten was suddenly killed, it "ripped everything open again within me, the grief and the wounds. . . . [E]very-where I saw my dying child. . . . [E]verything has been re-kindled."[30]

Alma's "small select"[31] circle in Beverly Hills now included Bruno Walter and his daughter, Lotte, who; were next-door neighbors; Erich Korngold and his wife, Alfred Döblin; the actor Ernst Deutsch and his wife, Anushka; the "sensitive, highly civilised" writer Bruno Frank; and Lion and Marta Feuchtwanger. Arnold Schoenberg, who lived nearby and had corresponded with Alma since he fled Europe in 1933, visited with his "dear, gifted, beautiful, overstrained, self-sacrificing" second wife Gertrud. Alma felt a particular affinity with her new German friends, Gustave O. Arlt, professor of German literature and language and chairman of the German Department at UCLA, and his wife, Gusti, who were "more truly brother and sister to me than the Bergs had been."[32] Thomas Mann's extremely succinct diaries record their regular evenings together. In October 1942 he reported, "A lavish meal, sparkling Californian burgundy, Benedictiner with the coffee."[33] When once asked how he could tolerate Alma, who represented "the kind of German who had become taboo to [him]," Mann "puzzled seriously for a few minutes . . . then smiled and said: 'She gives me partridges to eat, and I like them,'" Albrecht Joseph reported. Even Joseph conceded, "There was, altogether, a Viennese feminine softness about Alma, even in her most awful moments, that made it difficult to really dislike her."[34]

Outside her select circle, she could provoke very mixed, often powerful reactions. Dika Newlin, the composer and musicologist, met Alma at a 1941 performance of Werfel's poems that she had set to music. She was surprised to find Alma "quite excessively plump, with frizzly hair whose blondness seems to owe quite a bit to the beauty shop. . . . When she first came into the concert-room to sit down beside me, I thought, 'Why she looks like an ex-Follies queen!' But a few minutes of conversation with her utterly destroyed that impression; she is a charming person."[35] Not everyone was so generous; some mocked Alma. Writer Claire Doll likened her to "a bulging Germania. . . . To compensate for her fading charms, she wore gigantic hats festooned with ostrich feathers; nobody knew whether she was trying to impersonate a funeral horse pulling a hearse, or a new d'Artagnan. On top of that, she was painted, powdered, perfumed and inebriated. This bloated Valkyrie drank like a fish."[36]

The actress Marlene Dietrich, a political refugee after her declared opposition to the Nazis, was a fan who joined Alma's circle with her husband, Rudolf Sieber. The exiled and stateless German writer Erich Maria Remarque, author of *All Quiet on the Western Front*, who had recently been Dietrich's lover, became Alma's companion and drinking partner. Alma thought him "strikingly handsome, tall and slim (he was a racing driver in his youth) with tremendously expressive features, and a way of raising his black, bushy left eyebrow, which gives a satanic touch to his smile and laughter. He speaks little but with beautiful hand gestures."[37] To Carl Zuckmayer she confided, "He is quite a fellow and a great relief after the Manns, Ludwigs [sic] and Feuchtwängers [sic]."[38] Alma met Remarque at the actor Oskar Homolka's home on August 12, 1942: "We drank and talked together as if we had known each other for ages. We understood each other without speaking. After the second bottle of vodka he started saying 'Du,' describing Werfel as his brother."[39]

In Remarque's robust version of their "stormy vodka-rum downpour," Alma was "a wild, blond wench, violent, boozing. Has already put Mahler under the earth. She was with Gropius and Kokoschka, who seem to have escaped from her clutches. Werfel won't. We hit the bottle. She whistled to Werfel as if he were a dog, and was proud of the fact that he actually came. That got me mad, and, swimming in vodka, I gave her a piece of my mind."[40] Next day he sent her a charming letter offering "friendship for life or else an honest enmity" and with it a bottle of Russian vodka in a huge bouquet of flowers, a sign of his respect for her—the kind that "wolves have before lionesses."[41] Naturally, Alma forgave him, and their friendship blossomed.

While her friends and acquaintances appreciated her more majestic qualities, they did not ignore her prejudices. Alma was never particularly astute about politics; she did not support the "bacillus" of Nazism nor, despite her frequent distasteful remarks and anti-Semitic diatribes, was she a supporter of Hitler or of ideological anti-Semitism. But Alma loved to provoke, as Albrecht Joseph observed, and her frequently ill-informed and forthright opinions could prove too much, even for her close friends. He recalled a tea party with other émigrés toward the end of the war. When someone said "that nothing could ever make the world forget the horrors which the Nazis had committed, Alma . . . took issue and said that one must not generalise and that the Nazis, after all, had done a great many praiseworthy things." Joseph recalled that when someone replied that merely to think of the concentration camps was sufficient to make one sick for days, Alma asserted that "those horror stories are fabrications put out by the refugees," for she knew from a friend, a registered nurse in a top position, that "the camps have excellent medical care and that the Red Cross is conscientiously watching over the welfare of the prisoners."[42]

After a moment of paralyzed silence, Franz Werfel "jumped up, screaming, his face a deep purple, his eyes bulging . . . it was like the thunder of one of the Old Testament prophets. He was beside himself, had completely lost control. . . . Alma appeared unmoved." Very shortly afterward, however, she retracted her statement and agreed that the information, presumably from her former nurse, Sister Ida Gebauer (who would have been fed such Nazi propaganda in Vienna throughout the war) had been grotesquely inaccurate.[43]

ALMA HAD NOT seen Anna for five years when she heard in October 1943 that her daughter had married a Ukrainian conductor, Anatole Fistoulari, and was expecting a child—"this time with love and hope." Fistoulari, born in Kiev in 1907, had worked with the Ballets Russes in Paris before the war and escaped to London in 1940, where he became principal conductor of the London Philharmonic Orchestra. "It is strange that she has again returned to music, even though he is only a conductor," Alma reflected, somewhat haughtily. "Hopefully he will not soon become boring to her, which has been the case with all her relationships up till now."[44]

While Alma remained in Beverly Hills, Werfel was working in a rented bungalow on the grounds of the luxurious Biltmore Hotel in Santa Barbara on a play, *Jacobinsky and the Colonel,* which used his experience of flight and exile in a tragic farce about an army officer and a Polish Jew. Although he swiftly completed the first draft, the project from then on became an interminable burden as Werfel negotiated the treacherous tides of Broadway production. The theater producers demanded rewrites, the playwrights S. N. Behrens and then Clifford Odets were drafted in to "Americanize" the play for the Broadway stage—a collaboration with Odets that Werfel described as trying to "convey the European misery of France to an American deaf-mute by means of sign language." To cap it all, a Stuttgart banker, Stephan L. Jacobowicz, who had been a fellow refugee at the Hotel Vatican in Lourdes, took out a lawsuit, claiming Werfel had used one or two of his stories in the play and demanding compensation for his indirect assistance in its creation. "How lucky was Goethe! Where would his *Werther* have been if he was not allowed to create from life!!" Alma spluttered, clearly tired of the whole business.[45] "I had a ghastly time and fled to the sickbed."[46] That summer Werfel was on his fourth rewrite at Santa Barbara: "I can't turn an onion into a rose," he protested to Alma over the telephone: "I answered: 'You'll just have to make the onion as fragrant as possible.'"[47] Negotiations, rewrites, and finally rehearsals dragged on into the spring of 1944.

For her birthday in August, Alma joined Werfel in Santa Barbara, where he was working on a dystopian "travel novel," *Star of the Unborn*, set in the year 101943. It was "a paradise" Alma enthused. "Werfel behaved wonderfully towards me today and I shall remember it."[48] They went on beautiful rides and visited mansions "as full of culture, expensive simplicity, and boredom as befits the very rich."[49] But her birthday again prompted fear of aging and of mortality. "Dying is a contagious disease. I don't place pictures of the living next to those of the dead. And I don't place myself there."[50]

Their lives changed suddenly on the night of September 13, 1943. Three days after his fifty-fifth birthday, at their house in Beverly Hills, Werfel suffered a severe heart attack. Torberg was visiting and joined Werfel as he smoked "a coal black, heavy Havana cigar." Aware of his doctors' warnings about his smoking, Alma asked him to throw it away, but then he immediately lit another lighter one. "It was late and I went to my room, but only half an hour later he came to me with a completely altered face and I was hardly able to get him back to his room," Alma recalled.[51] He complained of fear of death and intense pain. She called a doctor, who administered digitalis and diagnosed nicotine poisoning. Werfel spent weeks in bed afflicted by a recurring lung embolism, bouts of high fever, and suffocation attacks, which required an oxygen tank to be installed in his room. Torberg often sat by his bed as he and Alma shared his care. During bouts of intense cold sweating she would "stand alongside him . . . in mortal agony . . . unable to help."[52] She was desperately anxious. "I can feel my strength ebbing away."[53]

He remained ill, his heart weak, his breathing heavy, attached to an oxygen tank for several hours each day: "Hopefully . . . hopefully we can help him over the worst. . . . This time he is afraid." He drifted between dreams and waking—had musical visions, and dreamed of the court ball, radiant officers, grandes dames, horses racing across the Steppe.[54] By October 18, Alma was more hopeful: "Franzl's patience is touching. He is YEARNING to get back to life and is doing everything that is asked of him . . . and he is above it all. Not a word of complaint . . . wonderful!"[55]

But three days later, on October 21, Werfel had another severe heart attack. The doctors suspected intestinal swelling, but when they tried to take an X-ray, he collapsed again. Alma was completely distraught: "His heart is *terribly* weak. I don't want to go on living without him. He is the whole meaning of my existence," she wailed.[56] "I ask God to keep my beloved Franzl alive! I can't live without him, without his wisdom—his generosity! . . . Now everything is destroyed—and so I live only for the strengthening of his weak body and hope . . . hope."[57] Once again Werfel was confined to bed. "Franzl simply said today: 'Perhaps IT will pass or I will pass.' He said it very calmly, standing above it all. . . . However he is afraid of death and God. In vain I try to convince him that he had never had any evil thoughts, let alone done anything wicked!" His spiritual torment confirmed to Alma that "at the centre of this is a deep Catholicism which he doesn't want to admit to himself or others."[58]

Death was stalking the exiles. On October 31 Alma heard that Max Reinhardt had died after suffering a heart attack, followed by the music historian Paul Stefan—"a friend and always prepared to fight for us."[59] Nor was Werfel out of the woods. On December 14, he suffered another heart attack: "He was more in the other world than in this one, but magnificent, as always," Alma wrote.[60] He was too ill to attend the film premiere of *The Song of Bernadette* in December, but they followed the excitement on his radio at home. By then the novel had sold more than a million copies. The US government bought up 50,000 copies to distribute to the army. The song of the film became a radio hit. A large portrait of Jennifer Jones as Bernadette by the painter and illustrator

Norman Rockwell was a huge success. Meanwhile, to Werfel's intense disapproval, S. N. Behrman's "Americanized" version of his play *Jacobinsky and the Colonel* was going ahead, with the young Elia Kazan as its director. In March 1944, the "comedy of a tragedy" was an immediate Broadway hit.

Werfel remained in a fragile state, cared for by Alma during most of the spring of 1944. "I don't know how much longer I will be able to endure this life under a cloud of anxiety. This over-exertion is costing me the last remnants of my youth," she opined to her diary. Werfel was being "horribly irascible, nervous, unpredictable. He can't see how miserable I am."[61] It had been "months of permanent torture. I wept through days and nights." Torberg "shared my nightly watch over him. Every evening he came . . . armed with a huge thermos of strong black coffee which he had laced with cognac." Gradually she "began to pull myself together. I realised I had to live on, whatever happened."[62]

As it did so often, music saved her. She felt her joy return as she "worked very seriously, studying Bach's Chromatic Fantasy and learning it by heart."[63] Werfel too returned to work on *Star of the Unborn*. Meanwhile, Marlene Dietrich, who was deeply fond of both Alma and Werfel, commissioned America's most famous astrologer, Carroll Righter, to cast Werfel's horoscope based only on his date and place of birth. Dietrich reported the results: he must keep strictly to his diet until March 12, he would be nervous until March 20 and rebellious until April, and he was "a genius as if I didn't know . . . furthermore your moon is in my venus stop first of all it sounds nice and secondly it means that you like me which makes me very happy. All my love to you both Marlene."[64] While she was on tour entertaining American troops in February, Dietrich wrote again: "All I wanted you to know is that I am thinking if you!"[65]

By July Werfel was well enough to move back to Santa Barbara, accompanied by a private physician, Bernard Spinak. Alma remained in Beverly Hills, where she heard by telegram that Anna had given birth in August to a daughter, Marina. Alma had regularly sent money and food parcels to Anna in London, but she feared that Anna "would never see any of us ever again."[66] The war had taken its toll: "I feel so shabby and old in general," Anna told her mother. "Unfortunately you didn't pass the eternal youth on to me."[67]

In the spring of 1944, Friedrich Torberg left Beverly Hills to take up a job with *Time* magazine in New York. He gave Alma a somewhat odd parting gift: a photo of Oskar Kokoschka, which jolted her into a new, harsher vision of the man who had so often haunted her: "The look of genius in his eye has given way to that of a cunning calculator, which also proves what a Russophoile total ass-kisser he is," she wrote. "In a word, I am not sorry that I left him, even though I still occasionally sighed for him later. He is, after all, the 'son of a serving maid'—and his working class manners were always strange to me."[68] It seemed that through her surge of love for Werfel she had at last reached a reckoning with Kokoschka. With Werfel "everything I might have wished for on earth has been fulfilled," she decided.[69]

Illness had brought Alma and Werfel closer. And now, despite his frail physical condition, "his sexuality is blossoming again," Alma confided to her diary. "But because of the terrible pains he has been getting after the joy of love for years, I try to distract him, which in turn gets on his nerves. . . . For the past two days, he has kept on saying: 'I'll go to the whorehouse to get myself titillated!' His eyes dwell on the sight of anything female with unquenchable lust. He has always been like that—but of course his art, its vigour and imagination flowed from the same sources!"[70] By August, his general health was also improving. Soon he was working productively for several hours a day on *Star of the Unborn*, his vision of America's future—"a humorous—cosmic-mystical world poem"—or, as he told Max Brod—"a monstrous mélange of philosophy and entertainment," which Alma believed to be "the strangest and strongest that Werfel had ever written. . . . To me it seemed a *Divine Comedy* of our time."[71] On weekdays he worked in Santa Barbara, then spent weekends with Alma at North Bedford Drive. On August 31, 1944, Alma celebrated her sixty-fifth birthday: "Franzl was waiting with [the Arlts] in the living room with *incredible* gifts, it was all lit up with candles, it was *breathtakingly* beautiful," she told Torberg.[72] But all day she had been unable to get rid of anxiety about Franz: "In his eyes there is such a fearful knowledge, a vision of everything and my throat tightens with tears but I cannot allow myself to cry."[73]

IN EUROPE THE tide of war turned. At the beginning of March 1945 the Allies crossed the Rhine. By mid-April, the Red Army had occupied Vienna after a long siege. News arrived that on April 28 Mussolini was shot by partisans near Milan, dumped in a town square, then hung upside down from a steel girder with his mistress, Claretta Petacci, to be beaten and spat at by crowds: "It was not a hero's death," Alma commented. "How do such men cling to hope until their dying hour? For him, as for Hitler all was lost long ago. What more did he want out of life, an old, poor, sick man, outlawed the world over?"[74] Two days later Hitler committed suicide with his mistress, Eva Braun, in his Berlin bunker. As the Allies advanced though Europe, they encountered the unimaginable horror of the Nazi concentration camps.

Alma had since 1940 had almost no contact with Carl Moll or her half sister, Maria, and her husband, Richard Eberstaller, who had all been early Nazi Party supporters. Eberstaller, a lawyer, had from time to time given her legal advice and, in October 1938, had acted as an intermediary when the Reich Propaganda Ministry attempted to buy her manuscript of Bruckner's Third Symphony, one of Hitler's particular favorites. In mid-June, Alma wrote to an American military chaplain stationed in Austria, asking him to inquire about the condition of her houses on the Hohe Warte and at Breitenstein, and the fate of her stepfather and half sister. It was too late. Although Alma did not find it out until much later, on April 12, as the Red Army marched into Vienna, all three had committed suicide by taking poison. When their tenants found them next morning, Moll was dead, Maria still breathing, and Eberstaller's throat was rattling. They died soon after.

As news filtered through from Europe, Alma was still preoccupied with Werfel, who had recovered sufficiently to commute to Santa Barbara. Though she had suffered a prolonged unexplained illness, which she attributed to constant worry over him, she was now visiting him regularly in Santa Barbara. On August 2 he was "looking splendid" as, "with deep emotion," she read through his manuscript. On her return she found an enchanting poem, "To Alma": "How much I love you was not known to me / Before the onset of these quick goodbyes," which he had sent to her by special delivery.

On August 17, Werfel finished the third and final part of *The Star of the Unborn*. He "called up radiantly" to tell Alma that now he wanted to get home as soon as possible. Alma suggested he come in the evening when it was cooler, but he insisted that Hess collect him the next morning. At 3 p.m. Alma met him at the house "in the midday furnace, tired and grey from the heat and exertion, struggling up the short path from the car to the house," Alma remembered.[75] He went immediately to bed while Alma called a doctor, who prescribed heart medicine and morphine.

That night, Werfel had another severe heart attack: "His hands were ice-cold and finally he lost all sensation in his hands and feet. He weakened steadily, approaching a state of collapse."[76] Doctors were summoned, but by early morning the danger seemed to have passed. During the three days of prescribed bed rest, Werfel noticed an owl sitting in a tree just outside his window that seemed to fix him with its gaze, day and night. "Werfel perceived its presence as an omen of death," his biographer Jungk noted.[77] Werfel reworked some poems, and seven days later, on August 25, he was well enough to go out with Alma, Bruno Walter, and his daughter Lotte to Romanoff's Restaurant. Walter arrived early, and, while he waited for them to get ready, he played Smetana's *Bartered Bride* on the piano. Werfel rushed out of his room and joined in, singing one of his favorite tunes and even managing a few dance steps. It was a convivial evening.

Next morning, Sunday, August 26, 1945, Werfel woke full of confidence. Alma and he discussed what he wanted to do in the next ten years and whether to take a boat or a plane when they went on their proposed trip to Europe. They joked about the drop in income his dentist would suffer now that his teeth had been seen to. It was a lovely day, and he joined Alma in the garden. In the afternoon Werfel had a nap, then dressed and went to work on revising his poems. Alma stayed with Gusti and Gustave Arlt in the sitting room.

When she opened his study door to look in on him, there was no sound: "I called his name . . . no response! I rushed forward—Franz was lying on the floor in front of his desk. My Franz, My Franz. . . . With a quiet, smiling face and unclenched, soft hands. I screamed!" August Hess came running in and saw what had happened. Alma refused to believe it. His body was still warm. She "put the oxygen mask over his mouth and massaged his heart, hands and feet," then helped Hess carry him to his bed. "But we all knew it was too late." She surmised, "It must have been over by the time he slid down from his swivel chair. The last change he had made to his poem was penned in a firm, clear hand—without agitation, without pain, without foreboding! Slowly turning to stone, his beautiful face grew more and more monumental and sublime."[78]

When his body was taken away that evening, Alma "felt as though my life were carried out."[79] She was prescribed sedatives as she lay inert on his bed—the only place where she thought she could rest. The Arlts stayed overnight. Next day Thomas and Katia Mann, Bruno and Lotte Walter, and several others visited Alma. "Painful and hard," Thomas Mann noted in his diary.[80] After two days, Alma started dictating Werfel's novel from his handwritten text: "Much of the manuscript was virtually illegible, and the strain of deciphering it through my tears helped me over the hours of the funeral," she recalled.[81]

The funeral was on August 29 in Beverly Hills. "The casket stood in a flower-laden chapel," Alma wrote. Werfel was dressed as he had requested in "a dinner jacket and a new silk shirt, with his glasses in the breast pocket and a spare silk shirt and several handkerchiefs in the coffin."[82] When Joseph went in a car to collect Alma, he found her sitting in a house dress writing at Werfel's desk. "'I'm not going.'—'What do you mean?'—She looked at me reprovingly: 'I never go.' It sounded as if she had been asked to break with a hallowed tradition, as if burying her husbands were a regular occurrence."[83]

Gathered at the funeral home were more than a hundred mourners—"the whole German republic of letters in exile in California," Joseph noted, including the Manns, the Schoenbergs, Otto Klemperer, and Igor Stravinsky.[84] Monsignor Georg Moenius was to conduct the ceremony. Neither he nor Alma was present when the organist began to play contemplative music nor when Bruno Walter played some short Schubert piano pieces, which were followed by silence. He played them again. After an hour, Monsignor Moenius finally arrived and the service went ahead—without Alma.

Mystery still shrouds what took place at North Bedford Drive to cause the delay, but it seems that Alma was altering Moenius's eulogy. It came as a surprise to many in the congregation when he emphasized the Catholic tendencies in Werfel's work and included a lengthy explanation of the three types of Catholic baptism—by water, by any practicing Christian in an emergency if there is no time to call a priest, and "baptism by desire"—when in their last moments someone who earnestly desires it can be received into the church by force of desire, without visible rites.

Moenius's eulogy led to speculation that he and Alma had baptized Werfel after his death. Professor Adolf Klarmann, a friend and expert on Werfel's work, reported that Alma had told him in October 1945 that a baptism by desire had been performed by Moenius after his death—but this was "a *secret*" that he must keep to himself. Alma always denied it. When Torberg later asked Alma directly, she replied, "Of course Werfel was not baptised. I could have had an *emergency* baptism when I found him—but I would never have *dared* do that. . . . Werfel was open to all *true* mysticism, but he would have told me, in one word, if he had wanted that. He told me . . . he wanted to be buried *that* way, inter-denominationally. And there were no symbols, no Talmud, no Cross."[85] The day after the funeral, Gustave and Gusti Arlt drove Alma to the cemetery, where Father Moenius, "with special permission from the arch-bishop, blessed the remains of Franz Werfel, an unbaptized Jew."[86]

The chasm left by his death was unbridgeable: "Why am I still alive? A week ago I lost my sweet man-child. I still can't grasp it. I keep think-ing that he must come home from Santa Barbara. But he will never come home," Alma wrote.[87] She would be forever haunted that she had not been there at the very end to help him, she confided to Torberg. "Such a sweet, pure and divine person the world will never see again. He was only kindness and love, and our partnership in love was more wonderful than ever."[88]

DURING "SEVEN WEEKS of torment," she lived in his room and slept in his bed while she dictated the rest of his handwritten *Star of the Unborn* to Werfel's new secretary, Wilhelm Melnitz: "And so I can in the meantime go on living," she told Torberg. Bruno Walter and Lotte were always with her and were "tremendous," the Arlts were there day and night, to the consternation of Albrecht Joseph, who found them unduly interfering and intrusive and was deeply suspicious of their motives and their influ-ence over Alma.[89]

When she finished dictating Werfel's manuscript in October, Alma set off for New York. But it was "changed without Franz." Once again, at this new phase in her life, she resolved "I must reconstruct my whole being, to be again what I was before his time."[90] Solitude was a new burden: "I have many people around me," she wrote to Lion and Marta Feuchtwanger, "but coming home in the evening and the irreversibility of being alone are dreadful."[91] Now she had no one, she wrote, and she lived in the past.

Alma moved from the St. Moritz Hotel into an apartment suite on Sixty-Fourth Street, where she remained until February 1946. She felt able to take up the threads of the past and had resumed contact with Sister Ida Gebauer, who had married and remained in Vienna throughout the war. In November, she learned from Gebauer that her house on the Hohe Warte had taken four direct hits in the Allied bombing. The top floor, where she had stored both Werfel's and Mahler's desks, had been destroyed. Fearing that all Werfel's manuscripts and letters had gone up in flames, she resolved to write down her memories of "this favourite of the Gods, whose journey on earth had paralleled mine."[92]

She saw much of Friedrich Torberg and his future wife, Marietta Bellak; dined and partied with Marlene Dietrich, Erich Maria Remarque, Alfred Polgar, and Carl Zuckmayer; and visited her old friend Fritz von Unruh, who had abandoned poetry and taken up painting. Concerts, operas, and exhibitions absorbed her time and revived her spirits.

With some trepidation, she returned to her Beverly Hills house in February 1946. Everything had remained unchanged since Werfel's death. "I don't feel very well, the house—the closeness of the awful experiences and I am dreaming daily of being with Franzl which is hardly bearable when I wake up," she confided to Torberg. "However I don't want to distance myself from him, who was my most beloved on earth. I try to get by day by day. My eyes are red from weeping."[93]

News came in of old friends. Gerhart Hauptmann died in June 1946. Though they had been estranged during the war, his wife, Margarete, wrote warmly to Alma in "a letter which ended our misunderstanding of years past."[94] Johannes Hollnsteiner wrote in the summer of 1945. Alma's reply to the former priest, delayed until June 1946, was dismissive: "Take good care of yourself—as an average citizen!"[95] But she renewed their correspondence in 1955; in reply to her letter asking after him, Hollnsteiner affirmed his "love and gratitude" to her for "all the unforgettable, beautiful years in Vienna, when you brought me out of my isolation, expanded my horizon and bestowed unforgettable experiences on me."[96] When they met in New York, in July 1955, Alma was "eternally happy to be seeing [him] again."[97]

Alma had resolved to write down the story of her life and, in the meantime, put Werfel's papers in order. At sixty-seven, her age troubled her: "I'm getting old. I'm to take it easy, not to walk too much, not to play the piano for too long a time." Her work arranging Werfel's writings, "which I do every day with a secretary, gives me a great deal of satisfaction. . . . It is hard work, but it keeps me near him. Some day, unfortunately, even this fount will run dry."[98]

The first anniversary of Werfel's death brought renewed grief. "Just as on the first day, I feel today I can't live without him. . . . He was un-spoilt . . . an angel and his excesses, which only I knew came from too much sensitivity and passion," she told Torberg.[99] Sometimes he appeared to her: "I saw him standing outside my window, cheerful, smiling, radiant. 'Why don't you let me in?' he called. 'I want to come home.' He looked as young as he did years ago, and ever so handsome. He must have had a wonderful experience in eternity and wished to tell me about it."[100] Other dreams were tortured, when he would pass her without a glance, and she woke up sobbing.

She needed to get away from the house that preserved so many mem-ories and decided to spend more time in New York. And she was planning another more difficult venture—a visit to Vienna. She did not intend to live there—"it must look awful, this Vienna, this poor Vienna!"[101] But she wanted to find out what had happened to her houses, her paintings, manuscripts, books, and possessions—all the things that had made up the past that she had abandoned so precipitously on that March day in 1938 before the conflagration.

— 15 —

La Grande Veuve
1946–1964

*I*t was nearly a year before Alma could return to Vienna, however. In September 1946, she traveled "incognito" to New York, as she did not want Werfel's family to know of her presence. Relations had deteriorated after Werfel's death when his mother, Albine, and sister, Hanna, disputed the will that named Alma as his sole heir: as immediate family, they claimed their entitlement to a share of the rights to his works. "It has unfortunately become clear that he had been right to leave his parents' home when he was a youngster," Alma informed Kokoschka, with whom she had resumed intermittent correspondence. "I do not wish to talk to them! What's the point?! . . . Werfel's family, to which he could never get close is now avenging itself on me—or trying to avenge itself—on me, whom he idolised for so many years."[1] Alma sought legal guidance to sort it out. When it emerged that Zsolnay Verlag had independently turned over all his rights to Alma, the dispute was resolved, but relations remained tense. "How fortunate for Franz Werfel not to know that he comes from a family of gangsters," Alma reflected acidly.[2]

She now enlisted Ida Gebauer to work and speak on her behalf in Vienna as she tried to track down and then reclaim her possessions and property. It was a frustrating process, conducted at long distance with an intransigent and unsympathetic bureaucracy in chaos. "People here talk of a gang of scoundrels who have stolen from me," Alma told Gebauer.[3]

She employed a Vienna attorney, Otto Hein, to deal with the complicated legal issues involving the return of her paintings and her dispute
over the will left by her half sister, Maria, which laid claim to the Breitenstein house. "Maria would never have had the right to inherit—only
after me, Anna and her children, it is pure theft, and should be treated as
such," she told Gebauer.[4] She enlisted Willy Legler, her sister Gretl's son,
to help her recover jewelry and furniture, the whereabouts and condition
of which were unknown.

When Alma's visa finally came through in September 1947, she set
off immediately and stopped off in London, where she saw Anna for the
first time in more than eight years. Wartime austerity in Britain had taken
its toll on Anna: "My daughter looked heart-rending, haggard and grey,
as though coming from hell," Alma recalled.[5] They agreed that Anna
would visit her in California in the spring. Alma arrived next day in Vienna, worn out and with swollen feet, to find a film crew waiting for her
as she emerged from the airplane. "I pulled myself together for a dignified

Figure 23. Alma with Ida Gebauer on her return to Vienna, 1947.

descent; but I had to hop up and down the steps ten times before they were satisfied."[6]

From September 17, she stayed at the Hotel Kranz, where she lived on the canned food she had sent ahead from California when she heard of the chronic food shortage in Vienna. Every night she slept with rats: "The hotel was bomb-damaged, and these vermin blithely came and went through the large holes between my room and the out-doors."[7] The entire city was "hell for me. The Opera, the Burgtheater, St Stephen's—everything lay in ruins." Her house on the Hohe Warte was "uninhabitable—the roof gone, the top floor collapsed, the interior in ashes, heating plant, water and electricity ruined, the marble panel-ling torn out, used for officers' bathrooms in the neighbouring villas." Both Mahler and Werfel's desks, with their "priceless" contents, had been burned to cinders; she retrieved only a couple of Mahler's small note-books. The manuscripts of all her songs, "my joy and grief of many years," had "fed the flames."

The process of untangling her private affairs was "unpleasantness itself," as she encountered "a Nazi-infested Austrian bureaucracy" that seemed determined to obstruct her: "How could you, a daughter of our great Schindler, marry a Gustav Mahler and a Franz Werfel?" thundered one old judge in the Justice Department.[8] Her father's pictures in the Belvedere Gallery were inaccessible to her. In 1937, Alma had loaned them three Schindler paintings for two years. But when Moll took over the administration of Schindler's estate, he had without telling Alma willed them for an indefinite period to the gallery, which now refused to return them. Moll had also sold Edvard Munch's *Summer Night at the Beach* to the Belvedere Gallery in 1940 for 7,000 Reichsmarks. Even though Alma had earlier asked him to sell it (the gallery's offer had not met her asking price) and in spite of Moll's claim that it was sold to pay for urgent repairs to the roof of her Breitenstein house, Alma main-tained throughout numerous hearings and court appearances that Moll had not been authorized to dispose of any of her property, and all the works should be returned to her.

She departed Vienna on September 23 with the major issues unre-solved, but she kept up persistent pressure on the authorities, with Ida Gebauer and her nephew Willy Legler as intermediaries. The experience had been so profoundly distressing that Alma vowed she would never return to her home city: "I could never be happy there," she wrote to Gebauer. "Everywhere is lawless and unjust. I seek nothing. I just want to live in peace with my dreams. When the house looks respectable, I will sell it. I cannot accept the small-mindedness of the people in Vienna," nor, she protested later, "the meanness of those who would rob me of everything."[9] As to the Edvard Munch painting, she was "beside herself that the Gallery should win!—I want my paintings back at any price," she told Gebauer.[10] Meanwhile she had been trying without success to persuade Ida Gebauer to join her in America. "I can't wait to have you here with me," she had written in April 1946 on the anniversary of Manon's death. "And I believe that together we could find some sort of happiness—with our memories and with the *present*. Because here it is really beautiful."[11]

Anna arrived in California in March 1948 on her planned visit and stayed for a month. It was a "great effort," Alma told Friedrich Torberg. "[Anna] is very clever and warm but I am very used now to being alone and the adjustment took its toll on my nerves."[12] Alma had taken against "this idiotic good-for-nothing man"—Anna's husband, the conductor Anatole Fistoulari.[13] Albrecht Joseph recalled how when Alma was angry with Anna, "mainly because she [Anna] had married a Jewish conductor whom she [Alma] considered an inferior creature, Alma would shrug her shoulders and say: 'What can one expect? Miscegenation.'"[14]

Anna was entirely familiar with her mother's capacity for offhand denigration; quite often she referred to Anna as a "bastard." Her animosity stemmed in part from jealousy: "Alma was wildly, possessively jealous," Anna told Marina, her daughter by Fistoulari. "She needed to be at the centre, and when she wasn't, she lashed out."[15] Their complex relationship left Anna in a state of constant suspense: "Every time I see your handwriting I feel a sharp blow in the pit of my stomach—in fear that your letter will be repugnant, and then I heave a sigh of relief when I find myself unscathed after reading it," Anna wrote to her mother.[16]

In May 1948, after Anna had left California, Alma fell into inertia, unable to decide whether to return to Vienna to sort out her affairs and what direction her life should take in America. "Franzerl had taken away what little energy there was in me," she told Torberg. "The *will* to go on living has gone."[17] She wanted to get away. "Here one goes on vegetating." Torberg was firm: "I think you should move. . . . You have to find a place where you can be Alma and not always be remembering Werfel. . . . You have to give up the house in Beverly Hills and find your place in New York, where you are much nearer to Europe and the atmosphere of European life."[18]

Now approaching seventy, Alma's unpredictability, her occasional intransigence, and her sensitivity to feeling undervalued or ignored led to rifts. Although she had retained cordial relations with Bruno Walter, ever since the Mahler days tensions had occasionally erupted. She had rapidly swatted away rumors circulating immediately after Werfel's death that she was about to marry Walter, who lived next door, but they fell out in 1948 over arrangements for the first postwar celebration in Vienna of Mahler's works. Alma pulled out when she felt that her contribution as the donor of her Rodin bust of Mahler for the occasion had been insufficiently acknowledged by Walter: "The attitude of B.W., the complete silence surrounding my name as the donor tells me enough!" she fumed to Ida Gebauer.[19] Accusations of bad behavior flew on both sides until Walter concluded finally, and rather cruelly, but possibly with a some truth, "If these things cause you to suffer to the point of tears, it just shows that you have a fondness for suffering, and not that any of this is my fault."[20]

Complications also developed in her dealings with Thomas Mann and Schoenberg over Mann's portrayal in his novel *Doctor Faustus* of a composer who invented a musical technique closely resembling Schoenberg's twelve-tone system. Alma alerted Schoenberg to the possibility of Mann's infringement of Schoenberg's intellectual property rights, which led to a dispute that lasted for two years, during which Alma fell out with both men. She even managed to cross swords with Torberg over the rights to a film script. Cordial relations were nevertheless restored in each case.

Alma's sixty-ninth birthday on August 31 was celebrated in style; sixty guests gathered as a chamber orchestra played a fugue of Mahler themes and the adagietto of his Fifth Symphony, and Erich Korngold dedicated a violin sonata to her. Thomas Mann had forgiven her: he inscribed in a copy of his latest novel, "To Alma, the personality, on her birthday, August 31 1948, from an old friend and admirer." It was "an odd feeling," Alma wrote, perhaps slightly disingenuously, "to be fêted on my own account after a lifetime of hiding behind my distinguished husbands!"[21]

In June 1949, she was overjoyed to receive from Vienna all of Werfel's letters that had been found in the burned-out house. "You will be *enraptured* when you read them. He was such a sweet soul, and for me he still is! I live again through those 27 years as if it were *today*!" She immediately started typing them out: "It is already 100 letters but this is just the beginning!" she told Torberg.[22] Her work kept her occupied until September 1949. She considered publishing them and assured Torberg, "Not one word, not one comma, will I change, except only, when letters are too similar, to omit the least strong."[23] Several of her own works had also been found in the destroyed house. Sometimes Alma sat at the piano "playing the last of my printed songs. . . . How beautiful my world had been then! It seemed empty now. Yet Werfel's letters brought joy to it, and a purpose."[24]

Hans Pfitzner, her "beloved, admired, dreaded friend," died in May 1949. "Gradually, inexorably, my loves turn into grey shadows," she mused sadly as, with something like pagan mysticism, she measured her loves against eternity. "But if they were strong, their shadows loom larger and longer. By now, Gustav Mahler's shadow has completely devoured his small human form, and it is growing still. Franz Werfel's shadow has not yet reached such dimensions; but he is also growing fast. Their stately advance is an epic." She reflected on all those she had loved: "Gustav Mahler and Franz Werfel were the essence and the substance of my life. The rest were clouds—some mighty thunder-claps, others mere curls on the horizon."[25]

In her widowed state, Alma relied more on women friends. Helene Berg wrote often from Austria. Gertrud Schoenberg was a confidante, as her daughter, Nuria Schoenberg Nono, recalled: "We were always in touch with them. My mother was very good friends with Alma, she was I think one of the few women who were not jealous of her . . . because of her success and her intelligence . . . and she really liked her."[26] Alma was "warm, friendly and generous to us." When Nuria's parents were away in Chicago on one of her birthdays, Alma invited her for dinner at Romanov's, "the most chic and expensive restaurant." She sent her chauffeur to pick Nuria up, "and then every time they brought another dish, she would give me a present, and then she sent me home with the chauffeur. It was such a lovely thing to do," Nuria recalled of this "fantastic figure" who, "when she walked into a room, you felt her presence." Yet, when she was with Thomas Mann or Bruno Walter or her father Arnold Schoenberg, "they were talking, mostly, and she was listening."[27]

Annelies Ehrlich Gottlieb was another close friend, who was married to German-born photographer, Ernst Gottlieb, cofounder of the Pacific Press, which showcased the works of émigré writers banned in Europe, including Werfel and Thomas Mann. "Alma was lonely," Annelies's daughter, Irene Hartzell, recalls, "She missed her soul-mate, she missed Franz Werfel." But Alma was rarely entirely alone, for "she was the focal point of a large group of people, because of who she was, because of her personality. . . . She loved nature, and she loved art, but above all she loved people." Irene, then a teenager, was beguiled by Alma: "She was charming, she was witty, she was engaging, she had these twinkly blue eyes . . . and she had an aura about her—she had an inner beauty and an inner glow that most people don't have." Alma was also very emotional and very perceptive, an "insightful thinker who could figure out people immediately," Irene believes, and she had "very definite ideas. . . . It would not occur to her to tell people what they wanted to hear." In every respect she was "a very advanced, independent thinking woman, a modern woman who lived out of her time."[28] As a token of their friendship, Alma gave Annelies a sketch from Mahler's Tenth Symphony with the note, "My dearest, You should not always give away what is dear to you but today I will give you something that I LOVE, and I ask you to honour it . . . With love always Alma."[29]

For Alma's seventieth birthday in August 1949, Gustave and Gusti Arlt asked her friends to contribute to a leather-bound book of appreciations. Seventy-seven people—companions from every stage of her life—responded, including Kurt von Schuschnigg from his exile in St. Louis; the writers Carl Zuckmayer, Franz Theodor Csokor, Lion Feuchtwanger, Heinrich Mann, Fritz von Unruh; composers Benjamin Britten, Ernst Krenek, Darius Milhaud, Igor Stravinsky; conductors Erich Kleiber, Eugene Ormandy, Leopold Stokowski, and Bruno Walter. Willy Haas, Werfel's boyhood friend, sent a tribute to this "timeless woman" with her "keen mind," "unfailing helpfulness," and charm, who "beautified the lives of everyone who has had the honour of loving and honouring you." Walter Gropius wrote from Cambridge, England, "Past and present join together! Heartfelt thoughts!"[30]

Schoenberg was not present, but he composed a birthday canon based on the text "The centre of gravity in your own solar system circled by glowing satellites, this is how your life appears to the admirer."

Figure 24. Alma in her New York apartment with a Mahler manuscript.

In a birthday letter, he explained, "It does me no good to move about in other people's solar systems. That is why even today you will not find me among the celebrities congratulating you."[31] Thomas Mann was unusually effusive as he praised "the joyful stimulation that exudes from your personality, a human nature in female form, a great woman . . . and the fact that you are additionally the widow of two wonderful men and great contemporaries, elevates the reverence with which I offer you my cordial felicitations."[32] Thomas Mann named Alma *La Grande Veuve*, the grand widow—a title she lived up to from then on.

Kokoschka invoked the erotic grandeur of their love in a long, fiery letter: "You are still a wild creature just like the first time you were swept away by *Tristan and Isolde* and used a quill pen to scrawl your comments about Nietzsche in your diary in that same hasty illegible script which I can only read because I know your rhythms. . . . Since the Middle Ages there has been nothing that could compare, for no loving couple ever breathed so passionately into each other. . . . Your Oskar."[33]

A visit by Anna in summer 1949 established a new harmony between them—"a gift from heaven that I hoped never to lose," Alma enthused.[34] By the following November, Anna had found a job teaching sculpture at UCLA and was separating from Fistoulari. She moved to California with seven-year-old Marina, who remembers her first impression of her grandmother: "I just thought she was beautiful. She had the most extraordinary skin—transparent, and the most amazing luminosity about her—the colour of her blue eyes was fantastic. . . . She seemed to have baby skin, baby eyes, and there were these golden locks piled up on top of her head. . . . She was in black, and had a large bust . . . and layers and layers of necklaces, some real, some not, and she was very regal." A friend up the street once told Marina wanly, "My granny's only a granny."[35]

The visit had not started well. Marina arrived in her gray school coat, which Alma took against, and she barely noticed the silent, concentrated child who had not as yet been told of her mother's decision to separate from her father but felt instinctively that the rupture had happened and they were not going back. To Alma's bewilderment, Marina refused for several months to eat the exotic pineapples and oranges (unavailable in Britain) that Alma provided for them. They managed to make their proximity work for a while, but the primal force of Alma's jealousy intervened. "She did not want to share my mother with me. . . . [S]he was jealous of my mother's love for me. My mother always loved me hugely, she loved me more than her mother, so there was jealousy," Marina realized.[36] At one point Alma wrote to Gusti Arlt, "Couldn't you exert some influence on [Anna], so she won't let the little brat tyrannize her all the time!?"[37]

Though Anna had escaped and spent years away from Alma "in a constant state of rebellion," she had never conquered the hold of her "Tiger-Mammy," as she called her. "Alma wanted to be adored, my mother always said, and my mother wasn't the adoring type. She couldn't manage to do that," Marina comments. Even so, Anna did adore her, like "a Greek goddess to whom one wanted to bring gifts and offerings.

Everybody did." And when Alma died, Anna lost her ambition, Marina reports. It seemed to Marina that her mother, Anna, was "a cross between a wounded lion and a Viking. It was so painful, there was nothing you could do. She had a wounded face, everything was bare, right there, and it was difficult to take. She had such depth. Her silence was so loud."[38]

Alma bought Anna and Marina a small house in Beverly Glen near the university at which Anna taught sculpture and "created works of strength and beauty," Alma wrote approvingly. "My headstrong daughter had mastered her art and made her way."[39] But Anna did not notice her approval—on the contrary, she was "positively gobsmacked at how horrible she could be," she told Peter Stephan Jungk.[40] "Mammi used to say, 'I know everybody at first glance.' But she didn't even know *me*. Much later, she confessed to me, 'If I had known you as I know you now, I wouldn't have treated you so miserably.' That really shocked me— because it showed she had done it consciously, all those years."[41] Not long after Anna moved to California, she began a relationship with Albrecht Joseph that lasted thirty-five years; he was her fifth husband.

In 1951, Alma left Los Angeles permanently for New York City, where she settled into the upper two stories of a house on 120 East 73rd Street, only a few blocks from Central Park and close enough to the Metropolitan Opera and Carnegie Hall, where she would spend much of her time. August Hess stayed on for a while as butler and handyman until he got tired of New York and returned to Los Angeles. Alma was not unduly upset because she found his temper difficult—and referred to him jokingly as "my murderer."[42]

Alma had found a safe haven in New York. "My flat is finally finished! A lot of work. But now really unique. . . . Today my grand piano is being seen to—then I will play!! It was right to come here," she told Annelies Ehrlich Gottlieb, while enjoining her, "Please look after Annerl a little!"[43] One part of Alma's third-floor apartment was dedicated to "the power of words, the other to that of music," she wrote. The living room walls were lined floor-to-ceiling with bookcases containing the German classics given to her as a young girl by Max Burckhard, Werfel's works in all languages, and the books of personal friends and of "those spirits I had admired over the centuries from Plato to Bernard Shaw." In between were hung Kokoschka's remaining six fans (the seventh had been burned by Gropius in a jealous rage), his portrait of her, and several of his drawings. A second room was dedicated to music and contained a grand piano, on which stood a large portrait of Gustav Mahler: in a safe beside the desk were the valuable original manuscripts of Bruckner, Mahler, and others. On the walls hung the paintings by her father of the Dalmatian coast, the Austrian mountains, and the Vienna Woods, which she had eventually recovered from Vienna.

Though living a quieter life, she still entertained: "I have champagne for my friends when something calls for a celebration—and something always does, for I believe in joy as the sovereign remedy for sickness and the sole preservative of youth," she declared.[44] Though troubled by her heart, she dismissed any serious health worries: "How I am doing? I don't know. Sometimes I get little warnings which I take no notice of—too trivial to consult the doctor. This seems the healthiest tactic," she told Torberg.[45] She went to concerts and the opera, attended exhibitions, and kept up with the cultural gossip. Friends visited. Gertrud Schoenberg,

Figure 25. Alma in her New York apartment, New Year's Eve, 1956. Anna Mahler (*far left*), Alma (*center*), and Ida Gebauer (*second from right*).
"I have champagne for my friends when something calls for a celebration—and something always does." —Alma Mahler-Werfel

who shared Alma's loneliness, came with her daughter, Nuria, who re-called Alma in the morning, unadorned, without her jewels, long ear-rings, and pearls, and likened her to "a beautiful picture, not beautiful like a film actress, but even in her older days her charisma was evident."[46] When Marina stayed, she felt she was in a different world: "From floor to ceiling there were books, and there were chests of drawers with things in them . . . everything piled in—photos, paintings, the piano and it was fascinating to me."[47] It was a complete contrast with her mother's spartan simplicity and a compelling reflection of their "completely different tem-peraments." Marina loved watching Alma in restaurants where everyone knew her and she hailed the waiter with an imperious gesture.

At the end of 1952, Alma returned with Gusti Arlt to Europe—not to Vienna, where the bureaucratic intransigence over her Munch paint-ing continued to enrage her, but to Paris where she stayed for two months at the familiar Hotel Royal Madeleine, and then to Rome where she im-mersed herself once again in Italian culture. "Great men somehow con-tinued to cross my path," she reported, for on the return journey to New York, as she sat alone reading on deck, "a tall, Apollonian figure of a man" had stood suddenly before her. "I'm Thornton Wilder," he said, and they began to talk. Still unable to resist the pull of intellectual genius, Alma's days "passed like minutes" with the eminent author of the Pulitzer Prize–winning novel *The Bridge of San Luis Rey:* "We seemed to go on talking until the ship docked in New York. His every word was a joy—and so, later, was his every letter. Since Werfel's passing, I have treasured nothing so much as Wilder's friendship."[48]

There would be one more trip to Rome in 1954, but she complained of tiredness and heart trouble and after that did not venture abroad again. When she cancelled a visit to Helene Berg in Vienna, a disappointed Helene wrote sadly, "I live as you do, with my loves, that I can only carry in my heart."[49]

From 1956, Alma worked on the autobiography she had begun in 1944. She had put aside the first draft, "Der schimmernde Weg" (The glittering path) in 1947 after several readers, including Werfel's publisher, Paul Zsolnay, advised her that it needed considerable revision because of "frequent references to racial issues" (meaning anti-Semitism) and the possibility of libel because of the unvarnished directness of Alma's comments on some of her contemporaries. In August 1956, Hutchinson

Publishers contracted the editor E. B. Ashton (the pen name of a fellow émigré, writer and translator Ernst Basch) to collaborate with Alma on an English edition.

Relations between ghostwriter and author were often fraught—as might be expected given her sensitivity to criticism, her personality, and her status in the project. She had also been unable to give it her full concentration as she had been ill with heart trouble and had suffered several minor strokes: "Since Franz Werfel left me . . . I've just been dragging myself along, until I got a coronary thrombosis from all the excitement about a year ago," she told Lion Feuchtwanger in June 1958.[50] By and large Alma agreed with Ashton's revisions. She had left him to make his own judgments on such issues as deleting statements "that might be unpleasant for the persons involved. . . . I don't want any lawsuits for defamation of character!"

The finished version, And the Bridge Is Love, was published in the spring of 1958 to a very mixed reception. Numerous inaccuracies and harsh judgments remained, elisions resulted in misrepresentations, and even her closest friends expressed discomfort or outright distaste at the degree of frankness with which she was prepared to divulge the private and intimate details of her marriages and relationships. Some believed that it was unduly self-serving, designed to glorify herself, sometimes at the expense of her husbands. A few friends kept their distance from then on.

Walter Gropius was particularly hurt: "The love story that you attribute to my name is not ours. The memory of Mutzi should have restrained you from revealing the content of our experience. . . . The rest is silence," he wrote coldly.[51] Although Alma's portrayal of their love is indeed edited and heavily truncated, she pleaded her innocence. She had been ill for a whole year and was unable "to pay as much attention to the book as I should have done," she explained, but she had in good faith instructed that the publisher send to him "everything concerning you, so that you can censor it. Not until I received your last letter did I realize that this had not occurred!"[52] Gropius was unappeased, and their friendship never recovered.

Alma blamed Ashton, possibly unfairly, for much of the furor around the book: "I asked 'Mr' Ashton to deal gently with the important people I number among my friends—but he pulled out all the positive points and developed everything with a negative touch!" she told Werfel's old friend, the writer and editor Willy Haas, who agreed to collaborate with her on the German version. She warned him, "We must go easy on still living persons and famous individuals who play leading roles in this history," adding, "Please eliminate all references to the Jewish question."[53] *Mein Leben* (*My Life*) came out in 1960 and continued to excite interest for its frankness. Albrecht Joseph recalled, "[It] was considered so hot that it was sold under the counter, like pornography. It helped to sustain and enhance the myth of Alma. She became one of the Great Lovers of the Ages, a superwoman in Renaissance style, a demi-goddess."[54]

In August 1959, Alma celebrated her eightieth birthday with a lunch at the St. Moritz Hotel with Anna, who had traveled to New York from California. Despite the uproar over her book, birthday greetings still arrived in huge numbers. Ida Gebauer had finally come over from Vienna and agreed to take care of her. Men still gathered around her, bestowing blessings. Benjamin Britten dedicated his Nocturne for Tenor and Small Orchestra, a setting of eight songs about sleep and dreams, to her.

Alma's correspondence with Kokoschka had revived. After Werfel's death she dwelled again on her remorse that she and Oskar had ever separated, even while acknowledging that it was "all over—you live a life that is alien to me—as mine is to you and so I am a poor soul!"[55] Kokoschka was now married to Olda Palkovská and lived in London before settling in Switzerland. He had kept the flame alive in his own unique way with a tribute in 1949 to her as the first to offer herself to him "so that I could be taught everything—happiness, misery, pain, delight, fury, and then perishing in wild frenzy."[56] Two years later, his flair for puppetry still intact, he offered to make a life-size wooden figure of himself that she could take to bed with her each night, which would "have a member . . . so you can remember me better and through practice can acquire a lust for the real thing again. We will get together again some time. Live for it, my unfaithful love."[57] Although there were numerous opportunities to meet, Alma always passed them up, as if to keep him confined in her imagination.

With continuing heart trouble and worsening deafness, Alma stayed more in her apartment. When she was diagnosed with diabetes, she gave up her favorite liqueur but "put a bottle of Benedictine beside her bed and said, 'that's for the day I die,'" Marina Mahler recalled.[58] In 1960 Leonard Bernstein held a Mahler festival to mark the centenary of his birth, which initiated the revival of his works and his reputation. Alma was invited to the rehearsals and was celebrated again as *La Grande Veuve*. Alma admired Bernstein—"a brilliant conductor . . . because he is also a very interesting composer," she wrote to Gusti Arlt.[59]

Over the years, reporters arrived to interview Alma. Often she would firmly admonish them, while simultaneously smothering them with charm. Toward her last days she was visited by Thilo Koch, a veteran reporter for ARD, the German radio and television network. He was greeted at the door by a silent, middle-aged woman (Ida Gebauer) and "thought he had walked into a dream": the room was darkened despite the sunny afternoon, with a few lamps "placed in such a way that only the person in the middle of the room was clearly visible, though not all that clearly." Alma was sitting in an armchair "shrouded in a cloud of heavy, sweet perfume" behind a table on which rested her "heavily bejewelled hands." Large scarves enveloped her voluminous body, on her ears were long, glistening ear clips, and she wore pearls. "Her eyes were glittering as she looked at

Figure 26. Alma at Carnegie Hall, 1960, listening to Mahler's Second Symphony. Music was always her salvation.

me expectantly." As she talked of Mahler and Werfel, Koch realized that she never directly answered his questions because she was almost entirely deaf, "but she did not want to admit it in order not to disappoint her guest. So she was acting out a game in front of me. It was a brilliant performance. Her strong personality, her forcefulness, her vitality and sensitivity, the excessiveness and courage of her character came through despite the the-atrical trappings she had chosen." Koch "would gladly have continued listening, but her sentences often just broke off. Then her hands and eyes would search the table for some specific reference point—and find none. I felt as if there were a lump in my throat that kept getting bigger. . . . She had carefully staged everything. The lighting. The make-up."[60] Despite her failing powers, Alma was no less determined to remain in control of her surroundings and of her image.

In the autumn of 1964, when an American friend, Suma Morgen-stern, visited, he found "the shadow of death was already upon her." She had suffered several strokes. Alma asked him about death: "'How is it now? Do you think often about death? Are you afraid?' 'Yes,' I said, 'I think often about death and have done for some time.'" Morgenstern left "feeling wretched. I had a premonition it would be the last parting. The time for grief was very near."[61] Her friend and adviser Adolf Klarmann saw her in October 1964: "It was already after her last strokes, after which nobody noticed anything physically wrong with her. Only in her face did she really look like an old lady for the first time. Gone were the little curls, and her eyes looked at me wanting a confirmation that nothing had changed. . . . Right to the end she remained clear and fought doggedly for the life that she was not about to give up gladly."[62] She was not always quite so clear. Sometimes she imagined she had met Crown Prince Ru-dolf, the doomed heir to the Habsburg throne, on a mountain top, and he wanted to have her child.

Alma died on December 11, 1964, in her New York apartment, sur-rounded by the mementos of her past in the rooms that "hold all my life."[63] She was in her eighty-sixth year. The funeral was two days later in the Frank E. Campbell Funeral Church nearby on Madison Avenue. When Adolf Klarmann saw Alma lying in her coffin, "her face . . . seemed to have the expression of somebody suspiciously curious, as if she were trying to figure out just where she was."[64] Alma was buried as she had wished, beside Manon in Grinzing cemetery, Vienna.

"MY LIFE WAS beautiful," Alma wrote in her own account of what had been important to her in her life. "God gave me to know the works of genius in our time before they left the hands of their creators. And if for a while I was able to hold the stirrups of those horsemen of light, my being has been justified and blessed."[65]

She did not mention her other legacy, her musical compositions. Although published and performed only intermittently in her lifetime, as interest in women composers has increased, her intense, beautiful, and technically complex songs are now appreciated as the work of an assured and highly accomplished and talented woman. She achieved a skillful range of color with notably enterprising harmonies and rich textures in her sensitive renderings of the poetic text.

Why she never returned to composing after Mahler's death, apart from a few lieder such as *Der Erkennende*, written in 1915, is not clear. The climate for female composers was certainly not encouraging, indeed it remained hostile for many decades, and the belittling of female talent, which in her case meant ascribing any work of quality to the influence or actual pen of a man—Mahler or Zemlinsky—had been common practice.

Her silence perhaps came about because after a gap of ten years, with no opportunity to practice, to hone or develop her talent, she no longer had the confidence to face the daunting opposition that her younger spirit had challenged. Or perhaps when she described carrying her songs around with her "in a coffin" for those ten years, it was because something had died inside her. Despite her burst of creativity when Mahler at last acknowledged her as a composer of talent, it was too late to revive it, the energy no longer burned, her confidence had drained, and her creative spirit dwindled. Life had taken over; she had found a different outlet for her creativity in the nurture of other creative spirits, a role she knew well from her childhood in her father's studio.

Her works are estimated to comprise perhaps as many as a hundred lieder and various instrumental pieces. Many of these have been lost, either incinerated in the ruins of wartime Vienna or mislaid during the flight that took her into exile in America. Her 1898–1902 diaries mention in all around seventy-three songs, and she also wrote piano music and chamber music, including a violin sonata and a fragmentary piano trio.[66] Some works have been published. Carl Moll included three lieder, *Liese weht ein erstes Bluhn*, *Meine Nächte*, and *Einsamer Gang*, in his private compilation for Alma's twenty-first birthday in 1900. At Mahler's instigation, five of her songs, all based on poems by eminent literary figures—Richard Dehmel, Rainer Maria Rilke, Heinrich Heine, Otto Hartleben, and Otto Julius Bierbaum—were published in 1910 and premiered by eminent singers in Vienna and New York. Alma arranged for Universal Edition to publish in 1915 four lieder composed between 1901 and 1911, and then in 1924 she published another five. Two more were published posthumously in 2000, and *Einsamer Gang* in 2018.

Although famous for her attraction to creative geniuses, throughout her life it was not the men who were her saviors. Composing, playing, or experiencing music in different forms was her crystalline core. It was the inner refuge to which she turned when life let her down and when the dreadful tragedies that shadowed her life struck her—the loss of her first husband and the awful deaths of three of her four children.

And music was the voice through which she could express her passionate spirit. Her own music is her lasting, and living, legacy.

Appendix

The Songs and Works of Alma Mahler-Werfel

Although Alma Mahler was a prolific composer, only seventeen of her songs survive in published form.

Published 1910

Die stille Nacht, text by Richard Dehmel
In meines Vaters Garten, text by Otto Erich Hartleben
Laue Sommernacht, text by Otto Julius Bierbaum
Bei dir ist es traut, text by Rainer Maria Rilke
Ich wandle unter Blumen, text by Heinrich Heine

Published 1915 (with a cover illustration by Oskar Kokoschka)

Licht in der Nacht, text by Otto Julius Bierbaum
Waldseligkeit, text by Richard Dehmel
Ansturm, text by Richard Dehmel
Emtelied, text by Gustav Falke

Published 1924

Hymne, text by Novalis
Ekstase, text by Otto Julius Bierbaum
Der Erkennende, text by Franz Werfel
Hymne an die Nacht, text by Novalis
Lobgesang, text by Richard Dehmel

Published 2000 by Hildegard Publishing Company, Philadelphia (ed. Susan Filler)

Kennst du meine Nächte? text by Leo Greiner
Leise weht ein erstes Blühn, text by Rainer Maria Rilke

Published 2018 by The Wagner Journal, London

Einsamer Gang, text by Leo Greiner

Acknowledgments

It is a particular challenge to write a biography of a figure who has already inspired several previous works. It demands deep delving to uncover new evidence, different facets of character, and new interpretations of known and perhaps familiar events. It is my good fortune to have been assisted throughout by researchers and experts of very high caliber. I am grateful to Michael Raleigh for his able research and translation and his technical acuity, and to John Pollack, David McKnight, and the staff at the Kislak Center for Special Collections, Rare Books and Manuscripts, at the University of Pennsylvania in Philadelphia. They gave us over a period of weeks unfettered access, friendly cooperation, and guidance in negotiating the impressively large and, in some parts, unmined Mahler-Werfel Papers. I thank Rosl Merdinger, who brought her previous knowledge of the subject to my research in Vienna, and the staff of the Belvedere Gallery, the Austrian National Library, and the Vienna City Library; also the Bauhaus Archive, Berlin, for the use of Walter Gropius's letters; the Fondation Oskar Kokoschka, Zurich, for the use of Oskar Kokoschka's works; and Stefan Weidle of Wiedle Verlag, Bonn, for those of Albrecht Joseph.

I am particularly grateful to my dear friend and agent, Caroline Michel, who matched me with Alma—an inspired act that has brought me years of pleasure, and to Leah Stecher, editor at Basic Books, for her expertise and clear editorial judgment and Brynn Warriner, Claire Potter, add Sharon Kunz for their steady support. My thanks to Dunja Noack and Thea Wrobbel, and to Jo Carlill for her outstanding picture research and Laurent Carré for photo images. I am especially grateful to Karin Gartzke for her excellent translations and to Nuria Schoenberg Nono and Irene Hartzell for their firsthand memories of Alma. It has been a special pleasure to work with Marina Mahler, and I thank her for her wonderful cooperation, for giving me access to all her family archives, and for permission to quote from the writings and archives of Alma Mahler-Werfel and Franz Werfel.

Many friends and colleagues have shared their expertise during long and always enthralling conversations. Tony Palmer, Howard Goodall, and Barry Millington and Deborah Calland of the Wagner Society gave me invaluable advice and background to Alma's musical accomplishments. I thank Peter Stephan Jungk for his warm, wise, and informed counsel; Hella Pick and Sally Doganis for their friendship, time, and helpfully astute comments on the manuscript; and Peter Ibbotson for his excellent photos.

I am grateful beyond measure for the friendship and love of friends and family who have steadfastly supported and advised me, kept me laughing, and encouraged me to continue writing this book through one of the most difficult and painful periods of my life. They include the late Tessa Jowell, Caroline Thomson, Roger Liddle, Jeremy Isaacs, Gillian Widdicombe, David Gilmore, Fiona Mollison, Nicholas and Kate Coulson, Diana Morant, Trevor Moore, Sandra Hepburn, Sue Howes, Rosemary Squire, Victoria Greenwood, Jenny Bland, Michael Prior, Hunter Davies, David Bassedow, Margreta de Grazia, Sally Emerson, Peter Taylor, Irene Barrett, Polly Lansdowne, Peter and Susie Ibbotson, Geraldine Sharpe-Newton, Julian Cooper, Linda Ryle, Hunter Davies, Tristram and Virginia Powell, Judy and the late Sir William McAlpine, Howard Jacobson and Jenny de Yong, and Jenna Davies. I thank Frances Haste and Helen Haste, and above all I thank Alice, my daughter, and Tom, my son, for the precious gift of their love and their support. To their respective sons, my grandsons, Arthur Bragg and Eric Flintoff, I dedicate this book.

Cate Haste
London, November 2018

Notes

Preface

1. Alma Mahler-Werfel, *Diaries 1898–1902*, ed. Antony Beaumont and Susanne Rode-Breymann (Ithaca, NY: Cornell University Press, 2000).

Chapter 1. Vienna Childhood 1879–1898

1. Albrecht Joseph, "Werfel, Alma, Kokoschka, the Actor George," unpublished manuscript, Mahler-Werfel Papers, Kislak Center for Special Collections, Rare Books and Manuscripts, University of Pennsylvania, 35.

2. Joseph, "Werfel, Alma, Kokoschka, the Actor George," 12.

3. Alma Mahler-Werfel, "Der schimmernde Weg," unpublished typescript, Mahler-Werfel Papers, 5.

4. Alma Mahler-Werfel, *And the Bridge Is Love* (London: Hutchinson, 1959), 12.

5. Mahler-Werfel, "Der schimmernde Weg," 5–6.

6. Mahler-Werfel, "Der schimmernde Weg," 6.

7. Mahler-Werfel, *Diaries*, October 25, 1899, 202.

8. Mahler-Werfel, "Der schimmernde Weg," 5.

9. Mahler-Werfel, "Der schimmernde Weg," 2.

10. Emil Jakob Schindler, Diary, March 14, 1879, March 20, 1879, cited in Heinrich Fuchs, *Emil Jakob Schindler* (Vienna: Selbst Verlag, 1970), 15.

11. Mahler-Werfel, *Diaries*, July 27, 1900, 307.

12. Emil Jakob Schindler, Diary, April 21, 1879, April 2, 1879, cited in Fuchs, *Emil Jakob Schindler*, 16.

13. Emil Jakob Schindler, Diary, October 15, 1879, cited in Fuchs, *Emil Jakob Schindler*, 19.

14. Emil Jakob Schindler, Diary, August 31, 1879, cited in Fuchs, *Emil Jakob Schindler*, 19.

15. Mahler-Werfel, *Diaries*, July 27, 1900, 307.

16. Carl Moll, *Eine Bildnisstudie* (1930), exhibition catalog, cited in *Poetic Realism* (Vienna: Belvedere, 2012), 40.

17. Mahler-Werfel, "Der schimmernde Weg," 8.

18. Moll, *Eine Bildnisstudie*, 40.

19. Carl Moll, "Memory of Plankenberg," cited in Mahler-Werfel, "Der schimmernde Weg," 4.

20. Mahler-Werfel, *And the Bridge Is Love*, 10.

21. Mahler-Werfel, *And the Bridge Is Love*, 10.

22. Mahler-Werfel, *And the Bridge Is Love*, 10.

23. Cited in Fuchs, *Emil Jacob Schindler*, 7, 8.

24. Mahler-Werfel, "Der schimmernde Weg," 6.

25. Mahler-Werfel, *Diaries*, September 5, 1899, 190–191.

26. Mahler-Werfel, "Der schimmernde Weg," 7.

27. Mahler-Werfel, "Der schimmernde Weg," 8.

28. Carl Moll, "Mein Leben," typescript, Belvedere Gallery Vienna, 96.

29. Mahler-Werfel, "Der schimmernde Weg," 8.

30. Mahler-Werfel, "Der schimmernde Weg," 9.

31. Mahler-Werfel, "Der schimmernde Weg," 9.

32. Mahler-Werfel, *Diaries*, September 5, 1899, 190.

33. Mahler-Werfel, "Der schimmernde Weg," 10.

34. Mahler-Werfel, "Der schimmernde Weg," 10.

35. Mahler-Werfel, "Der schimmernde Weg," 11.

36. Mahler-Werfel, "Der schimmernde Weg," 3.

37. Mahler-Werfel, *And the Bridge Is Love*, 17.

38. Mahler-Werfel, "Der schimmernde Weg," 10.

39. Mahler-Werfel, "Der schimmernde Weg," 11.

40. Carl E. Schorske, *Fin de Siecle Vienna* (London: Vintage 1981), 215.

41. Mahler-Werfel, *And the Bridge Is Love*, 17.

42. Franz Matsch, *Memoir*, cited in Frank Whitford, *Gustav Klimt, Artists in Context* (London: Collins and Brown, 1993), 32.

43. Cited in Schorske, *Fin de Siecle Vienna*, 215.

44. Stefan Zweig, *The World of Yesterday* (London: Cassell, 1943), 44.

45. Mahler-Werfel, *Diaries*, March 25, 26, 1898, 17.

46. Cited in Whitford, *Gustav Klimt*, 43.

47. Cited in Whitford, *Gustav Klimt*, 43.

48. J. M. Olbrich, "Das Haus der Sezession," *Der Architekt* 5 (January 1899): 5.

49. Mahler-Werfel, *Diaries*, October 12, 1898, 64.

50. Mahler-Werfel, *Diaries*, May 7, 1898, 30.

51. Mahler-Werfel, *Diaries*, May 18, 1898, 32, 31.

52. Mahler-Werfel, *Diaries*, May 22, 1898, 32.

53. Mahler-Werfel, *Diaries*, October 24, 1899, 201.

54. Mahler-Werfel, *Diaries*, February 9, 1898, 5.

55. Mahler-Werfel, *Diaries*, April 23, 1900, 279.

56. Mahler-Werfel, *Diaries*, December 16, 1899, 217.

57. Mahler-Werfel, *Diaries*, January 27, 1898, 3.

58. Mahler-Werfel, *Diaries*, November 29, 1898, 74.

59. Mahler-Werfel, *Diaries*, November 22, 1898, 72.

60. Mahler-Werfel, *Diaries*, December 20, 1898, 82.

61. Mahler-Werfel, *Diaries*, March 14, 1899, 104.

62. Mahler-Werfel, *Diaries*, January 5, 1899, 85.

63. Mahler-Werfel, *Diaries*, January 7, 1899, 85.

64. Mahler-Werfel, *Diaries*, February 9, 1898, 5.

65. Mahler-Werfel, *Diaries*, January 6, 1899, 85.

66. Mahler-Werfel, *Diaries*, February 9, 1898, 5.

67. Mahler-Werfel, *Diaries*, January 17, 1899, 88.

68. Mahler-Werfel, *Diaries*, February 28, 1899, 99.

69. Mahler-Werfel, *Diaries*, February 7, 1899, 93.

70. Mahler-Werfel, *Diaries*, January 13, 1899, 87.

71. Mahler-Werfel, *Diaries*, January 13, 1899, 87.

72. Mahler-Werfel, *Diaries*, January 24, 1899, 89.

73. Mahler-Werfel, *Diaries*, July 23, 1898, 40, 41.

74. Mahler-Werfel, *Diaries*, October 19, 1898, 66.

75. Mahler-Werfel, *Diaries*, August 9, 1898, 50.

76. Mahler-Werfel, *Diaries*, May 17, 1899, 137–138.

77. Mahler-Werfel, *Diaries*, December 1, 1898, 75.

78. Mahler-Werfel, *Diaries*, February 13, 1899, 94.

79. Mahler-Werfel, *Diaries*, March 12, 1899, 103.

80. Mahler-Werfel, *Diaries*, May 20, 1899, 141.

81. Mahler-Werfel, *Diaries*, July 20, 1899, 169.

82. Mahler-Werfel, *Diaries*, August 16, 1899, 180.

83. Mahler-Werfel, *Diaries*, September 6, 1899, 191–192.

Chapter 2. Awakening 1898–1899

1. Mahler-Werfel, *Diaries*, November 24, 1898, 73.

2. Mahler-Werfel, *Diaries*, February 9, 1898, 5.

3. Zweig, *World of Yesterday*, 22–23.

4. Zweig, *World of Yesterday*, 28.

5. Zweig, *World of Yesterday*, 28–29.

6. Mahler-Werfel, *Diaries*, April 14, 1900, 275; June 28–July 4, 1901, 414–415.

7. Mahler-Werfel, *Diaries*, April 28, 1898, 27–28.

8. Mahler-Werfel, *Diaries*, March 10, 1898, 12–13.

9. Mahler-Werfel, *Diaries*, March 27, 1898, 17–18.

10. Mahler-Werfel, *Diaries*, March 27, 1898, 18.

11. Mahler-Werfel, *Diaries*, April 17, 1898, 24.

12. Mahler-Werfel, *Diaries*, December 31, 1898, 84.

13. Mahler-Werfel, *Diaries*, April 26, 1898, 27.

14. Mahler-Werfel, *Diaries*, April 24, 1898, 26.

15. Mahler-Werfel, *Diaries*, August 4, 1898, 49.

16. Mahler-Werfel, *Diaries*, October 5, 1898, 64.

17. Mahler-Werfel, *Diaries*, November 12, 1898, 68.

18. Mahler-Werfel, *Diaries*, January 30, 1899, 90.

19. Mahler-Werfel, *Diaries*, January 14, 1899, 87.

20. Mahler-Werfel, *Diaries*, February 14, 1899, 95.

21. Mahler-Werfel, *Diaries*, February 14, 1899, 95.

22. Mahler-Werfel, *Diaries*, February 15, 1899, 95.

23. Mahler-Werfel, *Diaries*, March 2, 1899, 99.

24. Mahler-Werfel, *Diaries*, March 15, 1899, 104–105.

25. Mahler-Werfel, *Diaries*, March 18, 1899, 105.

26. Mahler-Werfel, *Diaries*, April 16, 1899, 120.

27. Mahler-Werfel, *Diaries*, April 20, 1899, 121.

28. Mahler-Werfel, *Diaries*, May 20, 1899, 141.

29. Mahler-Werfel, *Diaries*, April 29, 1899, 124.

30. Mahler-Werfel, *Diaries*, May 18, 1899, 139.

31. Mahler-Werfel, *Diaries*, May 1, 1899, 125–126.

32. Mahler-Werfel, *Diaries*, May 18, 1899, 139.

33. Mahler-Werfel, *Diaries*, May 24, 1898, 143–144.

34. Mahler-Werfel, *And the Bridge Is Love*, 17.

35. Mahler-Werfel, *Diaries*, May 4, 1899, 130.

36. Mahler-Werfel, *Diaries*, May 5, 1899. 131.

37. Mahler-Werfel, *Diaries*, May 5, 1899, 131–132.

38. Mahler-Werfel, *Diaries*, May 6, 1899, 132–133.

39. Mahler-Werfel, *Diaries*, May 8, 1899, 133.

40. Mahler-Werfel, *Diaries*, May 13, 1899, 135.

41. Mahler-Werfel, *Diaries*, May 13, 1899, 135–136.

42. Gustav Klimt to Carl Moll, May 19, 1899, cited in Henry-Louis de la Grange, *Gustav Mahler*, vol. 2, *Vienna: The Years of Challenge, 1897–1904* (Oxford: Oxford University Press, 1995), 695–697.

43. Mahler-Werfel, *Diaries*, May 15, 1898, 136.

44. Mahler-Werfel, *Diaries*, May 15, 1898, 137.

45. Mahler-Werfel, *Diaries*, May 17, 1899, 137.

46. Mahler-Werfel, *Diaries*, May 20, 1899, 141.

47. Mahler-Werfel, *Diaries*, July 22, 1899, 171.

48. Mahler-Werfel, *Diaries*, May 12, 1899, 135.

49. Mahler-Werfel, *Diaries*, June 9, 1899, 153.

50. Mahler-Werfel, *Diaries*, June 6, 1899, 151–152.

51. Mahler-Werfel, *Diaries*, June 30, 1899, 159.

52. Mahler-Werfel, *Diaries*, August 4, 1899, 178.

53. Mahler-Werfel, *Diaries*, August 4, 1899, 178.

54. Mahler-Werfel, *Diaries*, August 31, 1899, 186.

55. Mahler-Werfel, *Diaries*, January 21, 1900, 230.

Chapter 3. Love and Music 1899–1901

1. Mahler-Werfel, *Diaries*, September 9, 1899, 194.

2. Mahler-Werfel, *Diaries*, July 17, 1899, 164.

3. Mahler-Werfel, *Diaries*, July 18, 1899, 164.

4. Mahler-Werfel, *Diaries*, August 1, 1899, 176.

5. Mahler-Werfel, *Diaries*, August 9, 1899, 180.

6. Mahler-Werfel, *Diaries*, August 10, 1899, 180.

7. Mahler-Werfel, *Diaries*, October 3, 1899, 198–199.

8. Mahler-Werfel, *Diaries*, May 20, 1899, 142–143.

9. Mahler-Werfel, *Diaries*, October 12, 1898, 64.

10. Mahler-Werfel, *Diaries*, September 8, 1899, 193.

11. Mahler-Werfel, *Diaries*, August 9, 1899, 180.

12. Mahler-Werfel, *Diaries*, November 29, 1899, 210–211.

13. Mahler-Werfel, *Diaries*, December 1, 1899, 212.

14. Mahler-Werfel, *Diaries*, January 4, 1900, 221.

15. Mahler-Werfel, *Diaries*, September 20, 1900, 323.

16. Mahler-Werfel, *Diaries*, December 14, 1899, 216–217.

17. Mahler-Werfel, *Diaries*, October 23, 1900, 334.

18. Mahler-Werfel, *Diaries*, March 3, 1899, 100.

19. Mahler-Werfel, *Diaries*, December 3, 1899, 213.

20. Mahler-Werfel, *Diaries*, February 2, 1900, 242.

21. Mahler-Werfel, *Diaries*, April 24, 1900, 280.

22. Mahler-Werfel, *Diaries*, November 16, 1899, 71.

23. Mahler-Werfel, *Diaries*, March 10, 1900, 258.

24. Mahler-Werfel, *Diaries*, March 16, 1900, 263.

25. Mahler-Werfel, *Diaries*, February 7, 1900, 244.

26. Mahler-Werfel, *Diaries*, June 14, 1900, 293–294.

27. Mahler-Werfel, *Diaries*, January 4, 1900, 222.

28. Mahler-Werfel, *Diaries*, March 19, 1900, 265.

29. Berta Zuckerkandl, *Österreich intime* (Vienna: Amalthea Signum Verlag, 2013), 52.

30. Mahler-Werfel, *Diaries*, February 11, 1900, 245.

31. Mahler-Werfel, *Diaries*, February 26, 1900, 253–254.

32. Mahler-Werfel, *Diaries*, March 10, 1900, 258.

33. Mahler-Werfel, *Diaries*, April 23, 1900, 278–279.

34. Mahler-Werfel, *Diaries*, May 12, 1900, 283.

35. Mahler-Werfel, *Diaries*, May 12, 1900, 283.

36. Mahler-Werfel, *Diaries*, October 19, 1900, 332.

37. Mahler-Werfel, *Diaries*, June 23, 1900, 296; July 11, 1900, 299.

38. Mahler-Werfel, *Diaries*, July 11, 1900, 299; July 23, 1900, 305.

39. Mahler-Werfel, *Diaries*, July 24, 1900, 305.

40. Mahler-Werfel, *Diaries*, August 2, 1900, 308.

41. Mahler-Werfel, *Diaries*, September 4, 1900, 319.

42. Alexander Zemlinsky to Alma Schindler, August 9, 1900, cited in Mahler-Werfel, *Diaries*, August 10, 1900, 312.

43. Mahler-Werfel, *Diaries*, October 15, 1900, 331.

44. Mahler-Werfel, *Diaries*, October 18, 1900, 332.

45. Mahler-Werfel, *Diaries*, November 13, 1900, 343–344.

46. Mahler-Werfel, *Diaries*, December 27, 1901, 361.

47. Mahler-Werfel, *Diaries*, September 27, 1900, 326.

48. Mahler-Werfel, *Diaries*, November 12, 1900, 342–343.

49. Mahler-Werfel, *Diaries*, December 11, 1900, 355.

50. Mahler-Werfel, *Diaries*, December 14, 1900, 356.

51. Mahler-Werfel, *Diaries*, December 17, 1900, 357.

52. Mahler-Werfel, *Diaries*, December 24, 1900, 360.

53. Mahler-Werfel, *Diaries*, February 24, 1901, 377.

54. Mahler-Werfel, *Diaries*, September 22, 1900, 324.

55. Mahler-Werfel, *Diaries*, October 21, 1900, 333.

56. Mahler-Werfel, *Diaries*, February 28, 1901, 370, 378.

57. Mahler-Werfel, *Diaries*, March 2, 1901, 379.

58. Mahler-Werfel, *Diaries*, February 24, 1901, 377.

59. Alexander Zemlinsky to Alma Schindler, undated [1901], Mahler-Werfel Papers. Kislak Center for Special Collections, Rare Books and Manuscripts, University of Pennsylvania.

60. Mahler-Werfel, *Diaries*, January 7, 1901, 366.

61. Mahler-Werfel, *Diaries*, March 4, 1901, 380.

62. Mahler-Werfel, *Diaries*, March 13, 1901, 384.

63. Alexander Zemlinsky to Alma Schindler, March 20, 1901, Mahler-Werfel Papers.

64. Mahler-Werfel, *Diaries*, March 28, 1901, 393.

65. Mahler-Werfel, *Diaries*, March 25, 1901, 392.

66. Mahler-Werfel, *Diaries*, March 23, 1901, 391.

67. Mahler-Werfel, *Diaries*, March 28, 1901, 393.

68. Alexander Zemlinsky to Alma Schindler, c. April 3, 1901, Mahler-Werfel Papers.

69. Mahler-Werfel, *Diaries*, April 10, 1901, 395.

70. Mahler-Werfel, *Diaries*, April 11, 1901, 396.

71. Alexander Zemlinsky to Alma Mahler, undated, c. April 11, 1901, Mahler-Werfel Papers.

72. Mahler-Werfel, *Diaries*, April 18, 1901, 398.

73. Alexander Zemlinsky to Alma Schindler, c. April 19, 1901, Mahler-Werfel Papers.

74. Mahler-Werfel, *Diaries*, April 19, 1901, 398.

75. Mahler-Werfel, *Diaries*, April 19, 1901, 398–399.

76. Mahler-Werfel, *Diaries*, April 21, 1901, 399.

77. Mahler-Werfel, *Diaries*, April 22, 1901, 400.

78. Mahler-Werfel, *Diaries*, April 23, 1901, 400–401.

79. Mahler-Werfel, *Diaries*, February 27, 1900, 251.

80. Mahler-Werfel, *Diaries*, May 2, 1901, 403.

81. Mahler-Werfel, *Diaries*, May 17, 1901, 404.

82. Mahler-Werfel, *Diaries*, May 19, 1901, 405.

83. Mahler-Werfel, *Diaries*, May 21, 1901, 405.

84. Alexander Zemlinsky to Alma Schindler, May 22, 1901, Mahler-Werfel Papers.

85. Mahler-Werfel, *Diaries*, May 23, 1901, 409.

86. Mahler-Werfel, *Diaries*, May 25, 1901, 409.

87. Alexander Zemlinsky to Alma Schindler, May 27, 1901, Mahler-Werfel Papers.

88. Mahler-Werfel, *Diaries*, May 18, 1901, 404–405.

89. Mahler-Werfel, *Diaries*, May 4, 1901, 404.

90. Mahler-Werfel, *Diaries*, May 30, 1901, 409–410.

91. Mahler-Werfel, *Diaries*, May 30, 1901, 410.

92. Mahler-Werfel, *Diaries*, June 21, 1901, 413.

93. Mahler-Werfel, *Diaries*, June 21, 1901, 413.

94. Mahler-Werfel, *Diaries*, July 29, 1901, 422.

95. Mahler-Werfel, *Diaries*, July 14, 1901, 418.

96. Mahler-Werfel, *Diaries*, July 22, 1901, 419.

97. Mahler-Werfel, *Diaries*, July 23, 1901, 419–420.

98. Mahler-Werfel, *Diaries*, July 28, 1901, 421.

99. Mahler-Werfel, *Diaries*, July 24, 1901, 421.

100. Mahler-Werfel, *Diaries*, October 5, 1901, 435.

101. Mahler-Werfel, *Diaries*, October 7, 1901, 436.

102. Mahler-Werfel, *Diaries*, October 7, 1901, 436.

103. Mahler-Werfel, *Diaries*, October 27, 1901, 439.

104. Mahler-Werfel, *Diaries*, October 18, 1901, 439.

105. Mahler-Werfel, *Diaries*, November 9, 1901, 444.

Chapter 4. Divine Longing 1901–1902

1. Alma Mahler, *Gustav Mahler: Memories and Letters* (Seattle: University of Washington Press, 1975), 3.

2. Mahler-Werfel, *Diaries*, December 4, 1898, 76.

3. Mahler-Werfel, *Diaries*, February 19, 1899, 96.

4. Mahler-Werfel, *Diaries*, November 18, 1900, 345.

5. Mahler-Werfel, *Diaries*, July 11, 1899, 163.

6. Mahler-Werfel, *Diaries*, March 3, 1899, 101.

7. Mahler-Werfel, *Diaries*, February 26, 1900, 254.

8. Bert Blaukopf and Herta Blaukopf, *Mahler: His Life, Work and World* (London: Thames and Hudson, 1976), 17.

9. Zuckerkandl, *Österreich intime*, 48.

10. Zuckerkandl, *Österreich intime*, 52, 53.

11. Alma Mahler, *Gustav Mahler: Memories and Letters*, 4.

12. Berta Zuckerkandl to Sophie Clemenceau, November 30, 1901, in Zuckerkandl, *Österreich intime*, 53.

13. Zuckerkandl, *Österreich intime*, 53, 54.

14. Zuckerkandl, *Österreich intime*, 54.

15. Alma Mahler, *Gustav Mahler: Memories and Letters*, 4–5; *Gustav Mahler: Letters to His Wife*, ed. Henry-Louis de la Grange and Günther Weiss in collaboration with Knud Martner (Ithaca, NY: Cornell University Press, 2004), 34–35.

16. Mahler-Werfel, *Diaries*, November 7, 1901, 443.

17. Mahler-Werfel, *Diaries*, November 7, 1901, 443.

18. Zuckerkandl, *Österreich intime*, 54.

19. Alma Mahler, *Gustav Mahler: Memories and Letters*, 5.

20. Mahler-Werfel, *Diaries*, November 8, 1901, 444.

21. Gustav Mahler to Alma Schindler, Berlin, December 14, 1901, in *Gustav Mahler: Letters to His Wife*, 67.

22. Alma Mahler, *Gustav Mahler: Memories and Letters*, 15.

23. Mahler-Werfel, *Diaries*, November 19, 1901, 446.

24. Alma Mahler, *Gustav Mahler: Memories and Letters*, 17.

25. Alma Mahler, *Gustav Mahler: Memories and Letters*, 18.

26. Mahler-Werfel, *Diaries*, November 19, 1901, 446.

27. Alma Mahler, *Gustav Mahler: Memories and Letters*, 19.

28. Alma Mahler, *Gustav Mahler: Memories and Letters*, 19.

29. Carl Moll, *Erinnerungen*, unpublished manuscript, cited in *Gustav Mahler: Letters to His Wife*, 41.

30. Alma Mahler, *Gustav Mahler: Memories and Letters*, 19.

31. Alma Mahler, *Gustav Mahler: Memories and Letters*, 19–20.

32. Gustav Mahler to Alma Schindler, November 29, 1901, cited in *Gustav Mahler: Letters to His Wife*, 43.

33. Alma Schindler to Gustav Mahler, November 29, 1901, cited in *Gustav Mahler: Letters to His Wife*, 45.

34. Mahler-Werfel, *Diaries*, November 19, 1901, 447.

35. Mahler-Werfel, *Diaries*, December 1, 1901, 448.

36. Mahler-Werfel, *Diaries*, December 8, 1901, 455.

37. Mahler-Werfel, *Diaries*, December 3, 1901, 449.

38. Gustav Mahler to Alma Schindler, December 9, 1901, cited in *Gustav Mahler: Letters to His Wife*, 54.

39. Gustav Mahler to Alma Schindler, December 5, 8, 1901, cited in *Gustav Mahler: Letters to His Wife*, 49, 52.

40. Mahler-Werfel, *Diaries*, December 7, 1901, 451.

41. Gustav Mahler to Alma Schindler, December 11, 1901, cited in *Gustav Mahler: Letters to His Wife*, 57.

42. Gustav Mahler to Justine Mahler, Berlin, December 12, 1901, cited in *Gustav Mahler: Letters to His Wife*, 61.

43. Gustav Mahler to Justine Mahler, Berlin, December 14, 1901, cited in *Gustav Mahler: Letters to His Wife*, 62.

44. Gustav Mahler to Alma Schindler, December 16, 1901, cited in *Gustav Mahler: Letters to His Wife*, 73.

45. Gustav Mahler to Alma Schindler, December 12, 1901, cited in *Gustav Mahler: Letters to His Wife*, 61.

46. Gustav Mahler to Justine Mahler Berlin, December 15, 1901, cited in *Gustav Mahler: Letters to His Wife*, 72.

47. Gustav Mahler to Alma Schindler, December 14, 1901, cited in *Gustav Mahler: Letters to His Wife*, 65, 66.

48. Mahler-Werfel, *Diaries*, December 1, 1901, 459.

49. Mahler-Werfel, *Diaries*, December 15, 1901, 459.

50. Mahler-Werfel, *Diaries*, December 12, 1901, 458.

51. Mahler-Werfel, *Diaries*, December 13, 1901, 458.

52. Mahler-Werfel, *Diaries*, December 16, 1901, 459–460.

53. Mahler-Werfel, *Diaries*, December 9, 1901, 455–456.

54. Gustav Mahler to Alma Schindler, Berlin, December 16, 1901, cited in *Gustav Mahler: Letters to His Wife*, 74.

55. Mahler-Werfel, *Diaries*, December 18, 1901, 460–461.

56. Mahler-Werfel, *Diaries*, December 19, 1901, 461.

57. Alma Mahler, *Gustav Mahler: Memories and Letters*, 22.

58. *Gustav Mahler: Letters to His Wife*, 78–84.

59. *Gustav Mahler: Letters to His Wife*, 78–84.

60. Mahler-Werfel, *Diaries*, December 20, 1901, 462.

61. Alma Mahler, *Gustav Mahler: Memories and Letters*, 22.

62. Mahler-Werfel, *Diaries*, December 21, 1901, 462.

63. Gustav Mahler to Alma Schindler, December 21, 1901, cited in *Gustav Mahler: Letters to His Wife*, 86–87.

64. Mahler-Werfel, *Diaries*, December 21, 1901, 462.

65. Mahler-Werfel, *Diaries*, December 22, 1901, 462–463.

66. Mahler-Werfel, *Diaries*, December 24, 1901, 464.

67. Mahler-Werfel, *Diaries*, December 22, 23, 1901, 463, 464; Gustav Mahler to Alma Schindler, December 24, 1901, cited in *Gustav Mahler: Letters to His Wife*, 89.

68. Alma Mahler to Walter Gropius, August 17, 1910, Bauhaus Archive, cited in Henry-Louis de la Grange, *Gustav Mahler*, vol. 4, *A New Life Cut Short, 1907–1911* (Oxford: Oxford University Press, 2008), 877.

69. Mahler-Werfel, *Diaries*, December 21, 1901, 463–464.

70. Alma Mahler, *Gustav Mahler: Memories and Letters*, 23.

71. Mahler-Werfel, *Diaries*, December 28, 1901, 465.

72. Mahler-Werfel, *Diaries*, December 29, 1901, 466.

73. Mahler-Werfel, *Diaries*, New Year's Eve 1901, 467.

74. Mahler-Werfel, *Diaries*, December 30, 1901, 466.

75. Mahler-Werfel, *Diaries*, January 3, 1902, 467; January 4, 1902, 467.

76. Gustav Mahler to Alma Schindler, Vienna, January 3, 1902, cited in *Gustav Mahler: Letters to His Wife*, 95.

77. Bruno Walter to his parents, December 30, 1901, in *Bruno Walter Briefe, 1894–1962* (Frankfurt: Fischer Verlag, 1969), 52–53, cited in *Gustav Mahler: Letters to His Wife*, 92.

78. Mahler-Werfel, *Diaries*, January 5, 1902, 467; Alma Mahler, *Gustav Mahler: Memories and Letters*, 25–26.

79. Cited in de la Grange, *Gustav Mahler*, vol. 2, *Vienna: The Years of Challenge*, 463.

80. Alma Mahler, *Gustav Mahler: Memories and Letters*, 27.

81. Alma Mahler, *Gustav Mahler: Memories and Letters*, 31–32.

82. Mahler-Werfel, *Diaries*, January 6, 1902, 468.

83. Alma Mahler, *Gustav Mahler: Memories and Letters*, 29–30.

84. Mahler-Werfel, *Diaries*, January 16, 1902, 468.

85. Alma Mahler, *Gustav Mahler: Memories and Letters*, 14.

86. Gustav Mahler to Alma Schindler, February 1, 1902, cited in *Gustav Mahler: Letters to His Wife*, 101.

87. Alma Mahler, *Gustav Mahler: Memories and Letters*, 33.

88. Alma Mahler, *Gustav Mahler: Memories and Letters*, 34.

Chapter 5. A Nobler Calling 1902–1907

1. Alma Mahler, *Gustav Mahler: Memories and Letters*, 34.

2. Mahler-Werfel, *And the Bridge Is Love*, 27.

3. Alma Mahler, *Gustav Mahler: Memories and Letters*, 34.

4. Alma Mahler, *Gustav Mahler: Memories and Letters*, 36.

5. Gustav Mahler to Alma Schindler, December 1, 1901, cited in *Gustav Mahler: Letters to His Wife*, 73.

6. Bruno Walter to his parents, September 29, 1901, in *Bruno Walter Briefe*, 44.

7. Alma Mahler, *Gustav Mahler: Memories and Letters*, 39.

8. Alma Mahler, *Gustav Mahler: Memories and Letters*, 41.

9. Cited in de la Grange, *Gustav Mahler*, vol. 2, *Vienna: The Years of Challenge*, 528.

10. Alma Mahler, *Gustav Mahler: Memories and Letters*, 41.

11. Alma Mahler, *Gustav Mahler: Memories and Letters*, 47.

12. Mahler-Werfel, *And the Bridge Is Love*, 30–31.

13. Alma Mahler, *Gustav Mahler: Memories and Letters*, 45.

14. Alma Mahler, *Gustav Mahler: Memories and Letters*, 42.

15. Alma Mahler-Werfel, Tagebuch [diary], July 10, 1902, 2–3, Mahler-Werfel Papers.

16. Mahler-Werfel, Tagebuch, July 12, 1902, 2–3.

17. Mahler-Werfel, Tagebuch, July 13, 1902, 4; "Der schimmernde Weg," Mahler-Werfel Papers, 21.

18. Mahler-Werfel, Tagebuch, August 10, 1902, 4; "Der schimmernde Weg," 22.

19. Cited in de la Grange, *Gustav Mahler*, vol. 2, *Vienna: The Years of Challenge*, 638.

20. Mahler-Werfel, Tagebuch, November 25, 1902, 5.

21. Alma Mahler, *Gustav Mahler: Memories and Letters*, 49.

22. Mahler-Werfel, Tagebuch, December 13, 1902, 5.

23. Mahler-Werfel, Tagebuch, December 15, 1902.

24. Mahler-Werfel, Tagebuch, December 15, 1902, 5–6.

25. Mahler-Werfel, Tagebuch, December 13, 1902, 5.

26. Gustav Mahler to Alma Mahler, Wiesbaden, January 21, 1903, cited in *Gustav Mahler: Letters to His Wife*, 111.

27. Mahler-Werfel, Tagebuch, December 16, 1902, 6.

28. Mahler-Werfel, Tagebuch, January 8, 1903, 6–7.

29. Mahler-Werfel, Tagebuch, January 20, 1903, 7–8.

30. Mahler-Werfel, Tagebuch, March 17, 1903, 8.

31. Alma Mahler, *Gustav Mahler: Memories and Letters*, 76.

32. Alma Mahler, *Gustav Mahler: Memories and Letters*, 55.

33. Alma Mahler, *Gustav Mahler: Memories and Letters*, 58.

34. Alma Mahler, *Gustav Mahler: Memories and Letters*, 57.

35. Alma Mahler, *Gustav Mahler: Memories and Letters*, 58.

36. Gustav Mahler to Alma Mahler, April 2, 1903, cited in *Gustav Mahler: Letters to His Wife*, 117, 118.

37. Mahler-Werfel, Tagebuch, March 17, 1903, 8.

38. Mahler-Werfel, Tagebuch, March 29, 1903, 9–10.

39. Alma Mahler, *Gustav Mahler: Memories and Letters*, 60.

40. Mahler-Werfel, Tagebuch, June 15, 1903, 10.

41. Gustav Mahler to Alma Mahler, Vienna, August 30, 1903, cited in *Gustav Mahler: Letters to His Wife*, 125.

42. Mahler-Werfel, Tagebuch, February 25, 1904, 10–11.

43. Alma Mahler-Werfel, *Mein Leben* (Frankfurt: Fischer, 1960), 3, cited in de la Grange, *Gustav Mahler*, vol. 2, *Vienna: The Years of Challenge*, 694.

44. Alma Mahler, *Gustav Mahler: Memories and Letters*, 66.

45. Alma Mahler, *Gustav Mahler: Memories and Letters*, 83.

46. Gerhart Hauptmann to Gustav Mahler, undated, cited in de la Grange, *Gustav Mahler*, vol. 2, *Vienna: The Years of Challenge*, 701.

47. Alma Mahler, *Gustav Mahler: Memories and Letters*, 71.

48. Alma Mahler, *Gustav Mahler: Memories and Letters*, 68.

49. Alma Mahler, *Gustav Mahler: Memories and Letters*, 68.

50. Alma Mahler, *Gustav Mahler: Memories and Letters*, 70.

51. Alma Mahler, *Gustav Mahler: Memories and Letters*, 71.

52. Alma Mahler, *Gustav Mahler: Memories and Letters*, 70.

53. Erica Tietze's Maiernigg letters, August 1904, cited in de la Grange, *Gustav Mahler*, vol. 2, *Vienna: The Years of Challenge*, 716.

54. Erica Tietze to Ida Conrat, August 1904, cited in *Gustav Mahler: Letters to His Wife*, 176.

55. Alma Mahler, *Gustav Mahler: Memories and Letters*, 75.

56. Gustav Mahler to Alma Mahler, Cologne, October 15, 1904, cited in *Gustav Mahler: Letters to His Wife*, 180–181.

57. Alma Mahler, *Gustav Mahler: Memories and Letters*, 72.

58. Mahler-Werfel, Tagebuch, January 5, 1905, 12.

59. Mahler-Werfel, Tagebuch, January 5, 1905, 13.

60. Alma Mahler, *Gustav Mahler: Memories and Letters*, 77.

61. Alma Mahler, *Gustav Mahler: Memories and Letters*, 77; Mahler-Werfel, *Diaries*, January 27, 1905, 77.

62. Alma Mahler, *Gustav Mahler: Memories and Letters*, 77.

63. Alma Mahler, *Gustav Mahler: Memories and Letters*, 81.

64. Mahler-Werfel, Tagebuch, undated, [March 1905], 15.

65. Alma Mahler, *Gustav Mahler: Memories and Letters*, 82.

66. Mahler-Werfel, Tagebuch, June 5, 1905, 16.

67. Mahler-Werfel, Tagebuch, July 6, 1905, 16.

68. Gustav Mahler to Alma Mahler, June 8, 1910, cited in *Gustav Mahler: Letters to His Wife*, 357.

69. Alma Mahler, *Gustav Mahler: Memories and Letters*, 100.

70. Richard Specht, "Zu Mahlers Achte Symphonie," *Tagespost, Graz*, no. 150, June 14, 1914, cited in de la Grange, *Gustav Mahler*, vol. 3, *Vienna: Triumph and Disillusion, 1904–1907* (Oxford: Oxford University Press, 1999), 429–430.

71. "Bruno Walter erzählt von Mahler," *Neue Freie Presse*, November 16, 1935, cited in de la Grange, *Gustav Mahler*, vol. 3, *Vienna: Triumph and Disillusion*, 429.

72. Alma Mahler, *Gustav Mahler: Memories and Letters*, 101.

73. Oskar Fried, "Erinnerungen an Mahler," *Musikblätter des Anbruch*, 1919, 1, 16, cited in Henry-Louis de la Grange, *Gustav Mahler*, vol. 4, *A New Life Cut Short, 1907–1911*, 470.

74. Alfred Roller, *Die Bildnisse von Gustav Mahler* (Leipzig: Tal, 1922), cited in de la Grange, *Gustav Mahler*, vol. 3, *Vienna: Triumph and Disillusion*, 456.

75. Alma Mahler, *Gustav Mahler: Memories and Letters*, 87.

76. Alma Mahler, *Gustav Mahler: Memories and Letters*, 101.

77. Alma Mahler, *Gustav Mahler: Memories and Letters*, 109.

78. Alma Mahler, *Gustav Mahler: Memories and Letters*, 104.

79. Alma Mahler, *Gustav Mahler: Memories and Letters*, 105.

80. Gustav Mahler to Alma Mahler, Frankfurt, January 17, 1907, cited in *Gustav Mahler: Letters to His Wife*, 262; Gustav Mahler to Alma Mahler, Frankfurt, January 16, 1907, cited in *Gustav Mahler: Letters to His Wife*, 262.

81. Alma Mahler, *Gustav Mahler: Memories and Letters*, 106.

Chapter 6. Grief and Renewal 1907–1910

1. Alma Mahler, *Gustav Mahler: Memories and Letters*, 117–118.

2. Zuckerkandl, *Österreich intime*, 86.

3. *Gustav Mahler: Letters to His Wife*, 268.

4. Gustav Mahler to Arnold Berliner, July 17, 1907, in *Gustav Mahler Briefe, 1879–1911*, ed. Alma Maria Mahler (Vienna: Zsolnay, 1924), 365.

5. Alma Mahler, *Gustav Mahler: Memories and Letters*, 121.

6. Alma Mahler, *Gustav Mahler: Memories and Letters*, 121–22.

7. Alma Mahler, *Gustav Mahler: Memories and Letters*, 121–22.

8. Alma Mahler, *Gustav Mahler: Memories and Letters*, 121–122.

9. Alma Mahler, *Gustav Mahler: Memories and Letters*, 122.

10. Alma Mahler, *Gustav Mahler: Memories and Letters*, 122.

11. Alma Mahler to Alfred Roller, cited in *Gustav Mahler: Letters to His Wife*, 274.

12. Bruno Walter, *Gustav Mahler* (Vienna: Reichner, 1936), 42, cited in de la Grange, *Gustav Mahler*, vol. 3, *Vienna: Triumph and Disillusion*, 722.

13. Bruno Walter to his parents, September 13, 1907, *Bruno Walter Briefe*, 95.

14. Gustav Mahler to Alma Mahler, St. Petersburg, October 24, 1907, cited in *Gustav Mahler: Letters to His Wife*, 287, 288.

15. Zuckerkandl, *Österreich intime*, 48.

16. *Neue Freie Presse*, November 25, 1907, cited in *Gustav Mahler: Letters to His Wife*, 296.

17. Berta Zuckerkandl, undated diary extract, cited in Alma Mahler, *Gustav Mahler: Memories and Letters*, 303.

18. Zuckerkandl, *Österreich intime*, 84.

19. Alma Mahler, *Gustav Mahler: Memories and Letters*, 116.

20. Alma Mahler, *Gustav Mahler: Memories and Letters*, 126.

21. Paul Stefan, *Das Grab in Wien* (Berlin: Reiss, 1913), 92, cited in de la Grange, *Gustav Mahler*, vol. 2, *Vienna: The Years of Challange*, 792.

22. Alma Mahler, *Gustav Mahler: Memories and Letters*, 126.

23. Alma Mahler, *Gustav Mahler: Memories and Letters*, 127.

24. Alma Mahler, *Gustav Mahler: Memories and Letters*, 303.

25. Alma Mahler, *Gustav Mahler: Memories and Letters*, 127.

26. Alma Mahler, *Gustav Mahler: Memories and Letters*, 128.

27. Cited in de la Grange, *Gustav Mahler*, vol. 4, *A New Life Cut Short*, 41.

28. Alma Mahler, *Gustav Mahler: Memories and Letters*, 129.

29. Gustav Mahler to Carl Moll, February 16, 1908, cited in de la Grange, *Gustav Mahler*, vol. 4, *A New Life Cut Short*, 92; Gustav Mahler to Alexander Zemlinsky, undated, Philadelphia, 1907, cited in de la Grange, *Gustav Mahler*, vol. 4, *A New Life Cut Short*, 92.

30. Alma Mahler, *Gustav Mahler: Memories and Letters*, 129.

31. Alma Mahler, *Gustav Mahler: Memories and Letters*, 130.

32. Alma Mahler, *Gustav Mahler: Memories and Letters*, 130.

33. Alma Mahler, *Gustav Mahler: Memories and Letters*, 132.

34. Alma Mahler, *Gustav Mahler: Memories and Letters*, 131.

35. Alma Mahler, *Gustav Mahler: Memories and Letters*, 132, 131.

36. Alma Mahler, *Gustav Mahler: Memories and Letters*, 134.

37. Alma Mahler, *Gustav Mahler: Memories and Letters*, 136.

38. Alma Mahler, *Gustav Mahler: Memories and Letters*, 137.

39. Alma Mahler, *Gustav Mahler: Memories and Letters*, 135.

40. Alma Mahler, *Gustav Mahler: Memories and Letters*, 135.

41. Gustav Mahler to Countess Misa Wydenbruck, April 17, 1908, in Alma Maria Mahler, *Gustav Mahler Briefe* (Vienna: Paul Zsolnay Verlag, 1924), 428.

42. Alma Mahler, *Gustav Mahler: Memories and Letters*, 137.

43. Alma Mahler, *Gustav Mahler: Memories and Letters*, 139.

44. Gustav Mahler to Carl Moll, undated [summer 1908], in Alma Maria Mahler, *Gustav Mahler Briefe*, 382–383.

45. Mahler-Werfel, "Der schimmernde Weg," 35.

46. Alma Mahler-Werfel, *Mein Leben*, 44, cited de la Grange, *Gustav Mahler*, vol. 4, *A New Life Cut Short*, 209.

47. William Ritter, "Souvenirs sur Gustave [*sic*] Mahler," *Schweitzerische Musikzeitung* (Zurich: Cl, 1961), 34[–37], cited in *Gustav Mahler: Letters to His Wife*, 3.

48. Alma Mahler to Guido Adler, undated [July 1909], cited in de la Grange, *Gustav Mahler*, vol. 4, *A Life Cut Short*, 439.

49. Gustav Mahler to Guido Adler, January 1, 1910, in Alma Maria Mahler, *Gustav Mahler Briefe*, 461–463.

50. Alma Mahler, *Gustav Mahler: Memories and Letters*, 144.

51. Alma Mahler, *Gustav Mahler: Memories and Letters*, 146.

52. Alma Mahler, *Gustav Mahler: Memories and Letters*, 147.

53. Gustav Mahler to Carl Moll, March 10, 1909, in Alma Maria Mahler, *Gustav Mahler Briefe*, 381.

54. Alma Mahler, *Gustav Mahler: Memories and Letters*, 148–149.

55. Alma Mahler, *Gustav Mahler: Memories and Letters*, 151.

56. Gustav Mahler to Alma Mahler Toblach, undated [June 22] 1909, cited in *Gustav Mahler: Letters to His Wife*, 326.

57. Gustav Mahler to Alma Mahler, June 20, 1909, cited in *Gustav Mahler: Letters to His Wife*, 324.

58. Alma Mahler, *Gustav Mahler: Memories and Letters*, 142.

59. Alfred Roller to his wife, August 31, 1909, in Oskar Pausch, *Alfred Roller und Ladinien* (San Martin de Tor: Institut Ladin, 2005), 76, cited de la Grange, *Gustav Mahler*, vol. 4, *A New Life Cut Short*, 502–503.

60. Alma Mahler to Theobald Pollack, postcard, October 19, 1909, cited in de la Grange, *Gustav Mahler*, vol. 4, *A New Life Cut Short*, 552.

61. Alma Mahler, *Gustav Mahler: Memories and Letters*, 148.

62. Mahler-Werfel, *And the Bridge Is Love*, 46.

63. Alma Mahler, *Gustav Mahler: Memories and Letters*, 168.

64. Alma Mahler, *Gustav Mahler: Memories and Letters*, 160–161.

65. Alma Mahler, *Gustav Mahler: Memories and Letters*, 158–159.

66. Alma Mahler, *Gustav Mahler: Memories and Letters*, 160.

67. Alma Mahler, *Gustav Mahler: Memories and Letters*, 161–162.

68. Gustav Mahler to Anna Moll, undated [1910], in Alma Maria Mahler, *Gustav Mahler Briefe*, 379.

69. Gustav Mahler to Guido Adler, January 1, 1910, in Alma Maria Mahler, *Gustav Mahler Briefe*, 461.

70. Gustav Mahler to Alfred Roller, undated, postmarked January 6, 1910, in Alma Maria Mahler, *Gustav Mahler Briefe*, 443.

Chapter 7. "To Live for You, to Die for You," 1910–1911

1. Alma Mahler, *Gustav Mahler: Memories and Letters*, 170.

2. Mahler-Werfel, *And the Bridge Is Love*, 52.

3. Alma Mahler to Walter Gropius, undated, [Mittwoch], postmarked August 17, 1910, Bauhaus Archive, cited in de la Grange, *Gustav Mahler*, vol. 4, *A New Life Cut Short*, 875.

4. Gustav Mahler to Alma Mahler, Munich, June 21, 1910, cited in *Gustav Mahler: Letters to His Wife*, 64.

5. Gustav Mahler to Anna Moll, undated, [June] 1910, in Alma Maria Mahler, *Gustav Mahler Briefe*, 398.

6. Gustav Mahler to Anna Moll, undated postcard, July 2, 1910, in Alma Maria Mahler, *Gustav Mahler Briefe*, 399.

7. Anna Moll to Walter Gropius, postmarked July 22, 1910, Bauhaus Archive, cited in de la Grange, *Gustav Mahler*, vol. 4, *A New Life Cut Short*, 840.

8. Alma Mahler, *Gustav Mahler: Memories and Letters*, 172.

9. Alma Mahler to Walter Gropius, July 31, 1910, Bauhaus Archive, cited in Reginald Isaacs, *Walter Gropius: Der Mensch und sein Werk*, vol. 1 (Berlin: Gebr. Mann Verlag, 1983), 108.

10. Walter Gropius to Alma Mahler, undated draft letter [August 1 or 2, 1910], Bauhaus Archive, cited in Isaacs, *Walter Gropius*, 99.

11. Alma Mahler to Walter Gropius, undated, [Donnerstag], August 3, 1910, Bauhaus Archive, cited in Isaacs, *Walter Gropius*, 100.

12. Alma Mahler to Walter Gropius, undated, [Donnerstag], [August 3] 1910, Bauhaus Archive, cited in Isaacs, *Walter Gropius*, 100.

13. Walter Gropius to Alma Mahler, September 18, 1911, Bauhaus Archive, cited in Isaacs, *Walter Gropius*, 113.

14. Cited in Isaacs, *Walter Gropius*, 447 n118.

15. Alma Mahler, *Gustav Mahler: Memories and Letters*, 173.

16. Alma Mahler, *Gustav Mahler: Memories and Letters*, 173.

17. Alma Mahler, *Gustav Mahler: Memories and Letters*, 173.

18. Alma Mahler to Walter Gropius, undated, [Mittwoch], postmarked August 17, 1910, Bauhaus Archive, cited in de la Grange, *Gustav Mahler*, vol. 4, *A New Life Cut Short*, 875.

19. Alma Mahler, *Gustav Mahler: Memories and Letters*, 174.

20. Alma Mahler, *Gustav Mahler: Memories and Letters*, 174–175.

21. Alma Mahler to Walter Gropius, August 9, 1911, Bauhaus Archive, cited in de la Grange, *Gustav Mahler*, vol. 4, *A New Life Cut Short*, 871.

22. Alma Mahler, *Gustav Mahler: Memories and Letters*, 174.

23. Walter Gropius to Gustav Mahler, undated draft letter, c. August 5 or 6, 1910, Bauhaus Archive, cited in de la Grange, *Gustav Mahler*, vol. 4, *A New Life Cut Short*, 871.

24. Alma Mahler to Walter Gropius, August 7, 1910, Bauhaus Archive, cited in de la Grange, *Gustav Mahler*, vol. 4, *A New Life Cut Short*, 872.

25. Alma Mahler to Walter Gropius, undated, postmarked August 10, 1910, Bauhaus Archive, cited in de la Grange, *Gustav Mahler*, vol. 4, *A New Life Cut Short*, 872.

26. Alma Mahler to Walter Gropius, undated, [Mittwioch], August 10, 1910, Bauhaus Archive, cited in de la Grange, *Gustav Mahler*, vol. 4, *A New Life Cut Short*, 872.

27. Alma Mahler to Walter Gropius, undated, [Donnerstag], [August 11, 1910], Bauhaus Archive, cited in de la Grange, *Gustav Mahler*, vol. 4, *A New Life Cut Short*, 872–873.

28. Alma Mahler to Walter Gropius, undated, [Donnerstag], possibly August 11, 1910, Bauhaus Archive, cited in de la Grange, *Gustav Mahler*, vol. 4, *A New Life Cut Short*, 872–873.

29. Walter Gropius to Alma Mahler, draft letter, August 12, 1910, Bauhaus Archive, cited in de la Grange, *Gustav Mahler*, vol. 4, *A New Life Cut Short*, 873.

30. Anna Moll to Walter Gropius, Toblach, August 18, 1910, Bauhaus Archive, cited in de la Grange, *Gustav Mahler*, vol. 4, *A New Life Cut Short*, 875.

31. Gustav Mahler to Alma Mahler, undated, August 1910, cited in *Gustav Mahler: Letters to His Wife*, 377.

32. Gustav Mahler to Alma Mahler, undated, Toblach, August 1910, cited in *Gustav Mahler: Letters to His Wife*, 375.

33. Stuart Feder, "Mahler, Dying," *International Review of Psycho-analysis London* (1978), 125, cited in *Gustav Mahler: Letters to His Wife*, 381.

34. Alma Mahler, *Gustav Mahler: Memories and Letters*, 173.

35. Der Teufel tanzt es mit mir,
Wahnsinn, fass mich an, Vefluchten!
Vernichte mich
Dass ich vergesse, dass ich bin!
Dass ich aufhöre, zu sein
Dass ich ver.

36. Cited in de la Grange, *Gustav Mahler*, vol. 4, *A New Life Cut Short*, 849.

37. Cited in de la Grange, *Gustav Mahler*, vol. 4, *A New Life Cut Short*, 878.

38. Alma Mahler to Walter Gropius, undated, [August] 1910, cited in de la Grange, *Gustav Mahler*, vol. 4, *A New Life Cut Short*, 878.

39. Alma Mahler to Walter Gropius, August 17, 1910, Bauhaus Archive, cited in de la Grange, *Gustav Mahler*, vol. 4, *A New Life Cut Short*, 878–879.

40. Gustav Mahler to Alma Mahler, Toblach, August 1910, cited in *Gustav Mahler: Letters to His Wife*, 376.

41. Alma Mahler to Walter Gropius, undated, postmarked August 17, 1910, cited in de la Grange, *Gustav Mahler*, vol. 4, *A New Life Cut Short*, 879.

42. Alma Mahler, *Gustav Mahler: Memories and Letters*, 178.

43. Alma Mahler to Walter Gropius, undated, [August 27] 1910, Bauhaus Archive, cited in de la Grange, *Gustav Mahler*, vol. 4, *A New Life Cut Short*, 926.

44. Alma Mahler to Walter Gropius, undated letter postmarked July 21, 1910, Bauhaus Archive, cited in de la Grange, *Gustav Mahler*, vol. 4, *A New Life Cut Short*, 875; Alma Mahler to Walter Gropius, September 19, 1910, cited in Isaacs, *Walter Gropius*, 103.

45. Alma Mahler, *Gustav Mahler: Memories and Letters*, 174.

46. Gustav Mahler to Alma Mahler, telegram, August 27, 1910, cited in *Gustav Mahler: Letters to His Wife*, 380.

47. Alma Mahler, *Gustav Mahler: Memories and Letters*, 175.

48. Marie Bonaparte, unpublished diary manuscript, cited in Stuart Feder, *Gustav Mahler: A Life in Crisis* (New Haven, CT: Yale University Press, 2004), 229.

49. Gustav Mahler to Alma Mahler, Munich, c. September 4/5, 1910, in Alma Mahler, *Gustav Mahler: Memories and Letters*, 335.

50. Alma Mahler to Walter Gropius, undated, [August 26] 1910, Bauhaus Archive, cited in de la Grange, *Gustav Mahler*, vol. 4, *A New Life Cut Short*, 925.

51. Gustav Mahler to Alma Mahler Munich, [September 5] 1910, cited in *Gustav Mahler: Letters to His Wife*, 389.

52. Gustav Mahler to Alma Mahler Munich, September 5, 1910, cited in *Gustav Mahler: Letters to His Wife*, 388.

53. Alma Mahler to Walter Gropius, undated, Berlin, postmarked August 27, 1910, Bauhaus Archive, cited in de la Grange, *Gustav Mahler*, vol. 4, *A New Life Cut Short*, 879.

54. Alma Mahler to Walter Gropius, September 3, 1910, Bauhaus Archive, cited in de la Grange, *Gustav Mahler*, vol. 4, *A New Life Cut Short*, 931.

55. Gustav Mahler to Alma Mahler, September 4, 1910, cited in de la Grange, *Gustav Mahler*, vol. 4, *A New Life Cut Short*, 935.

56. From William Ritter diaries, September 10, 1910, in William Ritter, *William Ritter Chevalier de Gustav Mahler, Ecrits, correspondence, documents*, ed. Claude Meylan (Bern: Peter Lang, 2000), cited in de la Grange, *Gustav Mahler*, vol. 4, *A New Life Cut Short*, 957.

57. Alma Mahler, *Gustav Mahler: Memories and Letters*, 180.

58. Alma Mahler, *Gustav Mahler: Memories and Letters*, 180.

59. Walter Gropius to Alma Mahler, draft, undated, [September] 1910, cited in de la Grange, *Gustav Mahler*, vol. 4, *A New Life Cut Short*, 1027.

60. Walter Gropius to Alma Mahler, draft letter, dated January 23, 1911, Bauhaus Archive, cited in de la Grange, *Gustav Mahler*, vol. 4, *A New Life Cut Short*, 1099.

61. Walter Gropius to Alma Mahler, undated draft letter, Bauhaus Archive, cited in de la Grange, *Gustav Mahler*, vol. 4, *A New Life Cut Short*, 1028.

62. Walter Gropius to Alma Mahler, draft letter, undated, possibly September 1910, cited in de la Grange, *Gustav Mahler*, vol. 4, *A New Life Cut Short*, 1028.

63. Walter Gropius to Alma Mahler, draft letter, September 21, 1910, cited in de la Grange, *Gustav Mahler*, vol. 4, *A New Life Cut Short*, 1030.

64. Alma Mahler to Walter Gropius, [Friday] October 11 [or 12], 1910, postmarked October 12, Bauhaus Archive, cited in de la Grange, *Gustav Mahler*, vol. 4, *A New Life Cut Short*, 1032.

65. Alma Mahler to Walter Gropius, November 8, 1910, Bauhaus Archive, cited in de la Grange, *Gustav Mahler*, vol. 4, *A New Life Cut Short*, 1035.

66. Confidential letter, December 7, 1911, cited de la Grange, *Gustav Mahler*, vol. 4, *A New Life Cut Short*, 1193. Committee members including Mary Sheldon, Ruth Draper, Harriet C. Cheney, and Nelson S. Spencer informed the guarantors that total receipts increased from $63,323 to $91,640 average receipts per concert—1,376 up to 1,409. Total deficiency dropped from $118,566 to $98,006; deficit per concert down from $2,577 to $1,507. His tours produced a surplus of $15,891 for the second season compared with $4,044 for the first.

67. Alma Mahler, May 5, 1911, interview with critic Charles Meltzer in *American*, May 6, 1911, cited de la Grange, *Gustav Mahler*, vol. 4, *A New Life Cut Short*, 1194.

68. Alma Mahler, *Gustav Mahler: Memories and Letters*, 183.

69. Gustav Mahler to Alma Mahler, telegram, Syracuse, December 9, 1910, cited in *Gustav Mahler: Letters to His Wife*, 393.

70. Alma Mahler, *Gustav Mahler: Memories and Letters*, 184.

71. Alma Mahler, *Gustav Mahler: Memories and Letters*, 188.

72. Maurice Baumfeld, "Erinnerungen an Gustav Mahler," *New Yorker Staats-Zeitung*, May 21, 1911, cited in de la Grange, *Gustav Mahler*, vol. 4, *A New Life Cut Short*, 1222.

73. Alma Mahler, *Gustav Mahler: Memories and Letters*, 186.

74. Alma Mahler, *Gustav Mahler: Memories and Letters*, 187.

75. Alma Mahler to Walter Gropius, June 8, 1911, Bauhaus Archive, cited in de la Grange, *Gustav Mahler*, vol. 4, *A New Life Cut Short*, 1224.

76. Gustav Mahler to Anna Moll, undated [January/February 1910], in Alma Maria Mahler, *Gustav Mahler Briefe*, 396.

77. Alma Mahler, *Gustav Mahler: Memories and Letters*, 188.

78. Alma Mahler, *Gustav Mahler: Memories and Letters*, 187.

79. Alma Mahler, *Gustav Mahler: Memories and Letters*, 188.

80. Alma Mahler, *Gustav Mahler: Memories and Letters*, 191, 192.

81. Alma Mahler, *Gustav Mahler: Memories and Letters*, 190.

82. Alma Mahler, *Gustav Mahler: Memories and Letters*, 191.

83. Alma Mahler to Walter Gropius, March 11, 1911, Bauhaus Archive, cited in de la Grange, *Gustav Mahler*, vol. 4, *A New Life Cut Short*, 1254.

84. Alma Mahler to Walter Gropius, March 25, 1911, Bauhaus Archive, cited in de la Grange, *Gustav Mahler*, vol. 4, *A New Life Cut Short*, 1255.

85. Alma Mahler, *Gustav Mahler: Memories and Letters*, 194.

86. Alma Mahler, *Gustav Mahler: Memories and Letters*, 195.

87. Alma Mahler, *Gustav Mahler: Memories and Letters*, 196.

88. Alma Mahler, *Gustav Mahler: Memories and Letters*, 197.

89. Alma Mahler to Walter Gropius, April 28, 1911, Bauhaus Archive, cited in de la Grange, *Gustav Mahler*, vol. 4, *A New Life Cut Short*, 1255.

90. Alma Mahler, *Gustav Mahler: Memories and Letters*, 199.

91. Alma Mahler, *Gustav Mahler: Memories and Letters*, 199.

92. Alma Mahler, *Gustav Mahler: Memories and Letters*, 200.

93. Alma Mahler, *Gustav Mahler: Memories and Letters*, 201.

94. Alma Mahler, *Gustav Mahler: Memories and Letters*, 201.

95. cited in de la Grange, *Gustav Mahler*, vol. 4, *A New Life Cut Short*, 1276.

Chapter 8. Tempest 1911–1914

1. Mahler-Werfel, *And the Bridge Is Love*, 6.

2. Mahler-Werfel, "Der schimmernde Weg," 41.

3. Mahler-Werfel, *And the Bridge Is Love*, 66.

4. Alma Mahler to Walter Gropius, June 8, 1911, Bauhaus Archive, cited in de la Grange, *Gustav Mahler*, vol. 4, *A New Life Cut Short*, 1224.

5. Alma Mahler to Walter Gropius, July 15, 1911, Bauhaus Archive, cited in de la Grange, *Gustav Mahler*, vol. 4, *A New Life Cut Short*, 1224.

6. Walter Gropius to Alma Mahler, Timmendorfer Strand, June 4, 1911, cited in Isaacs, *Walter Gropius*, 1:111.

7. Alma Mahler to Walter Gropius, [August 15] 1911, cited in Isaacs, *Walter Gropius*, 113.

8. Walter Gropius to Alma Mahler, September 18, 1911, cited in Isaacs, *Walter Gropius*, 113.

9. Walter Gropius to Alma Mahler, December 1, 1911, cited in Isaacs, *Walter Gropius*, 113.

10. Alma Mahler to Walter Gropius, January 15, 1912, cited in Isaacs, *Walter Gropius*, 114.

11. Alma Mahler to Walter Gropius, November 21, 1912, cited in Isaacs, *Walter Gropius*, 114.

12. Walter Gropius to Alma Mahler, December 3, 1912, cited in Isaacs, *Walter Gropius*, 114–115.

13. Mahler-Werfel, *And the Bridge Is Love*, 68.

14. Mahler-Werfel, "Der schimmernde Weg," 42.

15. Alma Mahler to Walter Gropius, November 23, 1910, Bauhaus Archive, cited in de la Grange, *Gustav Mahler*, vol. 4, *A New Life Cut Short*, 1050.

16. Mahler-Werfel, *And the Bridge Is Love*, 67.

17. Mahler-Werfel, "Der schimmernde Weg," 39.

18. Mahler-Werfel, *And the Bridge Is Love*, 68.

19. Mahler-Werfel, Tagebuch, September 1914, 53.

20. Mahler-Werfel, *And the Bridge Is Love*, 70.

21. Dr. Paul Kammerer to Alma Mahler, October 31, 1911, Mahler-Werfel Papers.

22. Mahler-Werfel, *And the Bridge Is Love*, 70–71.

23. Mahler-Werfel, "Der schimmernde Weg," 46.

24. Mahler-Werfel, "Der schimmernde Weg," 48.

25. Quoted in Brassai, *Artists of My Life*, trans. Richard Miller (New York: Viking Press, 1982), 73, cited in Alfred Weidinger, *Kokoschka and Alma Mahler* (Munich: Prestel Verlag, 1996), 7.

26. Oskar Kokoschka to Alma Mahler, [April 15] 1912, in Oskar Kokoschka, *Briefe 1, 1905–1919* (Düsseldorf: Claasen, 1984), 29–30.

27. Mahler-Werfel, "Der schimmernde Weg," 51.

28. Cited in Susanne Keegan, *The Bride of the Wind* (New York: Viking, 1991), 178.

29. Cited in Keegan, *The Bride of the Wind*, 181–182.

30. Oskar Kokoschka to Lotte Franzos, Berlin, December 24, 1910, in Kokoschka, *Briefe 1*, 15.

31. Mahler-Werfel, "Der schimmernde Weg," 53.

32. Mahler-Werfel, "Der schimmernde Weg," 55.

33. Mahler-Werfel, "Der schimmernde Weg," 50.

34. Oskar Kokoschka to Alma Mahler, undated, [late May or early June] 1913, in Kokoschka, *Briefe 1*, 115–116.

35. Oskar Kokoschka to Alma Mahler, May 8, 1912, in Kokoschka, *Briefe 1*, 39–40.

36. Oskar Kokoschka to Alma Mahler, May 7, 1912, in Kokoschka, *Briefe 1*, 37–38.

37. Mahler-Werfel, "Der schimmernde Weg," 53.

38. Oskar Kokoschka to Alma Mahler, undated, [May] 1912, in Kokoschka, *Briefe 1*, 41.

39. Mahler-Werfel, "Der schimmernde Weg," 51.

40. Oskar Kokoschka to Alma Mahler, Vienna, July 9, 1912, in Kokoschka, *Briefe 1*, 44.

41. Mahler-Werfel, "Der schimmernde Weg," 54.

42. Alma Mahler, Tagebuch, June 4, 1920, 168, 169, Mahler-Werfel Papers.

43. Mahler-Werfel, *And the Bridge Is Love*, 75.

44. Cited in Weidinger, *Kokoschka and Alma Mahler*, 42.

45. Mahler-Werfel, "Der schimmernde Weg," 55.

46. Oskar Kokoschka to Alma Mahler, July 27, 1912, in Kokoschka, *Briefe 1*, 59.

47. Mahler-Werfel, *And the Bridge Is Love*, 75.

48. Cited in Brassai, *The Artists of My Life*, 74, cited in Weidinger, *Kokoschka and Alma Mahler*, 20.

49. Oskar Kokoschka to Alma Mahler, Vienna, June 1912, in Kokoschka, *Briefe 1*, 42.

50. Mahler-Werfel, "Der schimmernde Weg," 58.

51. Romana Kokoschka to a family member quoted in Oskar Kokoschka, *Erinnerungen: Ein Film von Albert Quendler*, cited in Weidinger, *Kokoschka and Alma Mahler*, 10.

52. Oskar Kokoschka, *My Life* (New York: Macmillan, 1974), 75.

53. Mahler-Werfel, Tagebuch, August 31, 1930, 243.

54. Mahler-Werfel, Tagebuch, August 31, 1930, 243.

55. Alma Mahler-Werfel, "Aus der Zeit meinier Liebe zu Oskar Kokoschka und der seinen zu mir" [From the days of my love for Oskar Kokoschka and of his love for me] (1913), part dictated by Kokoschka, part recorded by Alma Mahler [dated 1919], 44, Oskar Kokoschka Papers, Zentralbibliothek, Zürich, cited in Weidinger, *Kokoschka and Alma Mahler*, 20.

56. Mahler-Werfel, "Der schimmernde Weg," 55.

57. Cited in Weidinger, *Kokoschka and Alma Mahler*, 22, from Mahler-Werfel, "Aus der Zeit meiner Liebe zu Oskar Kokoschka und sein mit mir," 43.

58. Kokoschka, *My Life*, 77.

59. Mahler-Werfel, "Der schimmernde Weg," 56.

60. Oskar Kokoschka to Alma Mahler, undated, [December] 1912, Kokoschka, *Briefe 1*, 67.

61. Oskar Kokoschka to Alma Mahler, May 17, 1913, Kokoschka, *Briefe 1*, 105.

62. Oskar Kokoschka, May 20, 1913, Kokoschka, *Briefe 1*, 110.

63. Oskar Kokoschka to Alma Mahler, July 16, 1914, Kokoschka, *Briefe 1*, 171.

64. Oskar Kokoschka to Alma Mahler, July 1913, Kokoschka, *Briefe 1*, 128.

65. Mahler-Werfel, *And the Bridge Is Love*, 77.

66. Mahler-Werfel, *And the Bridge Is Love*, 76.

67. Cited in Weidinger, *Kokoschka and Alma Mahler*, 36.

68. Mahler-Werfel, *And the Bridge Is Love*, 77.

69. Mahler-Werfel, "Der schimmernde Weg," 71.

70. Oskar Kokoschka to Alma Mahler, May 10, 1914, Kokoschka, *Briefe 1*, 158.

71. Oskar Kokoschka to Alma Mahler, May 10, 1914, Kokoschka, *Briefe 1*, 160.

72. Mahler-Werfel, Tagebuch, May 17, 1914, 45.

73. Mahler-Werfel, Tagebuch, undated, [May] 1914, 45.

74. Oskar Kokoschka to Alma Mahler, undated, 1914, Mahler-Werfel Papers.

75. Mahler-Werfel, Tagebuch, undated, [c. July] 1914, 50.

76. Oskar Kokoschka to Alma Mahler, end of July 1914, 174–175.

77. Alma Mahler to Walter Gropius, undated, [May 6] 1914, cited in Isaacs, *Walter Gropius*, 115.

78. Mahler-Werfel, Tagebuch, undated, [August] 1914, 50.

Chapter 9. War and Marriage 1914–1917

1. Zweig, *World of Yesterday*, 173.

2. Alban Berg to Arnold Schoenberg, January 1, 1915, cited in Mosco Garner, *Alban Berg* (London: Duckworth, 1975) 40.

3. Mahler-Werfel, Tagebuch, September 1914, 51.

4. Mahler-Werfel, Tagebuch, undated, September 1914, 52.

5. Mahler-Werfel, Tagebuch, undated, [September] 1914, 51–52.

6. Mahler-Werfel, Tagebuch, end of October 1914, 54.

7. Oskar Kokoschka to Alma Mahler, end of July 1914, Kokoschka, *Briefe 1*, 177–178.

8. Oskar Kokoschka to Kurt Wolff, [late September] 1914, Kokoschka, *Briefe 1*, 182–183.

9. Interview with Anna Mahler, recorded by Peter Stephan Jungk, cited in Peter Stephan Jungk, *Franz Werfel: A Life in Prague, Vienna and Hollywood* (New York: Fromm International, 1991), 69.

10. Kokoschka, *My Life*, 84.

11. Oskar Kokoschka to Alma Mahler, December 5, 1914, in Kokoschka, *Briefe 1*, 185.

12. Mahler-Werfel, Tagebuch, October 6, 1914, 53–54.

13. Mahler-Werfel, Tagebuch, undated, [November 1914], 58–59.

14. Oskar Kokoschka to Alma Mahler, January 2, 1915, in Kokoschka, *Briefe 1*, 188.

15. Oskar Kokoschka to Alma Mahler, undated, [around April 1, 1915], cited in Kokoschka, *Briefe 1*, 216.

16. Oskar Kokoschka to Alma Mahler, undated, [end of June] 1915, cited in Kokoschka, *Briefe 1*, 222.

17. Kokoschka, *My Life*, 74.

18. Mahler-Werfel, Tagebuch, October 5, 1916, 88.

19. Kokoschka, *My Life*, 96–97.

20. Mahler-Werfel, Tagebuch, January 15, 1915, 62.

21. Alma Mahler to Walter Gropius, December 31, 1914, cited in Isaacs, *Walter Gropius*, 140.

22. Mahler-Werfel, Tagebuch, February 22, 1915, 62.

23. Mahler-Werfel, Tagebuch, February 22, 1915, 62–63.

24. Mahler-Werfel, Tagebuch, September 29, 1916, 95; Mahler-Werfel, Tagebuch, February 22, 1915, 64.

25. Alma Mahler to Walter Gropius, undated, [February or March] 1915, Bauhaus Archive, cited in Oliver Hilmes, *Malevolent Muse: The Life of Alma Mahler* (Boston: Northeastern University Press, 2015), 104.

26. Mahler-Werfel, Tagebuch, February 22, 1915, 63–64.

27. Mahler-Werfel, Tagebuch, undated, [April] 1915, 72.

28. Alma Mahler, Tagebuch, April 1, 1915, 73.

29. Alma Mahler, Tagebuch, March 5, 1915, 68.

30. Mahler-Werfel, Tagebuch, end of March 1915, 69.

31. Mahler-Werfel, Tagebuch, March 5, 1915, 67.

32. Mahler-Werfel, Tagebuch, April 1, 1915, 73.

33. Mahler-Werfel, Tagebuch, April 6, 1915, 73.

34. Walter Gropius to Manon Gropius, March 15, 1915, cited in Isaacs, *Walter Gropius*, 140.

35. Mahler-Werfel, Tagebuch, April 1, 1915, 72.

36. Mahler-Werfel, Tagebuch, April 6, 1915, 73.

37. Mahler-Werfel, Tagebuch, April 8, 1915, 74.

38. Mahler-Werfel, Tagebuch, April 1915, 74.

39. Mahler-Werfel, Tagebuch, April 9, 1915, 75.

40. Mahler-Werfel, Tagebuch, April 13, 1915, 75.

41. Mahler-Werfel, Tagebuch, June 8, 1915, 76.

42. Alma Mahler to Walter Gropius, undated, May or June 1915, cited in Isaacs, *Walter Gropius*, 142.

43. Alma Mahler to Walter Gropius, undated, c. June 1915, cited in Isaacs, *Walter Gropius*, 142.

44. Mahler-Werfel, Tagebuch, June 18, 1915, 76.

45. Manon Gropius to Walter Gropius, end of April 1915, cited in Isaacs, *Walter Gropius*, 141.

46. Walter Gropius to Manon Gropius, July 3, 1915, cited in Isaacs, *Walter Gropius*, 143.

47. Manon Gropius to Walter Gropius, June 7, 1915, cited in Isaacs, *Walter Gropius*, 143.

48. Mahler-Werfel, Tagebuch, August 19, 1915, 80.

49. Walter Gropius to Manon Gropius, September 13, 1915, cited in Isaacs, *Walter Gropius*, 156.

50. Mahler-Werfel, Tagebuch, August 19, 1915, 80.

51. Alma Mahler to Walter Gropius, undated, [end of September] 1915, cited in Isaacs, *Walter Gropius*, 156.

52. Alma Mahler to Walter Gropius, [end of September] 1915, cited in Isaacs, *Walter Gropius*, 156–157.

53. Alma Mahler to Walter Gropius, undated, Bauhaus Archive, cited in Oliver Hilmes, *Malevolent Muse*, 111.

54. Alma Mahler to Walter Gropius, undated, [end of September] 1915, cited in Isaacs, *Walter Gropius*, 157.

55. Alma Mahler to Walter Gropius, undated, [summer] 1916, cited in Isaacs, *Walter Gropius*, 161.

56. Alma Mahler to Walter Gropius, undated, Bauhaus Archive, cited in Hilmes, *Malevolent Muse*, 112.

57. Alma Mahler to Walter Gropius, undated, cited in Isaacs, *Walter Gropius*, 163.

58. Alma Mahler to Walter Gropius, undated, [September 1 or 2] 1915, cited in Isaacs, *Walter Gropius*, 147.

59. Walter Gropius to Manon Gropius [his mother], end of December 1915, cited in Isaacs, *Walter Gropius*, 158.

60. Mahler-Werfel, Tagebuch, New Year 1916, 86.

61. Mahler-Werfel, Tagebuch, February 10, 1916, 86.

62. Mahler-Werfel, Tagebuch, March 4, 1916, 86.

63. Mahler-Werfel, Tagebuch, undated, 1916, 87.

64. Alma Mahler to Walter Gropius, undated, Semmering, [June 6] 1916, cited in Isaacs, *Walter Gropius*, 162.

65. Manon Gropius to Walter Gropius, June 2, 1916, cited in Isaacs, *Walter Gropius*, 162.

66. Mahler-Werfel, Tagebuch, undated, [ca. September] 1916, 93.

67. Mahler-Werfel, Tagebuch, undated, 1916, 93.

68. Alma Mahler to Walter Gropius, undated, [September] 1916, cited in Isaacs, *Walter Gropius*, 167.

69. Mahler-Werfel, Tagebuch, undated, [October] 1916, 89.

70. Mahler-Werfel, Tagebuch, September 19, 1916, 87.

71. Walter Gropius to Manon Gropius, September 1916, cited in Isaacs, *Walter Gropius*, 169.

72. Mahler-Werfel, Tagebuch, October 5, 1916, 88.

73. Walter Gropius to Manon Gropius, October 5/6, 1916, cited in Isaacs, *Walter Gropius*, 168.

74. Walter Gropius to Manon Gropius, undated, 1916, cited in Isaacs, *Walter Gropius*, 170.

75. Mahler-Werfel, *And the Bridge Is Love*, 87.

76. Mahler-Werfel, Tagebuch, October 5, 1916. 88.

77. Alma Mahler to Manon Gropius, New Year's Eve 1916, cited in Isaacs, *Walter Gropius*, 170.

78. Mahler-Werfel, Tagebuch, undated, [July] 1917, 102.

79. Mahler-Werfel, Tagebuch, July 1917, 102.

80. Peter Stephan Jungk, interview with Anna Mahler, in Jungk, *Franz Werfel*, 69.

81. Mahler-Werfel, Tagebuch, undated, [September] 1917, 97.

82. Mahler-Werfel, Tagebuch, undated, November 1917, 97–98.

83. Mahler-Werfel, Tagebuch, November 1917, 97.

84. Mahler-Werfel, Tagebuch, undated, [winter] 1917, 90.

85. Mahler-Werfel, Tagebuch, undated, [winter] 1917, 90.

86. Mahler-Werfel, "Der schimmernde Weg," 166.

87. Mahler-Werfel, Tagebuch, undated, [November] 1917, 99.

Chapter 10. Intertwined Souls 1917–1920

1. Max Brod, "The Young Werfel and the Prague Writers," in *The Era of German Expressionism*, ed. Paul Raabe, trans. J. M. Ritchie (London: Calder & Boyars, 1974), 73, cited in Keegan, *The Bride of the Wind*, 215.

2. Brod, "The Young Werfel and the Prague Writers," in Raabe, *The Era of German Expressionism*, 53, cited in Keegan, *The Bride of the Wind*, 214–221.

3. Franz Kafka to Felice Bauer, December 12, 1912, in Franz Kafka, *Letters to Felice*, ed. Erich Heller and Jürgen Born (New York: Schocken, 1973), 102, cited in Jungk, *Franz Werfel*, 248n32.

4. Jungk, *Franz Werfel*, 31.

5. Franz Werfel to Gertrud Spirk, cited in Jungk, *Franz Werfel*, 49.

6. Franz Werfel to Gertrud Spirk, Deutsches Literaturarchiv, Schiller-Nationalmuseum, Marbach am Nekar, cited in Jungk, *Franz Werfel*, 57.

7. Correspondence Franz Werfel, Gertrud Spirk, Deutsches Literaturarchiv, cited in Jungk, *Franz Werfel*, 57.

8. Franz Werfel to Gertrud Spirk, [November 1917], cited in Jungk, *Franz Werfel*, 59.

9. Mahler-Werfel, Tagebuch, undated, [December] 1917, 105.

10. Mahler-Werfel, Tagebuch, December 8, 1917, 105.

11. Mahler-Werfel, Tagebuch, undated, [November/December] 1917, 106.

12. Mahler-Werfel, Tagebuch, undated, 1917, 107.

13. Mahler-Werfel, Tagebuch, undated, [December] 1917, 107.

14. Mahler-Werfel, Tagebuch, undated, [December] 1917, 107.

15. Mahler-Werfel, Tagebuch, undated, [December] 1917, 107.

16. Mahler-Werfel, Tagebuch, undated, [December] 1917, 107–108.

17. Walter Gropius to Karl Ernst Osthaus, December 19, 1917, cited in Isaacs, *Walter Gropius*, 176.

18. Walter Gropius to Manon Gropius, January 7, 1918, cited in Isaacs, *Walter Gropius*, 175.

19. Walter Gropius to Manon Gropius, January/February 1918, cited in Isaacs, *Walter Gropius*, 176.

20. Mahler-Werfel, Tagebuch, January 1, 1918, 109.

21. Mahler-Werfel, Tagebuch, January 5, 1918, 109.

22. Mahler-Werfel, Tagebuch, undated, [January 1918], 127.

23. Mahler-Werfel, *And the Bridge Is Love*, 93.

24. Franz Werfel to Alma Mahler, January 18, 1918, Mahler-Werfel Papers.

25. Franz Werfel to Alma Mahler, February 13, 1918, Mahler-Werfel Papers.

26. Franz Werfel to Alma Mahler, February 8, 1918, Mahler-Werfel Papers.

27. Mahler-Werfel, Tagebuch, undated, [February] 1918, 110–111.

28. Berta Zuckerkandl's Swiss diary, cited in Mahler-Werfel, *And the Bridge Is Love*, 96.

29. Mahler-Werfel, Tagebuch, undated, 119.

30. Walter Gropius to Manon Gropius, February 1918, cited in Isaacs, *Walter Gropius*, 176.

31. Alma Mahler to Manon Gropius, January 1918, cited in Isaacs, *Walter Gropius*, 177.

32. Alma Mahler to Manon Gropius, January 1918, cited in Isaacs, *Walter Gropius*, 177.

33. Walter Gropius to Manon Gropius, June 22, 1918, cited in Isaacs, *Walter Gropius*, 179.

34. Mahler-Werfel, Tagebuch, undated, 119.

35. Mahler-Werfel, Tagebuch, July 1918, 111.

36. Alma Mahler, Tagebuch, undated, 1918, 119.

37. Franz Werfel, "Secret Diary" [Geheimes Tagebuch], July 28/29, 1918, in Franz Werfel, *Zwischen Oben und Unten* (Munich: Langen Müller, 1975), 636.

38. Mahler-Werfel, Tagebuch, undated, 119–120, 634.

39. Mahler-Werfel, Tagebuch, undated, 120–121.

40. Walter Gropius to Manon Gropius, August 17, 1918, cited in Isaacs, *Walter Gropius*, 182.

41. Mahler-Werfel, Tagebuch, undated, 1918, 121.

42. Franz Werfel to Alma Mahler, August 2, 1918, cited in Hilmes, *Malevolent Muse*, 123.

43. Werfel, "Secret Diary," July 28/29, 1918, in Werfel, *Zwischen Oben und Unten*, 636–637.

44. Cited in Jungk, *Franz Werfel*, 66.

45. Alma Mahler to Franz Werfel, undated, Mahler-Werfel Papers.

46. Mahler-Werfel, Tagebuch, undated, [November 12, 1918], 121.

47. Mahler-Werfel, Tagebuch, undated, 1918, 112.

48. Werfel, "Secret Diary," August 26, 1918, in *Zwischen Oben und Unten*, 655.

49. Walter Gropius to Franz Werfel, September 10, 1918, cited in Jungk, *Franz Werfel*, 258.

50. Franz Werfel to Alma Mahler, undated, 1918, cited in Jungk, *Franz Werfel*, 67.

51. Walter Gropius to Manon Gropius, August 8, 1918, cited in Isaacs, *Walter Gropius*, 182.

52. Mahler-Werfel, Tagebuch, August 2, 1918, 112.

53. Mahler-Werfel, Tagebuch, September 1918, 112.

54. Mahler-Werfel, Tagebuch, September 26, 1918, 113.

55. Mahler-Werfel, Tagebuch, October 24, 1918, 114.

56. Mahler-Werfel, Tagebuch, November 4, 1918, 114–115.

57. Mahler-Werfel, Tagebuch, November 12, 1918, 117.

58. Mahler-Werfel, Tagebuch, November 12, 1918, 117.

59. Mahler-Werfel, *And the Bridge Is Love*, 121.

60. Mahler-Werfel, Tagebuch, December 15, 1918, 116.

61. Mahler-Werfel, Tagebuch, December 15, 1918, 116.

62. Mahler-Werfel, Tagebuch, February 1, 1919, 135.

63. Mahler-Werfel, Tagebuch, February 14, 1919, 136–137.

64. Mahler-Werfel, Tagebuch, March 9, 1919, 137.

65. Mahler-Werfel, Tagebuch, October 17, 1919, 152.

66. Mahler-Werfel, Tagebuch, January 1919, 128.

67. Mahler-Werfel, Tagebuch, February 14, 1919, 136.

68. Mahler-Werfel, Tagebuch, March 10, 1919, 137.

69. Werfel, "Secret Diary," cited in Jungk, *Franz Werfel*, 75.

70. Mahler-Werfel, Tagebuch, April 3, 1919, 142.

71. Gustav Klimt died on February 3, 1918.

72. Mahler-Werfel, Tagebuch, February 6, 1918, 111.

73. Mahler-Werfel, Tagebuch, March 10, 1919, 138–139.

74. Mahler-Werfel, Tagebuch, March 26, 1919, 138–139.

75. Mahler-Werfel, Tagebuch, March 26, 1919, 140.

76. Mahler-Werfel, Tagebuch, February 2, 1919, 135–136.

77. Mahler-Werfel, Tagebuch, January 1919, 128–129.

78. Mahler-Werfel, *And the Bridge Is Love*, 125.

79. Mahler-Werfel, Tagebuch, March 10, 1919, 138.

80. Oskar Kokoschka to Hermine Moos, August 20, 1918, in Kokoschka, *Briefe 1*, 294.

81. Brassai, *The Artists of My Life*, 74, cited in Weidinger, *Kokoschka and Alma Mahler*, 92.

82. Kokoschka, *My Life*, 118.

83. Mahler-Werfel, *And the Bridge Is Love*, 126.

84. Mahler-Werfel, *And the Bridge Is Love*, 127.

85. Mahler-Werfel, *And the Bridge Is Love*, 126.

86. Mahler-Werfel, Tagebuch, undated, [June] 1919, 144.

87. Mahler-Werfel, Tagebuch, July 12, 1919, 146.

88. Mahler-Werfel, Tagebuch, July 3, 1919, 146.

89. Alma Mahler to Walter Gropius, undated, Bauhaus Archive, cited in Hilmes, *Malevolent Muse*, 128.

90. Mahler-Werfel, Tagebuch, October 26, 1919, 153.

91. Mahler-Werfel, Tagebuch, November 11, 1919, 155.

92. Mahler-Werfel, Tagebuch, July 14, 1919, 147.

93. Franz Werfel to Alma Mahler, undated, cited in Jungk, *Franz Werfel*, 79.

94. Mahler-Werfel, Tagebuch, August 31, 1919, 148.

95. Mahler-Werfel, Tagebuch, May 1, 1919, 144.

96. Mahler-Werfel, Tagebuch, September, 16, 1919, 149.

97. Mahler-Werfel, Tagebuch, November 11, 1919, 154.

98. Mahler-Werfel, *And the Bridge Is Love*, 131.

99. Mahler-Werfel, Tagebuch, March 5, 1920, 160.

100. Mahler-Werfel, Tagebuch, March 7, 1920, 161.

101. Mahler-Werfel, Tagebuch, March 16, 1920, 163.

102. Mahler-Werfel, Tagebuch, March 20, 1920, 163.

103. Mahler-Werfel, Tagebuch, April 3, 1920, 164.

104. Mahler-Werfel, Tagebuch, undated, [May 9] 1920, 165.

105. Mahler-Werfel, Tagebuch, August 22, 1930, 174.

106. Mahler-Werfel, Tagebuch, June 4, 1920, 169.

107. Mahler-Werfel, Tagebuch, June 4, 1920, 168–169.

108. Mahler-Werfel, Tagebuch, July 27, 1920, 173.

109. Mahler-Werfel, Tagebuch, July 27, 1920, 170–171.

110. Mahler-Werfel, Tagebuch, July 27, 1920, 171.

Chapter 11. Conflict 1921–1931

1. Franz Werfel to Alma Mahler, undated, Franz Werfel Collection, Charles E. Young Research Library, University of California, Los Angeles, cited in Jungk, *Franz Werfel*, 86.

2. Franz Werfel to Alma Mahler, undated, Franz Werfel Collection, cited in Hilmes, *Malevolent Muse*, 132.

3. Mahler-Werfel, Tagebuch, September 24, 1921, 177.

4. Mahler-Werfel, Tagebuch, February 21, 1922, 180.

5. Mahler-Werfel, Tagebuch, undated, [1922], 183.

6. Mahler-Werfel, Tagebuch, undated, [1922], 182.

7. Ernst Krenek, *Im Atem der Zeit: Erinnerungen an die Moderne* (Hamburg: Hoffmann und Kampe, 1998), 395.

8. Krenek, *Im Atem der Zeit*, 395.

9. Author interview with Marina Mahler, April 30, 2018.

10. Krenek, *Im Atem der Zeit*, 395.

11. Jungk, interview with Anna Mahler, privately owned, cited in Hilmes, *Malevolent Muse*, 133.

12. Cited in Jungk, *Franz Werfel*, 98.

13. Mahler-Werfel, Tagebuch, April 24, 1924, 189.

14. Mahler-Werfel, Tagebuch, June 25, 1924, 189.

15. Mahler-Werfel, Tagebuch, March 23, 1923, 185–186.

16. Mahler-Werfel, Tagebuch, New Year's Eve [1923], 187

17. Mahler-Werfel, Tagebuch, January 22, 1924, 188.

18. Mahler-Werfel, Tagebuch, July 30, 1924, 190.

19. Mahler-Werfel, Tagebuch, August 2, 1924, 191.

20. Jungk, interview with Anna Mahler, cited in Jungk, *Franz Werfel*, 165.

21. Jungk, interview with Anna Mahler and Albrecht Joseph, cited in Jungk, *Franz Werfel*, 69, 70.

22. Joseph, "Werfel, Alma, Kokoschka, the Actor George," 12, 13.

23. Peter Stephan Jungk, interview with Milos Dubrovic, cited in Jungk, *Franz Werfel*, 94–95.

24. Jungk, interview with Milos Dubrovic, cited in Jungk, *Franz Werfel*, 94–95.

25. Mahler-Werfel, "Der schimmernde Weg," 287.

26. Mahler-Werfel, Tagebuch, November 9, 1925, 193.

27. Franz Werfel, *Ägyptisches Tagebuch* in *Zwischen Ober und Unten* (Munich: Langen Müller Verlag, 1975), cited in Jungk, *Franz Werfel*, 107.

28. Werfel, *Ägyptisches Tagebuch* in *Zwischen Ober und Unten*, cited in Jungk, *Franz Werfel*, 108.

29. Werfel, *Ägyptisches Tagebuch* in *Zwischen Ober und Unten*, February 11, 1925, 739.

30. Mahler-Werfel, Tagebuch, undated, [Summer 1925], 192.

31. Mahler-Werfel, Tagebuch, November 9, 1925, 193.

32. Cited in *Die schöne Literatur* (1926), cited in Jungk, *Franz Werfel*, 113.

33. Mahler-Werfel, Tagebuch, July 14, 1926, 194.

34. Mahler-Werfel, Tagebuch, July 15, 1927, 196.

35. Mahler-Werfel, Tagebuch, July 15, 1927, 196–197.

36. Mahler-Werfel, Tagebuch, undated, 1927, 201.

37. Mahler-Werfel, Tagebuch, July 15, 1927, 197.

38. Mahler-Werfel, Tagebuch, September 7, 1927, 202.

39. Mahler-Werfel, Tagebuch, undated, 1927, 204.

40. Mahler-Werfel, Tagebuch, February 21, 1927, 199.

41. Mahler-Werfel, *And the Bridge Is Love,* 164.

42. Mahler-Werfel, Tagebuch, April 19, 1924, 188–189.

43. Mahler-Werfel, Tagebuch, Venice, October 6, 1927, 205.

44. Mahler-Werfel, Tagebuch, undated, [October] 1927, 205.

45. Mahler-Werfel, Tagebuch, October 10, 1927, 206.

46. Mahler-Werfel, Tagebuch, undated, [October] 1927, 206.

47. Mahler-Werfel, Tagebuch, Vienna, November 5, 1927, 207.

48. Mahler-Werfel, Tagebuch, December 8, 1927, 207.

49. Mahler-Werfel, Tagebuch, December 8, 1927, 208.

50. Mahler-Werfel, Tagebuch, [December] 1927, 209.

51. Mahler-Werfel, Tagebuch, January 4, 1928, 211–212.

52. Mahler-Werfel, Tagebuch, January 4, 1928, 213.

53. Mahler-Werfel, *And the Bridge Is Love,* 177.

54. Mahler-Werfel, Tagebuch, March 31, 1928, 221–222.

55. Mahler-Werfel, Tagebuch, March 31, 1928, 222.

56. Mahler-Werfel, "Der schimmernde Weg," 340.

57. Mahler-Werfel, Tagebuch, Rome, April 15, 1928, 222–223.

58. Mahler-Werfel, "Der schimmernde Weg," 341.

59. Mahler-Werfel, Tagebuch, May 3, 1928, 225.

60. Mahler-Werfel, Tagebuch, August 1, 1928, 226.

61. Mahler-Werfel, Tagebuch, August 2, 1928, 228.

62. Mahler-Werfel, Tagebuch, August 13, 1928, 227.

63. Mahler-Werfel, Tagebuch, September 6, 1928, 228.

64. Mahler-Werfel, Tagebuch, Venice, October 7, 1928, 228.

65. Mahler-Werfel, Tagebuch, Venice, October 7, 1928, 229.

66. Mahler-Werfel, *And the Bridge Is Love,* 195.

67. Mahler-Werfel, Tagebuch, July 5, 1929, 231.

68. Mahler-Werfel, Tagebuch, August 13, 1929, 236–237.

69. Mahler-Werfel, Tagebuch, July 5, 1929, 231–232.

70. Mahler-Werfel, Tagebuch, August 14, 1929, 237.

71. Mahler-Werfel, Tagebuch, August 24, 1929, 239.

72. Mahler-Werfel, Tagebuch, August 15, 1929, 237.

73. Franz Werfel to Alma Mahler-Werfel, Breitenstein, undated, [1930], Mahler-Werfel Papers.

74. Mahler-Werfel, Tagebuch, August 21, 1929, 238.

75. Mahler-Werfel, "Der schimmernde Weg," 368.

76. Mahler-Werfel, *And the Bridge Is Love,* 184.

77. Mahler-Werfel, "Der schimmernde Weg," 369.

78. Mahler-Werfel, Tagebuch, August 19, 1930, 243.

79. Mahler-Werfel, Tagebuch, August 3, 1930, 242.

80. Mahler-Werfel, Tagebuch, October 23, 1930, 246.

81. Mahler-Werfel, Tagebuch, February 26, 1931, 257.

82. Mahler-Werfel, Tagebuch, March 29, 1931, 257.

83. Mahler-Werfel, Tagebuch, March 29, 1931, 257.

Chapter 12. Gathering Storms 1931–1936

1. Oliver Hilmes, interview with Johannes Trentini, cited in Hilmes, *Malevolent Muse,* 159.

2. Jungk, interview with Anna Mahler, cited in Jungk, *Franz Werfel,* 70.

3. Klaus Mann, *Der Wendepunkt, Ein Lebensbericht* (Munich: Spangenberg, 1989), 370, cited in Hilmes, *Malevolent Muse,* 167.

4. Joseph, "Werfel, Alma, Kokoschka, the Actor George," 2.

5. Joseph, "Werfel, Alma, Kokoschka, the Actor George," 6.

6. Joseph, "Werfel, Alma, Kokoschka, the Actor George," 2.

7. Joseph, "Werfel, Alma, Kokoschka, the Actor George," 8.

8. Joseph, "Werfel, Alma, Kokoschka, the Actor George," 13.

9. Joseph, "Werfel, Alma, Kokoschka, the Actor George," 12–13.

10. Mahler-Werfel, Tagebuch, May 26, 1931, 259.

11. Mahler-Werfel, Tagebuch, May 26, 1931, 259.

12. Mahler-Werfel, Tagebuch, undated, 1931, 263.

13. Mahler-Werfel, Tagebuch, December 1931, 263.

14. Mahler-Werfel, Tagebuch, December 31, 1931, 263.

15. Mahler-Werfel, Tagebuch, undated, 1931, 264.

16. Mahler-Werfel, Tagebuch, June 15, 1932, 266.

17. Mahler-Werfel, Tagebuch, March 20, 1932, 264a.

18. Mahler-Werfel, Tagebuch, April 8, 1932, 265.

19. Mahler-Werfel, Tagebuch, May 31, 1932, 265.

20. Franz Werfel, speech, New York, undated, in *Zwischen Oben und Unten*, cited in Jungk, *Franz Werfel*, 155.

21. Mahler-Werfel, Tagebuch, undated, [summer 1932], 266.

22. Mahler-Werfel, Tagebuch, August 6, 1932, 268.

23. Mahler-Werfel, Tagebuch, August 6, 1932, 267.

24. Mahler-Werfel, Tagebuch, August 6, 1932, 267.

25. Franz Werfel, *Can We Live Without Faith in God?* in *Between Heaven and Earth* (New York: Philosophical Library, 1944), 99–100.

26. Mahler-Werfel, Tagebuch, September 23, 1932, 268.

27. Mahler-Werfel, Tagebuch, July 27, 1933, 284.

28. Mahler-Werfel, Tagebuch, October 7, 1932, 269.

29. Mahler-Werfel, Tagebuch, December 16, 1932, 273.

30. Mahler-Werfel, Tagebuch, December 16, 1932, 273.

31. Mahler-Werfel, Tagebuch, December 16, 1932, 273b.

32. Mahler-Werfel, Tagebuch, February 5, 1933, 275.

33. Mahler-Werfel, Tagebuch March 3, 1933, 277.

34. Mahler-Werfel, Tagebuch, March 5, 1933, 277.

35. Mahler-Werfel, Tagebuch, March 5, 1933, 278.

36. Mahler-Werfel, Tagebuch, March 5, 1933, 278.

37. Cited in Hilmes, *Malevolent Muse*, 170.

38. Franz Werfel to Alma Mahler-Werfel, undated, 1933, Mahler-Werfel Papers.

39. Mahler-Werfel, Tagebuch, May 1, 1933, 280.

40. Mahler-Werfel, Tagebuch, June 28, 1933, 282.

41. Mahler-Werfel, *And the Bridge Is Love*, 278.

42. Mahler-Werfel, Tagebuch, July 27, 1933, 282–283.

43. Mahler-Werfel, Tagebuch, July 27, 1933, 282.

44. Mahler-Werfel, Tagebuch, undated, 1933, 284.

45. Mahler-Werfel, Tagebuch, undated, 1933, 284.

46. Mahler-Werfel, Tagebuch, November 16, 1933, 287–288.

47. Mahler-Werfel, Tagebuch, September 1, 1933, 285.

48. Mahler-Werfel, Tagebuch, October 8, 1933, 286.

49. Mahler-Werfel, Tagebuch, October 10, 1933, 286.

50. Franz Werfel to Anna Moll, undated, [c. February] 1934, Franz Werfel Collection, cited in Jungk, *Franz Werfel*, 146.

51. Mahler-Werfel, Tagebuch, June 25, 1933, 281.

52. Elias Canetti, *Das Augenspiel: Lebensgeschichte 1931–1937* (Frankfurt: Carl Hanser Verlag, 1985), 52–54.

53. Mahler-Werfel, Tagebuch, [beginning of] November 1933, 287.

54. Mahler-Werfel, Tagebuch, November 27, 1933, 288.

55. Mahler-Werfel, Tagebuch, December 24, 1933, 288.

56. Mahler-Werfel, Tagebuch, undated, [February] 1934, 289.

57. Mahler-Werfel, Tagebuch, March 3, 1941, 327.

58. Mahler-Werfel, Tagebuch, undated, February 1934, 289–290.

59. Mahler-Werfel, Tagebuch, undated, [February 1934], 290.

60. Mahler-Werfel, Tagebuch, March 28, 1934, 291.

61. Mahler-Werfel, Tagebuch, April 12, 1934, 291.

62. Bruno Walter, *Thema und Variationen: Erinnerungen und Gedanken* (Berlin: Bermann Fischer, 1947), 411, cited in James Reidel, "Manon's World," typescript, 101.

63. Mahler-Werfel, Tagebuch, October 22, 1933, 286.

64. Mahler-Werfel, Tagebuch, undated, 290.

65. Mahler-Werfel, Tagebuch, Easter Monday 1935, 293.

66. Mahler-Werfel, Tagebuch, Easter Monday 1935, 293.

67. Mahler-Werfel, Tagebuch, Easter Monday 1935, 293.

68. Mahler-Werfel, Tagebuch, Easter Monday 1935, 294.

69. Franz Werfel, "Manon," in *Erzählungen aus zwei Welten*, vol. 3 (Frankfurt am Main: S. Fischer Verlag, 1954), 397, cited in Reidel, "Manon's World," typescript, 121.

70. Mahler-Werfel, "Der schimmernde Weg," 443.

71. Manon Gropius to Walter Gropius, August 10, 1934, Bauhaus Archive, cited in Hilmes, *Malevolent Muse*, 178.

72. Werfel, "Manon," in *Erzählungen aus zwei Welten*, 397, cited in Reidel, "Manon's World," typescript, 154.

73. Cited in Reidel, "Manon's World," 130.

74. Mahler-Werfel, Tagebuch, Easter Monday 1935, 292.

75. Mahler-Werfel, Tagebuch, Easter Monday 1935, 292.

76. Mahler-Werfel, Tagebuch, Easter Monday 1935, 292.

77. Johannes Hollnsteiner, eulogy for "Mutzi," Mahler-Werfel Papers.

78. Reginald Isaacs, *Der Mensch und sein Werke*, vol. 2 (Berlin: Gebr. Mann Verlag, 1984), 740.

79. Canetti, *Das Augenspiel*, 190.

80. Bruno Walter to Alma Mahler-Werfel, April 22, 1935, Mahler-Werfel Papers.

81. Carl Zuckmayer to Alma Mahler-Werfel, April 28, 1935, Mahler-Werfel Papers.

82. Helene Berg to Alma Mahler-Werfel, April 23, 1935, in George Perle, "Mein Geliebtes Almschi, Briefe von Alban und Helene Berg an Alma Mahler-Werfel," *Österreichische Musikschrift* 35 (1980): 7.

83. Mahler-Werfel, *And the Bridge Is Love*, 210.

84. Mahler-Werfel, Tagebuch, July 7, 1935, 296.

85. Mahler-Werfel, Tagebuch, July 30, 1935, 296.

86. Mahler-Werfel, Tagebuch, undated, August 1935, 296.

87. Cited in Jungk, *Franz Werfel*, 153.

88. Mahler-Werfel, Tagebuch, September 11, 1935, 297.

89. Mahler-Werfel, Tagebuch, May 28, 1935, 295.

90. Mahler-Werfel, "Der schimmernde Weg," 457.

91. Mahler-Werfel, "Der schimmernde Weg," 453.

92. Mahler-Werfel, *And the Bridge Is Love*, 212.

93. Mahler-Werfel, Tagebuch, February 5, 1936, 297.

Chapter 13. Flight 1936–1941

1. Mahler-Werfel, Tagebuch, April 22, 1936, 298.

2. Thomas Mann, April 9, 1936, *Diaries 1918–1939* (London: Robin Clark, 1984), 258.

3. Mahler-Werfel, Tagebuch, April 22, 1936, 298.

4. Mahler-Werfel, Tagebuch, June 4, 1936, 299.

5. Mahler-Werfel, Tagebuch, June 2, 1936, 298.

6. Mahler-Werfel, Tagebuch, September 19, 1936, 300.

7. Jungk, interview with Anna Mahler, cited in Jungk, *Franz Werfel*, 165.

8. Jungk, interview with Anna Mahler, cited in Jungk, *Franz Werfel*, 165.

9. Mahler-Werfel, Tagebuch, September 19, 1936, 299.

10. Mahler-Werfel, Tagebuch, September 24, 1936, 300.

11. Mahler-Werfel, *And the Bridge Is Love*, 213.

12. Mahler-Werfel, Tagebuch, June 15, 1937, 302.

13. Mahler-Werfel, *And the Bridge Is Love*, 214.

14. Mahler-Werfel, "Der schimmernde Weg," 519.

15. Mahler-Werfel, Tagebuch, July 11, 1937, 303.

16. Mahler-Werfel, Tagebuch, July 11, 1937, 303.

17. Mahler-Werfel, Tagebuch, November 26, 1937, 307.

18. Mahler-Werfel, Tagebuch, undated, 1938, 309.

19. Mahler-Werfel, "Der schimmernde Weg," 479.

20. Carl Zuckmayer, *A Part of Myself* (New York: Carroll & Graf, 1984), 38.

21. Mahler-Werfel, "Der schimmernde Weg," 480.

22. Mahler-Werfel, *And the Bridge Is Love*, 218; Mahler-Werfel, "Der schimmernde Weg," 481.

23. Mahler-Werfel, "Der schimmernde Weg," 481.

24. Franz Werfel to Alma Mahler-Werfel, February 26, 1938, Mahler-Werfel Papers.

25. Mahler-Werfel, Tagebuch, undated, 332.

26. Cited in Keegan, *Bride of the Wind*, 271.

27. Mahler-Werfel, Tagebuch, undated, 332.

28. Franz Werfel, Tagebucheintragungen [diary entries], March 13, 1938, in Werfel, *Zwischen Oben und Unten*, 743.

29. Mahler-Werfel, Tagebuch, undated, 332.

30. Mahler-Werfel, Tagebuch, undated, 332.

31. Zuckmayer, *A Part of Myself*, 52.

32. Mahler-Werfel, Tagebuch, undated, 1938, 333.

33. Mahler-Werfel, Tagebuch, undated, 333.

34. Zuckmayer, *A Part of Myself*, 50–51.

35. Zuckmayer, *A Part of Myself*, 55.

36. Mahler-Werfel, Tagebuch, undated, 1938, 333.

37. Franz Werfel to Hanna von Fuchs-Robetin, August 22, 1942, cited in Jungk, *Franz Werfel*, 297.

38. Zuckmayer, *A Part of Myself*, 78.

39. Mahler-Werfel, Tagebuch, undated, 333.

40. Mahler-Werfel, Tagebuch, undated, 1938, 334.

41. Franz Werfel, diary, cited in Jungk, *Franz Werfel*, 172.

42. Werfel, Tagebucheintragungen, July 1, 1938, in Werfel, *Zwischen Oben und Unten*, 743.

43. Mahler-Werfel, Tagebuch, July 9, 1938, 312.

44. Mahler-Werfel, *And the Bridge Is Love*, 227.

45. Franz Werfel to his parents, October 14, 1938, cited in Jungk, *Franz Werfel*, 175.

46. Mahler-Werfel, Tagebuch, August 31, 1938, 313.

47. Mahler-Werfel, Tagebuch, September 1, 1938, 313.

48. Mahler-Werfel, Tagebuch, September 27, 1938, 313.

49. Mahler-Werfel, Tagebuch, Sanary, October 1, 1938, 314.

50. Mahler-Werfel, Tagebuch, October 9, 1938, 314.

51. Mahler-Werfel, Tagebuch, Sanary, October 1, 1938, 314.

52. Mahler-Werfel, Tagebuch, October 9, 1938, 314.

53. Mahler-Werfel, Tagebuch, October 16, 1938, 314–315.

54. Mahler-Werfel, Tagebuch, October 16, 1938, 315.

55. Mahler-Werfel, Tagebuch, November 28, 1938, 315.

56. Mahler-Werfel, Tagebuch, November 29, 1938, 316.

57. Mahler-Werfel, "Der schimmernde Weg," 501.

58. Mahler-Werfel, Tagebuch, January 24, 1939, 316.

59. Mahler-Werfel, Tagebuch, undated, [April] 1939, 319–320.

60. Mahler-Werfel, Tagebuch, undated, 337.

61. Mahler-Werfel, Tagebuch, undated, 338.

62. Mahler-Werfel, Tagebuch, November 11, 1939, 320.

63. Mahler-Werfel, Tagebuch, May 28, 1940, 339.

64. Mahler-Werfel, Tagebuch, May 28, 1940, 340.

65. Mahler-Werfel, Tagebuch, undated, [1940], 340.

66. Mahler-Werfel, Tagebuch, undated, 341.

67. Mahler-Werfel, "Der schimmernde Weg," 524.

68. Mahler-Werfel, Tagebuch, undated, [1940], 344.

69. Mahler-Werfel, Tagebuch, undated, [1940], 347a.

70. Mahler-Werfel, Tagebuch, July 2, 1940, 347a.

71. Mahler-Werfel, Tagebuch, July 2, 1940, 348.

72. Mahler-Werfel, "Der schimmernde Weg," 528.

73. Mahler-Werfel, "Der schimmernde Weg," 530.

74. Mahler-Werfel, Tagebuch, undated, [1940], 350.

75. Peter Stephan Jungk, interview with Golo Mann, cited in Jungk, *Franz Werfel*, 192.

76. Varian Fry, *Ausleiferung auf Verlangen—Die Rettung deutscher Emigraten in Marseille* (Munich: Carl Hanser Verlag 1986), 82.

77. Carl Zuckmayer to Albrecht Joseph, October 16, 1940, cited in Hilmes, *Malevolent Muse*, 213.

78. Jungk, interview with Golo Mann, cited in Jungk, *Franz Werfel*, 191.

79. Sheila Eisenberg, *A Hero of Our Own: The Story of Varian Fry* (New York: BackinPrint.com, 2005), 78.

80. Mahler-Werfel, Tagebuch, undated, 352.

81. Mahler-Werfel, Tagebuch, undated, [1940], 352.

82. Mahler-Werfel, Tagebuch, undated, [1940], 353.

83. Mahler-Werfel, Tagebuch, undated, [1940], 353a.

84. Mahler-Werfel, Tagebuch, undated, 353a.

85. Franz Werfel to Albine and Rudolf Werfel, October 13, 1940, cited in Jungk, *Franz Werfel*, 193.

86. Mahler-Werfel, "Der schimmernde Weg," 542.

87. Mahler-Werfel, Tagebuch, undated, 325.

88. Franz Werfel, "Unser Weg geht weiter," in *Zwischen Oben und Unten*, 333–337.

89. Franz Werfel to Rudolf and Albine Werfel, December 5, 1940, cited in Jungk, *Franz Werfel*, 194.

90. Mahler-Werfel, Tagebuch, undated, 325.

Chapter 14. Exile 1941–1946

1. Mahler-Werfel, Tagebuch, January 3, 1941, 325.

2. Franz Werfel to Rudolf and Albine Werfel, December 5, 1940, cited in Jungk, *Franz Werfel*, 194.

3. Mahler-Werfel, Tagebuch, January 11, 1941, 325.

4. Mahler-Werfel, Tagebuch, January 3, 1941, 325.

5. Mahler-Werfel, Tagebuch, January 12, 1941, 326.

6. Albrecht Joseph, *August Hess*, typescript, undated (Bonn: Weidle-Verlag, undated), cited in Hilmes, *Malevolent Muse*, 217.

7. Joseph, "Werfel, Alma, Kokoschka and the Actor George," 39.

8. Peter Stephan Junk, interview with Albrecht Joseph, cited in Jungk, *Franz Werfel*, 204.

9. Joseph, "Werfel, Alma, Kokoschka, the Actor George," 21–22.

10. Joseph, "Werfel, Alma, Kokoschka, the Actor George," 20–21.

11. Joseph, "Werfel, Alma, Kokoschka, the Actor George," 22.

12. Joseph, "Werfel, Alma, Kokoschka, the Actor George," 22–23.

13. Jungk, interview with Anna Mahler, cited in Jungk, *Franz Werfel*, 229.

14. Mahler-Werfel, Tagebuch, July 20, 1941, 354.

15. Alma Mahler-Werfel to Friedrich Torberg, October 29, 1941, in Friedrich Torberg, *Liebste Freundin und Alma: Briefwechsel mit Alma Mahler-Werfel* (Berlin: Ullstein Verlag, 1990), 32.

16. Friedrich Torberg to Alma Mahler-Werfel, May 29, 1942, quoted in Torberg, *Liebste Freundin und Alma*, 57.

17. Alma Mahler-Werfel to Friedrich Torberg, December 20, 1941, Vienna City Library [Wien Bibliothek im Rathaus].

18. Mahler-Werfel, *And the Bridge Is Love*, 250.

19. Alma Mahler, Tagebuch, February 16, 1942, 356.

20. Franz Werfel, "Stefan Zweig's Tod," memorial address, in Franz Werfel, *Zwichen Oben und Unten* (Munich: Langen Müller Verlag, 1975), 459.

21. Cited in Jungk, *Franz Werfel*, 200.

22. Franz Werfel, *A Personal Preface: The Song of Bernadette* (London: Hamish Hamilton, 1942), 5.

23. Franz Werfel to Francis J. Rummel, October 27, 1942, Franz Werfel Collection, cited in Hilmes, *Malevolent Muse*, 237.

24. Father Cyrill Fischer to Alma Mahler-Werfel, December 15, 1943, Mahler-Werfel Papers.

25. Mahler-Werfel, Tagebuch, June 23, 1942, 357.

26. Mahler-Werfel, Tagebuch, June 23, 1942, 357.

27. Alma Mahler, Tagebuch, August 31, 1942, 359.

28. Joseph, "Werfel, Alma, Kokoschka, the Actor George," 26.

29. Mahler-Werfel, Tagebuch, September 25, 1942, 360.

30. Mahler-Werfel, Tagebuch, October 1942, 360.

31. Mahler-Werfel, *And the Bridge Is Love*, 257.

32. Mahler-Werfel, "Der schimmernde Weg," 601.

33. Thomas Mann, October 11, 1942, *Tagebücher 1940–1943* (Berlin: S. Fischer Verlag, 1982), 484.

34. Joseph, "Werfel, Alma, Kokoschka and the Actor George," 35.

35. Dika Newlin, *Schoenberg Remembered Diaries: and Recollections (1938–1976)* (New York: Pendragon Press, 1980), 296, cited in Keegan, *The Bride of the Wind*, 306.

36. Claire Goll, *Ich verzeihe keinem: Eine literarische chronique scandaleuse unserer Zeit* (Berlin: S. Fischer Verlag 1987), 229.

37. Mahler-Werfel, Tagebuch, August 25, 1942, 359.

38. Alma Mahler-Werfel to Carl Zuckmayer, cited in Hilmes, *Malevolent Muse*, 226.

39. Mahler-Werfel, Tagebuch, August 21, 1942, 358.

40. Erich Maria Remarque, diary, August 13, 1942, in Erich Maria Remarque, *Das unbekannte Werk: Briefe und Tagebücher*, vol. 5 (Cologne: Kiepenheuer & Witsch, 1998), 368, cited in Hilmes, *Malevolent Muse*, 226.

41. Mahler-Werfel, Tagebuch, August 21, 1942, 358; Erich Maria Remarque to Alma Mahler-Werfel, undated, [1942], Mahler-Werfel Papers.

42. Joseph, "Werfel, Alma, Kokoschka, the Actor George," 26–27.

43. Joseph, "Werfel, Alma, Kokoschka, the Actor George," 26–27.

44. Mahler-Werfel, Tagebuch, October 1942, 359.

45. Mahler-Werfel, Tagebuch, May 1943, 363.

46. Mahler-Werfel, Tagebuch, May 1943, 363.

47. Mahler-Werfel, Tagebuch, May 1943, 368.

48. Mahler-Werfel, Tagebuch, August 31, 1943, 369.

49. Mahler-Werfel, "Der schimmernde Weg," 572.

50. Mahler-Werfel, Tagebuch, April 1943, 362.

51. Mahler-Werfel, Tagebuch, October 1943, 371.

52. Mahler-Werfel, Tagebuch, September 1943, 371.

53. Mahler-Werfel, Tagebuch, September 17, 1943, 371.

54. Mahler-Werfel, Tagebuch, October 3, 5, 1943, 372.

55. Mahler-Werfel, Tagebuch, October 18, 1943, 372.

56. Mahler-Werfel, Tagebuch, October 1943, 371.

57. Mahler-Werfel, Tagebuch, November 23, 1943, 374.

58. Mahler-Werfel, Tagebuch, November 3, 1943, 373–374.

59. Mahler-Werfel, Tagebuch, November 12, 1943, 374.

60. Mahler-Werfel, Tagebuch, December 14, 1943, 375.

61. Mahler-Werfel, Tagebuch, January 21, 1944, 377.

62. Mahler-Werfel, "Der schimmernde Weg," 587.

63. Mahler-Werfel, "Der schimmernde Weg," 587.

64. Marlene Dietrich to Franz Werfel, Western Union telegram, February 10, 1944, Mahler-Werfel Papers.

65. Marlene Dietrich to Alma Mahler-Werfel, and Franz Werfel, February 5, 1944, Mahler-Werfel Papers.

66. Mahler-Werfel, Tagebuch, January 1, 1944, 376.

67. Anna Mahler to Alma Mahler-Werfel, undated, Mahler-Werfel Papers,

68. Mahler-Werfel, Tagebuch, July 24, 1944, 587.

69. Mahler-Werfel, "Der schimmernde Weg," 596.

70. Mahler-Werfel, "Der schimmernde Weg," April 1945, 600.

71. Franz Werfel to Ben Huebsch, his American publisher, undated, Mahler-Werfel Papers, cited in Jungk, *Franz Werfel*, 224; Franz Werfel to Max Brod, undated, Mahler-Werfel Papers, cited in Jungk, *Franz Werfel*, 225; Mahler-Werfel, "Der schimmernde Weg," 606.

72. Alma Mahler-Werfel to Friedrich Torberg, August 31, 1944, in Torberg, *Liebste Freundin und Alma*, 133.

73. Alma Mahler-Werfel to Freidrich Torberg, August 31, 1944, in Torberg, *Liebste Freundin und Alma*, 133.

74. Mahler-Werfel, "Der schimmernde Weg," April 29, 1945, 602.

75. Mahler-Werfel, "Der schimmernde Weg," 608.

76. Mahler-Werfel, "Der schimmernde Weg," August 19, 1945, 608.

77. Jungk, *Franz Werfel*, 227.

78. Mahler-Werfel, "Der schimmernde Weg," August 2, 1945, 611.

79. Mahler-Werfel, "Der schimmernde Weg," August 2, 1945, 613.

80. Thomas Mann, August 27, 1945, *Tagebücher 1944–1946*, ed. Inge Jens (Berlin: S. Fischer Verlag 1986), 246.

81. Mahler-Werfel, *And the Bridge Is Love*, 270.

82. Mahler-Werfel, *And the Bridge Is Love*, 270.

83. Joseph, "Werfel, Alma, Kokoschka, the Actor George," 35–36.

84. Joseph, "Werfel, Alma, Kokoschka, the Actor George," 35–36.

85. Alma Mahler to Friedrich Torberg, September 16, 1955, cited in Jungk, *Franz Werfel*, 232.

86. Mahler-Werfel, *And the Bridge Is Love*, 270.

87. Mahler-Werfel, *And the Bridge Is Love*, 269.

88. Alma Mahler to Friedrich Torberg, September 4, 1945, Vienna City Library [Wienbibliothek im Rathaus].

89. Alma Mahler-Werfel to Friedrich Torberg, September 1, 1945, in Torberg, *Liebste Freundin und Alma*, 243.

90. Mahler-Werfel, *And the Bridge Is Love*, 270.

91. Alma Mahler-Werfel to Lion and Marta Feuchtwanger, November 14, 1945, cited in Hilmes, *Malevolent Muse*, 243.

92. Mahler-Werfel, *And the Bridge Is Love*, 270.

93. Alma Mahler-Werfel to Friedrich Torberg, March 29, 1946, Vienna City Library.

94. Mahler-Werfel, *And the Bridge Is Love*, 272.

95. Alma Mahler-Werfel to Johannes Hollnsteiner, June 30, 1946, quoted in Friedrich Buchmayr, *Der Priester in Almas Salon: Johannes Hollnsteiners Weg von der Elite Ständestaats zur NS-Bibliothekar* (Vienna: Verlag Bibliothek der Provinz, 2003), 263, cited in Hilmes, *Malevolent Muse*, 233.

96. Johannes Hollnsteiner to Alma Mahler-Werfel, May 23, 1955, Mahler-Werfel Papers.

97. Alma Mahler-Werfel to Johannes Hollnsteiner, July 29, 1955, quoted in Buchmayr, *Der Priester in Almas Salon*, 13.

98. Mahler-Werfel, *And the Bridge Is Love*, 273.

99. Alma Mahler-Werfel to Friedrich Torberg, September 11, 1946, Vienna City Library.

100. Mahler-Werfel, *And the Bridge Is Love*, 273.

101. Alma Mahler-Werfel to Friedrich Torberg, September 11, 1946, Vienna City Library.

Chapter 15. La Grande Veuve 1946–1964

1. Alma Mahler-Werfel to Oskar Kokoschka, November 20, 1946, Oskar Kokoschka Estate, Zentralbibliothek Zurich, cited in Hilmes, *Malevolent Muse*, 244.

2. Alma Mahler-Werfel, "Meine vielen Leben," unpublished manuscript, October 1946, privately owned, 674, cited in Hilmes, *Malevolent Muse*, 244.

3. Alma Mahler-Werfel to Ida Gebauer, December 17, 1945, Austrian National Library.

4. Alma Mahler-Werfel to Ida Gebauer, March 1, 1946, Austrian National Library.

5. Mahler-Werfel, *And the Bridge Is Love*, 273.

6. Mahler-Werfel, *And the Bridge Is Love*, 273.

7. Mahler-Werfel, "Meine vielen Leben," Autumn 1947, 684, privately owned, cited in Hilmes, *Malevolent Muse*, 245.

8. Mahler-Werfel, *And the Bridge Is Love*, 273–274.

9. Alma Mahler-Werfel to Ida Gebauer, April 29, 1948, Austria National Library; Alma Mahler-Werfel to Ida Gebauer, May 17, 1948, Austria National Library.

10. Alma Mahler-Werfel to Ida Gebauer, November 26, 1947, Austria National Library.

11. Alma Mahler-Werfel to Ida Gebauer, April 22, 1946, Austria National Library.

12. Alma Mahler-Werfel to Friedrich Torberg, May 13, 1948, Torberg, *Liebste Freundin und Alma*, 265.

13. Alma Mahler-Werfel to Ida Gebauer, undated, [June] 1948, Austria National Library.

14. Joseph, "Werfel, Alma, Kokoschka, the Actor George," 27.

15. Author interview with Marina Mahler, April 30, 2018.

16. Anna Mahler to Alma Mahler-Werfel, undated, Mahler-Werfel Papers.

17. Alma Mahler-Werfel to Freidrich Torberg, May 13, 1948, in Torberg, *Liebste Freundin und Alma*, 265.

18. Friedrich Torberg to Alma Mahler-Werfel, May 30, 1948, in Torberg, *Liebste Freundin und Alma*, 266.

19. Alma Mahler-Werfel to Ida Gebauer, May 17, 1948, Austria National Library.

20. Bruno Walter to Alma Mahler-Werfel, May 19, 1948, Mahler-Werfel Papers.

21. Mahler-Werfel, *And the Bridge Is Love*, 277.

22. Alma Mahler-Werfel to Friedrich Torberg, June 23, 1949, Torberg, *Liebste Freundin und Alma*, 269.

23. Alma Mahler-Werfel to Friedrich Torberg, May 14, 1950, Torberg, *Liebste Freundin und Alma*, 273.

24. Mahler-Werfel, *And the Bridge Is Love*, 278.

25. Mahler-Werfel, *And the Bridge Is Love*, 277.

26. Author interview with Nuria Schoenberg Nono, April 13, 2018.

27. Author interview with Nuria Schoenberg Nono, April 13, 2018.

28. Author interview with Irene Hartzell, April 13, 2018.

29. Alma Mahler-Werfel to Annelies Ehrlich Gottlieb, undated, in Irene Hartzell Papers, privately owned.

30. Walter Gropius in Birthday Book to Alma Mahler, Pennsylvania State University Libraries, cited in Hilmes, *Malevolent Muse*, 260.

31. Arnold Schoenberg to Alma Mahler-Werfel. Message from the Arnold Schoenberg Centre, Vienna, cited in Hilmes, *Malevolent Muse*, 260.

32. Thomas Mann in Birthday Book to Alma Mahler, Pennsylvania State University Libraries, cited in Hilmes, *Malevolent Muse*, 259.

33. Cited in Weidinger, *Kokoschka and Alma Mahler*, 95–96.

34. Mahler-Werfel, *And the Bridge Is Love*, 280.

35. Author interview with Marina Mahler, April 30, 2018.

36. Author interview with Marina Mahler, April 30, 2018.

37. Alma Mahler-Werfel to Gusti Arlt, March 14, 1951, cited in Hilmes, *Malevolent Muse*, 262.

38. Author interview with Marina Mahler, April 30, 2018.

39. Mahler-Werfel, *And the Bridge Is Love*, 280.

40. Jungk, interview with Anna Mahler, cited in Hilmes, *Malevolent Muse*, 262.

41. Jungk, interview with Anna Mahler, cited in Jungk, *Franz Werfel*, 166.

42. Joseph, Albrecht, *August Hess*, typescript, undated (Bonn: Weidle Verlag).

43. Alma Mahler-Werfel to Annelies Ehrlich Gottlieb, undated, 1951, Irene Hartzell Archive, Private Papers.

44. Mahler-Werfel, *And the Bridge Is Love*, 281.

45. Alma Mahler-Werfel to Freidrich Torberg, June 23, 1949, in Torberg, *Liebste Freundin und Alma*, 269–270.

46. Author interview with Nuria Schoenberg Nono, April 13, 2018.

47. Author interview with Marina Mahler, April 30, 2018.

48. Mahler-Werfel, *And the Bridge Is Love*, 81.

49. Helene Berg to Alma Mahler-Werfel, June 10, 1956, Mahler-Werfel Papers.

50. Alma Mahler-Werfel to Lion Feuchtwanger, June 5, 1958, cited in Hilmes, *Malevolent Muse*, 269.

51. Walter Gropius to Alma Mahler-Werfel, August 17, 1958, cited in Hilmes, *Malevolent Muse*, 269.

52. Alma Mahler-Werfel to Walter Gropius, August 20, 1958, cited in Hilmes, *Malevolent Muse*, 269.

53. Alma Mahler-Werfel to Willy Haas, January 4, 1959, Mahler-Werfel Papers.

54. Joseph, "Werfel, Alma, Kokoschka, the Actor George," 10.

55. Alma Mahler-Werfel to Oskar Kokoschka, September 25, 1946, Oskar Kokoschka Estate, Central Library Zurich.

56. Oskar Kokoschka to Alma Mahler-Werfel, October 5 [1949], Oskar Kokoschka Estate, Central Library Zurich.

57. Oskar Kokoschka to Alma Mahler-Werfel, June 7, 1951, Oskar Kokoschka Estate, Central Library Zurich.

58. Author interview Marina Mahler, April 30, 2018.

59. Alma Mahler-Werfel to Gusti Arlt, undated, privately owned, cited in Hilmes, *Malevolent Muse*, 274.

60. Thilo Koch, *Ähnlichkeit mit lebenden Personen* (Berlin: Rowohlt, 1975), 208–210.

61. Suma Morgenstern Obituary of Alma Mahler, December 13, 1964, typescript, private collection, cited in Keegan *The Bride of the Wind,* 309.

62. Adolf Klarmann to Friedrich Torberg, December 24, 1964, Friedrich Torberg Estate, Municipal and Rural Library, Vienna.

63. Mahler-Werfel, *And the Bridge Is Love,* 281.

64. Adolf Klarmann to Friedrich Torberg, December 24, 1964, Friedrich Torberg Estate, Municipal and Rural Library, Vienna.

65. Mahler-Werfel, *And the Bridge Is Love,* 282.

66. Deborah Calland and Barry Milington, "'Lonely Walk,' an Unpublished Song by Alma Schindler-Mahler," *Wagner Journal* 12, no. 3, November 2018.

Bibliography

Barea, Ilsa. *Vienna: Legend and Reality.* London: Pimlico, 1966.

Bauer-Lechner, Natalie. *Recollections of Gustav Mahler.* Translated by Dika Newlin. London: Faber, 1980.

Baumfeld, Maurice. *Erinnerungen an Gustav Mahler.* New York: Staats-Zeitung, May 21, 1911.

Blaukopf, Bert, and Herta Blaukopf. *Mahler: His Life, Work and World.* London: Thames and Hudson, 1976.

Brassai. *Artists of My Life.* Translated by Richard Miller. New York: Viking Press, 1982.

Brendon, Piers. *The Dark Valley: A Panorama of the 1930s.* London: Jonathan Cape, 2000.

Brod, Max. "The Young Werfel and the Prague Writers." In *The Era of German Expressionism.* Edited by Paul Raabe. Translated by J. M. Ritchie. Calder & Boyars, 1974.

Buchmayr, Friedrich. *Der Priester in Almas Salon: Johannes Hollnsteiners Weg von der Elite Ständestaats zur NS-Bibliothekar.* Vienna: Verlag Bibliothek der Provinz, 2003.

"Bruno Walter erzählt von Mahler." *Neue Freie Presse,* November 16, 1935.

Canetti, Elias. *Das Augenspiel: Lebensgeschichte 1931–1937.* Frankfurt: Carl Hanser Verlag, 1985.

de la Grange, Henry-Louis. *Gustav Mahler.* Vol. 2, *Vienna: The Years of Challenge, 1897–1904.* Oxford: Oxford University Press, 1995.

de la Grange, Henry-Louis. *Gustav Mahler.* Vol. 3, *Vienna: Triumph and Disillusion 1904–1907.* Oxford: Oxford University Press, 1999.

de la Grange, Henry-Louis. *Gustav Mahler.* Vol. 4, *A New Life Cut Short, 1907–1911.* Oxford: Oxford University Press, 2008.

Feder, Stuart. *Gustav Mahler: A Life in Crisis.* New Haven, CT: Yale University Press, 2004.

Feder, Stuart. "Mahler, Dying." *International Review of Psycho-Analysis,* 5:125, London (1978).

Fried, Oskar. "Erinnerungen an Mahler." *Musikblätter des Anbruch,* 1919.

Fry, Varian. *Ausleiterung auf Verlangen— Die Rettung deutscher Emigraten in Marseille.* Munich: Carl Hanser Verlag, 1986.

Fuchs, Heinrich. *Emil Jakob Schindler.* Vienna: Selbst Verlag, 1970.

Garner, Mosco. *Alban Berg.* London: Duckworth, 1975.

Giroud, Françoise. *Alma Mahler: Or the Art of Being Loved.* Oxford: Oxford University Press, 1991.

Goll, Claire. *Ich verzeihe keinem: Eine literarische chronique scandaleuse unserer Zeit.* Berlin: S. Fischer Verlag, 1987.

Hilmes, Oliver. *Malevolent Muse: The Life of Alma Mahler.* Boston: Northeastern University Press, 2015.

Isaacs, Reginald. *Walter Gropius: Der Mensch und sein Werk*. Vol. 1. Berlin: Gebr. Mann Verlag, 1983.

Isaacs, Reginald. *Walter Gropius: Der Mensch und sein Werke*. Vol. 2. Berlin: Gebr. Mann Verlag, 1984.

Joseph, Albrecht. *August Hess* (typescript). Bonn:Weidle-Verlag, n.d.

Joseph, Albrecht. "Werfel, Alma, Kokoschka, the Actor George." Unpublished manuscript. Mahler-Werfel Papers, Kislak Center for Special Collections, Rare Books and Manuscripts. University of Pennsylvania.

Jungk, Peter Stephan. *Franz Werfel: A Life in Prague, Vienna and Hollywood*. New York: Fromm International, 1991

Kafka, Franz. *Letters to Felice*. Edited by Erich Heller and Jürgen Born. New York: Schocken, 1973.

Keegan, Susanne. *The Bride of the Wind*. New York: Viking, 1991.

Kershaw, Ian. *Hitler 1889–1936: Hubris*. London: Allen Lane, 1998.

Kershaw, Ian. *Hitler, 1936–1945: Nemesis*. London: Allen Lane, 2000.

Koch, Thilo. *Ähnlichkeit mit lebenden Personen*. Berlin: Rowohlt, 1975.

Kokoschka, Oskar. *Briefe 1, 1905–1919*. Düsseldorf: Claasen, 1984.

Kokoschka, Oskar. *My Life*. New York: Macmillan, 1974.

Krenek, Ernst. *Im Atem der Zeit: Erinnerungen an die Moderne*. Hamburg: Hoffmann und Kampe, 1998.

Lebrecht, Norman. *Why Mahler?* London: Faber and Faber, 2010.

Mahler, Alma. *Gustav Mahler: Memories and Letters*. Seattle: University of Washington Press, 1975.

Mahler, Alma Maria. *Gustav Mahler Briefe*. Vienna: Paul Zsolnay Verlag, 1924.

Mahler-Werfel, Alma. *And the Bridge Is Love*. London: Hutchinson, 1959.

Mahler-Werfel, Alma. "Der schimmernde Weg." Unpublished typescript. Mahler-Werfel Papers, Kislak Center for Special Collections, Rare

Books and Manuscripts. University of Pennsylvania.

Mahler-Werfel, Alma. *Diaries 1898–1902*. Edited by Antony Beaumont and Susanne Rode-Breymann. Ithaca, NY: Cornell University Press.

Mahler-Werfel, Alma. *Mein Leben*. Frankfurt am Main: S. Fischer Verlag, 1960.

Mahler, Gustav. *Gustav Mahler: Letters to His Wife*. Edited by Henry-Louis de la Grange and Günther Weiss in collaboration with Knud Martner. Ithaca, NY: Cornell University Press, 2004.

Mann, Katia. *Meine ungeschreibene Memoiren*. Frankfurt: S. Fischer Verlag, 1995.

Mann, Thomas. *Diaries 1918–1939*. London, Robin Clark, 1984.

Mann, Thomas. *Tagebücher, 1940–1943*. Edited by Peter Mandelssohn. Frankfurt am Main: S. Fischer Verlag, 1978.

Mann, Thomas. *Tagebücher, 1944–1946*. Edited by Inge Jens. Frankfurt am Main: S. Fischer Verlag, 1986

Moll, Carl. *Eine Bildnisstudie* (1930). Exhibition catalog, in *Poetic Realism*. Vienna: Belvedere, 2012.

Moll, Carl. "Mein Leben." Typescript. Belvedere Gallery Library, Vienna.

Moll, Carl. "Memory of Plankenberg." Mahler-Werfel Papers, Kislak Center for Special Collections, Rare Books and Manuscripts. University of Pennsylvania.

Monson, Karen. *Alma Mahler: Muse to Genius*. London: Collins, 1984.

Néret, Gilles. *Gustav Klimt, 1862–1918: The World in Female Form*. Cologne: Taschen, 2007.

Newlin, Dika. *Schoenberg Remembered: Diaries and Recollections (1938–1976)*. New York: Pendragon Press, 1980.

Pausch, Oskar. *Alfred Roller und Ladinien*. San Martin de Tor: Institut Ladin, 2005.

Peham, Helga. *Die Salonièren und die Salons in Wien*. Vienna: Styria Premium, 2013.

Perle, George. "Mein Geliebtes Almschi, Briefe von Alban und Helene Berg an

Alma Mahler Werfel." *Österreichische Musikschrift* 35 (1980).

Pynsent, Robert B., ed. *Decadence and Innovation*. London: Weidenfeld and Nicolson, 1989.

Remarque, Erich Maria. *Das unbekannte Werk: Briefe und Tagebücher*. Vol. 5. Cologne: Kiepenheuer & Witsch, 1998.

Ritter, William. *William Ritter Chevalier de Gustav Mahler: Ecrits, correspondence, documents*. Edited by Claude Meylan. Bern: Peter Lang, 2000.

Roller, Alfred. *Die Bildnisse von Gustav Mahler*. Leipzig: Tal, 1922.

Schorske, Carl E. *Fin de Siecle Vienna*. London: Vintage, 1981.

Schulte, Michael. *Berta Zuckerkandl: Saloniere, Journalistin, Geheimdiplomatin*. Zurich: Atrium Verlag, 2006.

Specht, Richard. "Zu Mahlers Achte Symphonie." *Tagespost, Graz*, no. 150, June 14, 1914.

Stefan, Paul. *Das Grab in Wien*. Berlin: Reiss, 1913.

Stuckenschmidt, H. H. *Arnold Schoenberg: His Life, World and Work*. London: John Calder, 1977.

Tietze, Erica. Letters to Ida Conrat, August 1904. Mahler-Werfel Papers, Kislak Center for Special Collections, Rare Books and Manuscripts. University of Pennsylvania.

Torberg, Friedrich. *Liebste Freundin und Alma: Briefwechsel mit Alma Mahler-Werfel*. Berlin: Ullstein Verlag, 1990.

Waal, Edmund de. *The Hare with Amber Eyes: A Hidden Inheritance*. London: Vintage, 2011.

Walter, Bruno. *Briefe, 1894–1962*. Frankfurt: Fischer Verlag, 1969.

Walter, Bruno. *Gustav Mahler*. Vienna: Reichner, 1936.

Walter, Bruno. *Thema und Variationen: Erinnerungen und Gedanken*. Berlin: Bermann Fischer, 1947.

Weidinger, Alfred. *Kokoschka and Alma Mahler*. Munich: Prestel Verlag, 1996.

Werfel, Franz. "Manon." In *Erzählungen aus zwei Welten*. Vol. 3. Frankfurt am Main: S. Fischer Verlag, 1954.

Werfel, Franz. *A Personal Preface: The Song of Bernadette*. London: Hamish Hamilton, 1942.

Werfel, Franz. *Zwischen Oben und Unten*. Munich: Langen Müller, 1975.

Whitford, Frank. *Gustav Klimt, Artists in Context*. London: Collins and Brown, 1993.

Zuckerkandl, Berta. *Österreich intime, Erinnerungen 1892–1942*. Vienna: Amalthea Signum Verlag, 2013.

Zuckmayer, Carl. *A Part of Myself*. New York: Carroll & Graf, 1984.

Zweig, Stefan. *The World of Yesterday*. London: Cassell, 1943.

Archival Sources

Albertina Museum, Vienna.

Bauhaus Archive, Berlin.

Belvedere Library, Vienna.

Division of Handwritten Documents, Austria National Library, Vienna.

Franz Werfel Collection, Charles E. Young Research Library, University of California, Los Angeles.

Mahler-Werfel Papers, Kislak Center for Special Collections, Rare Books and Manuscripts, University of Pennsylvania, Philadelphia.

Municipal and Rural Library, Vienna.

Oskar Kokoschka Papers, Zentralbibliothek, Zürich.

Wienbibliothek im Rathaus (Vienna City Library).

Figure Credits

1. Photo: akg-images/INTERFOTO/picturedesk.com/ÖNB.

2. Photo: Mahler-Werfel Papers, Kislak Center for Special Collections, Rare Books and Manuscripts, University of Pennsylvania.

3. Alma Production Fotoarchiv, Vienna.

4. Photo: akg-images/ullstein bild.

5. Mahler family albums, photos Laurent Carré / MaxPPP.

6. Photo: Mahler-Werfel Papers, Kislak Center for Special Collections, Rare Books and Manuscripts, University of Pennsylvania.

7. Alma Production Fotoarchiv, Vienna.

8. Mahler family albums, photos Laurent Carré / MaxPPP.

9. Photo: Getty Images.

10. Photo: Mahler-Werfel Papers, Kislak Center for Special Collections, Rare Books and Manuscripts, University of Pennsylvania.

11. Photo: Mahler-Werfel Papers, Kislak Center for Special Collections, Rare Books and Manuscripts, University of Pennsylvania.

12. Photo: Getty Images.

13. Photo: Hugo Erfurth (1874–1948), private collection, Stapleton Collection, Bridgeman Images.

14. Photo: Self-portrait with Alma Mahler, 1913 (Coal and black chalk on paper), Oskar Kokoschka (1886–1980), Sammlung Leopold, Vienna, Bridgeman Images © Fondation Oskar Kokoschka / DACS 2019.

15. Photo: Mahler-Werfel Papers, Kislak Center for Special Collections, Rare Books and Manuscripts, University of Pennsylvania.

16. Photo: Mahler-Werfel Papers, Kislak Center for Special Collections, Rare Books and Manuscripts, University of Pennsylvania.

17. Mahler family albums, photos Laurent Carré/MaxPPP.

18. Photo: Mahler-Werfel Papers, Kislak Center for Special Collections, Rare Books and Manuscripts, University of Pennsylvania.

19. Mahler family albums, photos Laurent Carré/MaxPPP.

20. Mahler family albums, photos Laurent Carré/MaxPPP.

21. Mahler family albums.

22. Photo: Mahler-Werfel Papers, Kislak Center for Special Collections, Rare Books and Manuscripts, University of Pennsylvania.

23. Photo: Mahler-Werfel Papers, Kislak Center for Special Collections, Rare Books and Manuscripts, University of Pennsylvania.

24. Photo: Mahler-Werfel Papers, Kislak Center for Special Collections, Rare

Books and Manuscripts, University of Pennsylvania.

25. Photo: Mahler-Werfel Papers, Kislak Center for Special Collections, Rare

Books and Manuscripts, University of Pennsylvania.

26. Photo: Alfred Eisenstaedt, Time Life Pictures / Getty Images.

Index

Cate Haste is a biographer, historian, and filmmaker. She is the author of several books, including the award-winning biography *Sheila Fell: A Passion for Paint*, as well as *Rules of Desire* and *Nazi Women*. Haste lives in London.